William Barrack

Lexicon to xenophon's anabasis

For the use of schools

William Barrack

Lexicon to xenophon's anabasis
For the use of schools

ISBN/EAN: 9783337146634

Hergestellt in Europa, USA, Kanada, Australien, Japan

Cover: Foto ©Paul-Georg Meister /pixelio.de

Weitere Bücher finden Sie auf **www.hansebooks.com**

LEXICON

TO

XENOPHON'S ANABASIS

FOR THE USE OF SCHOOLS.

BY THE

REV. WILLIAM BARRACK, M.A.

PRINCIPAL OF DOLLAR INSTITUTION.

LONDON:

LONGMANS, GREEN, AND CO.

1872.

PREFACE.

THIS LEXICON has been prepared to supply a want that has been long felt in our Grammar Schools. The Anabasis of Xenophon is the first Greek book put into the hands of beginners for translation, and it is of the greatest importance to convey correct information at the very beginning of the pupil's course. Many of our youths in Scotland are self-taught. They cannot afford to buy expensive books, and they have not access to correct sources of information at the outset; and hence they often learn forms which have no existence, or slip into errors which have to be unlearned, and which often follow them through life. In the Lexicon the endeavour has been to give, in a cheap form, all the information a reader of the Anabasis may require from such books as are not readily available for beginners. The passages where the words occur have been noted, and varieties of construction have been given, so that the Lexicon will serve both as an *index verborum* and an *index Græcitatis*. It is hoped that the book will be found useful to those preparing for entrance to the Universities, and the medical and other professions.

The books consulted have been numerous. Constant reference has been made to Liddell and Scott's Greek

Lexicon, Veitch's 'Irregular Greek Verbs,' Krüger's 'Lexicon zu Xenophon's Anabasis' (Berlin, 1849), Dr. Friedrich Carl Theiss's 'Wörterbuch zu Xenophon's Anabasis' (Leipzig, 1863), Vollbrecht's 'Anabasis für den Schulgebrauch' (Leipzig, 1861), Kuhner's 'Anabasis' (Gothae, 1852), Anthon's 'Anabasis' by Doran (London, 1856), and other English editions, and Smith's valuable dictionaries.

My best thanks are due to my friends the Rev. J. W. Legge, one of the Classical Masters in the Grammar School, Aberdeen, and Mr. T. A. Stewart, the principal Classical Master in George Watson's College Schools, Edinburgh, for revising the proof sheets.

I may say with a distinguished writer, that 'I have conscientiously striven to be accurate, which no one knows the difficulty of being till he has earnestly made the attempt.' Some errors, I am afraid, have escaped notice, but I hope they are few and far between.

DOLLAR: *September* 20, 1872.

XENOPHON

was born at Athens, B.C. 444,[1] and was the son of Gryllus, a well-to-do citizen of the class of 'knights.' He was a pupil of Socrates, and we have his 'Notes of his Master's Conversations' in the Memorabilia. Socrates was put to death B.C. 399, during Xenophon's absence in Persia with the 'Ten Thousand.' Xenophon, probably on account of his connection with Cyrus, was banished from Athens ; and he joined Agesilaus and the Spartans in the battle of Coronēa, B.C. 394, when the Athenians and Thebans were defeated. As a reward for his services, he received from the Spartans an estate at Scillus, a village two miles from Olympia. Here he lived with his wife (Philesia) and family the quiet life of a country gentleman, occupying his time with literary work, farming, hunting, and dispensing a generous hospitality, particularly when eminent men assembled from all parts of Greece to witness the Olympic games in the neighbourhood. When he was an old man, the Athenians revoked the decree of banishment against him ; but, so far as we can gather, he never returned to Athens, but died at Scillus, or, as some say, at Corinth, at the advanced age of 90. He had two sons Gryllus and Diodorus ; but Gryllus died before his father, having been killed at the battle of Mantinea, B.C. 362.

Xenophon's principal works, besides the Anabasis, are the *Hellenica*, or 'History of Greece' from 411 to 362 B.C. ; the *Cyropædĭa*, or 'The Education of Cyrus,' the Elder,—a historical romance ; and the *Memorabilia*, or 'Recollections of Socrates.' For further particulars see Art. *Xenophon* in Smith's *Dictionary of Biography*, Mure's *History of Grecian Literature*, vol. v., and Sir A. Grant's *Xenophon* in *Ancient Classics for English Readers*.

CYRUS

was born B.C. 422, and was the son of Darius Nothus and Parysatis. At seventeen years of age he was appointed satrap of Lydia, Phrygia, and Cappadocia. His father died B.C. 404, and his elder brother, Artaxerxes Mnemon, became king. Cyrus, dissatisfied with the

---

[1] Mure makes the date B.C. 435 (*History of Grecian Lit.* v. 182) ; Sir A. Grant makes it B.C. 431 (*Ancient Classics*, p. 4).

inferior position he occupied, wished to supersede his brother on the throne. When he went to Babylon, at his father's death, he was accused of plotting against his brother, was arrested, and would have been put to death, had not his mother (Parysatis) obtained his pardon. Cyrus afterwards made war openly upon his brother, but was killed at the battle of Cunaxa,[1] September 7, 401 B.C., at the age of 21.

---

[1] The place where the battle was fought is not mentioned by Xenophon, but Plutarch (Artax. 8) says : Ὁ μὲν οὖν τόπος, ἐν ᾧ παρετάξαντο, Κούναξα καλεῖται, καὶ Βαβυλῶνος ἀπέχει σταδίους πεντακοσίους. He thus makes Cunaxa about 57 miles from Babylon ; but Xenophon says (2. 2. 6) that the battle was fought only 360 stadia from Babylon, or about 40 miles.

DATES OF THE PRINCIPAL EVENTS IN THE ANABASIS.

THE ANABASIS, BOOK I.

B.C.

Departure from Ephesus seven months be-⎱ about Feb. 7, 401.
fore the battle . . . . ⎰

Departure from Sardis (1. 2. 5.) . . . ,, Mar. 6, 401.
Arrival at Celænæ (1. 2. 7.) . . . ,, Mar. 20, 401.
,, Caÿstrus (1. 2. 11.) . . . ,, May 1, 401.
,, Tarsus (1. 2. 23.) . . . ,, June 6, 401.
,, Myriandrus (1. 4. 6.) . . . ,, July 6, 401.
Fording the Euphrates at Thapsacus (1. 4. 11.) ,, Aug. 5, 401.
At the Pylæ (1. 5. 5.) . . . . . ,, Sep. 1, 401.
Battle of Cunaxa (1. 7. 20.) . . . ,, Sep. 7, 401.

The Anabasis occupied seven months, from February 7 to September 7, B.C. 401, from Ephesus to Cunaxa, a distance of 535 parasangs, more than 1,800 miles.

THE KATABASIS, BOOK II. TO THE END.

B.C.

Arrival at the truce villages (2. 2. 16.) . about Sep. 10, 401.
At Sitace (2. 4. 13.) . . . . . ,, Oct. 11, 401.
Massacre at the Zabatus (2. 5. 1.) . . ,, Oct. 29, 401.
Ascent of the Karduchian mountains (4. 1. 4.) ,, Nov. 20, 401.
First snow in Armenia (4. 4. 8.) . . . ,, Dec. 6, 401.
Fording the Eastern Euphrates (4. 5. 2.) . ,, Dec. 13, 401.
Arrival at the villages of refreshment (4. 5. 23.) ,, Dec. 18, 401.
,, the Harpasus river (4. 7. 18.) . ,, Jan. 19, 400.
,, Mount Theches, 'θάλαττα, ιάλαττα'⎱ ,, Feb. 1, 400.
(4. 7. 24.) . . . . ⎰
,, Trapezus (Trebizond) (4. 8. 22.) . ,, Feb. 13, 400.
,, Cotyora (5. 5. 3.) . . . ,, Apr. 13, 400.

B.C.

Arrival at Heraclea (6. 2. 1. or 5. 9. 1.)   .   about July 1, 400.
,,   Chrysopolis (*Scutari*) (7. 1. 1.)   .   ,,   Aug. 7, 400.
Joining Seuthes in Thrace (7. 3. 14.) . .   ,,   Dec. 5, 400.
,, Thimbron (7. 8. 24.) .   .   .   .   ,,   Mar. 5, 399.

The Katabasis (5. 5. 4.) occupied about seven months, from September 7, B.C. 401, to April 13, B.C. 400, from Cunaxa to Cotyora, a distance of 620 parasangs, more than 2,000 miles. The number of Greek troops at the review near Babylon (1. 7. 10.) was 12,900, and at Cerasus (5. 3. 3.), after surmounting all their difficulties, they were found to be 8,600.

*** The figures denote book. chapter, and paragraph. Thus 1. 2. 3. would be the first book, second chapter, third paragraph ; and 1. 2. 3, 4. 4, would be the fourth chapter and fourth paragraph of the same first book, while 1. 2. 3, 4, would be the third and fourth paragraphs of the second chapter of the first book. There are two ways of numbering the chapters in the sixth book. Some give ten chapters to the fifth book, and only four chapters to the sixth ; while others give eight chapters to the fifth, and six to the sixth. The first mode has been adopted in the present work. Hence the quotation 6. 2. 4. will be in most editions 6. 4. 4. and so on. This discrepancy arises from the want of an introductory paragraph in the sixth book. All the other books have a short preface, and the omission in the sixth would lead one to infer that Xenophon intended the fifth and sixth books to be considered one book.

Errata.

LEXICON

TO

XENOPHON'S ANABASIS.

—◦◦—

Ἄβατος, ος, ον, or η, ον (ἀ priv. | diligo ; φιλέω=amo : στέονω.

ERRATUM

Page 163, line 2, for ἀκοράτος read ἄκράτος

υ. 41.   τὸ ἀγαϑὸν, τὸ πᾱγιστι good (*summum bonum*). ἀμεί-νων, ἄριστος; βελτίων, βέλτι-στος; κρείσσων, κράτιστος, etc.

Ἀγάλλομαι τινί, ἐπί τινι, to glory, exult in a thing, be proud of it (only pres. and impf.), 2. 6. 26.

Ἄγαμαι, ἀγάσομαι, 1 aor. ἠγάσ-θην, to admire, wonder at, 1. 1. 9.

Ἄγαν, adv. *too much*, 7. 6. 39.

Ἀγαπάω (ἄγαμαι), ήσω, etc., to *love*, founded on esteem=

ᾰγγελλω (ἄγω), ελῶ, ἤγγελκη, ἤγγελμαι, 1 aor. ἤγγειλα, to bring news, report, proclaim, 2. 3. 19.

Ἄγγελος, ου, ὁ, *a messenger*, 2. 1. 5, 3. 6, etc.

Ἀγείρω (ἀγερῶ), ἀγήγερκα, ἀγή-γερμαι, 1 aor. ἤγειρα, p. ἠγέρθην (ἄγω), to *collect, gather*.

Ἀγένειος, ος, ον (ἀ priv. γένειον, γένυς), *beardless*, 2. 6. 28.

Ἀγησίλαος, ου, ὁ (ἡγέομαι, λαός)· *Agesilaus*, king of Sparta, 5. 3. 6·

* Bopp gives Sansc. agâdhas, *deep* ; Passow, ἄγαν ; Donaldson (Crat. § 323), ἀ euph. and root *ga*, 'joy.' Cf. Eng. *good*, Ger. *gut*.

B

B.C.

Arrival at Heraclea (6. 2. 1. or 5. 9. 1.)   .   about July 1, 400.
,,   Chrysopolis (*Scutari*) (7. 1. 1.)   .   ,,   Aug. 7, 400.
Joining Seuthes in Thrace (7. 3. 14.) .   .   ,,   Dec. 5, 400.
,,   Thimbron (7. 8. 24.) .   . . .   ,,   Mar. 5, 399.

The Katabasis (5. 5. 4.) occupied about seven months, from September 7, B.C. 401, to April 13, B.C. 400, from Cunaxa to Cotyora, a distance of 620 parasangs, more than 2,000 miles. The number of Greek troops at the review near Babylon (1. 7. 10.) was 12,900, and at Cerasus (5. 3. 3.), after surmounting all their difficulties, they were found to be 8,600.

Errata.

Page 34, head line,   *for* Διαγγελλω   *read* Διαγγέλλω.
,,   36, head line,   ,, Διασφειδοναω   ,,   Διασφενδονάω.
,,   65, head line,   ,, ῾Ηδομαι-῾Ημισυς   ,,   ῞Ηδομαι-῞Ημισυς.
,,   65, col. 1, line 1,   ,, Ηδομαι, ἡσθησομαι   ,,   ῞Ηδομαι, ἡσθήσομαι.
,,   65, col. 1, last line, ,, Ηλιος   ,,   ῞Ηλιος.
,,   72, head line,   ,, Καιναι   ,,   Καιναί.
,,   91, col. 2, line 1,   ,, νεός   ,,   νέος.
,,   94, col. 2, line 10,   ,, ἀνηρ   ,,   ἀνήρ.
,,   95, col. 2, line 31,   ,, οἱος   ,,   οἱός.
,,   95, col. 2, last line, insert after ὅϊς *a sheep.*
,,   137, head line, *for* Ταμιενομαι *read* Ταμιενόμαι.
,,   140, col. 2, line 27, *for* Τλήμων, ων, ων, *read* Τλήμων, ων, ον.
,,   144, col. 1, line 22, ,, Υἱός, ου,   ,,   Υἱός, οὗ.

LEXICON

TO

XENOPHON'S ANABASIS.

—◦◦—

Ἄβατος, ος, ον, or η, ον (ἀ priv. βαίνω), *impassable, unfordable*, 5. 6. 9.

Ἀβροζέλμης, ου, ὁ, *Abrozelmes*, a Thracian, Seuthes' interpreter, 7. 6. 43.

Ἀβροκόμας, α, ὁ, *Abrocomas*, satrap of Phœnicia, 1. 3. 20, 1. 4. 3.

Ἄβῦδος, ου, ἡ, *Abydus,* a town on the Asiatic side of the Hellespont, opposite Sestos, 1. 1. 9.

Ἀγαθός, ἡ, όν (ἄγω*), *good, brave, noble.* τὰ ἀγαθά (bona, opes), *goods, wealth,* 3. 5. 1, 4. 4. 9, 6. 27. τὸ ἀγαθόν, *the highest good* (summum bonum). ἀμείνων, ἄριστος; βελτίων, βέλτιστος; κρείσσων, κράτιστος, etc.

Ἀγάλλομαι τινί, ἐπί τινι, *to glory, exult in a thing, be proud of it* (only pres. and impf.), 2. 6. 26.

Ἄγαμαι, ἀγάσομαι, 1 aor. ἠγάσθην, *to admire, wonder at,* 1. 1. 9.

Ἄγαν, adv. *too much,* 7. 6. 39.

Ἀγαπάω (ἄγαμαι), ἠσω, etc., *to love,* founded on esteem =

diligo; φιλέω=*amo*; στέργω, *parental love*; ἐράω, *sexual love,* 5. 5. 13.

Ἀγασίας, ου, ὁ (ἄγαμαι), *Agasias,* a general from Stymphalus in Arcadia, 4. 1. 27, 7. 11.

Ἀγασίας, ου, ὁ, *Agasias,* a seer from Elis, *aliter* Βασίας, 7. 8. 10.

Ἀγαστός, ἡ, όν (ἄγαμαι), *admired, admirable,* 1. 9. 24.

Ἀγγεῖον, ου, τό (ἄγγος, εος, τό), *a vessel, pail,* 6. 4. 23.

Ἀγγελία, ας, ἡ (ἄγγελος), *a message, news.*

Ἀγγέλλω (ἄγω), ελῶ, ἤγγελκα, ἤγγελμαι, 1 aor. ἤγγειλα, *to bring news, report, proclaim,* 2. 3. 19.

Ἄγγελος, ου, ὁ, *a messenger,* 2. 1. 5, 3. 6, etc.

Ἀγείρω (ἀγερῶ), ἀγήγερκα, ἀγήγερμαι, 1 aor ἤγειρα, p. ἠγέρθην (ἄγω), *to collect, gather.*

Ἀγένειος, ος, ον (ἀ priv. γένειον, γένυς), *beardless,* 2. 6. 28.

Ἀγησίλαος, ου, ὁ (ἡγέομαι, λαός), *Agesilaus,* king of Sparta, 5. 3. 6.

---

* Bopp gives Sansc. agâdhas, *deep*; Passow, ἄγαν; Donaldson (Crat. § 323), ἀ euph. and root *ga,* ' joy.' Cf. Eng. *good,* Ger. *gut.*

B

'Αγίας, ov, ὁ (ἄγω), Agias, an Arcadian, one of the Greek generals, 2. 5. 31, 2. 6. 30.

Ἄγκος, εος, τό, a glen or valley, 4. 1. 7.

Ἄγκυρα, Lat. ancŏra, an anchor. ἄγκυραν βάλλειν, ἀφιέναι, to cast anchor. αἴρεσθαι, to weigh anchor. ἐπ' ἀγκύρας ὁρμεῖν, to ride at anchor.

'Αγνοέω, ήσω, ηκα (ἀ priv. νοῦς), Lat. ignorare, not to know.

'Αγνωμοσύνη, ης, ἡ (ἀ priv. γνώμη), want of sense, pl. misunderstandings, 2. 5. 6.

'Αγνώμων, ων, ον, gen. ονος (ἀ priv. γνώμη), senseless, inconsiderate, 7. 6. 23, 38.

'Αγορά, ᾶς, ἡ (ἀγείρω), Lat. forum, a market-place, a market, provisions. ἀγορὰ πλήθουσα, the forenoon, from 9 to 12, when the market is full, 2. 3. 24, 3. 1. 2, etc. ἀγοράν ἄγειν, to bring provisions, 5. 7. 33; πέμπειν, 5. 5. 19; παρέχειν, 2. 3. 24, 3. 1. 2, 5. 5. 6, 18; ἔχειν, 5. 5. 16 : ἀγορᾷ χρῆσθαι, 7. 6. 24; ἀπὸ τῆς ἀγ. ζῆν, to live on what was bought in the market, 5. 9. 1; οἱ ἐκ τῆς ἀγ., the market people, 1. 2. 18; ἀγ. συνάγειν, to call a meeting, 5. 7. 3.

'Αγοράζω, άσω (ἀγορά), to be in the market, to buy or sell, 1. 3. 14, 1. 5. 10.

'Αγορανόμος, ov, ὁ (ἀγορά, νέμω), a clerk of the market, 5. 7. 2.

'Αγορεύω, εύσω (ἀγορά), to harangue in the assembly, proclaim, assert.

'Αγρεύω (ἄγρα), εύσω, to hunt, 5. 3. 8.

Ἄγριος, ία, ιον (ἀγρός), living in the fields, wild, 1. 5. 2.

'Αγρός, οῦ, ὁ, Lat. ager, a field, land, 5. 3. 9.

'Αγρυπνέω, ήσω (ἄγρυπνος, ἀ priv. ὕπνος), to lie awake, to be attentive. τινί, to anything, 7. 6. 36.

Ἄγω, ἄξω, ἦχα or ἀγήοχα, ἦγμαι, 2 aor. ἤγαγον (conj. ἀγάγω), 1 aor. pass. ἤχθην, fut. p. ἀχθήσομαι, to lead, take with one, 2. 4. 8, 5. 4. 33; ἄγειν καὶ φέρειν (ferre et agere), to plunder a country completely. ἄγειν refers to men and cattle, φέρειν, to things, 5. 5. 13, 2. 6. 5; ἄγειν εἰς δίκην (rapere in jus), to carry one to a court of justice, 6. 6. 7, 17; to lead an army, to march, 1. 3. 19, 2. 2. 16, etc.; εἰρήνην, ἡσυχίαν, to keep the peace, 3. 1. 14; βίον, to lead a life (vitam agere); ἄγεσθαι, to take to oneself, γυναῖκα = uxorem ducere; ἄγε, well, come then, 2. 2. 10, so ἄγετε δή in pl., 5. 4. 9, 7. 6. 33.

'Αγώγιμος, ος, ον (ἄγω), easy to be led, or carried, τὰ ἀγώγιμα, goods, wares, a cargo, 5. 1. 16.

'Αγών, ῶνος, ὁ (ἄγω) (ἄγων, οντος, pres. part. of ἄγω), an assembly, a contest, a place of contest. ἀγῶνα ἄγειν, ποιεῖν, τιθέναι, to hold or propose games, 1. 2. 10. The games were πυγμή, boxing, πάλη, wrestling, δρόμος, running, δίσκος, quoits, ἄλμα, leaping (πένταθλον).

'Αγωνίζομαι, ίσομαι, or ιοῦμαι, ἠγώνισμαι, to contend in the games, περί τινος, for anything, πρός τινα, with anyone; ἀγωνίζεσθαι στάδιον, to run in the racecourse, 4. 8. 27.

'Αγωνοθέτης, ου, ὁ (ἀγών, τίθημι), a president in the games, a judge, 3. 1. 21.

"Αδειπνος, ος, ον (ἀ priv. δεῖπνον), dinnerless (incœnatus), unfed, 1. 10. 19.

'Αδελφός, οῦ, ὁ (ἀ cop. δελφύς), a brother, an intimate friend, 7. 2. 25.

'Αδεῶς, adv. (ἀ priv. δέος, fear), without fear, fearlessly, 1. 9. 13, 6. 6. 1.

"Αδηλος, ος, ον (ἀ priv. δῆλος), uncertain, unknown, 5. 1. 10.

'Αδιάβατος, ος, ον (ἀ priv. διά, βαίνω), impassable, 2. 1. 11, 3. 1. 2.

'Αδικέω, ήσω, ἠδίκηκα, ἠδίκημαι (ἀ priv. δίκη), to do wrong, to injure, τινά, anyone, τί, in anything, 1. 6. 7, 2. 6. 20, 5. 7. 5, 7. 6. 14, etc. The pres. has often the force of a perf. I have done wrong, I am in the wrong, 2. 6. 20, 5. 7. 29.

'Αδικία, ας, ἡ, wrong, injustice.

Αδικος, ος, ον (ἀ priv. δίκη), unjust, εἴς τι, in a thing, περί τινα, towards a person; adv. ἀδίκως, unjustly, wrongly, 1. 6. 8, 2. 6. 25.

'Αδόλως, adv. (ἀ priv. δόλος), without fraud or treachery, Lat. sine dolo malo.

'Αδύνατος, ος, ον (ἀ priv. δύναμαι), unable to do a thing, impossible, with inf.; λόγοι ἀδ., ineffectual, 7. 7. 24, πορεία ἀδ., impracticable, 5. 6. 10.

Αἴδω, or ἄδω, poet. ἀείδω, ᾄσομαι, ᾖσμαι, to sing, to praise, 5. 9. 6.

'Αεί, and αἰεί, adv. always, ever, 3. 2. 38, 7. 3. 37; οἱ ἀεὶ τοῦτ' ἔχοντες, they who at any time were in possession of this, 5. 4. 15.   ἀεὶ τὸ ὑπερβάλλον, 4. 1.

7, the part that gained the height from time to time.

'Αετός, and αἰετός ὁ (ἄημι), an eagle, δεξιός, 5. 9. 23; αἴσιος, 6. 3. 2; χρυσοῦς, 1. 10. 12.

"Αθεος, ος, ον (ἀ priv. θεός), without god, godless, reckless, 2. 5. 39.

'Αθῆναι, ῶν, αἱ, Athens, dat. 'Αθήνῃσι, at Athens, 'Αθήναζε, to Athens, the capital of Attica, 7. 3. 19.

'Αθηναία, ας, ἡ, or 'Αθήνη, 'Αθηνᾶ, 'Αθηνάα, Minerva, 7. 3. 39.

'Αθηναῖος, αία, αῖον, Athenian, 7. 1. 27.

Αθλον, ον, τό, a prize, 1. 2. 10, 3. 1. 21.

'Αθροίζω, ίσω, ἤθροισμαι (ἀθρόος), to gather together, collect, assemble, 1. 2. 1, etc.

'Αθρόος, α, ον (ἀ cop. and θρόος from θρέω), collected, gathered together, in crowds, 1. 10. 13, 5. 2. 1, 6. 3. 22, 7. 3. 9.

'Αθυμέω, ήσω, to be ἄθυμος, downhearted, desponding, τινί, 5. 10. 14. ἐπί τινι, πρός τι, at or for a thing, 7. 1. 9.   Vb. ἀθυμητέος, 3. 2. 23.

'Αθυμία, ας, ἡ, faintheartedness, despondency, 3. 2. 8.

Αθυμος, ος, ον (ἀ priv. θυμός), downhearted, desponding. εἴ τις ἀθυμότερος ἦν, if anyone was rather backward, or disinclined, 1. 4. 9. ἀθύμως, adv., 3. 1. 3.

Αἰγιαλός, οῦ, ὁ (ἀΐσσω, ἅλς), the beach, the sea-shore, 6. 4. 1.

Αἰγύπτιος, α, ον, Egyptian, 1. 8. 9.

Αἴγυπτος, ου, ἡ, Egypt, 2. 1. 14.

Αἰδέομαι, έσομαι, ᾖδεσμαι (αἰδώς), to fear, respect, 3. 2. 5.

Αἰδήμων, ων, ον, g. ονος (αἰδώς), bashful, modest, 1. 9. 5.

Αἰδοῖον, ου, τό, mostly in pl. τὰ αἰδοῖα, the loins, 4. 3. 12 ; from

Αἰδώς, όος, contr. οὖς, ἡ, shame, modesty, regard, respect, 2. 6. 19.

Αἰετός, for ἀετός, an eagle.

Αἰήτης, ου, ὁ, Æetes, son of Helios, father of Medea, and king of Colchis, 5. 6. 37.

Αἰθρία, ας, ἡ, poet. αἴθρη, the open sky ; ὑπὸ τῆς αἰθρίας, Lat. sub divo, in the open air, 4. 4. 14.

Αἴθω, only pres. and impf. ᾖθον, to burn (urere) ; αἴθεσθαι, to blaze (ardere), 4. 7. 20, 6. 3. 19.

Αἰκίζομαι, ίσομαι, ἤκισμαι (αἰκία), to outrage, torment, plague, 3. 1. 18, 3. 4. 5, 2. 6. 29.

Αἷμα, ατος, τό (ἄἴσσω or αἴθω), blood (sanguis) ; βρότος (ῥέω), (cruor), gore.

Αἰνέας, or Αἰνείας, α, ὁ (αἰνέω), Æneas, a captain from Stymphalus in Arcadia, 4. 7. 13.

Αἰνιᾶνες, ων, οἱ, sing. Αἰνιάν, ᾶνος, the Ænianians, a Thessalian tribe, in the upper valley of the Sperchīus, separated from the Dolopians by Mt. Othrys, 1. 2. 6, 5. 9. 7.

Αἴξ, αἰγός, ὁ, ἡ (ἀΐσσω), a goat.

Αἰολίς, ίδος, ἡ (sc. γῆ), Æolia, in Asia Minor, on the Ægean coast, 5. 6. 24.

Αἱρετέος, verbal fr. αἱρέω, must be taken, 4. 7. 3.

Αἱρετός, ή, όν (αἱρέω), desirable, chosen; οἱ αἱρετοί, the delegates, 1. 3. 21.

Αἱρέω, ήσω, ᾕρηκα, ᾕρημαι, 2 aor. εἷλον, 1 aor. pass. ᾑρέθην, to take, seize, 1. 6. 2, 3. 4. 8, 4. 2. 13 ; Mid. to choose, 1. 3. 14, 2. 2. 5, 6. 11, τι ἀντί τινος, to prefer one thing to another, 1. 9. 9, 7. 6. 15. The pass. is ἁλίσκομαι, to be caught, 1. 4. 7.

Αἴρω, from ἀείρω, ἀρῶ, ᾖρκα, ᾖρμαι, to raise, lift, 5, 6. 33. Mid. to win.

Αἰσθάνομαι, old form αἴσθομαι, αἰσθήσομαι, ᾔσθημαι, 2 aor. ᾐσθόμην, to perceive, understand, learn, usually acc., 1. 8. 22, 1. 2. 21, 1. 4. 16, sometimes gen., 1. 1. 8, 6. 3. 10.

Αἴσθησις, εως, ἡ, perception, sense; μὴ αἴσθησιν παρέχειν, to escape observation, 4. 6. 13.

Αἴσιος, α, ον, or ος, ον (αἶσα), propitious, lucky, 6, 3, 2.

Αἰσχίνης, ου, ὁ, Æschines, an Acarnanian, who led a company of peltasts, 4. 3. 22, 8. 18.

Αἰσχρός, ά, όν (αἶσχος), shameful, disgraceful, base, 4. 6. 14.

Αἰσχύνη, ης, ἡ, (αἶσχος) (ῡ), shame, τινος, in regard to a person, 3. 1. 10; ἄτευ, 2. 6. 6, ὑπό, 7. 7. 11; disgrace, reproach.

Αἰσχύνω, υνῶ (ᾔσχυγκα), ᾔσχυμμαι, to put to shame, disgrace; Pass. to be ashamed, τινά, before anyone, 2. 5. 39, 2. 3. 22. αἰσχύνομαι ποιῶν, 7. 6. 21, I am ashamed to do it, and yet I do it; αἰσχύνομαι ποιεῖν, I am ashamed to do it, and therefore I refrain from doing it.

Αἰτέω, ήσω, ᾔτηκα, ᾔτημαι, to ask, τινά τι, 1. 1. 10, 1. 3. 14. anyone for anything, also τί παρά τινος, 1. 3. 16, 5. 1. 11,

6, 4. 22; with inf. ζοῦναι, 2. 3. 18, 6. 6. 31.

Αἰτία, ας, ἡ, a cause, a fault, blame, accusation, αἰτίαν ἔχειν τινός, to be accused of a thing, 7. 1. 8, 7. 6. 15, 7. 7. 56.

Αἰτιάομαι, ἄσομαι, (ᾶ), ᾐτίαμαι, to blame, τινά τινος and τινά τι, 1. 2. 20, or acc. and inf. 5. 5. 19, 3. 1. 7, 3. 3. 12.

Αἴτιος, α, ον, causing ill, guilty, τινός τινι, being the cause of a thing to a person. τὸ αἴτιον, the cause, 4. 1. 17. ὁ αἴτιος, the accused (reus), 7. 7. 48. αἴτιος οὐδὲν, guiltless, in no respect to blame, 7. 1. 25.

Αἰχμάλωτος, ος, ον (αἰχμή, ἁλίσκομαι), taken in war, οἱ αἰχ., prisoners; τὰ αἰχ., booty, 4. 1. 13, 5. 9. 4.

Ἀκαρνάν, ᾶνος, ὁ, an Acarnanian.

Ἄκαυστος, ος, ον (ἁ priv. καίω), unburnt, 3. 5. 13.

Ἀκέραιος, ος, ον (ἁ priv. κεράω, κεράννυμι), unmixed, pure, fresh, 6. 5. 9.

Ἀκήρυκτος, ος, ον (ἁ priv. κῆρυξ), without heralds, when no overtures would be listened to, 3. 3. 5.

Ἀκινάκης, ου, ὁ, Lat. acinaces, a Persian word, a short straight sword, worn on the right side, a scimitar, 1. 8. 29.

Ἀκίνδυνος, ος, ον (ἁ priv. κίνδυνος), without danger, free from danger, 2. 6. 6.

Ἄκληρος, ος, ον (ἁ priv. κλῆρος), without lot or portion, poor, needy, 3. 2. 26.

Ἀκμάζω, άσω (ἀκμή), to be in full bloom or vigour, with inf. to be strong enough to do, 3. 1. 25.

Ἀκμήν, in a moment, in an instant, in a twinkling (Ger. Augenblicklich), (Lat. in puncto temporis), 4. 3. 26.

Ἀκόλαστος, ος, ον (ἁ priv. κολάζω), unpunished, unchecked, unbridled, 2. 6. 9.

Ἀκολουθέω, ήσω, etc. (ἀκόλουθος), to follow, go along with, τινί; and σύν τινι, 7. 5. 3.

Ἀκόλουθος, ος, ον (ἁ cop. κέλευθος, ἡ, a way), following. οὐκ ἀκόλουθα, inconsistent, 2. 4. 19.

Ἀκοντίζω, ίσω, (ἀκόντιον), to hurl a javelin at one, τινα, 1. 10. 7, 7. 4. 18.

Ἀκόντιον, ον, τὸ (ἄκων, ἀκή), a javelin (jaculum); δόρυ, the shaft; αἰχμή, the point (of iron); ἀγκύλη (amentum), the strap for hurling it, 4. 2. 28; hence

Ἀκόντισις, εως, ἡ, the throwing the javelin, 1. 9. 5, and

Ἀκοντιστής, οῦ, ὁ, a javelin-thrower, 4. 3. 28.

Ἀκούω, οὐσομαι, ἀκήκοα, ἤκουσμαι, to hear, σάλπιγγος, 4. 2. 8; θορύβου, 1. 8. 16; λόγου, 5. 7. 27; τί or τινός, 1. 10. 5, 4. 1. 3; and τί παρά τινος, or τί τινος, to hear anything from one; with inf. 1. 3. 20, and part. 1. 2. 21; τινός, to obey one, 2. 6. 11, 3. 5. 16; εὖ, κακῶς ἀκούειν, to be well or ill spoken of (Lat. bene, male audire); βαρέως, to hear anything with painful feelings, 2. 1. 9.

Ἄκρα, ας, ἡ (ἀκή), a point, a peak, a citadel, 5, 2. 17, 7. 1. 20.

Ἄκρᾱτος, ος, ον (ἁ priv. κεράννυμι), unmixed. οἶνος ἄκρατος, *wine without water, strong wine,* 4. 5. 27, 5. 4. 29.

Ἄκρῑτος, ος, ον (ἀ priv. κρίνω), *unjudged, untried,* 5. 7. 28.

Ἀκροβολίζομαι, ἰσομαι (ἄκρος, βάλλω), *to throw from afar, to skirmish,* 3. 4. 33, 5. 2. 10.

Ἀκροβόλισις, εως, ἡ, *a skirmishing,* 3. 4. 18.

Ἀκρόπολις, εως, ἡ (ἄκρος, πόλις), *the upper city, the citadel, castle,* 1. 2. 8.

Ἄκρος, α, ον (ἀκή), *highest, topmost, the peak, top,* 1. 2. 21, 3. 4. 27, 4. 7. 25, τὸ ἀκρότατον, *the highest point,* 5. 4. 15.

Ἀκρωνυχία, ας, ἡ (ἄκρος, ὄνυξ), *the tip of the nail, the ridge, a top,* 3. 4. 37, 38.

Ἀκτή, ῆς, ἡ (ἄγνυμι), *the beach, where the waves break.*

Ἄκῡρος, ος, ον (ἀ priv. κύρω), *without authority, obsolete,* ἄκυρον ποιεῖν, *to set aside,* 6. 1. 28.

Ἄκων, ουσα, ον, gen. ἄκοντος (ἀ priv. ἕκων) (ᾰ), *unwilling,* ἄκοντος Κύρου, *against the will of Cyrus,* Lat. *Cyro invito,* 1. 3. 17.

Ἀλαλάζω, άξω, *to raise the ἀλαλά, or war-cry,* 5. 2. 14, 4. 2. 7, etc.

Ἀλεεινός, ή, όν (ἀλέα), *warm, hot,* 4. 4. 11.

Ἀλέξω, ήσω, 1 aor. mid. ἠλεξάμην, fut. ἀλέξομαι from ἀλέκω, *to ward off, repel an attack,* 3. 4. 33, 5. 5. 21, 7. 7. 3, τί τινι, *anything from anybody;* τινί, dat. of person, *to help, defend.* ἀλέξασθαί τινα, *to keep one off from oneself,* ἐχθρόν, *to defend oneself against an enemy,* 1. 3. 6,

ἀλεξόμενος, *by making them a suitable return,* 1. 9. 11.

Ἀλέτης, ου, ὁ (ἀλέω), *a grinder,* ἀλ. ὄνος, *a millstone,* 1. 5. 5.

Ἄλευρα, ων, τα (ἀλίω), *wheaten flour;* ἄλφιτα, *coarser meal,* 1. 5. 6.

Ἀλήθεια, ας, ἡ (ἀληθής), *truth,* 2. 6. 25; τῇ ἀληθείᾳ, *in very truth,* 5. 10. 10.

Ἀληθεύω, εύσω, *to speak truth,* 1. 7. 18; *report truly,* 4. 4. 15, τι *about a thing,* 5. 6. 18, *to prove true,* 7. 7. 25.

Ἀληθής, ής, ές (ἀ priv. λανθάνω), *true, truthful, frank,* τὸ ἀ., *the truth,* 2. 6. 22.

Ἀληθινός, ή, όν, *honest, trusty, genuine, real,* 1. 9. 17.

Ἀλιευτικός, ή, όν (ἀλιεύς, ἅλς), *of or belonging to fishing;* πλοῖον ἀλ., *a fishing boat,* 7. 1. 20.

Ἀλίζω, ἴσω (ἀλής), *to gather together, to assemble,* 2. 4. 3, 6. 3. 3.

Ἄλιθος, ος, ον (ἀ priv. λίθος), *without stones, not stony,* 6.4.5.

Ἅλις, adv. *enough,* ἅλις τούτων ἔχειν, 5. 7. 12.

Ἀλισάρνη, ης, ἡ, *Halisarne,* a town in Mysia, 7. 8. 17.

Ἁλίσκομαι, ἁλώσομαι, ἑάλωκα and ἥλωκα, 2 aor. ἑάλων and ἥλων (ἁλῶ, ἁλοίην, ἁλούς, ἁλῶναι [ᾰ]), *to be taken, caught,* 4. 4. 19, 3. 4. 17, 7. 1. 36, pass. of αἱρέω; with part. *to be caught doing a thing.*

Ἄλκιμος, ος, ον (ἀλκή), *strong, stout, brave,* 4. 3. 4, 4. 7. 15.

Ἀλλά, conj. *but* (ἄλλα (alia), *other things*). At the beginning of a speech, *now, well, now then,* 1. 7. 6, 2. 1. 4; ἀλλὰ γάρ, *but really (at enim*

or *enimvēro*), 3. 2. 25, 5. 7. 8;
ἀλλά γε, 3. 2. 3, *but still, at
least*; ἀλλὰ καί, after οὐδέν or
οὐ μόνον, *but also*; alone, *nay,
even*, 2. 6. 10, 3. 5. 16, ἀλλὰ
μήν (*at vero*), *but really*, 2. 5.
12, 2. 2. 16; ἀλλὰ μήν γε
(*atqui certe*), *but at least*, 1. 9.
18, 2. 5. 14; ἀλλ' ὅμως (*sed
tamen*), *but yet, nevertheless*, 5.
8. 19.
'Αλλαχῆ, adv. (ἄλλος), *elsewhere,
in another place*, 7. 3. 47;
ἄλλος ἀλ., *one here, another
there*; ἄλλοτε ἀλλαχῆ, *now
here, now there*.
'Αλλαχοῦ = ἀλλαχῆ.
"Αλλῃ, adv. sc. ὁδῷ, *in another
way*, 4. 2. 4; sc. χώρᾳ, *in
another place*, 5. 2. 29, 6. 1. 7;
ἄλλῃ καὶ ἄλλῃ, *here and there*,
5. 2. 29.
'Αλλήλων, wants nom. and sing.,
one another, 4. 7. 25.
"Αλλοθεν, adv. (ἄλλος), *from
another place*, 1. 10. 13; ἄλλοι
ἄλλοθεν, *one from one place
another from another*; ἄλλοσε
=*to another place*.
"Αλλομαι, ἀλοῦμαι, 1 aor. ἡλάμην,
2 aor. ἡλόμην (ἄλωμαι, ἀλοί-
μην), *to leap, jump, dance*, 5.
9. 5.
"Αλλος, η, ο, *another*, Lat. *alius*.
ἄλλος ἄλλα λέγει, *one says
this another that*, 2. 1. 15;
ἄλλος ἀλλαχῆ, 7. 3. 47, ἄλλοι
ἄλλως; οἱ ἄλλοι Κρῆτες, *the
others, namely the Cretans*, 5.
2. 31; τῇ ἄλλῃ ἡμέρᾳ, *on the
next day*, 2. 1. 3, 3. 4. 1. ὁ
ἄλλος, τὸ ἄλλο, οἱ ἄλλοι, *the
rest* (*cæteri*); οὐδὲ ἄλλο δένδρον
οὐδέν, *there was not a tree at
all*, 1. 5. 5; τἆλλα for τὰ
ἄλλα (*cætera, reliqua*, not *alia*),

in other respects, 1. 3. 3, 1. 7.
4, 4. 8. 20; ἄλλοτι ἤ, *what
else would we do than, would
we not*, 2. 5. 10.
"Αλλοτε, adv. (ἄλλος ὅτε), *at another time*; ἄλλοτε . . . τότε
δέ, *at other times . . . but at
that time*, 4. 1. 17; ἄλλοτε καὶ
ἄλλοτε, *now and then, from
time to time*, 2. 4. 26, 5. 2.
29.
'Αλλότριος, ία, ιον (ἄλλος), *belonging to another, foreign,
strange*, Lat. *alienus*; κρα-
τουμένων μὲν γὰρ ἐπίστασθε
ὅτι πάντα ἀλλότρια, *for you
know that all things belonging
to the vanquished become the
property of others*, 3. 2. 28.
"Αλλως, adv., *in another way,
otherwise*, 3. 1. 20, 3. 2. 37;
ἄλλως τε καί, *especially, above
all*, 5. 6. 9, 7. 7. 40; *heed-
lessly, at random*, Lat. *temere*,
5. 1. 7.
'Αλόγιστος, ος, ον (ἀ priv. λογίζομαι), *unreasoning, thoughtless,
silly, rash*, 2. 5. 21.
"Αλσος, εος, τό (ἄλδω, *to nourish*,
or ἄλλομαι, *to leap*, as *saltus*,
salio), *a grove*, 5. 3. 12.
"Αλυς, υος, ὁ, *the river Halys* in
Asia Minor, 5. 6. 9.
"Αλφιτον, ου, τό, generally pl.
ἄλφιτα, *barley meal, coarse
meal*, opp. to ἄλευρα, *fine meal*,
1. 5. 6.
'Αλωπεκίς, ίδος, ἡ (ἀλώπηξ), *a
fox-skin cap*, 7. 4. 4.
'Αλώσιμος, ος, ον (ἀλίσκομαι),
easy to take; οὐχ ἀλώσιμον,
impregnable, 5. 2. 3, 7. 8. 10.
"Αμα, adv. *at the same time*, 6. 1.
5, 3. 3. 10, 4. 1. 19; ἅμα μέν
. . . ἅμα δέ, *partly . . .
partly*, 3. 4. 19, 4. 1. 4; ἅμα

τε . . . καί (simul atque), as
soon as, 7. 1. 7, 5. 2. 14;
prep. together with, gov. dat.
ἅμα τῇ ἡμέρᾳ, at daybreak, 2.
1. 2, 4. 3. 3; ἅμα εἰπὼν ἀνέστη,
as soon as he spoke he stood up,
3. 1. 47.

'Αμαζόνες, ὦν, αἱ (sing. 'Αμαζών,
όνος, ἡ), (ἀ, μαζός, breastless,
because they cut off the right
breast, or Circassian maza, the
moon, because they were the
priestesses of Artemis). The
Amazons, a race of female
warriors, living on the river
Thermōdon, in Asia Minor, 4.
4. 16.

Ἅμαξα, ης, ἡ (ἅμα, ἄγω, or ἅμα,
ἄξων, ονος, an axle), a waggon,
1. 5. 7. βοῦς ὑφ' ἁμάξης, a
draught-ox.

Ἁμαξιαῖος, αία, αῖον (ἅμαξα),
fit for a waggon; λίθοι, stones
large enough to fill a waggon,
4. 2. 3.

Ἁμαξιτός, ός, όν (ἅμαξα, εἶμι),
traversed by waggons; ὁδός,
a carriage road, a highway,
1. 2. 21.

Ἁμαρτάνω, ἁμαρτήσομαι, ἡμάρ-
τηκα, ἡμάρτημαι, 2 aor. act.
ἥμαρτον, 1 aor. pass. ἡμαρ-
τήθην, to err, fail, miss, 5. 8.
20; περί τινά τι, to do some
wrong in regard to a person,
3. 2. 20; τινός, to miss one,
1. 5. 12, 3. 4. 15. ἁμαρτη-
θέντα, Lat. peccata, even slight
mistakes, 5. 8. 20.

Ἁμαχεί, adv. (ἀ priv. μάχη),
without fighting, 1. 7. 9, 3. 4.
46, 6. 3. 15.

Ἁμαχητί, adv.=ἁμαχεί, 4. 2. 15.

Ἁμβρακιώτης, ου, ὁ, an inhabitant of Ambracia, 1. 7. 18.

Ἀμείνων, ων, ον, comp. of ἀγα-

θός (Lat. amœnus), better,
abler, braver, 1. 7. 3, 5. 6. 28,
7. 7. 54.

'Αμέλεια, ας, ἡ (ἀ priv. μέλει),
neglect, carelessness, 4. 6. 3.

'Αμελέω, ήσω, ἠμέληκα, ἠμέλη-
μαι, to be careless, negligent
of, Gen. 7. 2. 7, 1. 3. 11.

Ἀμελῶς, adv. carelessly, 5. 1. 6.

Ἄμετρος, ος, ον (ἀ priv. μέτρον),
without measure, immense, 3.
2. 16.

'Αμήχανος, ος, ον (ἀ, μηχανή),
without means, in trouble, 1.
5. 21. ὁδὸς ἀμήχανος εἰσελ-
θεῖν, a road hard, or impossible, to enter on, 1. 2. 21.
κακά, evils without remedy,
irremediable, 2. 3. 18.

'Αμιλλάομαι, ήσομαι, ημαι (ἅμιλ-
λα, ἅμα), to contend, struggle
for anything, ἐπί τι, 3. 4. 46;
ἐπὶ τὸ ἄκρον, to reach the
height, 3. 4. 44.

Ἄμπελος, ου, ἡ (ἀμφί), a vine,
a vineyard, 1. 2. 22.

'Αμπρακιώτης, ου='Αμβρακιώτης.

'Αμυγδάλινος, η, ον, of almonds;
ἔλαιον, almond oil, 4. 4. 13.

Ἀμύζω, see μύζω.

'Αμύνω, ἀμύνω, 1. aor. ἤμυνα, to
ward off (ἀ euph. μύνη, an
excuse). Mid., to ward off
from oneself, to defend, guard
oneself, 5. 4. 25; τινα, against
one, 2. 3. 23; punish.

'Αμφί, prep., round, on both sides,
but περί, all round, gov. gen.
(rarely in prose), 4. 5. 17,
dat. and acc. (usually in
prose); οἱ ἀμφὶ Τισσαφέρνην,
Tissaphernes and his retinue,
3. 5. 1, 4. 3. 21; sometimes
the retinue alone, 1. 8. 21;
sometimes the person alone.
ἀμφί τι ἔχειν or εἶναι, to be oc-

cupied with, be busy about, 3. 5. 14, 5. 2. 26, 6. 4. 1. ἀμφί τι δαπανᾶν, 1. 1. 8, to spend money on anything; τὰ ἀμφὶ τάξεις, the things relating to tactics, 2. 1. 7; ἀμφὶ τοὺς δισχιλίους, about, of number, 1. 2. 9; of time, ἀμφὶ ἀγοράν, 1. 8. 1, 1. 10. 17.

Ἀμφιγνοέω, ἥσω (ἀμφί, νοέω, Æol. γνοέω), to be doubtful. ἠμφιγνόουν ὅ, τι ἐποίουν, they did not know what they were doing, 2. 5. 33.

Ἀμφίδημος, ου, ὁ, Amphidemus, an Athenian, father of Amphicrates, 4. 2. 13.

Ἀμφικράτης, ους, ὁ, an Athenian, Amphicrates, 4. 2. 13.

Ἀμφιλέγω, ξω, to dispute, 1. 5. 11, τι about anything.

Ἀμφίπολις, εως, ἡ, Amphipolis, a city in Thrace, on both sides of the Strymon, and hence the name, 1. 10. 7.

Ἀμφιπολίτης, ου, ὁ, a citizen of Amphipolis.

Ἀμφορεύς, έως, ὁ (ἀμφί, φέρω), a jar, 5. 4. 28. Lat. amphŏra.

Ἀμφότερος, α, ον (ἄμφω), both, Lat. ambo, 1. 5. 17.

Ἀμφοτέρωθεν, on both sides, 1. 10. 9, 3. 4. 29.

Ἄμφω, οιν, both, 4. 2. 21.

Ἄν (ᾱ)=ἐάν=ἤν=if, takes the conjunctive. (ἄν=ἂ ἤν.)

Ἄν, the conditional particle, joined to ind. of past tenses, to conj., to opt., to part., to inf., but not to imperat. or presential indicatives. It never stands at the beginning of a sentence. With ind. of historical tenses, 1. 5. 2, 1. 9. 19, 2. 3. 11, 3. 4. 22; ὡς τις ἂν ᾤετο, 1. 5. 8; ἔφην

ἄν, 3. 2. 24; ἐπέτρεπον, 3. 5. 12; ἐπορεύθησαν, 4. 2. 10. With fut., ἀπαλλάξετε, but better reading is ἀπαλλάξαιτε, 5. 6. 32. With opt., 1. 3. 19, 1. 7. 2, 3. 1. 7; after ὅτι, 1. 6. 2, 2. 1. 10, ὡς, 3. 2. 4; after rel., 3. 2. 12, 2. 5. 11, 1. 5. 9, 7. 2. 6. With conj., ὡς δ' ἂν μάθῃς, 2. 5. 16, 2. 5. 18, 1. 3. 5, 1. 3. 15; πρίν, 1. 1. 10. With inf. 1. 3. 6, 2. 1. 12, 3. 1. 17, 5. 9. 31. With part., 1. 1. 10, 7. 7. 30, 5. 2. 8, 6. 2. 7, 4. 7. 16.

Ἀνά, prep. gov. acc. up, opp. to κατά, down, 3. 5. 16, 7. 4. 2. With numerals it has a distributive force, ἀνὰ πέντε παρασάγγας τῆς ἡμέρας, five parasangs each day, 3. 4. 21, 4. 6. 4. Of time, through; ἀνὰ κράτος, with all one's might, vigorously, like κατὰ κράτος, 1. 8. 1, 4. 3. 20.

Ἀναβαίνω, βήσομαι, βέβηκα, βέβαμαι, 2 aor. ἀνέβην, to go up from the coast into the interior, 1. 1. 2, 3. 4. 25; mount, 1. 8. 3; go on board, 5. 9. 14.

Ἀναβάλλω, βαλῶ, βέβληκα, βέβλημαι, to throw up, 5. 2. 5; ἐπὶ τὸν ἵππον, to put on horseback, in equum inferre (Cæs.), 4. 4. 4.

Ἀνάβασις, εως, ἡ (ἀνά, βαίνω), a going up, mounting, an expedition or journey from the coast into the interior of a country, 1. 4. 9, 3. 1. 1, 4. 1 10, 7. 8. 26.

Ἀναβιβάζω, άσω, to make go up, take up, 1. 10. 14.

Ἀναβοάω, ήσομαι, to cry aloud, shout out, 5. 4. 31.

Ἀναβολή, ῆς, ἡ (ἀνά, βάλλω), a mound of earth, an embankment, 5. 2. 5.

Ἀναγγέλλω, ελῶ, ἀνήγγελκα, ἀνήγγελμαι, to carry back tidings, to report, 1. 3. 21.

Ἀναγιγνώσκω, γνώσομαι, ἀνέγνωκα, ἀνέγνωσμαι, 1 aor. ἀνέγνωσα, I persuaded, 2 aor. ἀνέγνων, to know well, to read, 1. 6. 4.

Ἀναγκάζω, άσω, ἠνάγκασμαι (ἀνάγκη), to force, compel; τινά τι, anyone to do a thing, 6. 2. 6, inf. 4. 5. 21.

Ἀναγκαῖος, ος, ον (ἀνάγκη), necessary. τὸ ἀν., necessity, 1. 5. 9. οἱ ἀναγκαῖοι, relatives, Lat. necessarii, 2. 4. 1.

Ἀνάγκη, ης, ἡ (ἀνά, ἄγχω), necessity, need, 4. 5. 15. ἀνάγκη ἐστί, with inf., it is necessary that, 5. 4. 20; often without ἐστί.

Ἀνάγω, άξω, ῆχα, ῆγμαι, 2 aor. ἀνήγαγον (ἀνά, ἄγω), to lead up, bring up, 3. 4. 28, 2. 3. 21, 2. 6. 1; Mid. to put to sea, Lat. ferri in altum, 5. 7. 17, 9. 33.

Ἀναζεύγνυμι, ζεύξω, to yoke again; στρατόπεδον, to break up the camp, Lat. castra movere, to march off, 3. 4. 37, 4. 6. 1.

Ἀναθαρρέω, or θαρσέω, ήσω, τεθάρρηκα, to regain courage, 6. 2. 12.

Ἀνάθημα, ατος, τὸ (ἀνά, τίθημι), that which is set up, a votive offering, as tripods, statues, etc., 5. 3. 5.

Ἀναθορυβέω (ἀνά, θόρυβος), to cry out loudly, applaud, 5. 1. 3, 9. 30.

Ἀναιρέω, ήσω, ἀνήρηκα, μαι, 2 aor. ἀνεῖλον (ἀνά, αἱρέω), to take up, Lat. tollere, to lift

one's voice; φωνήν, to answer as an oracle, to give a response, 3. 1. 6, 5. 3. 7; with inf. θύεσθαι, 3. 1. 8, 7. 6. 44. ἀναιροῦμαι πόλεμον, to undertake a war, begin, 5. 7. 27. νεκροὺς ἀναιρεῖσθαι, to take up the dead for burial, 4. 1. 19, 5. 7. 30.

Ἀνακαίω, καύσω, to kindle, light up, 3. 1. 3.

Ἀνακαλέω, έσω, κέκληκα, κέκλημαι, to call upon, to summon; τῇ σάλπιγγι ἀνακαλεῖσθαι, to sound a retreat, Lat. receptui canere, 4. 4. 22.

Ἀνακοινόω, ώσω, to communicate something to another, τινί τι, communicare aliquid cum aliquo, 5. 6. 36, or τινὶ περί τινος, 3. 1. 5, 5. 9. 22; ἀνακοινοῦσθαι, 5. 6. 36.

Ἀνακομίζω, κομίσω, κεκόμισμαι, to carry up, store up, 4. 7. 1, 17.

Ἀνακράζω, κράξομαι, κέκραγα, 2 aor. ἀνέκραγον, to cry out, shout aloud, 4. 4. 20, 7. 3. 33.

Ἀναλαλάζω, ξω, to raise the war-cry ἀλαλά, 4. 3. 19.

Ἀναλαμβάνω, λήψομαι, εἴληφα, εἴλημμαι, 2 aor. ἀνέλαβον, to take up ὅπλα, 6. 3. 1, or with one, ἱερεῖα, 7. 1. 41, 5. 2. 32, 1. 10. 6, 4. 7. 24.

Ἀναλάμπω, ψω to flame up, take fire, 5. 2. 24.

Ἀναλέγω, ξω, ἀνείλοχα, ἀνείλεγμαι, to gather, recount, 2. 1. 17.

Ἀναλίσκω, λώσω, ἀνήλωκα and ἀνάλωκα, ἀνήλωμαι and ἀνάλωμαι, to spend, to squander.

Ἀνάλωτος, ος, ον (ἀ priv. ἁλίσκομαι), not taken, impregnable, 5. 2. 20.

Ἀναμένω, μενῶ, μεμένηκα, to wait for, await, τινά or τί, 6. 4.

1, with acc. and inf. 3. 1. 14, 24.

Ἀναμίγνῦμι, or -ύω, μίξω, μέμιχα, μέμιγμαι, to mix up, ἐν among, 4. 8. 8.

Ἀναμιμνήσκω, ἀναμνήσω, μέμνηκα, μέμνημαι, to remind one of a thing, τινά τι or τινά τινος; Mid. to call to mind, recollect, τί, 7. 1. 26, or part. 6. 1. 23.

Ἄνανδρος, ος, ον (ἀ priv. ἀνήρ), unmanly, cowardly, 2. 6. 25.

Ἀναξίβιος, ου, ὁ, Anaxibius, a Spartan admiral, 7. 1. 10, 13.

Ἀναξυρίδες, ων, αἱ (ἀνά, σύρω, to draw, Eustath.; probably Persian), trousers, ποικίλαι, tartan, 1. 5. 8.

Ἀναπαύω, σω, κα, μαι, to make to cease, give rest; Mid. to rest, to cease, desist, 1. 10. 16, 4. 1. 14, 2. 2. 4, 3. 1. 3, 5. 6. 31.

Ἀναπείθω, πείσω, πέπεικα, πέπεισμαι, to persuade, τινά τι, one of a thing, 5. 7. 1; inf. to do a thing, 1. 4. 11.

Ἀναπετάννυμι, πετάσω, πεπέτασμαι or πέπταμαι, to spread out, open; ἀναπεπταμέναι πύλαι, open gates, 7. 1. 17.

Ἀναπηδάω, ήσω, to leap up, spring, mount on horseback, 7. 2. 20. Lat. conscendere, often without equum.

Ἀναπνέω, πνεύσω, to breathe again, take breath, revive, 4. 1. 22.

Ἀναπράττω, πράξω, πέπραχα, πέπραγμαι, to exact, levy, 7. 7. 31.

Ἀναπτύσσω, ύξω, to unfold; τὸ κέρας, to extend the front, to deploy, Lat. explicare, 1. 10. 9. Others say, to increase

the depth, in 1. 10. 9. Fr. réplier, to fold back the wing.

Ἀνάπτω, ψω, to make fast, fasten, to light up, kindle, 5. 2. 24.

Ἀναπυνθάνομαι, πεύσομαι, πέπυσμαι, to search out, inquire into, learn by inquiry, ταῦτα πραττόμενα, that these things were being done, 5. 7. 1.

Ἀναρίθμητος, ος, ον (ἀ priv. ἀριθμός), innumerable, countless, 3. 2. 13.

Ἀνάριστος, ος, ον, without breakfast (ἀ priv. ἄριστον), 1. 10. 19, 4. 2. 4.

Ἁρπάζω, ξω and σω, ἀνήρπακα, ἀνήρπασμαι and αγμαι, to snatch up; 7. 1. 15, carry off, plunder.

Ἀναρχία, ας, ἡ (ἀ priv. ἀρχή), lawlessness, anarchy, 3. 2. 29.

Ἀνασκευάζω, άσω, ἀνεσκεύασμαι (opp. to κατασκευάζω), to pack up, 6. 2. 8, often the baggage, σκεύη, Lat. vasa colligere; Mid. to march away.

Ἀνασταυρόω, ώσω (ἀνά, σταυρός, a stake, ἵστημι), to impale, crucify, fix on a stake, 3. 1. 17.

Ἀναστέλλω, στελῶ, ἔσταλκα, ἔσταλμαι, to send up, to check, keep back, 5. 4. 23.

Ἀναστρέφω, ψω, ἀνέστροφα, ἀνέστραμμαι, to turn upside down, turn back, 1. 4. 5, 4. 3. 29; Mid. face about, 1. 10. 12; to act, 2. 5. 14.

Ἀναταράττω or άσσω, άξω, τετάραγμαι, to stir up, confuse, throw into confusion, 1. 7. 20.

Ἀνατείνω, τενῶ, τέτακα, τέταμαι, to stretch up, lift up, hold up, 3. 2. 9, 33, 38; syn. αἴρειν, 5. 6. 33, 7. 3. 6. ἀετὸς ἀνατεταμένος, a spread eagle, 1. 10. 12; stretch out, 7. 4. 9.

'Ανατέλλω, τελῶ, τέταλκα, τέταλ-
μαι, 1 aor. ἀνέτειλα (ἀνά,
τέλλω), trans. to make rise,
intr. to rise, of the sun, 2. 3.
1; so ἀνίσχω.
'Ανατίθημι, θήσω, τέθεικα, τέθειμαι, 1 aor. ἀνέθηκα, 2 aor.
mid. ἀνεθέμην, to lay upon, 3.
1. 30, 2. 2. 4; to consecrate,
deposit, 5. 3. 5, 4. 7. 26.
'Ανατρέφω, θρέψω, τέτροφα, τέθραμμαι, to bring up, to fatten,
4. 5. 35.
'Αναφεύγω, ξομαι, to escape, flee
up, 2 aor. ἀνέφῦγον, 6. 2. 24.
'Αναφρονέω, ήσω, to come back
to one's senses (resipiscere),
4. 8. 21.
'Αναχάζω, άσω, 2 aor. ἐχᾰδον,
to drive back; Mid. to draw
back, retire, 4. 7. 10. In 4. 1.
16, Act. as Mid.
'Αναχωρέω, ήσω, κεχώρηκα, to
retire, draw back; ἐπὶ πόδα,
to retreat backwards, leisurely,
Lat. pedetentim, 5. 2. 32.
'Αναχωρίζω, ίσω, to make to
go back, cause to retire, 5. 2.
10.
'Ανδραγαθία, ας, ἡ (ἀνήρ, ἀγαθός),
the character of a brave, good
man, manly virtue, courage, 5.
2. 11.
'Ανδράποδον, ου, τὸ (ἀνήρ, πούς,
better from ἄνδρα ἀποδόσθαι),
a slave taken in war; Lat.
mancipium, 4. 1. 12.
'Ανδρεῖος, εία, εῖον (ἀνήρ), manly,
courageous; comp. -ότερος,
superl. -ότατος.
'Ανδρειότης, ητος, ἡ, manliness
(virtus)=ἀνδρεία, 6. 5. 14.
'Ανδρίζω, ίσω, to make a man of,
make strong; Mid. to act man-
fully, 5. 8. 15; showing manliness, 4. 3. 34.

'Ανεγείρω, εγερῶ, εγήγερκα, εγή-
γερμαι, 1 aor. act. ἀνήγειρα;
pass. ἀνηγέρθην (ἀνά, ἐγείρω),
to wake up, rouse.
'Ανειπεῖν (ἀνά, εἰπεῖν), to proclaim, make a proclamation
that, with inf. Pass. form ἀν-
ερρήθην 2. 2. 20, 5. 2. 18.
'Ανεκπίμπλημι, ἀνεκπλήσω (ἀνά,
ἐκ, πίμπλημι), to fill up or
again, 3. 4. 22.
"Ανεμος, ου, ὁ (ἄημι, to blow),
the wind, hence Lat. animus.
'Ανεπίληπτος, ος, ον (ἀ priv. ἐπί,
λαμβάνω), adv. -τως, not open
to be attacked, blameless, fault-
less, 7. 6. 37.
'Ανερεθίζω, ίσω, to provoke; Pass.
to be excited; Lat. irritare, 6.
6. 9.
'Ανερωτάω, ήσω, to ask again or
repeatedly, 2. 3. 4, 4. 5. 34.
"Ανευ, adv. or prep., without, gov.
gen. 1. 3. 13.
'Ανευρίσκω, ευρήσω, εὕρηκα, εὕρημαι, 2 aor. act. ἀνεῦρον, 1 aor.
pass. ἀνευρέθην, to find out,
discover, 7. 4. 14.
'Ανέχω, ἕξω or ἀνασχήσω, ἀνέ-
σχηκα, ἀνέσχημαι, 2 aor. act.
ἀνέσχον, to hold up, lift up,
to put up with, endure, 1.
7. 4, 1. 8. 11, 7. 7. 47.
Intrans. to rise as the sun,
pres. ἀνίσχω. αὐτοῦ βασιλεύ-
οντος ἀνέχεσθαι, to endure his
being king, 2. 2. 1; to restrain
oneself, 1. 8. 26, 5. 6. 34.
Impf. mid. ἠνειχόμην, 2 aor.
ἠνεσχόμην, double augm.
'Ανεψιός, οῦ, ὁ (ἀ cop. and νέπο-
δες, Lat. nepotes, ' grandsons
together,' Don.), a cousin, a
kinsman, 7. 8. 9.
'Ανήκεστος, ος, ον (ἀ priv. ἀκέο-
μαι), incurable, fatal. ἀν

κακόν τινα ποιεῖν, to inflict, irremediable evils, ruin utterly 2. 5. 5.

'Ανήκω, ξω, to come up to, reach up to, 6. 4. 3.

'Ανήρ, ἀνδρός, ὁ, a man, vir, opp. to woman, (ἄνθρωπος, homo, opp. to beast). ἄνδρες στρατιῶται, 1. 3. 3, 7. 1. 25; ἅ. εὐεργέται, 7. 7. 23. οἱ ἄνδρες, the enemy, 3. 1. 23; ὁ ἀνήρ=ἀνήρ, τοῦ ἀνδρός= τἀνδρός, 7. 7. 3.

'Ανθέμιον, ον, τὸ (ἄνθος, εος, τὸ), a flower, a spiral line, 5. 4. 32.

'Ανθίστημι, ἀντιστήσω, ἀνθέστηκα, ἀνθέσταμαι (ἀντί, ἵστημι), to set against; Mid. to oppose, resist, τινί anyone.

Ανθρώπινος, η, ον (ἄνθρωπος), of or belonging to man. τὰ ἀνθρώπινα, human remedies, 2. 5. 8.

Ἄνθρωπος, ου, ὁ, man, Lat. homo, opp. to beast, 1. 7. 4, 3. 3. 5, 4. 2. 7, 7. 3. 43, 6. 2. 23.

'Ανιάω, άσω, 1 aor. pass. ἠνιάθην, to vex, grieve; (ἀνία, ας, ἡ, grief), 3. 3. 19, 4. 8. 26.

'Ανίημι, ἀνήσω, ἀνεῖκα, ἀνεῖμαι, 1 aor. ἀνῆκα (ἀνά, ἵημι), to send up, let go, let loose, 7. 6. 30.

'Ανιμάω, ήσω, usu. ἥσομαι (ἀνά, ἱμάς, άντος, ὁ, a leather strap), to draw up, to pull up, 4. 2. 8.

'Ανίστημι, ἀναστήσω, ἀνέστηκα, ἀνέσταμαι, to set or raise up ; Mid. to rise up, so 2 aor. act. ἀνέστην, and pf. and plp. act. intrans. 4. 5. 19, 21, 1. 5. 3, 1. 3. 13, 4. 5. 8, 3. 1. 15, 4. 8. 21, 5. 9. 5.

'Ανίσχω (ἀνά, ἴσχω) = ἀνέχω, intr. to rise, as the sun, 2. 1. 3, 5. 7. 6 ; so ἀνατέλλω.

Ἄνοδος, ου, ἡ (ἀνά, ὁδός), the way up, specially into Central Asia, like ἀνάβασις, 2. 1. 1.

Ἄνοδος, ος, ον, (ἀ priv. ὁδός), without a road, impassable, 4. 8. 10.

'Ανόητος, ος, ον (ἀ priv. νοέω), without understanding, senseless, silly.

'Ανοίγω or ἀνοίγνυμι, ἀνοίξω, ἀνέῳχα, ἀνέῳγμαι, to open, 2 pf. ἀνέῳγα, intr. am or stand open, impf. ἀνέῳγον, 1 aor. act. ἀνέῳξα, pass. ἀνεῴχθην, 5. 5. 20.

'Ανομία, ας, ἡ (ἀ priv. νόμος), sin, lawless conduct, 5. 7. 34.

'Ανόμοιος, ος and α, ον (ἀ priv. and ὅμοιος), unlike. ἀνομοίως, ἔχειν, to be differently situated, 7. 7. 49.

Ἄνομος, ος, ον (ἀ priv. νόμος), without law, lawless, impious, 6. 4. 13.

'Ανταγοράζω, άσω (ἀντί, ἀγοράζω), to buy in return, 1. 5. 5.

'Αντακούω, οὐσομαι (ἀντί, ἀκούω), to hear in turn, 2. 5. 16.

Ἄντανδρος, ου, ἡ, Antandrus, a city in Mysia, 7. 8. 7.

'Αντεμπλέω or ἀντεμπίπλημι, ἀντεμπλήσω, etc. (ἀντί, ἐν, πλέω, or πίμπλημι), to fill in turn, in requital, 4. 5. 28.

'Αντεπιμελέομαι, ἥσομαι (ἀντί, ἐπιμελέομαι,) to attend or give heed in turn, 3. 1. 16.

'Αντευποιέω, ήσω, ηκα, ημαι (ἀντί, εὖ, ποιέω), to do good in turn, 5. 5. 21.

'Αντί, a prep. gov. the gen. over against, opposite, 4. 7. 6 ; in return for, instead of, 1. 1. 4. ἀνθ᾽ ὧν εὖ ἔπαθον=ἀντὶ τούτων ἅ, in return for the favours I received, 1. 3. 4; in exchange for, 1. 7. 3.

Ἀντιδίδωμι, δώσω, δέδωκα, δέδομαι (ἀντί, δίδωμι), to give in return, 3. 3. 19.

Ἀντιθέω, θεύσομαι (ἀντί, θέω), to run opposite, 4. 8. 17.

Ἀντικαθίστημι, καταστήσω, καθέστηκα, καθέσταμαι (ἀντί, κατά, ἵστημι), to place or appoint instead of, 3. 1. 38.

Ἀντιλέγω, ξω (ἀντί, λέγω), to speak against, oppose, 2. 3. 25, 7. 3. 14; μὴ ἰέναι, 2. 5. 29.

Ἀντιλέων, οντος, ὁ (ἀντί, λέων) Antileon, a native of Thurii, in Italy, 5. 1. 2.

Ἀντίος, α, ον (ἀντί), opposite, against. οἱ λόγοι ἀντίοι εἰσὶν ἢ οὓς ἤκουον, the words are the very reverse of those I heard, 6. 4. 34; ἰέναι, ἐλαύνειν, 1. 8. 17, 24.

Ἀντιπαραθέω, θεύσομαι, (ἀντί, παρά, θέω), to run to either side opposite, 4. 8. 17.

Ἀντιπαρασκευάζομαι, άσομαι, παρέσκευασμαι (ἀντί, παρά, σκευάζω), to prepare oneself in turn, in opposition, 1. 2. 5.

Ἀντιπαρατάττω, τάξω, τέταχα, τέταγμαι (ἀντί, παρά, τάττω), to draw out in array against. ἀντιπαρατάττεσθαι φάλαγγα, to draw up in battle array opposite; κατὰ φάλαγγα, 4. 8. 9, in line, with a greater front than depth.

Ἀντιπάρειμι (ἀντί, παρά, εἶμι), to march over against, or alongside, parallel with, 4. 3. 17.

Ἀντιπάσχω, πείσομαι, πέπονθα (ἀντί, πάσχω), to suffer in turn, 2. 5. 17.

Ἀντιπέρας (ἀντί, πέρας), adv. over against, opposite, 4. 8. 3.

Ἀντιποιέω, ήσω, ηκα, ημαι (ἀντί, ποιέω), to do in return, 3. 3. 7; Mid. c. gen., to seek after, lay claim to, ἀρετῆς, 4. 7. 12; to contend for ἀρχῆς empire τινί with one, 2. 1. 11; or περί τινος, 5. 2. 11, for anything.

Ἀντιπορεύομαι, εύσομαι (ἀντί, πορεύω), to march against, false reading, 4. 8. 17.

Ἀντίπορος, ος, ον (ἀντί, πόρος), over against, 4. 2. 18.

Ἀντιστασιάζω (ἀντί, στασιάζω), to form a party against one, τινί, 4. 1. 27.

Ἀντιστασιώτης, ου, ὁ, one of the opposite party. οἱ ἀν. 1. 1. 10, the opposite faction.

Ἀντιστοιχέω, ήσω (ἀντί, στοιχέω), to stand opposite in rows or pairs, as in a dance, 5. 4. 12.

Ἀντιστρατοπεδεύω, εύσω (ἀντί, στρατοπεδεύω), to encamp opposite, 7. 7. 33.

Ἀντιτάττω, τάξω, τέταχα, τέταγμαι (ἀντί, τάττω), to draw up opposite, to range in battle against, λιμόν τινι, 2. 5. 19; ἀντιτετάχαται, Ion. for ἀντιτεταγμένοι εἰσί, 4. 8. 5.

Ἀντιτιμάω, ήσω, ηκα, ημαι (ἀντί, τιμάω), to honour in turn, 5. 5. 14.

Ἀντιτοξεύω, εύσω (ἀντί, τοξεύω), to shoot arrows in turn, 3. 3. 15, 5. 2. 32.

Ἀντιφυλάττω, άξω (ἀντί, φυλάττω), to watch in turn; Mid. to be on one's guard against one, τινά, 2. 5. 3.

Ἄντρον, ον, τό, Lat. antrum, a cave, cavern.

Ἀντρώδης, ης, ες (ἄντρον, εἶδος), full of caves, 4. 3. 11.

Ἀνυστός, ός, όν (ἀνύω), possible,

σιγῇ ὡς ἀνυστόν, as silently as possible, 1. 8. 11.

Ἀνύω or ἀνύτω (ῠ), ὗσω, ἤνῠκα, ἤνυσμαι, to accomplish, 7. 7. 24.

Ἄνω (ἀνά), adv. up, above; comp. ἀνωτέρω, higher, 1. 4. 17; superl. ἀνωτάτω, 7. 4. 11. τὸ ἄνω, the party above, 4. 6. 26. ὁ ἄνω βασιλεύς, the king of the upper country, 7. 7. 3; the Persian king, 7. 1. 28; 4. 1. 6, 1. 7. 15. Of countries, inland (opp. to κάτω), from the coast, to the interior. οἱ ἄνω, the living, sometimes, our ancestors. οἱ κάτω, the dead. ἡ ἄνω ὁδός, 3. 1. 8.

Ἀνώγαιον, ου, τό (ἄνω, γαῖα), anything raised above the ground, a room, the upper floor, 5. 4. 29.

Ἄνωθεν (ἄνω), adv. from above, 4. 7. 12; from the interior of a country, 7. 7. 2.

Ἀξία, ας, ἡ, worth, value, deserts, 6. 4. 33; κατ' ἀξίαν, according to one's desert, duly.

Ἀξίνη, ης, ἡ (ῐ) (ἄγνυμι), an axe, 1. 5. 12, 7. 1. 17. In 4. 4. 12 it is understood.

Ἄξιος, ία, ιον, adj. (ἄγω), worth, worthy, with gen. πολλοῦ ἄξιος, valuable, worth much, 1. 3. 12, 4. 1. 28. παντὸς ἄξιος, worthy of all esteem, all important, 7. 3. 13. ἄξιόν ἐστι, operæ pretium est, æquum est, decet, with inf. and dat. pers. 7. 3. 19; it is worth while, 5. 8. 7; it is right, proper, becoming, 5. 7. 5, 2. 3. 25, 7. 3. 19.

Ἀξιοστράτηγος, ος, ον, adj. worthy of being commander, worthy of a great general, 3. 1. 24.

Ἀξιόω, ώσω (ἄξιος), to think one

worthy, τινά τινος, 3. 2. 7; to think it right, Lat. æquum censere, 1. 9. 15; to ask, Lat. postulare, 1. 3. 19; to request, Lat. petere, acc. c. inf. 1. 1. 8; to wish, with inf., Lat. cupere, velle, 1. 7. 8; εἶναι, to claim to be, 3. 1. 37.

Ἀξίωμα, ατος, τό (ἄξιος), that of which one is thought worthy, dignity, reputation, 5. 9. 28.

Ἄξων, ονος, ὁ (ἄγω), an axle, 1. 8. 10; (ἄξων, οντος, fut. part. of ἄγω).

Ἄοπλος, ος, ον (ἀ priv. ὅπλον), unarmed, 2. 3. 3.

Ἀπαγγέλλω, ελῶ, ἤγγελκα, ἤγγελμαι (ἀπό, ἀγγέλλω), τί τινι or τι πρός τινα, to report, announce, bring back word, report in answer; 1 aor. ἀπήγγειλα, 1. 3. 19, 7. 2, 10. 14, 2. 4. 23, 3. 9; εἰς τὴν Ἑλλάδα, 2. 4. 4, 6. 2. 25.

Ἀπαγορεύω, εύσω, to forbid, τῷ πολέμῳ, to give up, renounce, takes part. of vb.; like ἀπείρηκα, to be unable to speak, be wearied, 1. 5. 3, 5. 8. 3.

Ἀπάγω, άξω, ἀπῆχα, ἀπῆγμαι, 2 aor. ἀπήγαγον, to lead away, bring back; τὴν ἐπὶ θανάτῳ ἀπάγειν (sc. ὁδόν), to lead to death, 1. 6. 10; sc. ἑαυτόν, to make off, go away, 1. 10. 6; Mid. to take away with them, 6. 4. 1.

Ἀπαγωγή, ῆς, ἡ, a leading away.

Ἀπαθής, ής, ές (ἀ priv. πάθος), without suffering, c. gen. κακῶν, 7. 7. 33; apathetic, calm.

Ἀπαίδευτος, ος, ον (ἀ priv. παιδεύω), untaught, ignorant, rude, 2. 6. 26.

Ἀπαίρω, ἀρῶ (ἀπό, αἴρω), to lift off, take away; sc. ναῦς, to sail away; στρατόν, march away, 7. 6. 33.

'Απαιτέω, ήσω, ήτηκα, ημαι (ἀπό, αἰτέω), to ask, demand back, τίνα τι, 1. 2. 11, 7. 7. 21, 6. 17.

'Απαλλάττω, άξω, ἀπήλλᾰχα, ἀπήλλαγμαι, to get rid of, 3. 2. 28; to set free, τίνα τινος, 4. 3. 2; to put away from, τί τινος, remove; intr. to get off, 1. 10. 8, escape, 5. 6. 32; Mid. depart, 7. 1. 4, 6, βίου, from life, escape from, get rid of, 5. 1. 14.

'Απαλός, ή, όν (ἅπτομαι, I touch), tender, soft, 1. 5. 2.

'Απαμείβομαι, ψομαι (ἀπό, ἀμείβω), to reply, 1 aor. pass. ἀπημείφθη, he answered, 2. 5. 15.

'Απαντάω, ήσω or ήσομαι, 1 aor. ἀπήντησα, to come to meet, to encounter, τινί, anyone; to fall in with, 2. 3. 17, 4. 6. 24, 2. 4. 25.

'Άπαξ, adv. once, Lat. semel, 1. 9. 10, 4. 7. 12.

'Απαρασκεύαστος, ος, ον (ἀ priv. παρά, σκεύαζω), unprepared, 1. 1. 6, 1. 5. 9.

'Απαράσκευος, ος, ον, unprepared.

'Άπας, ασα, αν (ἅμα, πᾶς), all together, 4. 4. 1; ἅπαν τὸ μέσον, 1. 4. 4; τὸ στράτευμα ἅπαν, 2. 5. 28 (yet next line, ἅπαν τὸ στρ. 2. 5. 29), 4. 3. 19, 1. 4. 17; πεδίον ἅπαν, 4. 4. 1.

'Απαυθημερίζω(ἀπό,αὐτός,ἡμέρα), to do a thing on the same day, to return the same day, 5. 2. 1.

'Απειθέω, ήσω, to disobey, to be ἀπειθής (ἀ priv. πείθομαι), 2. 6. 4.

'Απειλέω, ήσω, to threaten, takes inf. or ὅτι, ὡς, 5. 5. 22.

'Απειλή, ῆς, ἡ, a threat, 7. 7. 24.

'Άπειμι (ἀπό, εἶμι), to go away, depart, part. ἀπιών, 1. 9. 29, 2. 1. 21, 1. 4. 7, 4. 6. 1.

'Άπειμι (ἀπό, εἰμί), to be away, to be absent, part. ἀπών.

'Απειπεῖν (ἀπό, εἶπον), 2 aor., fut. ἀπερῶ, perf. ἀπείρηκα, p. p. ἀπείρημαι, fut. ἀπορρηθήσομαι, to forbid, 7. 2. 12; renounce, give up, 7. 1. 41; intr. to give up, be wearied, sink from exhaustion, 2. 2. 16; 5. 1. 2; 6. 5. 30.

'Άπειρος, ος, ον (ἀ priv. πεῖρα), inexperienced, ignorant, 2. 2. 5, 5. 1. 8, 5. 6. 29; unacquainted with, c. gen. 3. 2. 16.

'Απελαύνω, ελάσω and ελῶ, ελήλᾰκα, ελήλᾰμαι (ἀπό, ἐλαύνω), to drive away, τί τινι; sc. στρατίαν, to march, depart, 1. 4. 5, 7. 8. 11; sc. ἵππον, to ride away, 1. 8. 17, 2. 3. 6.

'Απερύκω, ξω (ἀπό, ἐρύκω), to keep away from, τί τινι, or ἀπό τινος, 5. 8. 25.

'Απέρχομαι, ελεύσομαι, ελήλυθα, to go away, depart from, go back, return, 1. 1. 4, 9. 29, 4. 6. 13, 8. 6, 5. 2. 20.

'Απεχθάνομαι, ἀπεχθήσομαι, ἀπήχθημαι, 2 aor. ἀπηχθόμην, to be hated, become hateful, 2. 6. 19, 5. 8. 25, 7. 6. 34.

'Απέχω, ἀφέξω or ἀποσχήσω, ἀπέσχηκα, ἀπέσχημαι, imp. ἀπεῖχον, 2 aor. ἀπέσχον (ἀπό, ἔχω), to keep off, or away from, ἀγαθῶν, 3. 1. 22, 5. 9. 31, 6. 4. 14, 2. 6. 10; to be away or distant from, 1. 3. 20, 3. 2. 34, ἀλλήλων, 2. 4. 10, τῆς 'Ελλάδος, 3. 1. 2.

Ἀπιστέω, ήσω (ἄπιστος, ἀ priv. and πίστις), to disbelieve, distrust, τινί τι, 2. 5. 6, 7. 2. 31, 2. 6. 19, 6. 4. 13.

Ἀπιστία, ας, ἡ (ἀ priv. πίστις), distrust, disbelief, 2. 5. 4, 7. 7. 30, 2. 5. 21; faithlessness, 3. 2. 4.

Ἄπιστος, ος, ον, untrustworthy, faithless, 2. 4. 7, 7. 7. 23, 24.

Ἀπιτέον, verbal fr. ἄπειμι, one must, or it is necessary to, go away, 5. 3. 1.

Ἄπλετος, ος, ον, collat. form ἄπλᾶτος (ἀ priv. πελάω), unapproachable, immense, terrible, 4. 4. 11.

Ἀπλοῦς, ῆ, οῦν (ἅμα, simul), Lat. simplex, single, plain, simple, opp. to διπλοῦς, duplex, double, 5. 8. 18, 2. 6. 22.

Ἀπό, prep. gov. the gen., Lat. ab, from, away from, 7. 3. 12, 6. 1. 8, 3. 4. 38, of place; of time, after, from, since, 7. 5. 8, 1. 7. 18, 6. 1. 23. ἀπὸ ἵππου, on horseback, 1. 2. 7. ἄρχεσθαι ἀπό, to begin with, 6. 1. 18.

Ἀποβαίνω, βήσομαι, βέβηκα, βέβαμαι, 2 aor. ἀπέβην, to step off, dismount, disembark, go away, 5. 7. 9, 6. 1. 2 ; to come true, be verified, 7. 8. 22.

Ἀποβάλλω, βαλῶ, βέβληκα, βέβλημαι, to throw away, cast off, 5. 9. 21, 4. 6. 10.

Ἀποβιβάζω, άσω, Att. βιβῶ, causative of ἀποβαίνω, to make to get off, disembark, set on land, 1. 4. 5.

Ἀποβλέπω, ψω, to look steadfastly at one, τινά, to direct one's eyes to one, εἴς τινα, 1. 8. 14, 7. 2. 33.

Ἀπογιγνώσκω or γινώσκω, γνώσομαι, ἀπέγνωκα, ἀπέγνωσμαι, to give up an intention, τοῦ μάχεσθαι, of fighting, 1. 7. 19.

Ἀποδείκνυμι, δείξω, δέδειχα, δέδειγμαι, to point out, τινί τι, 5. 8. 7 ; appoint, 1. 1. 2, 1. 9. 7. ἀποδέξασθαι γνώμην, to deliver one's opinion, 5. 5. 3, 5. 6. 37. ἀποδεδειγμένοι πολέμιοι, declared enemies, 7. 1. 26.

Ἀποδέρω, δερῶ, to flay, skin, 2 aor. pass. ἀπεδάρην, 3. 5. 9.

Ἀποδέχομαι, δέξομαι, δέδεγμαι, to accept, 6. 1. 24.

Ἀποδημέω, ήσω, ἀποδεδήμηκα (ἀπό, δῆμος), to be away from home, to be or go abroad, 7. 8. 4.

Ἀποδιδράσκω, δράσομαι, δέδρακα, 2 aor. ἀπέδραν, to escape, so as not to be found; ἀποφεύγειν, to escape, so as not to be caught, 1. 4. 8, 2. 5. 7, 6. 3. 16.

Ἀποδίδωμι, δώσω, δέδωκα, δέδομαι, to give back, restore, pay, 1. 7. 5, 18; Mid. to sell, 7. 2. 3, 6.

Ἀποδοκέω, δόξω, δέδογμαι, to resolve not to do, ποιεῖν or μὴ ποιεῖν; used impers., 2. 3. 9.

Ἀποδύω, δύσω, δέδυκα, δέδυμαι, 1 aor. ἀπέδυσα, trans., 2 aor. ἀπέδυν, intrans. 4. 3. 17, to strip, τί τινος. Perf. is trans. 5. 8. 23.

Ἀποθαρρέω, ήσω, to take courage, have confidence, 5. 2. 22, usually ἀποχωρεῖν.

Ἄποθεν, old Att. ἄπωθεν, from afar, 1. 8. 14.

Ἀποθνήσκω, θανοῦμαι, τέθνηκα, 2 aor. ἀπέθανον, to die, to be put to death, ὑπό τινος, by anyone, 2. 6. 29, 5. 1. 15.

Ἀποθύω, θύσω, τέθῦκα, τέθῦμαι, to offer up a sacrifice, in ful-

filment of a vow, 3. 2. 12, 4.
8. 25, 5. 1. 1.

'Αποικία, ας, ἡ (ἀπό, οἶκος), a
colony, settlement. στέλλειν,
ἄγειν, ἐκπέμπειν, to plant a
colony, 4. 8. 22, etc.

Ἄποικος, ος, ον, away from home,
abroad, sc. πόλις, a colony =
ἀποικία, 5. 3. 2, 10. 1; ἄποικοι,
settlers, colonists, 5. 5. 10, 10.
15.

'Αποκαίω, καύσω (κέκαυκα, κέκαυμαι), to burn off; also of intense
cold, like Lat. uro, aduro. ἀπε-
καίοντο αἱ ῥῖνες, their noses
were frozen off, frost-bitten, 7.
4. 3; to wither up, 4. 5. 3.

'Αποκαλέω, έσω, κέκληκα, κέκλημαι, to call back, recall, call
away or aside, 7. 3. 35.

'Αποκάμνω, καμοῦμαι, κέκμηκα,
to grow quite weary, fail or
flag utterly, 4. 7. 2.

'Απόκειμαι, κείσομαι, to be laid
away, to be laid up in store,
τινί, reserved for one's use, 2.
3. 15, 5. 4. 27, 7. 7. 46.

'Αποκλείω, κλείσω, κέκλεικα, κέκλειμαι and εισμαι, 1 aor. pass.
ἀπεκλείσθην, to shut, 7. 6. 24;
shut off, cut off, 6. 6. 13, 4. 3.
20, 21.

'Αποκλίνω, κλϊνῶ, κέκλϊκα, κέκλῖ-
μαι, to turn aside, off the road,
2. 2. 16.

'Αποκόπτω, κόψω, κέκοφα, κέκομμαι, to cut off, beat off, knock
off, 7. 4. 15, 3. 4. 39, 4. 2. 10,
17.

'Αποκρίνομαι, κρινοῦμαι, κέκριμαι, to answer, reply; Att.
ἀπεκρίνατο; Hellenistic, ἀπε-
κρίθη, 2. 1. 22; Ion. ὑπεκρίν-
ατο; Epic, ἠμείψατο, or ἠμεί-
φθη, ἀπημείφθη, 2. 5. 15.
Act. to separate.

'Αποκρύπτω, ὑψω, κέκρυφα, κέκρυμμαι, to hide from, τινί τι or
τινά τι. Mid. conceal, 1. 9.
19.

'Αποκτείνω, κτενῶ, ἔκτονα or
εκτόνηκα or ἔκταγκα, 1 aor.
ἔκτεινα, 2 aor. ἔκτανον, poet.
ἔκταν, to kill, put to death, 1.
1. 3, 2. 1. 11. Pass. ἀποθνήσκω. Bye-forms ἀποκτίννυμι,
ὑω, 6. 5. 5, 7. 28.

'Αποκωλύω, ὑσω (ῡ), κεκώλῡκα,
κεκώλῡμαι, to hinder, τινά
τινος, one from anything, 3. 3.
3; ποιεῖν or μὴ ποιεῖν, to prevent doing, 6. 2. 24.

'Απολαμβάνω, λήψομαι, ἀπεί-
ληφα, ἀπείλημμαι, 2 aor. ἀπέ-
λαβον, to take or receive from,
1. 2. 27, 7. 7. 14, 55, τι
παρά τινος, to cut off, intercept,
2. 4. 17.

'Απολείπω, λείψω, λέλοιπα, λέλειμμαι, 2 aor. ἀπέλιπον, to
leave behind, forsake, 4. 2. 15,
1. 4. 8, 2. 6. 12; leave a space
open, 6. 5. 11; τῆς τάξεως, to
abandon military order, 5. 4.
20.

'Απόλεκτος, ος, ον (ἀπό, λέγω),
chosen out, picked, 2. 3. 15.

'Απόλλυμι, ὀλέσω or ὀλῶ, ὀλώ-
λεκα, 1 aor. ἀπώλεσα, 2 aor.
ἀπωλόμην, 2 perf. ἀπόλωλα,
I am undone; to destroy, kill,
2. 5. 39, 3. 2. 4; τι ὑπό
τινος, to have anything de-
stroyed by anyone, 3. 4. 11,
7. 2. 22; ὑπὸ χιόνος ἀπόλλυσ-
θαι, to perish in the snow, 5.
3. 3; λιμῷ, ὑπὸ λιμοῦ, to die
of hunger, 1. 5. 5, 2. 2. 11,
7. 4. 5.

'Απόλλων, ωνος, ὁ, Apollo, acc.
'Απόλλω, voc. Ἄπολλον, 1.
2. 8, 5. 3. 4, 7. 8. 3.

Ἀπολλωνία——Ἀποστρατοπεδεύω 19

Ἀπολλωνία, ας, ἡ, Apollonia, a city in Mysia, 7. 8. 15.

Ἀπολλωνίδης, ου, ὁ, Apollonides, a Bœotian, 3. 1. 26.

Ἀπολογέομαι, ήσομαι, to speak in defence of oneself, in regard to a thing, περί τινος, 5. 6. 3.

Ἀπολύω, λύσω, λέλυκα, λέλυμαι, to set free, release from, τινά τινος; τῆς αἰτίας, free one from blame, acquit, 6. 6. 15.

Ἀπομάχομαι, μαχέσομαι and μαχοῦμαι, to fight off a thing, decline it, 6. 2. 6.

Ἀπόμαχος, ος, ον (ἀπό, μάχη), unfit to fight, disabled, horsde-combat, 3. 4. 32, 4. 1. 13.

Ἀπονοστέω, ήσω, to return, come home, 3. 5. 16.

Ἀποπέμπω, ψω, πέπομφα, πέπεμμαι, to send off, despatch, release, discharge, 1. 1. 3, 5, 8, etc.

Ἀποπέτομαι, πετήσομαι, 2 aor. ἀπεπτόμην, to fly away, 1. 5. 3.

Ἀποπήγνυμι, πήξω, πέπηχα, πέπηγμαι, 2 aor. ἀπεπάγην, to make to freeze; Pass. to freeze, be frozen, 5. 8. 15.

Ἀποπηδάω, ήσω, to leap off from, start away, 3. 4. 27.

Ἀποπλέω, πλεύσομαι or οῦμαι, to sail away, sail off, 1. 3. 14, 1. 4. 7, 7. 1. 4.

Ἀπόπλοος, contr. ἀπόπλους, πλόου, ὁ, a sailing away, a voyage, 5. 6. 20.

Ἀποπορεύομαι, εύσομαι, to depart, go away, 7. 6. 33, 7. 7. 8.

Ἀπορέω, ήσω, to be ἄπορος, without means, to be at a loss, to be in doubt, 1. 5. 13; to be perplexed, 1. 3. 8, 7. 3. 20, 29. μή, to fear lest; τινός, to be in want of anything, 1. 7. 3, 5. 6. 30, 5. 8. 25.

Ἀπορία, ας, ἡ, difficulty, perplexity, embarrassment, 2. 5. 9, 3. 5. 7, 3. 1. 2, 11, 12, 6. 4. 11, 1. 3. 13. τροφῆς, a want of food, 2. 5. 9; scarcity, 7. 7. 31.

Ἄπορος, ος, ον (ἀ priv. πόρος, πείρω), impassable, pathless, impracticable, 2. 4. 4, 2. 5. 18. ἐν ἀπόροις εἶναι, to be in great straits, 5. 6. 20, 7. 6. 11; helpless, 2. 5. 21; τὰ ἄπορα, difficulties.

Ἀπόρρητος, ος, ον (ἀπερῶ, ἀπό, ἐρεῖν), not to be spoken, that should not be spoken, forbidden, secret, 1. 6. 5. ἐν ἀπορρήτῳ ποιησάμενος, having made the communication as a secret, 7. 6. 43.

Ἀπορρώξ, ῶγος, ὁ, ἡ (ἀπό, ῥήγνυμι), broken, rugged, steep, 6. 4. 3.

Ἀποσήπομαι, ψομαι, σέσηπα, to rot off, be frost-bitten, 4. 5. 12.

Ἀποσκάπτω, ψω, to cut off or intercept by trenches, 2. 4. 4.

Ἀποσκεδάννυμι, άσω or σκεδῶ, ἐσκέδασμαι, to scatter, disperse, straggle, 4. 4. 15.

Ἀποσκηνέω, ήσω (ἀπό, σκηνή), to encamp apart, 3. 4. 35.

Ἀποσπάω, άσω, ἔσπακα, ἔσπασμαι, to take or draw away, 1. 8. 13, 7. 2. 11, τινά τινος, separate, 2. 2. 12, 7. 3. 41.

Ἀποσταυρόω, ώσω, to fence off with a palisade, 6. 3. 1.

Ἀποστέλλω, στελῶ, ἔσταλκα, ἔσταλμαι, to send away from, send off, despatch, 2. 1. 5.

Ἀποστερέω, ήσω, ἐστέρηκα, ἐστέρημαι, to rob, despoil, defraud, τινά τινος or τινά τι, 7. 7, 48, 6. 4. 23, 7. 6. 9.

Ἀποστρατοπεδεύω, εύσω, or dep. ἀποστρατοπεδεύομαι, εύσομαι, ἀπεστρατοπέδευμαι, to encamp away from, at a distance from, 7. 7. 1, 3. 4. 34.

Ἀποστρέφω, ψω, ἀπέστροφα, ἀπέστραμμαι, to turn back, bring back, recall; or intr. sc. ἑαυτόν, ναῦν, to turn back.

Ἀποστροφή, ῆς, ἡ, a turning back, resource, refuge, 7. 6. 34, 2. 4. 22.

Ἀποσυλάω, ήσω, to strip off, rob, defraud, τινά τινος or τινά τι, 1. 4. 8.

Ἀποσώζω, σώσω, to save or restore again, οἴκαδε, bring safe home, 2. 3. 18.

Ἀποταφρεύω, εύσω (ἀπό, τάφρος, θάπτω), to fence off with a ditch, intrench, 6. 5. 1.

Ἀποτείνω, τενῶ, τέτἄκα, τέτἄμαι, to stretch out, extend, 1. 8. 10.

Ἀποτειχίζω, ίσω, Att. ιῶ, to wall off, to cut off or shut out by a wall, 2. 4. 4.

Ἀποτέμνω, τεμῶ, τέτμηκα, τέτμημαι, to cut off, 3. 4. 29; ἀποτμηθέντες τὰς κεφαλάς, having had their heads cut off, 2. 6. 1.

Ἀποτίθημι, θήσω, τέθεικα, τέθειμαι, to put away, stow away, 2. 3. 15.

Ἀποτίνω, τίσω, τέτἴκα, τέτισμαι, to pay back, repay, 7. 6. 16. Mid. avenge oneself on one, τινά, punish, take vengeance, 3. 2. 6.

Ἀπότομος, ος, ον (ἀπό, τέμνω), cut off, abrupt, precipitous, steep, 4. 1. 2.

Ἀποτρέπω, ψω, τέτροφα, τέτραμμαι, to turn back or aside, 3. 5. 1, 7. 3. 7, 6. 11.

Ἀποτρέχω, θρέξομαι and δραμοῦμαι, 2 aor. ἀπέδραμον, to run off or away.

Ἀποφαίνω, φανῶ, πέφαγκα, πέφασμαι, to show, display, 5. 7.

12; ἀποφαίνεσθαι γνώμην, to declare one's opinion, 1. 6. 9.

Ἀποφεύγω, φεύξομαι and οὖμαι, πέφευγα, πέφυγμαι, to escape, get clear off (without being caught), vid. ἀποδιδράσκω, 1. 4. 8, 2. 5. 7, 5. 7. 19, 6. 2. 25.

Ἀπόφραξις, εως, ἡ (ἀπό, φράττω), a blocking up. ἔλυε ἀπ. τῆς παρόδου, he removed the obstruction of the pass, 4. 2. 25.

Ἀποχωρέω, ήσω, to go away from, depart, retire, retreat, 5. 7. 16, 4. 2. 21, 6. 5. 17.

Ἀποψηφίζομαι, ίσυμαι, Att. ιοῦμαι; to vote against, νόμον, a law, hence reject it; μὴ ποιεῖν, to vote against doing, 1. 4. 15 = ἀποχειροτονέω.

Ἀπρόθυμος, ος, ον (ἀ priv. πρόθυμος), not eager, disinclined, 5. 10. 7.

Ἀπροσδόκητος, ος, ον (ἀ priv. προσδοκάω), unexpected, unlooked for; adv. ἐξ ἀπροσδοκήτου, ex improviso, 4. 1. 10.

Ἀπροφασίστως, adv. (ἀ priv. πρόφασις, πρό, φαίνω), offering no excuse, unhesitatingly, 2. 6. 10.

Ἅπτω, ἅψω, ἧμμαι, to fasten, kindle, τί, anything; Mid. to touch, τινός, 1. 5. 10, anything, take part in, 5. 6. 28.

Ἄρα, ergo; ἄρα, num; ἀρά, imprecatio. ἄρα (ἄρω), then, 1. 7. 18, 2, 2. 3, 4. 2. 15, 5. 7. 5, 5. 1. 13, cannot begin a sentence, but ἄρα in Prose always begins a sentence. τίς ἄρα λέξει, who then will say? ἄρά τις λέξει, will any one say? implying that no one will. ἆρ᾽ οὐ, nonne, 3. 1. 18; ἆρα μή, num vero, 7. 6. 5.

Ἀραβία, ας, ἡ, Arabia, (1) ἡ

πετραία, Arabia Petræa; (2) ἡ ἔρημος, A. Deserta; (3) ἡ εὐδαίμων, A. Felix, 1. 5. 1, 7. 8. 25.

Ἀράξης, ου, ὁ, the Araxes, a river in Armenia, flowing into the Caspian sea, hod. Aras, called by Xenophon the Phasis, 4. 6. 4. The Araxes of Xen. 1. 4. 19 is a branch of the Euphrates in Mesopotamia, and called by other writers Aborras, hod. Khabur.

Ἀρβάκας, ου, ὁ, Arbacas, the ruler of Media, 7. 8. 25.

Ἀρβάκης, ου, ὁ, Arbaces, one of Artaxerxes' generals, 1. 7. 12.

Ἀργεῖος, α, ον Argive, from Argos in the Peloponnesus.

Ἀργός, ός, όν (ἀ priv. ἔργον), lazy, slothful; ἀργός, ή, όν, white, bright.

Ἀργύρεος, α, ον, contr. οὖς, ᾶ, οῦν, made of silver, 4. 7. 27.

Ἀργύριον, ου, τὸ (ἄργυρος, silver; ἀργός, white), a piece of silver money, Scoticè, ' siller,' 2. 6. 16.

Ἀργυρόπους, οδος, ὁ, ἡ (ἄργυρος, πούς), silver-footed, with silver feet, 4. 4. 21.

Ἀργώ, οῦς, ἡ (ἀργός, swift), Argo, the ship in which Jason sailed for the golden fleece, 6. 2. 1.

Ἄρδην, adv. (ἀείρω, lifted up on high), utterly, wholly; πάντες, entirely, all, all together, 7. 1. 12.

Ἄρδω, ἄρσω, to water, irrigate, 2. 3. 13.

Ἀρέσκω, ἀρέσω (ἄρω), to please, gratify, τινί, anyone, 2. 4. 2.

Ἀρετή, ῆς, ἡ (Ἄρης, Mars), virtue, bravery, goodness; περὶ ἐμέ, services to me, 1. 4. 8.

Ἀρήγω, ξω, (ἀρκέω), to help, succour, τινί, 1. 10, 5.

Ἀρηξίων, οντος, ὁ, Arexion, an Arcadian soothsayer, 6. 4. 13, 5. 8.

Ἀριαῖος, ου, ὁ, Ariæus, who commanded under Cyrus, 1. 8. 5, etc.

Ἀριθμός, οῦ, ὁ, number, ἐξέτασιν καὶ ἀριθμὸν ποιεῖν, to hold a review and muster, 1. 2. 9, 14, 7. 1. 7; ἀριθμὸς τῆς ὁδοῦ, the length of the journey, 2. 2. 6.

Ἀρίσταρχος, ου, ὁ, Aristarchus, the Spartan harmost of Byzantium, 7. 2. 13.

Ἀριστάω, ήσω (ἄριστον), to take luncheon (prandēre), 3. 3. 6.

Ἀριστέας, ου, ὁ, Aristeas, a Chian commanding the light-armed, 4. 1. 28.

Ἀριστερός, ά, όν, the left; ἐν ἀριστερᾷ, on the left hand, 5. 2. 25, ἐξ ἀριστερᾶς, 4. 8. 2; in augury, unpropitious.

Ἀρίστιππος, ου, ὁ, Aristippus, a Thessalian from Larissa, who supported Cyrus, 1. 1. 10.

Ἄριστον, ου, τὸ (ᾱ) (ἦρι, early), the mid-day meal, luncheon, prandium. The Greek meals were, (1) ἀκράτισμα (ἄκρατος, unmixed wine), breakfast, jentaculum; (2) ἄριστον, luncheon, prandium; (3) δεῖπνον, dinner, cœna; (4) δόρπον, supper. (ἄριστον, best, has ᾰ.)

Ἀριστοποιέω, ήσω, to prepare luncheon; Mid. to take luncheon, 3. 3. 1, 4. 3. 9.

Ἄριστος, η, ον, superl. of ἀγαθός (Ἄρης), (ᾰ, but ἄριστον, prandium, has ᾱ), best, bravest, 1. 5. 7, 1. 6. 4, 3. 1. 6.

Ἀρίστων, ωνος, ὁ, Aristo, an Athenian, 5. 6. 14.

'Αριστώνυμος, ου, ὁ, Aristonymus, an Arcadian from Methydrium, 4. 6. 20.

'Αρκαδικός, ή, όν, of or belonging to Arcadia, Arcadian.

'Αρκάς, άδος, ὁ, an Arcadian.

'Αρκέω, έσω, 1 aor. p. ἠρκέσθην, to be sufficient, 5. 1. 13, with inf. 2. 6. 20, 7. 5. 3; Lat. arceo. ὅσοις μὲν ἤρκει σώζεσθαι δι' ἡμᾶς, as many as were content to be saved by us, 5. 8. 13; ἀρκοῦσαν, plentiful,5.9.4.

Ἄρκτος, ου, ὁ and ἡ, a bear; ἡ, the constellation Ursa major, also called ἅμαξα, The Wain, hence the North, 1. 9. 6.

Ἅρμα, ατος, τὸ (ἄρω), a chariot; ἅρ. δρεπανηφόρα, scythe-bearing chariots, 1. 7. 10.

'Αρμάμαξα, ης, ἡ (ἅρμα, ἅμαξα), a covered carriage, a waggonette, 1. 2. 16, 18.

'Αρμενία, ας, ἡ, Armenia, 4. 3. 1, 4. 4. 1, 4.

'Αρμένιος, α, ον, Armenian, 4. 5. 33.

'Αρμήνη, ης, ἡ, Harmene, a harbour near Sinōpe, 6. 1. 15.

'Αρμοστής, οῦ, ὁ (ἁρμόζω), a director, a harmost, one sent by the Spartans to govern their dependencies, 5. 5. 19.

Ἄρνειος, α, ον (ἀρνός), of or belonging to a lamb, 4. 5. 31.

'Αρπαγή, ῆς, ἡ, plunder, booty, 3. 5. 2, 5. 4. 16.

'Αρπάζω, άσω, ἥρπάκα, ἥρπασμαι, non Attic ἁρπάξω, ἥρπαγμαι (αἱρέω), to seize, plunder, carry off; to seize hastily, snatch up, Lat. rapio, 1. 2. 27, 4. 3. 6, 5. 9. 8, 4. 6. 11.

Ἄρπασος, ου, ὁ, Harpasus, a branch of the Araxes in Armenia, 4. 7. 18.

'Αρταγέρσης, ου, ὁ, Artagerses, a Persian cavalry officer, 1. 7. 11.

'Αρτακάμας, α, ὁ, Artacamas, a Persian satrap, 7. 8. 25.

'Αρτάοζος, ου, ὁ, Artaozus, a friend of Cyrus, 2. 4. 16.

'Αρταξέρξης, ου, ὁ (arta khshatra, honoured warrior or king, Sansc.), Artaxerxes Mnemon, the son of Darius, was king of Persia from 404 to 361 B.C., 1. 1. 1, 3, 4, &c.

'Αρταπάτας or ης, ου, ὁ, Artapatas, one of Cyrus' attendants, 1. 6. 11.

'Αρτάω, ἥσω, ἥρτηκα, ἥρτημαι, to fasten to, attach, 3. 5. 10.

Ἄρτεμις, ιδος, ἡ, acc. ιν or ιδα, Artemis, the Roman Diana, 5. 3. 6, 12.

Ἄρτι, adv., just, just now, 4. 6. 1.

'Αρτίμας, α, ὁ, Artimas, the ruler of Lydia, 7. 8. 25.

'Αρτοκόπος, ου, ὁ and ἡ (ἄρτος, κόπτω), a bread-cutter, a baker. Butt. approves of ἀρτοπόπος, from πέσσω, to bake, 4. 4. 21.

Ἄρτος, ου, ὁ, bread, a loaf, 4. 5. 31, 7. 3. 21.

'Αρτούχας, ου, ὁ, Artuchas, a Persian general, 4. 3. 4.

'Αρύστας, ου, ὁ, Arystas, an Arcadian, 7. 3. 23.

'Αρχαγόρας, ου, ὁ, Archagoras, an Argive, 4. 2. 13.

'Αρχαῖος, α, ον (ἀρχή), old, 4. 5. 14, 7. 3. 28, 3. 1. 4. Κῦρος ὁ ἀρχαῖος, the elder Cyrus, 1. 9. 1; τὸ ἀρχαῖον, formerly, 1. 1. 6.

'Αρχή, ῆς, ἡ, the beginning; ἀρχήν, at first; with a neg. not at all, 7. 7. 28; government, rule, empire, 1. 5. 9, etc.

'Αρχηγός, ός, όν (ἀρχή, ἄγω), beginning, originating; as subst. a leader, prince, chief, 3. 1. 26.

Ἀρχικός, ή, όν (ἀρχή), fit to rule, qualified to command, 2. 6. 8, 20.

Ἄρχω, ξω, ἦρχα, ἦργμαι, to command; Mid. to begin, takes gen., 3. 2. 7; ἀπό, 6. 1. 18, 6. 2. 1; λέγειν, 3. 1. 26, 7. 2. 24, 2. 6. 14. οἱ ἄρχοντες, the rulers, the commanders; οἱ ἀρχόμενοι, the ruled, those under authority, 2. 6. 19, 3. 2. 30.

Ἄρωμα, ατος, τό, a sweet smelling, fragrant herb, 1. 5. 1.

Ἀσέβεια, ας, ἡ (ἀσεβής), ungodliness, impiety, 3. 2. 4.

Ἀσεβής, ής, ές (ἀ priv. σέβομαι), irreverent, ungodly, godless, profane, 2. 5. 20.

Ἀσθενέω, ήσω (ἀ priv. σθένος), to be weak, feeble, sick, 1. 1. 1, 5. 3. 1.

Ἀσθενής, ής, ές (ἀ priv. σθένος), weak, feeble, sickly, 1. 5. 9.

Ἀσία, ας, ἡ, Asia; ἡ ἄνω, Upper Asia; ἡ κάτω, Lower Asia, 6. 4. 1, 7. 1. 2.

Ἀσιδάτης, ου, ὁ, Asidates, a Persian, 7. 8. 9.

Ἀσιναῖος, α, ον, of or belonging to Asine, a town in Laconia, 5. 6. 36.

Ἀσινῶς, adv. (ἀ priv. σίνομαι), without injury, without doing damage, 2. 3. 27, 3. 3. 3.

Ἄσιτος, ος, ον (ἀ priv. σῖτος), without food, 2. 2. 16, 4. 5. 11.

Ἀσκέω, ήσω, ἤσκηκα, ημαι, to work, cultivate, practise, train, 2. 6. 25, 7. 7. 24.

Ἀσκός, οῦ, ὁ, a leather bag, a bottle, 3. 5. 9.

Ἄσμενος, η, ον (ἥδομαι), well-

pleased, glad; ἀκούω, ὁρῶ, I am glad to hear, see, 2. 1. 16, 5. 6. 22, 7. 6. 8.

Ἀσπάζομαι, άσομαι, ἤσπασμαι, to welcome, 6. 1. 24; to salute, 7. 1. 40, 7. 2. 23 ; to bid farewell, 7. 1. 8.

Ἀσπένδιος, ου, ὁ, an inhabitant of Aspendus, 1. 2. 12.

Ἀσπίς, ίδος, ἡ, a shield (round) (clypeus) ; θυρεός, oblong (scutum); πέλτη, a small light shield used by the Thracians; γέῤῥον, a large Persian shield usually of wicker-work covered with ox-hide. ἀσπὶς μυρία, 10,000 men-at-arms, for ἀσπιδηφόροι, 1. 7. 10; παρ' ἀσπίδας, to the left hand; opp. to ἐπὶ δόρυ, to the right, 4. 3. 26.

Ἀσσυρία, ας, ἡ, Assyria, in Asia, capital Νῖνος, Nineveh, 7. 8. 25.

Ἀσσύριος, ία, ιον, of or belonging to Assyria, Assyrian.

Ἀσταφίς, ίδος, ἡ (ἀ euphonic, σταφίς), raisin-wine, raisins, 4. 4. 9.

Ἀστράπτω, ψω (ἀστραπή, ἀ euph. στεροπή, στρέφω), there is lightning, to flash like lightning, 1. 8. 8.

Ἀσφάλεια, ας, ἡ (ἀσφαλής), safety, security, 7. 6. 30.

Ἀσφαλής, ής, ές (ἀ priv. σφάλλω), not liable to fall, safe, firm, secure; ἐν ἀσφαλεῖ εἶναι, to be in safety, 5. 6. 33; ἐν ἀσφαλεστέρῳ εἶναι, 3. 2. 36; ἐν ἀσφαλεστάτῳ, 1. 8. 22 ; ὡς ἀσφαλέστατα, as securely as possible, 1. 3. 11.

Ἄσφαλτος, ου, ἡ (ἀ priv. σφάλλω), asphalt, bitumen, 2. 4. 12.

Ἀσφαλῶς, adv. fr. ἀσφαλής, Comp. ἔστερον, Superl. ἔστατα.

Ἀσχολία, ας, ἡ (ἀ priv. σχολή), want of time, hindrance, engagement, 7. 5. 16.

Ἀτακτέω, to be ἄτακτος, 5. 8. 21.

Ἄτακτος, ος, ον (ἀ priv. τάσσω), undisciplined, disorderly, 1. 8. 2.

Ἀταξία, ας, ἡ (ἀ priv. τάσσω), disorder, confusion, opp. εὐταξία, 3. 1. 38, 2. 29, 5. 8. 13.

Ἀτάρ, conj. but, yet, however, Lat. at, 4. 6. 14, 7. 7. 10.

Ἀταρνεύς, έως, ὁ, Atarneus, a city of Æolis, opp. Lesbos, 7. 8. 8.

Ἀτασθαλία, ας, ἡ (ἄταις, dat. of ἄτη, θάλλω), blind folly, rashness, akin to ἄτη, implying deliberate wickedness, 4. 4. 14.

Ἄτυφος, ος, ον (ἀ priv. θάπτω), unburied, 6. 5. 6.

Ἄτε, acc. pl. neut. of ὅστε, ob quæ, quippe, utpote, inasmuch as, seeing that, c. part. 4. 2. 13, 5. 2. 1, 4. 5. 18.

Ἀτέλεια, ας, ἡ (ἀ priv. τέλος), exemption from public burdens, immunity, privilege, 3. 3. 18.

Ἀτιμάζω, άσω (ἄτιμος), not to hold in honour, to esteem lightly, dishonour, 1. 9. 4.

Ἄτιμος, ος, ον (ἀ priv. τιμή), without honour, dishonoured, 7. 7. 24.

Ἀτμίζω, ίσω (ἀτμός), to smoke, steam, 4. 5. 15.

Ἀτραμύττιον or Ἀδραμυττεῖον, Adramyttium, a town in Mysia, 7. 8. 8.

Ἀτρϊβής, ής, ές (ἀ priv. τρίβειν), not rubbed, not traversed, untrodden, 4. 2. 8, 7. 3. 42.

Αὖ, adv. again, 1. 6. 7, 1. 10. 11; on the contrary, 2. 4. 20; in turn (vicissim), 2. 5. 26.

Αὐαίνω, ἄνω (αὔω), to wither away, 2. 3. 16.

Αὐθαίρετος, ος, ον (αὐτός, αἱρέω), self-elected, 5. 7. 29.

Αὐθημερόν (αὐτός, ἡμέρα), on the same day, 4. 4. 22.

Αὖθις (αὖ), adv. again, 1. 10. 10; afterwards (deinde), 5. 6. 25; hereafter, 5. 4. 20.

Αὐλέω, ήσω (αὐλός), to play on the flute; κέρασι, to blow the horns; αὐλεῖσθαι, to be played to, to get music, 5. 9. 11.

Αὐλίζομαι, ίσομαι, ηὔλισμαι (αὐλή), to be in the courtyard, to bivouac, 4. 3. 1, 2. 2. 17.

Αὐλός, οῦ, ὁ (ἄω, ἄημι, to blow), a flute, or rather a flageolet, because it had a mouthpiece. One person often played two, one in each hand, tibia dextra et sinistra, αὐλοὶ ἀνδρήϊοι καὶ γυναικήϊοι, bass and treble, 5. 9. 5.

Αὐλών, ῶνος, ὁ, poet. ἡ (ἄω), a hollow, a glen, a canal, a channel, 2. 3. 10.

Αὐξάνω and αὔξω, αὐξήσω, ηὔξηκα, ηὔξημαι, to increase, Lat. augere.

Αὔριον, adv. to-morrow, ἡ αὔ. sc. ἡμέρα, 7. 6. 6.

Αὐστηρότης, τητος, ἡ (αὐστηρός, ἄω or αὔω, making the tongue dry), harshness, bitterness, 5. 4. 29.

Αὐτίκα (αὐτός; cf. Lat. illico, ille), adv. immediately, 2. 1. 9; αὐτίκα μάλα, instantly, 6. 2. 5, 7. 6. 17.

Αὐτόθεν, adv. (αὐτός), from thence, 4. 2. 6, 5. 1. 10 (inde).

Αὐτόθι, adv. (αὐτός), there (ibi), 1. 4. 6=αὐτοῦ.

Αὐτοκέλευστος, ος, ον (αὐτός,

κελεύω), *unbidden, of one's own accord* (*ultro*), 3. 4, 5.

Αὐτοκράτωρ, *ορος*, ὁ (αὐτός, κρατέω), *one's own master, absolute*; used for Lat. *dictator* or *imperator*, 6. 1. 21.

Αὐτόματος, η, ον (αὐτός, μάω; or better, αὐτός alone), *acting of one's own will*; ἀπὸ or ἐκ τοῦ αὐτομάτου, *of one'e own accord, naturally*, 1. 2. 17, 1. 3. 13, 6. 4. 18.

Αὐτομολέω, ήσω, *to be an αὐτόμολος, ἐκ* or *παρά τινος, πρός* or *εἴς τινα, to desert*, 1. 7. 13.

Αὐτόμολος, ου, ὁ (αὐτός, μολεῖν fr. βλώσκω, *to go*), *a deserter*, 1. 7. 2; Lat. *transfuga*.

Αὐτόνομος, ος, ον (αὐτός, νέμω), *living by one's own laws, free, independent, autonomous*.

Αὐτός, ή, ό, pron. reflex., *self*, 1. 10. 17, 4. 2. 1, 2. 4. 10, 1. 6. 7; in the oblique cases often for pers. pron. *him, her, it*, but never at the beginning of a sentence, 1. 1. 5, 3. 4. 44, &c.; with art. before it, ὁ αὐτός, *the same*, 1. 8. 14; with dat., 2. 6. 22, 3. 1. 27. αὐτὸς ἔφη, *ipse dixit, the master said it*, a common Pythagorean expression; ἐν ταὐτῷ εἶναί τινι, *to be in the same place with one*, 3. 1. 27.

Αὐτόσε, adv. *thither* (αὐτός).

Αὐτοῦ, adv. *there, just there*, in full, ἐπ' αὐτοῦ τοῦ τόπου, 2. 2. 1, 1. 10. 17, 4. 2. 22.

Αὐτοῦ, Attic for ἑαυτοῦ.

Αὕτως or αὔτως, adv. *even so, just so*; ὡς δ' αὔτως, *in just the same manner*, 5. 6. 9.

Αὐχήν, ένος, ὁ, *the neck, throat*; also *an isthmus*, 6. 2. 3.

'Αφαιρέω, ήσω, ήρηκα, ήρημαι,

2 aor. ἀφεῖλον (ἀπό, αἱρέω), *to take away, deprive*, τί τινι or τί τινος, 6. 4. 21; τί τινα, 1. 3. 4, 3. 4. 48.

'Αφανής, ής, ές (ἀ priv. φαίνω), *unseen, invisible, out of sight*; ἀφανής εἰμι ποιῶν τι, *I do a thing without being noticed*, 4. 2. 4, 2. 6. 28, 1. 4. 7.

'Αφανίζω, ίσω, Att. ιῶ, *to cause to disappear, make away with, annihilate*, 3. 2. 11, 4. 8.

'Αφαρπάζω, άσω, *to snatch away from*, τί τινος, *snatch eagerly, to rob, plunder*, 1. 2. 27.

'Αφειδής, ής, ές (ἀ priv. φείδομαι), *unsparing*; adv. ἀφειδῶς, *severely*, 1. 9. 13.

'Αφελύμενος, see ἀφαιρέω.

'Αφηγέομαι, ήσομαι, ήγημαι, *to lead away, relate, explain*, 7. 2. 26.

'Αφθονία, ας, ἡ (ἄφθονος), *plenty, abundance*, 6. 4. 3, 1. 9. 15; εἰς ἀφθονίαν παρέχειν, *to give a plentiful supply*, 7. 1. 33.

"Αφθονος, ος, ον (ἀ priv. φθόνος, *without envy*), *plentiful, abundant*, 5. 6. 25, 6. 2. 4; ἐν ἀφθόνοις βιοτεύειν, *to live in plenty*, 3. 2. 25, 4. 5. 29, 7. 6. 31.

'Αφίημι, ήσω, εἶκα, εἶμαι (ἀπό, ἵημι), *to send away, let go, let loose*, τινά τινος; κύνας, 5. 8. 24; ὄνον, 2. 2. 20; ὕδωρ, 2. 3. 13.

'Αφικνέομαι, ίξομαι, ῖγμαι, 2 aor. ἀφικόμην, *to come to, to reach*, 6. 4. 26.

'Αφιππεύω, εύσω (ἀπό, ἱππεύω), *to ride off* or *away*, 1. 5. 12.

'Αφίστημι, ἀποστήσω, ἀφέστηκα, ἀφέσταμαι, trans. pres. fut. 1 aor. (intrans. p. plp. 2 aor. act. and fut. mid. and pass.), to put away, remove, cause to revolt. Intrans. to stand aloof from, to shun, revolt, πρός or εἴς τινα, 1. 1. 6, 1. 6. 7.

Ἄφοδυς, ου, ἡ (ἀπό, ὁδός), departure, 6. 4. 13.

Ἀφροντιστέω, ήσω (ὰ priv. φροντίζω), to be heedless, to have no care of a thing, τινός, 5. 4. 20.

Ἀφροσύνη, ης, ἡ (ἄφρων), folly, thoughtlessness, 5. 1. 14.

Ἄφρων, ων, ον, gen. ἄφρονος (ὰ priv. φρήν), foolish, thoughtless, senseless, silly, 7. 1. 28. Comp. ἀφρονέστερος, ἐσταπος.

Ἀφυλακτέω, ήσω, to be ἀφύλακτος.

Ἀφύλακτος, ος, ον (ὰ priv. φυλάττω), off one's guard, unguarded, 2. 6. 24; adv. 5. 1. 6.

Ἀχαιός, ά, όν, Achaian, an Achaian.

Ἀχάριστος, ος, ον (ὰ priv. χάρις), unpleasant, 2. 1. 13; ungrateful, 7. 6. 23; unrewarded, 1. 9. 18; adv. ἀχαρίστως, from want of gratitude, 2. 3. 18.

Ἀχερουσιάς, άδος, ἡ, and Ἀχερουσίς, ίδος, ἡ, Acherusia, a town near Heraclea in Bithynia, 6. 2. 2.

Ἄχθομαι, ἔσομαι, ήχθημαι (ἀχθήσομαι is fut. pass. of ἄγω), 1 aor. pass. ἠχθέσθην, to be displeased at, τοῦτο, 3. 2. 20; αὐτῶν πολεμούντων, 1. 1. 8; τοῖς γεγενημένοις, 5. 7. 20; ἐπὶ τοῖς πεπονημένοις, 7. 6. 10. Lat. ægre ferre.

Ἀχρεῖος, ος, ον (ὰ priv. χρεία), useless, unprofitable, unserviceable, 5. 2. 21, 4. 6. 26.

Ἄχρηστος, ος, ον (ὰ priv. χράομαι), useless, unprofitable, unserviceable, 3. 4. 26.

Ἄχρι, before a vowel ἄχρις, prep. with gen. until; ἄχρις οὖ, conj. until; also ἄχ. ἄν, 2. 3. 2.

Ἀψίνθιον, ον, τό, wormwood, 1. 5. 1.

B.

Βαβυλών, ῶνος, ἡ, Babylon, the capital of the Persian empire, 2. 2. 6, 1. 5. 5.

Βαβυλωνία, ας, ἡ, Babylonia, and adj. 1. 7. 1, 2. 2. 13.

Βάδην (βαίνω), adv. slowly, at a slow pace, 4. 8. 28.

Βαδίζω, ίσω or βαδιοῦμαι (βαίνω), to walk or go slowly, opp. to τρέχω, 5. 1. 2; applied to horsemen, 6. 3. 19.

Βάθος, εος, τό (βαθύς), depth (altitudo) or height.

Βαθύς, εῖα, ύ, deep, high (like altus); βαθύτερος, βαθύτατος, βαθίων, poet., Dor. βάσσων, βάθιστος.

Βαίνω, βήσομαι, βέβηκα, βέβαμαι, 2 aor. ἔβην (βήσω, ἔβησα, are trans.; causative βιβάζω), to go, step, depart. ἐπὶ γῆς βεβηκότες, standing firmly on the ground, 3. 2. 19.

Βακτηρία, ας, ἡ (βαίνω)=βάκτρον, a staff, baton, 2. 3. 11.

Βάλανυς, ου, ἡ, an acorn: βάλανοι τῶν φοινίκων (glandes palmarum), dates, 2. 3. 15, 1. 5. 10.

Βάλλω, βαλῶ, βέβληκα, βέβλημαι, 2 aor. ἔβαλον, to throw, hit, shoot, 4. 6. 12, 5. 7. 21. βαλλόμενοι τὰς κεφαλάς, struck on the head, 4. 6. 12.

Βάπτω, ψω, βέβαμμαι, 2 aor. pass. ἐβάφην, to dip in water, immerse, 2. 2. 9.

Βαρβαρικός, ή, όν, barbarian, strange, foreign, not Greek, applied to all who did not speak Greek. Adv. βαρβαρικῶς, in the Persian language, 1. 8. 1.

Βάρβαρος, ος, ον, barbarian, strange, not Greek, outlandish, rude, 1. 7. 3, 2. 5. 32.

Βαρέως, adv. from βαρύς; βαρέως φέρειν τι, moleste, ægre ferre, to take a thing ill, suffer impatiently, be vexed or annoyed at it, 2, 1. 4; βαρέως ἀκούειν, to be annoyed by hearing, 2. 1. 9.

Βασίας, ου, ὁ, Basias, a seer from Elis, 7. 8. 11; also an Arcadian, 4. 1. 18.

Βασίλειᾰ, ας, ἡ, a queen, but—

Βασιλεία, ας, ἡ, sovereignty, kingdom, dominion; κατέστη εἰς τὴν β., was made king, ascended the throne, 1. 1. 3.

Βασίλειος, ος, ον (βασιλεύς), of or belonging to a king, royal (regius); βασιλικός (regalis), fit for a king, kingly. βασίλειον sc. δῶμα (domus regia), a palace, 3. 4. 24, 4. 4. 2; frequently pl. 1. 2. 7. ἦν, one building, but ἦσαν, scattered buildings, 1. 2. 23.

Βασιλεύς, έως, ὁ (βάσις, λαός), a hereditary king, opp. to τύραννος, a usurper; ἄναξ (ἄνω), a prince. Without the article, as if a proper name, βασιλεύς signified the king of Persia, 2. 3. 17, 2. 4. 3; sometimes μέγας β., 1. 2. 8, 1. 7. 2, 2. 3. 17; sometimes β. μέγας, 1. 4. 11, 1.7.16, 2.4.3.

Βασιλεύω, εύσω, to be king, reign, rule over, with gen. 5. 6. 37.

Βασιλικός, ή, όν (βασιλεύς), like a king, kingly, princely, βασιλικώτατος, 1. 9. 1; royal, 2. 2. 16.

Βάσιμος, ος, ον (βαίνω), passable, accessible, τινί, 3. 4. 49.

Βατός, ή, όν (βαίνω), passable, τινί, 4. 6. 17.

Βέβαιος, α, ον (βαίνω), firm, steady, sure, certain, 1. 9. 30.

Βεβαιόω, ώσω, to make firm, establish, secure; τὴν πρᾶξίν τινι (alicui pactum servare), to redeem one's word, 7. 6. 17.

Βέλεσις, ιος, ὁ, or Βέλεσυς, υος, ὁ, Belesis, a Persian, 1. 4. 10, 7. 8. 25.

Βέλος, εος, τό (βάλλω), a missile, esp. an arrow, dart, stone, 3. 3. 16, 4. 3. 6.

Βέλτιστος, η, ον (βέλος), Superl. of ἀγαθός, 5. 6. 19; Comp. βελτίων, 3. 2. 32.

Βῆμα, ατος, τό (βαίνω), a step, pace = 30 in., hence βῆμα διπλοῦν is 5 ft.

Βία, ας, ἡ, bodily strength, power, force, might; βίᾳ τινός, against one's will, 7. 8. 17; βίᾳ, by force, 7. 3. 3, 3. 4. 12.

Βιάζομαι, άσομαι, βεβίασμαι, to overpower by force, compel; βιασάμενοι παρέλθοιεν, to force their way through, 1. 4. 5; βιασάμενοι ξυνεξέρχονται, they force their way out in a body, 7. 8. 11.

Βίαιος, α, ον, or ος, ον (βία), forcible, violent, ποιεῖν, 6. 6. 15. Adv. ως, by force.

Βίβλος, ου, ἡ, the inner bark of a tree, paper, a book; Lat. liber, 7. 5. 14.

Βιθυνοί, ῶν, οἱ, the Bithynians, in Asia Minor, 6. 4. 2.

Βίκος, ου, ὁ, Oriental word for πίθος, a wine-jar, 1. 9. 25.

Βίος, ου, ὁ, life (but βιός, a bow), living, 5. 5. 1, 7. 7. 9, 6. 4. 8.

Βιωτεύω, to live, get a living, 3. 2. 25.

Βισάνθη, ης, ἡ, Bisanthe, a Thracian city, 7. 2. 38.

Βίτων, ωνος, ὁ, Bito, a Greek mentioned 7. 8. 6.

Βλάβη, ης, ἡ (βλάπτω), injury, hurt, 2. 6. 6.

Βλάβος, εος, τό,=βλάβη, 7. 7. 28.

Βλακεύω (βλάξ), to be slack, lazy, 2. 3. 11, 5. 8. 15.

Βλάπτω, ψω, βέβλαφα, βέβλαμμαι, 2 aor. pass. ἐβλάβην, to injure, hurt, 3. 3. 14, 16.

Βλέπω, ψω, βέβλεφα, βέβλεμμαι, to see, look on, εἰς τι, 4. 1. 20, 1. 8. 10.

Βοάω, βοήσομαι, βεβόημαι, Dor. βοάσομαι, Ep. βώσομαι (βοή), to shout, cry out, τινί τι, 1. 8. 12.

Βυεικός, ή, όν (βοῦς)=βόειος, of ox-hide. ζεύγη β. waggons drawn by oxen, 7. 5. 2, 4.

Βοή, ῆς, ἡ, a cry, a shout, the battle-cry, the slogan.

Βοήθεια, ας, ἡ (βοηθέω), help, relief, succour, 3. 5. 4, 2. 3. 19.

Βοηθέω, ήσω, βεβοήθηκα, ημαι, (βοή, θέω), to help, aid, succour, come to the rescue, ἐπί τινα, 3. 5. 6, usually τινί.

Βόθρος, ου, ὁ (βόθω=Lat. fodio), a ditch, trench, hole, 4. 5. 6, 5. 8. 9.

Βοΐσκος, ου, ὁ, (βοῦς), Boiscus (Eng. Cowie), a Thessalian, 5. 8. 23.

Βοιωτιάζω (Βοιωτός), to act as a Bæotian, to speak Bæotian, 3. 1. 26.

Βοιωτός, οῦ, ὁ (βοῦς), a Bæotian, an inhabitant of Bæotia, 5. 3. 6.

Βορέας, and βορρᾶς, ου, ὁ, the north wind (Aquilo), strictly the NNE. wind, 5. 7. 7.

Βόσκημα, ατος, τό (βόσκω), that which is fed or fatted, pl. cattle, fatted cattle.

Βουλεύω, εύσω, βεβούλευκα, ευμαι (βουλή), to take counsel, deliberate, determine, resolve, purpose, plan, κακόν τινι, 2. 5. 16; τί, 2. 3. 8, 6. 2. 4; ὑπέρ τινος, 5. 7. 12, and περί, 5. 9. 3; πρός τι, 1. 3. 19, 2. 3. 21; ὑπέρ τινος and πρό τινος (consulere alicui), 7. 6. 27. Inf. to resolve to, 3. 2. 8.

Βουλιμιάω, άσω (βοῦς, λιμός, a ravenous hunger), to suffer from bulimy, 4. 5. 7.

Βούλομαι, ήσομαι, βεβούλημαι, 2 p. βέβουλα, Ep. pres. βόλομαι=Lat. volo, to will, to wish, with the notion of choice or preference. Butt., however, says βούλομαι denotes mere inclination; while ἐθέλω expresses will combined with choice or purpose. ὁ βουλόμενος, quivis, anyone who wishes, 1. 3. 9, 5. 2. 18, 5. 6. 20, c. inf.

Βουπόρος, ος, ον (βοῦς, πείρω), ox-piercing; ὀβελίσκος, a fork that would spit a whole ox, 7. 8. 14, a long spear.

Βοῦς, βοός, ὁ and ἡ (βοάω), an ox or cow; ὑφ᾽ ἁμάξης, yoke-oxen. It stands for (δορά), an ox-hide, corium bovinum, or ἀσπίς, a shield covered with ox-hide, 4. 7. 22, 5. 4. 12.

Βραχέως, adv. fr. βραδύς, slowly.

Βραδύς, εῖα, ύ, slow, heavy, sluggish (tardus); βραδύτερος, βραἔντατος, or poet. βραΐων and βράσσων, βράδιστος, 7. 3. 37.

Βραχύς, εῖα, ύ, short, Lat. brevis, of space and time; few, of number; trifling, of value. βραχύτερος, βραχύτατος; βραχίων, βράχιστος.

Βρέχω, βέβρεγμαι, to wet, 1 aor. pass. ἐβρέχθην, 2 aor. ἐβράχην, 1. 4. 17.

Βροντή, ῆς, ἡ, thunder.

Βρωτός, ή, όν (βρώσκω), eatable; τὸ βρωτόν, food, 4. 5. 5.

Βυζάντιον, ου, τό, Byzantium, aft. Constantinople, 7. 1. 2; adj. Βυζάντιος, ία, ιον, 7. 1. 19.

Βωμός, οῦ, ὁ (βαίνω), any raised place (suggestus), an altar, 4. 8. 28.

Γ.

Γαλήνη, ης, ἡ, a calm, stillness of the sea, 5. 7. 8.

Γαμέω, γαμῶ or γαμήσω, γεγάμηκα, γεγάμημαι, to marry, applied to the man, ducere in matrimonium; Mid. γαμέομαι, to marry, applied to the woman, nubere. γαμεῖσθαι γυναῖκά τινι, to bestow a female subject or relation in marriage, collocare in matrimonium. 1 aor. ἔγημα, 4. 5. 24.

Γάμος, ου, ὁ, a marriage, marriage, a marriage-feast; ἐπὶ γάμῳ, upon marriage, 2. 4. 8.

Γάνος, ου, ἡ, Ganos, a town in Thrace, 7. 5. 8.

Γάρ=γὲ ἄρα, conj. for; καὶ γάρ, etenim, namque; never stands at the beginning of a sentence; ἔχει γὰρ ἡ χώρα, epexegetic, now the country has, 5. 6. 6.

In questions why, οἴει γάρ; why, do you think? 1. 7. 9. εἴθε γάρ, O that. ἀλλὰ γάρ— γάρ gives the reason of a clause to be supplied by ἀλλά, 3. 1. 24, 3. 2. 32, 25. καὶ γὰρ οὖν, wherefore, 1. 9. 12.

Γαστήρ, έρος, sync. γαστρός, ἡ, d. pl. γαστράσι and γαστῆρσι, the belly.

Γαυλικός, ή, όν (γαῦλος, a galley), of or belonging to a trading ship; χρήματα γ. a ship's cargo, 5. 8. 1; opp. to μακρὰ ναῦς, navis longa, a war-vessel.

Γαυλίτης, ου, ὁ, Gaulites, a Samian exile, 1. 7. 5.

Γαυλιτικός, ή, όν=γαυλικός.

Γέ, adv. at least, Lat. quidem, saltem, vi minuendi; even, indeed, vi augendi, σὺ δ᾽ οὐ λέγεις γε, true, you do not say. εἷς γε ἀνήρ, most of all, 1. 9. 12; δῶρα πλεῖστα εἷς γε ὧν ἀνὴρ ἐλάμβανε, he used to receive more presents than any other man, 1. 9. 22; γὲ ίή, 4. 6. 3, sane quidem, really; γὲ μήν, 1. 9. 16, moreover; ἐπεί γε, since at least, 1. 3. 9; καὶ ἀδελφοί γε, and brothers too, 7. 2. 38, 7. 47.

Γείτων, ονος, ὁ, ἡ (γῆ), a neighbour, τινί, 2. 3. 18, and τινός, 3. 2. 4.

Γελάω, ἄσομαι, γεγέλασμαι, to laugh, ἐφ᾽ ἑαυτοῖς, at themselves, 5. 4. 34, also τί, τινά.

Γελοῖος, α, ον (γέλως), laughable, ridiculous, absurd, 5. 6. 25.

Γέλως, ωτος, ὁ (γελάω, acc. γέλωτα, γέλων and γέλω), laughing, laughter, 7. 3. 25.

Γελωτοποιός, ός, όν (γέλως, ποιέω),

exciting laughter; as a subst. a jester, a clown, 7. 3. 33.

Γέμω, to be full, τινός, 4. 6. 27, used only in pres. and impf.

Γενεά, ᾶς, ἡ (γένος), birth, 2. 6. 30.

Γενειάω, ήσω=γενειάζω (γένειον, the chin), to get a beard, to have a beard, to be bearded (barbatum esse), 2. 6. 28.

Γένος, εος, τό (γίγνομαι, γένω), race, descent, offspring, 5. 2. 29, 1. 6. 1.

Γεραιός, ά, όν (γῆρας), old, γεραίτερος, γεραίτατος; οἱ γεραίτεροι, the elders, the senators, 5. 7. 17.

Γερόντιον, ου, τό, dim. of γέρων, a little old man, 6. 3. 22.

Γέρρον, ου, τό (εἴρω, sero,to knit); Lat. gerra, anything made of wickerwork, a shield, 2. 1. 6, 4. 3. 4; oblong, of wickerwork covered with ox-hide; the soldiers who had them were called γερροφόροι, 1. 8. 9.

Γέρων, οντος, ὁ, an old man (senex), 4. 3. 11.

Γεύω, γεύσω, to give a taste; Mid. γεύομαι, γεύσομαι, γίγευμαι, to taste, τινός, 3. 1. 3.

Γέφυρα, ας, ἡ (γῆ, φέρω), a bridge; ἐζευγμένη πλοίοις, a bridge of boats, 1. 2. 5.

Γεώδης, ης, ες (γῆ, εἶδος), earthlike, earthy, 6. 2. 5.

Γῆ, γῆς, ἡ, the earth (terra), land, ground; καὶ κατὰ γῆν, καὶ κατὰ θάλασσαν (terra marique), by sea and land, 1. 1. 7; κατὰ γῆς, under the earth, 7. 1. 30.

Γήϊνος, ος, ον (γῆ), of earth, earthen, 7. 8. 14.

Γήλοφος, ου, ὁ (γῆ, λόφος), a hill, a rising ground, 1. 5. 8.

Γῆρας, αος, contr. γήρως τό, old age, but γέρας, αος, τό, a prize.

Γίγνομαι and γίνομαι, γενήσομαι, γεγένημαι, 2 aor. ἐγενόμην, perf. γέγονα,1. 6.8; Lat. gigno, to come into being, be born, become, be; ἐν ἑαυτῷ γίγνεσθαι, to be himself, to be master of himself; Lat. apud se esse, 1. 5. 17; τὰ ἱερὰ γίγνεται, the sacrifices are favourable, 6. 2. 9, 2. 2. 3; τὰ γεγενημένα, what had happened, 2. 5. 33; ἀργύριον γενόμενον, the money realised, 5. 3. 4; οἱ γιγνόμενοι δασμοί, the accruing tribute, 1. 1. 8. γ. ἐπί τινι, to be under one's power, 3. 1. 13, 17; μετά τινος, on one's side. Causative γεννάω, to beget, and ἐγεινάμην from γείρομαι.

Γιγνώσκω and γινώσκω, γνώσομαι, ἔγνωκα, ἔγνωσμαι, 2 aor. ἔγνων, Lat. nosco, to learn, know, have an opinion, περί τινος, about a thing, 2. 5. 8, 6. 1. 19; know, perceive, like scio, οἶδα, 1. 7. 4.

Γλοῦς, Γλοῦός, ὁ (like βοῦς), Glus, the son of Tamos, 1. 4. 16, 2. 1. 3, 4. 24.

Γνήσιππος, ου, ὁ, (γνήσιος, γένος, real, ἵππος) Gnesippus, an Athenian, 7. 3. 28.

Γνούς, 2 aor. part. of γιγνώσκω.

Γνώμη, ης, ἡ (γιγνώσκω), the judgment, the will, a judgment, an opinion; γνώμῃ, with good reason, from principle, 2. 6. 9; γνώμην ἔχειν, to hold an opinion, 2. 2. 10, 12; γ. ἐ. πρὸς ἑαυτόν, to follow him, to favour, support him, 2. 5. 29.

Γογγύλος, ου, ὁ, Gongylus, a Euboean from Eretria, 7. 8, 17.

Γονεύς, έως, ὁ (γένω), a father, a parent; pl. γονεῖς.

Γόνυ, ατος, τό, the knee; pl. γόνατα, dat. γόνασι, the joints in grasses, 4. 5. 26.

Γοργίας, ου, ὁ, Gorgias of Leontini, a famous sophist, 2. 6. 16.

Γοργίων, ωνος, ὁ, Gorgio, the brother of Gongylus, 7. 8. 8.

Γοῦν=γε οὖν, at least then, at any rate, at all events, 7. 1. 30.

Γρᾴδιον, ου, τό, dim. of γραῦς, for γραΐδιον, a little old woman, 6. 3. 22.

Γράμμα, ατος, τό (γράφω), that which is written, a written character (litera), and so in pl. a piece of writing, an inscription, 5. 3. 13.

Γράφω, ψω, γέγραφα, γέγραμμαι, to write, draw, engrave, 1. 6. 3, 7. 8. 1.

Γυμνάζω, άσω (γυμνός), to train, exercise, practise, 1. 2. 7.

Γυμνής, ῆτος, ὁ, pl. οἱ γυμνῆτες, the light-armed foot soldiers, 4. 1. 6, 6. 17, &c.

Γυμνήτης, ου, ὁ, pl. οἱ γυμνῆται, another form of γυμνής.

Γυμνίας, ἡ, Gymnias, the chief city of the Scythini, 4. 7. 19.

Γυμνικός, ή, όν (γυμνός), belonging to gymnastic exercises; ἀγών, a gymnastic contest, 4. 8. 25.

Γυμνός, ή, όν, naked, 4. 3. 12; exposed, 4. 3. 6; lightly clad, without the upper garment, 1. 10. 3, 4. 4. 12.

Γυνή, γυναικός, ἡ, voc. γύναι, d. pl. γυναιξί, a woman (femina), opp. to man, ἀνήρ, vir; a wife, spouse, opp. to παρθένος, 1. 2. 12, 3. 2. 25.

Γωβρύας, a or ου, ὁ, Gobryas,

one of Artaxerxes' four generals, 1. 7. 12.

Δ.

Δάκνω, δήξομαι, δέδηχα, δέδηγμαι, 2 aor. ἔδακον, to bite, 3. 2. 18.

Δακρύω, ύσω (ῡ) (δεδάκρυκα), δεδάκρυμαι, to weep, 1. 3. 2.

Δακτύλιος; ου, ὁ, a ring, finger-ring, prop. an adj. sc. κύκλος, 4. 7. 27, from

Δάκτυλος, ου, ὁ, a finger; ὁ μέγας δ. the thumb; δ. τοῦ ποδός, a toe, 4. 5. 12; a finger's breadth=$\frac{1}{10}$ths of an inch.

Δαμάρᾶτος, ου, ὁ, Demaratus, king of Sparta, 2. 1. 3, 7. 8. 17.

Δάνα, ης, ἡ, Dana, a town in Cappadocia; Rennell would read Τύανα, 1. 2. 20.

Δαπανάω, ήσω (δεδαπάνηκα), δεδαπάνημαι (δαπάνη, δάπτω), spend, waste, τὶ εἴς τι, 1. 3. 3, 2. 6. 6; ἀμφί τι, 1. 1. 8; δ. τὰ ἑαυτῶν, to live at their own expense, 5. 5. 20, 7. 6. 31.

Δάπεδον, ου, τό (γῆ, πέδον), any level surface, the ground, 4. 5. 6.

Δαραδάξ, ακος, ὁ, the Daradax, a tributary of the Euphrates, 1. 4. 10.

Δαρδανεύς, έως, ὁ, a Dardanian, an inhabitant of Dardanos, a town in the Troad, 3. 1. 47, 5. 6. 21.

Δαρεικός, ή, όν, of or belonging to Darius; as a subst. (sc. στατήρ) a Persian gold coin, so called because first coined by Darius, so Napoleon, Louis d'or, 1. 1. 9. It was equal to 20 Attic silver drachmæ=16s. 3d., or, computing from its weight in gold =21s., a guinea. Five darics make a mina, 300 darics a talent.

Δαρεῖος, ου, ὁ, Darius Nothus, king of Persia, reigned 423-404 B.C. Acc. to Hdt.=ἐρξείης, a worker, probably Persian dara, a king, 1. 1. 1.

Δάσμευσις, εως, ἡ (δασμεύω), a dividing, distributing, 7. 1. 37.

Δασμός, οῦ, ὁ (δάζω, δαίω), a division, distribution, tribute, tax, 1. 1. 8, 4. 5. 24.

Δασύς, εῖα, ύ, thick, hairy, rough, shaggy; hence, γέρρα βοῶν δασέα, shields covered with skins with the hair on, 5. 4. 12; so, γέρρα βοῶν δασέων ὠμοβόϊνα, shields covered with raw (untanned) hides with the hair on, 4. 7. 22; thickly covered with leaves, bushes, wood, 2. 4. 14; bushy, 4. 8. 26; τὸ δασύ, the bush, the bushy country, 4. 7. 7.

Δαφναγόρας, ου, ὁ (δάφνη, ἀγείρω), Daphnagoras, a Mysian, 7. 8. 10.

Δαψιλής, ής, ές (δάπτω), abundant, plentiful; of persons, liberal, profuse, lavish, 4. 2. 22, 4. 4. 2.

Δέ (δέω, I bind), a connective particle answering to μέν, on the other hand, but; resuming a narrative, now, 1. 1. 1, 2, &c.; οἱ μέν... οἱ δέ, alii... alii, some... others; καὶ δέ, and too, and also; δ' ἀλλά, but at least. It never stands at the beginning of a sentence. It is also an enclitic put after the acc. of nouns signifying direction, as οἰκόνδε or οἴκαδε, home-

wards, 3. 2. 24. Ἀθήναζε for Ἀθήνασδε, to Athens.

Δεῖ, δεήσει, impers. it concerns, it is necessary, one must, c. acc. and inf. 3. 2. 28, 30, or dat. and inf. 3. 4. 35. With gen. there is need of, there is want of, 3. 3. 16. δεῖ μοί τινος, I am in want of something; πολλοῦ δεῖ, there wants much, far from, 5. 4. 32; ὀλίγου δεῖ, there wants little, all but, 1. 5. 14; τὸ δέον, necessity, what must be, 4. 7. 7; εἰς τὸ δέον, that these things would come right, 1. 3. 8.

Δείδω, δείσομαι, δέδοικα, 2 p. δέδια, to fear, to be afraid, 5. 6. 36; δέδοικα μή=timeo ne, I fear he will; δέδοικα μὴ οὐ, timeo ut, I fear he wont.

Δείκνυμι and δεικνύω, δείξω, δέδειχα, δέδειγμαι, to show, point out, explain.

Δείλη, ης, ἡ (akin to εἵλη, the heat of the sun, Butt.), the time when the day is hottest, the afternoon; δείλη πρωΐα, early in the afternoon, close after twelve; δείλη ὀψία, late in the afternoon, approaching sunset, 3. 3. 11, 1. 8. 8.

Δειλός, ή, όν (δέος), cowardly, worthless, wretched, 1. 4. 7.

Δεινός, ή, όν (for δεεινός, δέος), awful, fearful, terrible; δεινὸν or δεινὰ ποιεῖν τινα, to treat one ill, 5. 7. 23; ποιεῖσθαι, to consider wonderful, 6. 1. 11 clever, 1. 9. 19; c. inf. δεινὸς λέγειν, φαγεῖν, a terrible, powerful speaker, eater, clever at speaking, eating, 5. 5. 7, 7. 3. 23, 4. 6. 16. Adv. δεινῶς, awfully, &c.; δεινῶς ἔχειν, to be in straits, 6. 4. 23.

Δειπνέω——Δή   33

ἵπνηκα, sync.
dinner, 7. 8.

e chief meal,
See ἄριστον.
to prepare
ι dine, 6. 1.

decl. ten (δέ,
:, two hands
. 2. 10.

lj. indecl. fif-

κα), to exact
h part, 5. 3. 9.
·α), ord. adj.
it. δεκάτη, sc.
ırt, sc. ἡμέρα,

given to land
mouths of a
hape, applied
peninsula in

·, ἵνος, ὁ, a
se, 5. 4. 28.
lphi, a town
·ated for the
5. 3. 5.
tree, dat. pl.
and δένδρεσι,
poetic form

ιι (δεξιός), to
hand, shake

ιι), Lat. dex-
t hand; τὸ
ing, sc. κέρας,
sc. χείρ, the
ν διδόναι, 2.
λαβεῖν καὶ
3. 1; φέρειν,
ledges. ἀετός,
ι on the right,

Δέξιππος, ου, ὁ (δέχομαι, ἵππος),
Dexippus, a Spartan, 6. 1. 32,
6. 6. 9, 5. 1. 15.
Δέομαι, δεήσομαι, δεδέημαι, to
need, want, beg, ask, τινός, 2.
6. 13, 1. 9. 21, 2. 6. 5, &c.
Δερκυλλίδας, ου, ὁ, Dercyllidas,
a Spartan, 5. 6. 24.
Δέρμα, ατος, τό (δέρω), a skin,
hide, leather; Lat. pellis, 1.
2. 8, 4. 8. 26.
Δερμάτινος, η, ον (δέρμα), of
skin, leathern, 4. 7. 26.
Δέρνης, ους, ὁ, Dernes, satrap of
Phœnicia and Arabia, 7. 8.
25.
Δεσμεύω (δεσμός), to bind in
fetters, 5. 8. 24, put for διδέασι.
Δεσμός, οῦ, ὁ (δέω), a band,
bond, fetter, 3. 5. 10.
Δεσπότης, ου, ὁ, a master, Lat.
dominus, lord, owner, 7. 4. 14.
Δεῦρο (δέω), adv. hither, in pl.
δεῦτε, come hither.
Δεύτερος, α, ον (δύο), ord. adj.
second, in time, place, order;
δεύτερον, 1. 8. 16, and τὸ δ.,
2. 2. 4, a second time, again
(iterum).
Δέχομαι, δέξομαι, δέδεγμαι (δέκα,
'two hands'), to receive, accept, 1. 8. 17; receive hospi-
tably, 4. 8. 23, 5. 5. 20; in a
hostile sense, 1. 10. 6; δέχεσθαι εἰς χεῖρας, to come to close
quarters, 4. 3. 31, Lat. manus
conserere.
Δέω, δήσω, δέδεκα, δέδεμαι, to
bind, tie, fasten. τὼ χεῖρε δε-
δεμένος, with both his hands
tied, 5. 9. 8.
Δέω, δεήσω, δεδέηκα, δεδέημαι, to
need, want, request. See ἱεῖ,
δέομαι, c. gen. τινός, 1. 5. 14.
Δή, strengthened form of δέ,
assuredly, some say shortened

D

for ἤδη, now, 1. 10. 8, *then*; τί δή; *why then?* 2. 5. 22, 7. 3. 47. ἔνθα δή, *then I assure you*, 2. 1. 10; ὅσῳ δή, *then*, 4. 7. 23; νῦν δὲ δή, 7. 1. 28, *but now I ask you*=quæso.

Δηλονότι (δῆλος, ὅτι), *doubtless, manifestly, clearly*, 1. 3. 9.

Δῆλος, η, ον (δαίελος, δαίω, I *shine), clear, manifest, certain*; δῆλος ἦν σπεύδων, *he was manifestly making haste*, 1. 5. 9, 2. 6. 21, 2. 5. 27; δῆλοι ὅτι, 5. 2. 26.

.Δηλίω, ώσω, δεδήλωκα, δεδήλωμαι (δῆλος), *to show, manifest, indicate, point out,* τί τινι, 2. 5. 26; πρός τινα, 7. 7. 35.

Δημαγωγέω, *to be a* δημαγωγός (δῆμος, ἄγω), *to lead the people* ; τινά, *to curry favour with one*, 7. 6. 4.

Δημάρατος=Δαμάρατος.

Δημοκράτης, ου, ὁ (δῆμος, κράτος), *Democrates*, a Greek from Temenium in Argolis, 4. 4. 15.

Δημοσάδης, ου, ὁ=Μηδοσάδης.

Δημόσιος, α, ον (δῆμος, δέω), *belonging to the community, public*, 6. 4. 2. τὰ δημόσια, *the public property*, 4. 6. 16.

.Δηόω—δηϊόω, ώσω (δήϊος), *to cut down, destroy, plunder*, 5. 5. 7.

Δήποτε, adv. (δή, ποτε), *at some time*, strengthened form of ποτε, τί δήποτε ; *what in the world?*

Δήπου, *perhaps, doubtless, no doubt, of course, I presume*, 3. 2. 15, 5. 7. 6, 7. 6. 13.

Διά, prep. gov. gen. and acc.: (1) with gen., (a) place, *through, right through*, 1. 4. 6, 4. 4. 1, 7, 4 5. 1; (b) time, *through, throughout, during*, διὰ νυκτός,

4. 6. 22 ; δι' ὅλης τῆς νυκτός, 4. 2. 4; διὰ τέλους, *all through, from the beginning to the end*, 6. 4. 11; (c) cause, *through, by means of*, 2. 3. 17, 5. 21 ; διὰ ταχέων=adv. ταχίως, 1. 5. 9. (2) with acc. as Lat. *propter, ob, on account of, for the sake of, by reason of*, 7. 2, 18, 6. 30, 7. 49.

Διαβαίνω, βήσομαι, βέβηκα, βέβαμαι, *to go through, pass over, cross*; Lat. *transire*, 1. 4. 14, 3. 4. 1.

Διαβάλλω, βαλῶ, βέβληκα, βέβλημαι, *to throw over* or *across, carry over*, Lat. *trajicere* ; *to attack a man's character, slander, accuse falsely*, Lat. *traducere*, hence διάβολος, Eng. *devil*, lit. *accuser*, τινά πρός τινα, 7. 5. 11; *state slanderously*, τί, 7. 5. 8.

Διάβασις, εως, ἡ (διά, βαίνω), *a going over* or *across, a passage*, 3. 5. 9; ποταμοῦ, *a ford*, 1. 5. 12, 4. 3. 16; *a bridge*, 2. 3. 10; *a narrow passage*, 3. 4. 20.

Διαβατέος, έα, έον, verb adj. from διαβαίνω, *to be crossed*, 2. 4. 6; so also

Διαβατός, ή, όν, *transeundus*.

Διαβιβάζω, άσω, *to carry over* or *across, take across*, 3. 5. 8, 5. 2. 8, 10.

Διαβολή, ῆς, ἡ (διαβάλλω), *false accusation, slander*, 2. 5. 5.

Διαγγέλλω, ελῶ, διήγγελκα, διήγγελμαι, 1 aor. διήγγειλα, *to give notice by a messenger, to send a message*, 1. 6. 2 ; *to give notice, inform*. Mid. *to pass the word from man to man*, 3. 4. 36.

Διαγελάω, άσομαι, to laugh at, τινά, 2. 6. 26.

Διαγίγνομαι, γενήσομαι, γεγένημαι, to go through, to pass, 1. 10. 19; to live, continue, with part., 1. 5. 6, 2. 6. 5.

Διαγκυλίζομαι, ίσομαι, διηγκύλισμαι (διά, ἀγκύλη, the thong of a javelin), to be ready to throw or shoot, to hold the javelin by the thong, 4. 3. 28, 5. 2. 12.

Διαγκυλόω=διαγκυλίζομαι.

Διάγω, άξω, ῆχα, ῆγμαι, to carry over or across, 2. 4. 28, 7. 2. 12; to pass, spend, Lat. degere, 4. 2. 7; to continue, keep, with part., 1. 2. 11.

Διαγωνίζομαι (διά, ἀγωνίζομαι), to contend, struggle against, τινί and πρός τινα, 4. 7. 12.

Διαδέχομαι, δέξομαι, δέδεγμαι (διά, δέχομαι), to receive one from another; λόγον, to speak next; τινά, to succeed one, take his place, hence διαδεδεγμένος, in turns, vicissim, 1. 5. 2.

Διαδίδωμι, δώσω, &c., to give from hand to hand, hand over, distribute, τινί τι, 1. 10. 18, 1. 9. 22.

Διάδοχος, ου, ὁ, ἡ, taking another's place, succeeding, 7. 2. 5.

Διαζεύγνυμι, ζεύξω, to disjoin, part, separate, 4. 2. 10.

Διαθεάομαι, άσομαι, τεθέαμαι, to look through or see everywhere, 3. 1. 19.

Διαιθριάζω, άσω (διά, αἰθρία, fine weather), to be clear and fine, ἐδόκει διαιθ., it seemed likely to be fine weather, 4. 4. 10.

Διαιρέω, ήσω, ῆρηκα, ῆρημαι, 2 aor. διεῖλον, 1 aor. pass.

διῃρέθην, to divide, tear away, pull down, σταυρούς, 5. 2. 21; break down, γέφυραν, 2. 4. 22.

Διάκειμαι, κείσομαι, pass. of διατίθημι, to be in a certain state of mind, to be disposed, πρός τινα, 2. 6. 12, 7. 7. 38. φιλικῶς τινι διακεῖσθαι, to be friendly disposed to one, 2. 5. 27, 7. 7. 30. ἄμεινον ὑμῖν διακείσεται, it will be better for you, 7. 3. 17.

Διακελεύομαι, εύσομαι, κεκέλευσμαι, to exhort, direct, encourage, τινί, 4. 7. 26; ἀλλήλοις διεκελεύοντο, they cheered one another on, 4. 8. 3.

Διακινδυνεύω, εύσω, κεκινδύνευκα, κεκινδύνευμαι; to run all risks, to hazard, encounter danger, 6. 3. 17, 1. 8. 6.

Διακλάω, άσω, κέκλασμαι, to break in twain, κατὰ μικρόν, to break into small pieces, 7. 3. 22.

Διακονέω, ήσω, δεδιακόνηκα (διάκονος), to wait on, serve, supply, 4. 5. 33.

Διακόπτω, ψω, κέκοφα, κέκομμαι, to cut through, break or burst through, 1. 8. 10, 4. 8. 13.

Διακόσιοι, αι, α, num. adj. two hundred, 1. 2. 9.

Διακρίνω, κρινῶ, κέκρικα, κέκριμαι, to separate, distinguish, settle, decide, 6. 1. 22.

Διαλαγχάνω, λήξομαι, to divide or part by lot, 4. 5. 23.

Διαλαμβάνω, λήψομαι, είληφα, είλημμαι, to take each his share, 5. 3. 4; to take separately, 4. 1. 23.

Διαλέγω, λέξω, διείλοχα, είλεγμαι, to pick out; Mid. to discourse, converse with, τινί, 1. 7. 9, 4. 8. 4.

Διαλείπω, λείψω, λέλοιπα, λέλειμμαι, 2 aor. διέλιπον, to leave an interval or gap, to be placed at intervals, 4. 7. 6, 1. 8. 10, 4. 8. 12; τὸ διαλεῖπον, the gap, interval, 4. 8. 13.

Διαμαρτάνω, ἥσομαι, to miss entirely, fail completely; τῶν ἐξόδων, having failed to discover the way out, 7. 4. 17.

Διαμάχομαι, μαχέσομαι or μαχοῦμαι, or poet. μαχήσομαι, μεμάχημαι, to fight or strive with, τινί, struggle, resist strongly, fight obstinately, μή, 5. 6. 25, 5. 8. 23.

Διαμένω, μενῶ, μεμένηκα, to remain by, continue, 5. 4. 22, often ἔμειναν.

Διαμετρέω, ήσω, μεμέτρηκα, μεμέτρημαι, to measure out, give out rations, τινί, 7. 1. 40.

Διαμπερές, adv. (διά, ἀνά, πείρω), through and through, right through, 7. 8. 14.

Διανέμω, νεμῶ, νενέμηκα, νενέμημαι, to distribute, apportion, divide, 7. 5. 2.

Διανοέομαι, νοήσομαι, νενόημαι, to think over, intend, purpose, 6. 1. 19, 7. 7. 48, 2. 4. 17.

Διάνοια, ας, ἡ (διά, νοέω), thought, intention, purpose, 5. 6. 31.

Διαπαντός, adv. (διά, πᾶς), throughout, δ.=ἀεί, 7. 8. 11, always.

Διαπέμπω, πέμψω, πέπομφα, πέπεμμαι, to send off, 4. 5. 8.

Διαπεράω, άσω, πεπέρᾱκα, to go over or across, pass through, 4. 3. 21.

Διαπλέω, πλεύσομαι or πλευσοῦμαι, πέπλευκα, πέπλευσμαι, to sail over or across, 7. 3. 3.

Διαπολεμέω, ήσω, ηκα, ημαι, to carry the war through to the end, Lat. debellare, fight it out with, τινί, 3. 3. 3.

Διαπορεύω, εύσω, &c., to carry over, set across, 2. 5. 18; Pass. to pass across, go through, 2. 5. 18.

Διαπορέω, ήσω, &c., Act. and Mid. (διά, ἀπορέω), to be quite at a loss, in difficulty, or in doubt, 6. 1. 22.

Διαπράττω, ξω, &c., to accomplish, bring about, effect, settle, τινί τι, 7. 1. 38, 2. 37; παρά τινος, 2. 6. 2. φιλίαν διαπράττεσθαι πρός τινα, to make friendship with; διαπράττεσθαί τι πρός τινα περί τινος, to effect something with some one about something, 7. 2. 7, 7. 4. 12; stipulate, negotiate, 3. 5. 5.

Διαρπάζω, άσομαι, &c., to tear in pieces, spoil, plunder, 1. 2. 26, 7. 1. 25.

Διαρριπτέω and διαρρίπτω, ψω, &c., to cast through, throw about, scatter, 7. 3. 23, 5. 8. 6.

Διάρριψις, εως, ἡ (διά, ρίπτω), a scattering about (disjectio), 5. 8. 7.

Διασημαίνω, σημᾰνῶ, &c., to mark out, to point out, 2. 1. 23.

Διασκηνέω, σκηνάω or σκηνόω (διά, σκηνή), vb. διασκηνητέον, 4. 4. 14; to place in separate tents, quarter, 4. 4. 8, and neut. to encamp separately, 4. 5. 29.

Διασπάω, άσομαι, &c., to tear asunder, scatter, separate, 1. 5. 9, 3. 4. 20, 5. 6. 32.

Διασπείρω, σπερῶ, &c., to scatter or spread about, 1. 8. 25.

Διασφενδοράω, ήσω, &c., to scatter as by a sling; Pass. to fly in pieces as if hurled from a sling, 4. 2. 3.

Διασώζω, σώσω, &c., to preserve, keep safe; Pass. with εἰς or πρός, to get safe to a place, 5. 4. 5, 6. 2. 8.

Διατάρττω, τάξω, &c., to arrange, set in order, draw up in battle array, 3. 4. 5.

Διατείνω, τενῶ, &c., to stretch out, accomplish; Mid. exert oneself, 7. 6. 36.

Διατελέω, έσω, &c., to end, accomplish, 1. 5. 7, 4. 5. 11, with part. ποιῶν, to continue to do or do constantly, 4. 3. 2, 3. 4. 17.

Διατήκω, ξω, to melt, soften by heat, 4. 5. 6.

Διατίθημι, θήσω, &c., to place separately, arrange, treat, dispose of, 1. 1. 5, 4. 7. 4, 6. 6. 37.

Διατρέφω, θρέψω, &c., to feed, support, sustain, 4. 7. 17.

Διατρῐβή, ῆς, ἡ (διά, τρίβω), a wasting away, waste of time, delay, 5. 9. 1.

Διατρίβω, ψω, &c. (ι except in 2 aor. pass. διετρῑβην), to waste, χρόνον (tempus terere), 7. 2. 3; to lose time, delay, 1. 5. 9, 2. 3. 9.

Διαφαίνω, φανῶ, &c., to show through; Mid. to appear, show itself, 5. 2. 29, 7. 8. 14.

Διαφανῶς, adv. (διά, φαίνω), manifestly, clearly.

Διαφερόντως, adv. (διά, φέρω), differently from, in a distinguished manner, 1. 9. 14.

Διαφέρω, διοίσω, διενήνοχα, διενήνεγμαι, 1 aor. διήνεγκα, 2 aor. διήνεγκον, to carry over, carry through, bear, sustain; intr. to differ from, 2. 3.

15; surpass, excel, τινός τι, 3. 1. 37. Often impers. πολὺ διαφέρει, there is a great difference, 3. 4. 33. Pass. to differ, quarrel about, ἀμφί τινος, 4. 5. 17; πρός τινα, 7. 6. 15.

Διαφεύγω, φεύξομαι, &c., to flee through, get away, escape, 6. 5. 4.

Διαφθείρω, φθερῶ, &c., to destroy utterly, make away with, kill, 3. 3. 5.

Διάφορος, ος, ον (διαφέρω), different, unlike, at variance with, opp. to φίλος, 7. 6. 15; as a subst. ὁ, an enemy, an opponent, τὸ δ., a difference, disagreement, 4. 6. 3.

Διαφυή, ῆς, ἡ (διά, φύω), any natural partition or break, a joint in grasses, a cleft in nuts, 5. 4. 29.

Διαφυλάττω, άξω, &c., to watch closely, preserve, maintain, 7. 6. 22.

Διαχάζω (διά or δίς, χάζω), only in 4. 8. 18, usually διαχάζομαι, to draw back, separate.

Διαχειμάζω, άσω (διά, χειμών), to pass the winter, 7. 6. 31.

Διαχειρίζω, ίσω or Att. ιῶ (διά, χείρ), to have in hand, manage, 1. 9. 17.

Διαχωρέω, ήσω, &c., to go through, pass through; κάτω διεχώρει αὐτοῖς, they were affected with diarrhœa, 4. 8. 20.

Διδάσκαλος, ου, ὁ, a teacher, 2. 6. 12, from

Διδάσκω, διδάξω, δεδίδαχα, δεδίδαγμαι (δάω), to teach, τινά τι or ὡς, 2. 5. 6, 3. 3. 4; to show, prove, 5. 7. 11; Mid. caus. to have one taught (docendum curare).

Δίδημι, rare in prose=δέω, *to bind*, 3 pl. διδέασι, 5. 8. 24. •

Δίδωμι, δώσω, δέδωκα, δέδομαι, 1 aor. act. ἔδωκα, 2 aor. ἔδων, not in ind. sing., *to give, grant*, 6. 6. 19, 7. 3. 13, 2. 3. 25, 3. 4. 42.

Διείργω, ξω (διά, εἴργω), *to keep asunder, separate*; intr. *lie between*, 3. 1. 2.

Διελαύνω, ελάσω or ελῶ, &c. (διά, ἐλαύνω), *to drive through, thrust through*, sc. ἵππον, *to ride through, charge*, 1. 5. 12, 10. 7, 2. 3. 19.

Διεξέρχομαι, ελεύσομαι (διά, ἐξ, ἔρχομαι), *to go out through, pass right through, get to the end of*, 6. 6. 38.

Διέρχομαι, ελεύσομαι, &c. (διά, ἔρχομαι), *to go through, pass through*, *arrive at*, λόγος διῆλθε, *a report spread*, 1. 4. 7, 4. 1. 3, 4. 7. 15, 3. 5. 17, 6. 5. 19.

Διερωτάω, ήσω, &c. (διά, ἐρωτάω), *to cross-question*, 4. 1. 26.

Διέχω, ἕξω or διασχήσω, &c. (διά, ἔχω), trans. *to divide, keep apart*; intr. *to go through, be separate, be distant, stand apart*, 1. 10. 4, 3. 4. 20. τὸ διέχον, *the interval*, 3. 4. 22.

Διηγέομαι, ήσομαι, ημαι (διά, ἡγέομαι), *to set out in detail, describe, narrate*, 4. 3. 13.

Διηγκυλισμένος, see διαγκυλίζομαι.

Διίημι, ήσω, &c. (διά, ἵημι), *to send through, let people go through*, 3. 2. 23 (*transmittere*), 5. 4. 2.

Διίστημι, διαστήσω, &c. (διά, ἵστημι), *to divide*; Pass. with 2 aor. pf. and plp. act. *to stand apart, stand aside*, 1. 5. 2, 8. 20, 10. 7.

Δίκαιος, αία, αιον (δίκη; δίχα, Aristotle), *just, righteous*; τὰ δίκ. λαμβάνειν, *to receive what is right*, 7. 7. 17. ἐκ τοῦ δικαίου = δικαίως, *according to justice*, 1. 9. 19, so σὺν τῷ δικαίῳ, 2. 6. 18.

Δικαιοσύνη, ης, ἡ (δίκαιος), *justice, righteousness*, 1. 9. 16, 7. 7. 41.

Δικαιότης, τητος, ἡ (δίκη)=δικαιοσύνη, 2. 6. 26.

Δικαίως, adv. fr. δίκαιος, 5. 1. 9, 2. 3. 19.

Δικαστής, οῦ, ὁ (δίκη), *a judge*, or rather *juryman=judex*; *the presiding judge*=ὁ κριτής, 5. 7. 34.

Δίκη, ης, ἡ (ι), *custom, right, justice*; δ. ἐσχάτη, *the severest punishment*, 6. 6. 15; δίκην λαβεῖν, *inflict punishment* (*sumere pœnam*), 5. 8. 17, so also δίκην ἐπιτιθέναι, 1. 3. 10, 3. 2. 8, 5. 6. 34. εἰς δίκας καταστῆσαι (*in judicium vocare*, *summon to trial*, 5. 7. 34; δίκην ὑπέχειν, *to stand trial, suffer punishment, be punished* (*pœnas dare, solvere*), 5. 8. 18, 6. 6. 15, so also δίκην διδόναι, *to be punished*, 2. 6. 21, 5. 4. 20. ὑπό τινος, 4. 4. 14, *by one*; τινός, *for a thing*, 7. 6. 10; δίκην ἔχειν, *to have punishment, be punished*, 2. 5. 38, 41, 7. 4. 24. Cf. δείκνυμι.

Διμοιρία, ας, ἡ (δίς, *twice*, μοῖρα, *a share*), *a double share*, 7. 2. 36, 6. 1.

Δινέω, ήσω, &c. (δίνη, *a whirlpool*), *to whirl round*, 6. 1. 9.

Διό=δι' ὅ, *wherefore*, 5. 5. 10.

Δίοδος, ου, ἡ (διά, ὁδός), the
way through, the passage, 5.
4. 9.

Διοράω (διά, ὁράω), to see through,
5. 2. 30.

Διορύττω, ξω, &c. (διά, ὁρύττω),
to dig through, 7. 8. 13.

Διότι=διὰ τοῦτο ὅτι, for this
reason that, because, since, 2.
2. 14.

Δίπηχυς, υς, υ (δίς, πῆχυς), two
cubits long, 4. 2. 28.

Διπλάσιος, α, ον (δίς), double, a
double supply, twice as much
or as far, 4. 1. 13, 6, 5. 17,
3. 3. 16.

Δίπλεθρος, ος, ον (δίς, πλέθρον),
two plethra long or broad=
202 feet, 4. 3. 1.

Διπλόος, οῦς, ῆ, οῦν (δίς), two-
fold, double, twice as much,
7. 6. 7.

Δίς, adv. twice.

Δισχίλιοι, αι, α (δίς, χίλιοι), two
thousand.

Διφθέρα, ας, ἡ (δέφω, to tan), a
prepared hide, leather, a wal-
let, 5. 2. 12 ; skins, used as
tent-coverings, 1. 5. 10.

Διφθέρινος, η, ον, adj. (διφθέρα),
made of leather, leathern, 2.
4. 28.

Δίφρος, ου, ὁ (for δίφορος, δίς,
φέρω), pl. δίφροι and δίφρα, the
foot-board in the war-chariot
for two (the driver, ἡνίοχος,
and the combatant, παραιβά-
της), a chariot, a seat, 7. 3.
29.

Δίχα (δίς), adv. in two, apart,
δίχα ποιεῖν, to divide, 6. 4.
11.

Διχάζω, άσω (δίχα), to divide,
separate, for διαχάζω, 4. 8.
18.

Διψάω, ήσω, δεδίψηκα, contr.

with η (δίψα), to thirst, 4. 5.
27 ; to thirst after, τινός, like
Lat. sitio.

Διωκτέος, vb. from

Διώκω, διώξω and διώξομαι (δίω,
to flee), to pursue, chase, make
to run, 3. 2. 35, 3. 8; in law,
to prosecute ; ὁ διώκων, the
prosecutor ; ὁ φεύγων, the de-
fendant.

Δίωξις, εως, ἡ (διώκω), a pur-
suing, following after, pursuit,
3. 4. 5.

Διῶρυξ, υχος and υγος, ἡ (διορύττω), a trench, canal, 1. 7.
15, 2. 4. 13.

Δόγμα, ατος, τό (δοκέω), an opinion ; δόγμα ἦν τῶν στρατιωτῶν, it was resolved on by the
soldiers, 6. 6. 27. δόγμα
ποιεῖσθαι, to make a decree, to
come to a resolution, c. acc.
and inf. 6. 4. 11.

Δοκέω, δόξω, δέδογμαι (δοκήσω,
δεδόκηκα, δεδόκημαι, poet.), to
think, expect ; intr. to seem,
appear ; impers. δοκεῖ μοι, it
seems good to me, I think (mihi
videtur), with inf., 1. 2. 1, 4.
5. 1. τὸ δόξαν, 6. 1. 18 ; τὰ
δόξαντα, 1. 3. 20 ; τὸ δεδογ-
μένον, 5. 6. 35 ; τὰ δεδογμένα,
3. 2. 39 (quod visum est), what
was resolved on ; ἔδοξε ταῦτα,
these things were agreed to,
resolved on, this proposal was
adopted, 1. 3. 20 ; δόξαν ταῦτα,
these things having been resolved upon, nom. abs. 4. 1.
13. καὶ τούτους τί δοκεῖτε ;
et hos quid putatis fecisse ? 5.
7. 26.

Δοκιμάζω, άσω (δόκιμος), to examine, prove, test, then to
approve, sanction, inspect, 3.
3. 20.

Δόλιος, α, ον (δόλος), *crafty, deceitful, treacherous*, 1. 4. 7.

Δολιχός, ή, όν, *long* ; as subst. ὁ, *the long race*, 4. 8. 27.

Δόλος, ου, ὁ (δέλυς, *a bait*), Lat. *dolus, a bait, stratagem ; cunning, craft, deceit*, 5. 6. 29.

Δόλοψ, οπος, ὁ, *a Dolopian, living in Epire, between Acarnania, Ætolia, and Pindus*, 1. 2. 6.

Δόξα, ης, ἡ (δοκέω), *the opinion one has*, παρὰ δόξαν or ἀπὸ δόξης, *contrary to expectation*, opp. to κατὰ δόξαν; *the opinion others have of one, estimation, esteem, honour, glory*, 6. 5. 14.

Δοξάζω, άσω (δόξα), *to think, imagine, magnify, extol.*

Δοράτιον, ου, τό (δόρυ), *a little spear, a lance*, 6. 4. 23.

Δορκάς, άδος, ἡ (δέρκομαι, *to see*), *a gazelle, antelope, an animal of the deer kind with large bright eyes*, 1. 5. 2, 5. 3. 10.

Δόρπηστος, ου, ὁ, and δορπηστός (δόρπον), *supper-time*, 1. 10. 17.

Δόρυ, ατος, τό, *a spear* ; ἐπὶ δόρυ, *ad dextram, to the right hand*, opp. ἐπ᾿ ἀσπίδα, 4. 3. 29.

Δορυφόρος, ου, ὁ (δόρυ, φέρω), *spearmen*, 5. 2. 4.

Δουλεία, ας, ἡ (δοῦλος), *slavery*, 7. 7. 32.

Δουλεύω, εύσω, δεδούλευκα (δοῦλος), 4. 8. 4, *to serve, be a slave (servire)* ; δουλόω, *to enslave (in servitutem redigere).*

Δοῦλος, ου, ὁ (δέολος, δέω, *to bind*), *a slave, bondsman*, opp. δεσπότης, *subject, vassal*, 1. 9. 29, 2. 5. 38.

Δουπέω, ήσω, 2 pf. δέδουπα (δοῦπος), *to give a dull heavy sound*, like a corpse, *thud, strike, dash*, 1. 8. 18 ; in 4. 5. 18, κρούω is used.

Δοῦπος, ου, ὁ, *a dead heavy sound, noise, din*, 2. 2. 19.

Δρακόντιος, ου, ὁ (δράκων), *Dracontius*, a Spartan, 4. 8. 25, 6. 6. 30.

Δρεπανηφόρος, ος, ον (δρέπανον φέρω), *scythe-bearing*, δρεπανηφόρα, sc. ἅρματα, *scythe-bearing chariots*, 1. 8. 10.

Δρέπανον, ου, τό (δρέπω, *to pluck*), *a scythe*, 1. 8. 10.

Δρίλαι, ων, αἱ, *the Drilæ*, a people in Pontus, 5. 2. 1.

Δρόμος, ου, ὁ (δραμεῖν, τρέχω), *a race, a running*, 4. 8. 26 ; δρόμῳ θεῖν, *to run at full speed*, 1. 8. 18, 19, so δρόμῳ φεύγειν, 5. 7. 25.

Δύναμαι, δυνήσομαι, δεδύνημαι, impf. ἐδυνάμην, ἐδύνω, ἐδύνατο (ὁ, τι ἐδύνω, 1. 6. 7, *as much as you could*), *to be able, can (possum)*, 2. 6. 2, 7. 6. 37. οἱ μέγιστα δυνάμενοι, *the most powerful*, 2. 6. 21. οὐδὲν ἄλλο δυνάμενος, *was equivalent to*, 2. 2. 13 ; *to be worth of money*, 1. 5. 6.

Δύναμις, εως, ἡ, *power, means, resources (potentia, opes)*, 2. 5. 11 ; *a force (copiæ)*, 1. 3. 12, 5. 4. 7. εἰς δύναμιν, *according to our ability*, 2. 3. 23 ; *implied weakness*, 1. 6. 7.

Δυνάστης, ου, ὁ (δύναμαι), *a lord, master, ruler* ; οἱ δυνάσται, *the chief men (optimates)* ; δ. τῶν ὑπάρχων, *the chief of the viceroys*, 1. 2. 20, Eng. *dynasty.*

Δυνατός, ή, όν (δύναμαι), *power-*

ful, strong, influential, possible, with inf. 4. 1. 24.

Δύνω, δύσομαι, δέδῦκα, 2 aor. ἔδυν, intr. to sink (trans. δύω), set of the sun, 2. 2. 3.

Δύη, δυοῖν (or δύο, indecl.), two, 1. 2. 23.

Δύσβατος, ος, ον (δυς, βαίνω), inaccessible, impassable, 5. 2. 2.

Δυσδιάβατος, ος, ον (δυς, διά, βαίνω), difficult to get through.

Δυσμή, ῆς, ἡ (δύνω), sinking, setting, in pl. 6. 2. 26, 7. 3. 34.

Δυσπάρἴτος, ος, ον (δυς, πάρειμι), hard or difficult to pass, 4. 1. 25.

Δυσπορευτός, ός, όν (δυς, πορεύω), hard to pass, 1. 5. 7.

Δυσπορία, ας, ἡ (δυς, πόρος), difficulty of passing, 4. 3. 7.

Δύσπορος, ος, ον, hard to pass, scarcely passable, ποταμός, 2. 5. 9 ; νάπος, 6. 5. 12 ; ὁδοί, 5. 1. 13.

Δυσπρόσιτος, ος, ον (δυς, πρός, εἶμι), hard to get at.

Δύσχρηστος, ος, ον (δυς, χράομαι), hard to use or manage, useless, 3. 4. 19.

Δυσχωρία, ας, ἡ (δυς, χῶρα), difficult ground, the roughness of the country, 3. 5. 16.

Δύω, δύσω, δέδυκα, δέδυμαι, to cause to enter, put on another ; Mid. to sink, set, 5. 7. 6, 1. 10. 15 ; δύς, 2 aor. part. act.

Δώδεκα (δύο, δέκα), num. adj. twelve.

Δωρέομαι, ήσομαι (δῶρον), to give presents, 7. 3. 18, 5. 3.

Δωροδοκέω (δῶρον, δέκω, δέχομαι), to accept presents, receive gifts, 7. 6. 17.

Δῶρον, ου, τό (δίδωμι), a gift, a present, 1. 9. 22.

E.

'Εάν= εἰ ἄν, contr. ἤν, ἄν (ἅ), conj. if, takes always conjunctive, 3. 1. 23, 2. 20. ἐάν τε—ἐάν τε or εἴτε—εἴτε=(sive—sive), whether—or, 5. 5. 16, 7. 3. 37. ἐὰν μή=(nisi), unless ; ἐάνπερ; if at all events, 4. 6. 17.

'Εαρίζω, ίσω (ἔαρ), to pass the spring, Lat. vernare, 3. 5. 15.

'Εαυτοῦ, ῆς, οῦ, Lat. sui, sibi, se, of himself, herself, itself, sometimes αὑτοῦ, αὑτῆς, 6. 6. 16, 7. 6. 14. οἱ ἑαυτοῦ, his own men, 1. 2. 15 ; τὰ ἑαυτῶν, their own affairs, 3. 1. 16, 7. 7. 44 ; ἐν ἑαυτῷ ἐγένετο, he came to himself, 1. 5. 17,

'Εάω, ἐάσω, εἴακα, εἴαμαι (ᾰ pres. and impf., ᾱ everywhere else), to let, leave alone, suffer, allow, c. acc. and inf. 5. 2. 10, 7. 4. 11. οὐκ ἐᾶν, to forbid (prohibere), 7. 4. 10.

'Εβδομήκοντα, num. adj. seventy.

'Εβοζέλμιος, ου, ὁ='Αβροζέλμης.

'Εγγίγνομαι, ἐγγενήσομαι, 2 aor. ἐνεγενόμην, to be born in, to be engendered, 5. 8. 3.

"Εγγονος, ος, ον, a grandchild, a descendant, 3. 2. 14.

'Εγγυάω, ήσω, ἐγγεγύηκα, ἐγγεγύημαι (ἐγγύη, a pledge), to pledge (spondēre) ; Mid. to promise, engage, acc. and inf. 7. 4. 13.

'Εγγύθεν, adv. (ἐγγύς), from close at hand, near, 4. 2. 27.

'Εγγύς, adv. near, nearly, 2. 2. 15. ἐ. εἶναι, 1. 10. 10, 2. 5. 36 ; ἐ. προσιέσθαι, 4. 2. 12 ; ἐ. γίγνεσθαι, 4. 2. 15, 7. 23, 4. 5. 16 ; ἐγγυτέρω or ον, ἐγγυτάτω or a, or ἔγγιον, ἔγγιστα; αἱ ἐγγυτάτω κῶμαι, 2. 2. 16; οἱ ἐγγύτατα τῶν πολεμίων, 2. 2. 17, 5. 4. 13, 7. 13.

'Εγείρω, ἐγερῶ (ἐγήγερκα), ἐγήγερμαι (2 p. ἐγρήγορα, I am awake, keep watch), to awaken, rouse, stir up, 4. 6. 22, 5. 7. 10.

'Εγκαλέω, ἔσω, &c. (ἐν, καλέω), to call in, claim, τι, 7. 7. 33; τινί, to bring a charge or accusation against one, 7. 7. 44, 47; ὅτι or acc. of subst. 7. 5. 7.

'Εγκαλύπτω, ψω, ἐγκεκάλυμμαι (ἐν, καλύπτω), to hide closely, cover up, 4. 5. 19.

"Εγκειμαι, κείσομαι (ἐν, κεῖμαι), to lie or be in, 4. 5. 26.

'Εγκέλευστος, ος, ον (ἐν, κελεύω), ordered, commanded, 1. 3. 13.

'Εγκέφαλος, ος, ον (ἐν, κεφαλή), within the head, sc. μυελός, the brain, the pith of the palm, 2. 3, 16.

'Εγκεχαλινωμένως, see ἐγχαλινόω, better ἐγκεχαλινωμένοι, 7. 2. 21.

'Εγκρατής, ής, ές (ἐν, κρατέω), holding fast, strong, master of, c. gen. 5. 4. 15, 1. 7. 7.

'Εγχαλινόω, ώσω, &c. (ἐν, χαλινός, a bridle, χαλάω), to put a bit in the mouth of, ἵππον; Pass. to have the bit in, to be ready bridled, 7. 2. 21, 7. 6.

'Εγχειρέω, ήσω (ἐν, χείρ), to put one's hand to, undertake, attempt, c. dat. 5. 1. 8.

'Εγχειρίδιος, ος, ον (ἐν, χείρ), in the hand, τό, a dagger, 4. 3. 12; a handle, a hand-book.

'Εγχειρίζω, ίσω, Att. ιῶ (ἐν, χείρ), to put into one's hands, to trust, τινά τινι, 3. 2. 8.

'Εγχέω, ἐγχεῶ, to pour in, 4. 3. 13.

'Εγώ, 1 pers. pron. I; ἔγωγε, I for my part, 1. 4. 8, 4. 1. 22.

"Εἔω, see ἐσθίω.

'Εθελοντής, οῦ, ὁ (ἐθέλω), a volunteer, acc. pl. ἐθελοντάς, but part. ἐθέλοντας, willing, 1. 6. 9, 4. 1. 26, 27.

'Εθελοντί, adv. willingly, 3. 3. 18, but ἐθέλοντι is dat. part. of ἐθέλω.

'Εθελούσιος, ος, ον, adj. willing, 4. 6. 19.

'Εθέλω, ἐθελήσω, ἠθέληκα, to wish, be willing, 5. 10. 6, 1. 9. 14.

"Εθνος, εος, τό (ἔθος, a custom), a nation, tribe, 4. 5. 28.

Εἰ, conj. if, with ind. 3. 2. 39, 3. 3. 16, 5. 4. 6, 6. 37; with opt. 4. 8. 11, 5. 1. 11, 6. 4. It is never joined in Attic with the conjunctive. After verbs interrogandi, dubitandi et deliberandi, 1. 8. 15, 2. 1. 15, 4. 1. 25, 1. 3. 5, 5. 1. 12, 1. 10. 5; εἴγε, if at least, 7. 6. 22; εἰ δὲ μή, 5. 7. 32; εἰ καί, 6. 6. 27; καὶ εἰ, 3. 2. 24; εἰ μή, 1. 5. 2, 4. 2. 4, 5. 5; εἴπερ γε, if at all events, 1. 7. 9; εἴπως, if by any means, 2. 3. 18, 5. 2, 4. 1. 8; εἴτε—εἴτε = sive—sive, whether—or whether, 2. 1. 14; εἴ τε, and if, 1. 3. 11; εἴ τις = si quis, if any one, 1. 5. 9, 4. 5. 17. εἴθε, εἰ γάρ, particles of wishing, O that = utinam. εἰ = if; εἶ = es, thou art.

Εἶδος, εος, τό (εἶδον, ὁράω), appearance, form, 2. 3. 16.

Εἶδον, see ὁράω.

Εἰκάζω, άσω, εἴκασμαι (εἰκώς), to make like, conjecture, guess, 1. 6. 11, 10. 16, 5. 4. 12.

Εἰκώς, εἰκότος, τό, neut. of the
perf. εἶκα or ἔοικα, fr. εἴκω, to
be like, adj. likely, reasonable,
probable, 3. 1. 13, 2. 26, 5. 1.
12. εἰκότα λέγειν, to say what
is reasonable, 2. 3. 6; ὡς
εἰκός, as was likely, 3. 4. 24,
7. 6. 13.

Εἴκοσι (εἴκατι, ὀνο-ἔκατι, dvi-
ginti, two-tens, Don.), num.
adj. twenty.

Εἰκότως, adv. fr. εἰκός=κατὰ τὸ
εἰκός, in all likelihood, with
good reason, 2. 2. 3, 6. 4. 18.

[Εἴκω], εἴξω, ἔοικα, to be or look
like, 2. 1. 13; ὡς ἔοικε, as it
seemed, apparently, 2. 2. 18;
οὐδενὶ καλῷ ἔοικε, it is not at
all like a brave man, 6. 5. 17.
Imp. it seems, beseems, it is
right, reasonable, likely.

Εἴκω, εἴξω, to yield, give way.

Εἰμί, ἔσομαι, impf. ἦν, to be,
with μή, οὐ, μηδέν, οὐδείν, to be
impossible, 4. 2. 10; εἶναί τι,
to be something; εἶναί τινος,
or ἔκ τινος, 3. 2. 13; ἔστι μοι,
I have, 1. 7. 8, 2. 1. 10; εἶναι
περί τι, to be busy, 3. 5. 7;
ἐπί and πρός τινι, 5. 4. 2, 25,
κατά, 1. 10. 9; for ἔξεστι,
it is allowable, possible, Lat.
licet, 1. 5. 2, 2. 2. 3. ἦν
δυναμένη, 2. 2. 13; ἔστιν ὅστις,
whoever, 1. 8. 20; ἔσθ' ὅτε,
at times, sometimes, 2. 6. 9;
ἔστιν ὁπόθεν, there is a place
from which, 6. 2. 4; οὐκ ἔστιν
ὅπως, 2. 4. 3, it cannot but
be that; τὰ ὄντα, things
really existing, 4. 4. 15, also
=χρήματα, property, 7. 8. 22;
τὸ κατὰ τοῦτον εἶναι, as regards this man, 1. 6. 9; τῷ
ὄντι, really, in reality.

Εἶμι, I shall go, Lat. ibo, 7. 3.

34; imp. ἴθι, 3 pl. ἰόντων, 1.
4. 8; impf. ἤειν and ᾔα, and
ᾖα; inf. ἰέναι, 1. 3. 1, 2. 6. 10,
1. 8, 16. ἐπί τινα, τινὶ διὰ φιλίας, to be on friendly terms
with, 3. 2. 8. διὰ πολέμου, 3.
2. 8. τοῦ πρόσω ἰέναι, to go a
bit farther, gen. of portion, 1.
3. 1. ἴθι=Lat. age, come then,
well then, 7. 2. 26, 7. 27. ἰτέον,
we must go, 3. 1. 7, 6. 3. 30.

Εἰπεῖν, 2 aor. of φημί, which
see.

Εἴργω, for ἔεργω, excludo (εἴργω, includo), εἴρξω, εἴργμαι,
f. mid. as pass. 6. 6. 16, to
shut out.

Εἴρηκα fr. εἴρω, pf. for λέγω, I
have said; εἴρω, ἐρῶ, εἴρηκα,
εἴρημαι, 1 aor. pass. ἐρρήθην,
fut. ῥηθήσομαι.

Εἰρήνη, ης, ἡ (εἴρω, to bind),
peace, 2. 6. 6.

Εἰς or ἐς, a prep. to or into,
gov. acc. PLACE, 1. 2. 22, 4.
7. 1, 5. 5. 14; PERSON, 3. 3.
19, 5. 3. 6, 5. 6. 28; TIME, 1.
7. 1, 2. 3. 25; NUMBER,
about=circiter, 3. 3. 6, 4. 8.
15; also distributively εἰς δύο,
two each. εἰς δικαιοσύνην, as
to, as regards, 1. 9. 16; φιλίαν, 2. 6. 30; ἀφθονίαν, 7. 1.
33; δύναμιν, 2. 3. 23. παρῆ-
σαν εἰς Σάρδεις, constructio
prægnans=they came to Sardis
and were in it, 1. 2. 2, so, 2. 2.
16, 7. 2. 5. εἰς ὑμᾶς λέγειν,
5. 6. 28, 5. 6. 37, to speak to
or before.

Εἷς, μία, ἕν, gen. ἑνός, μιᾶς, ἑνός,
num. adj. one; εἷς τις, some
one; εἷς ἕκαστος (unusquis-
que), each one, 6. 6. 12; εἷς
γε ἀνήρ (unus omnium max-
ime), 1. 9. 12.

Εἰσάγω, άξω, &c. (εἰς, ἄγω), to lead into, πρὸς Σεύθην, 7. 5. 19; εἰς σκηνήν, 1. 6. 11.

Εἰσακοντίζω, ίσω (εἰς, ἀκοντίζω), to throw javelins in, 7. 4. 15.

Εἰσβαίνω, βήσομαι, &c. (εἰς, βαίνω), to go into, go on board.

Εἰσβάλλω, βαλῶ, &c. (εἰς, βάλλω), to throw into, bring into quickly; as if intrans., make an inroad into, to enter, 1. 2. 21; to fall of a river, εἰς τὸν Εὐφράτην, 1. 7. 15.

Εἰσβιβάζω, άσω (εἰς, βαίνω), to make to go into, put on board, 5. 3. 1.

Εἰσβολή, ῆς, ἡ (εἰς, βάλλω), entrance, passage, pass, 1. 2. 21; εἰσβολὴν ποιεῖσθαι, to force a passage, 5. 6. 7.

Εἰσδύομαι, δύσομαι (εἰς, δύω), 2 aor. εἰσέδυν, to enter into, 4. 5. 14.

Εἴσειμι (εἰς, εἶμι), to go into, enter, 7. 2. 30. εἰσήει αὐτοὺς ὅπως, it came into their minds that, 5. 9. 17.

Εἰσελαύνω, ελάσω, &c. (εἰς, ἐλαύνω), to drive into, sc. ἵππον, ἄρμα, ναῦν, στρατόν, &c. to ride, drive, sail, march into, 1. 2. 26.

Εἰσέρχομαι, ελεύσομαι, &c. (εἰς, ἔρχομαι), to go into, enter, enter upon, 7. 1. 27.

Εἴσοδος, ου, ἡ (εἰς, ὁδός), an entrance, 6. 5. 1.

Εἰσπηδάω, ήσω, &c. (εἰς, πηδάω), to leap into, εἰς τὸν πηλόν, 1. 5. 8.

Εἰσπίπτω, πεσοῦμαι, &c. (εἰς, πίπτω), to fall into, fall upon, 7. 1. 19.

Εἰσπλέω, πλεύσομαι, &c. (εἰς, πλέω), to sail into, 6. 2. 1.

Εἰσπορεύομαι, εύσομαι, &c. (εἰς, πορεύω), to march, proceed, enter into.

Εἰστρέχω, θρέξομαι, &c., 2 aor. εἰσέδραμον (εἰς, τρέχω), to run into, 5. 2. 16.

Εἰσφέρω, οἴσω, &c. (εἰς, φέρω), to bring, carry into, 7. 3. 21.

Εἰσφορέω, ήσω, &c. (εἰς, φέρω), to carry, bring into, 4. 6. 1.

Εἴσω (εἰς), adv. within, τῶν ὀρέων, 1. 2. 21; τῶν ὅπλων, 3. 3. 7, 4. 26.

Εἰσωθέω, ωθήσω and ώσω, &c. (εἰς, ὠθέω), to thrust into; Mid. to force, press, push in, 5. 2. 18.

Εἶτα, adv. afterwards, then, next, Lat. deinde, πρῶτον μέν —εἶτα δέ, 1. 3. 2, 6. 10. Often joined to a part. 1. 2. 25, and then they wandered about and perished.

Εἴτε—εἴτε = (εἴ τε) sive—sive—whether—or, with ind. 6. 6. 20; with opt. in or. obliq. 2. 1. 14, 7. 7. 18.

Εἴωθα, perf. with pres. meaning from ἔθω, I am wont, with inf. 7. 8. 4.

Ἐκ, prep. gov. gen. out, out of PLACE, ἐκ Φοινίκης, 1. 7. 12; ἐκ τοῦ πεδίου, 3. 4. 25; TIME, ἐξ οὗ (χρόνου), from the time that, since; ἐκ τούτου, 1. 2. 17, 6. 8, after this; ἐκ τοῦ ἀρίστου, 4. 6. 21; ἐκ τούτων, 1. 3. 11, 7. 6. 10; ἐκ τῶν παρόντων, 3. 2. 3; in consequence of, ἐκ τῆς νικώσης sc. γνώμης, 5. 9. 18; ἐκ τοῦ ἀδίκου, 1. 9. 16; ἐκ τῆς ψυχῆς φίλος, a friend from the heart, 7. 7. 43; φῶς ἐκ Διός, 3. 1. 12; φόβος ἐκ τῶν Ἑλλήνων, 1. 2. 18; ἐκ παντὸς τρόπου, in every way, 3. 1.

43; ἐξ ἐπιβουλῆς, *per insidias*, 6. 2. 7; ἐξ ὑποψίας, 2. 5. 5.

'Εκασταχόσε, adv. (ἕκαστος), *to each side*, 3. 5. 17.

Ἕκαστος, η, ον (ἑκάς, ἑκάτερος, *each of two* (*uterque*); ἕκαστος, *each of many* (*quisque*), 1. 7. 15, 4. 2. 12; ἕκαστός τις, *each one*, 6. 1. 19.

'Εκάστοτε, adv. *each time, always*, 2. 4. 10.

'Εκάτερος, α, ον (ἑκάς), *each of two* (*uterque*), 1. 8. 27, 3. 2. 36; καθ' ἑκάτερα (*ab utraque parte*), *on both sides*, 5. 6. 7.

'Εκατέρωθεν, adv. *from or on both sides* (*utrimque*), 1. 8. 13, 6. 2. 3.

'Εκατέρωσε, adv. *to each side, each way*, 1. 8. 14.

'Εκατόν, num. adj. indecl. *a hundred*, 1. 2. 25.

'Εκατώνυμος, ου, ὁ (ἑκατόν, ὄνομα), *Hecatonymus*, a citizen of Sinope, 5. 5. 7.

'Εκβαίνω, βήσομαι, &c. (ἐκ, βαίνω), *to go out, disembark*, 5. 4. 11, 4. 3. 23.

'Εκβάλλω, βαλῶ, &c. (ἐκ, βάλλω), *to throw, drive out*, ἐκ τῆς φιλίας, 7. 5. 6.

Ἕκβασις, εως, ἡ (ἐκ, βαίνω), *a going out, a way out, pass*, 4. 2. 1, 3. 20, 21.

'Εκβάτανα, ων, τά, *Ecbatana*, the capital of Media, 2. 4. 25.

'Εκβοηθέω, ήσω, &c. (ἐκ, βοή, θέω), *to march out to aid*, 7. 8. 15.

Ἕκγονος, ος, ον (ἐκ, γίγνομαι), *born of, sprung from*; subst. ὁ, ἡ, *a child*, son or daughter; pl. *descendants* (*posteri*), 3. 2. 14; τὰ ἔκγονα, *the off-spring*, 4. 5. 25.

'Εκδέρω, δερῶ (ἐκ, δέρω), 1 aor.

ἐξέδειρα, *to strip off the skin, to flay*, 1. 2. 8.

'Εκδίδωμι, δώσω, &c. (ἐκ, δίδωμι), *to give out, give up*, 6. 4. 10; *to give out of one's house, give one's daughter in marriage* (*nuptum dare*), πυρ' ἀνδρί, 4. 1. 24.

'Εκδύω or ἐκδύνω, ἐκδύσω, &c. (ἐκ, δύω), *to strip, put off*, 4. 3. 12.

'Εκεῖ, adv. *there* (*ibi*), 7. 2. 30, 4. 1. 24.

'Εκεῖθεν, adv. *thence* (*inde*), 5. 6. 24.

'Εκεῖνος, η, ο (ἐκεῖ), *the man there, that man*, 1. 7. 18.

'Εκεῖσε, adv. *thither* (*illuc*).

'Εκθλίβω, ψω, &c., *to press or push out*, 3. 4. 19, 20.

'Εκκαθαίρω, αρῶ, ἐκκεκάθαρμαι (ἐκ, καθαίρω), *to cleanse, burnish*, 1. 2. 16.

'Εκκαλύπτω, ύψω, ἐκκεκάλυμμαι (ἐκ, καλύπτω), *to uncover*, 1. 2. 16.

'Εκκλησία, ας, ἡ (ἐκ, καλέω), *an assembly, the legislative assembly of citizens*; in Anab. *an assembly of soldiers*, 1. 3. 2, 4. 12; in Eccl. Gr. *a church*, Fr. *église*.

'Εκκλησιάζω (ἐκκλησία), *to hold an assembly, convene, summon to an assembly*, 5. 6. 37.

'Εκκλίνω, κλινῶ, &c. (ἐκ, κλίνω), *to bend out of the regular line*, 1. 8. 19.

'Εκκομίζω, ίσω, &c. (ἐκ, κομίζω), *to carry, fetch, take out* (*exportare*), 5. 2. 19.

'Εκκόπτω, ψω, &c. (ἐκ, κόπτω), *to cut out, knock out, cut down*, 1. 4. 10.

'Εκκυβιστάω, ήσω (ἐκ, κυβιστάω, κυβή, *the head*), *to tumble* headlong, to throw a summer-set, 6. 1. 9.

Ἐκκυμαίνω, ανῶ (ἐκ, κυμαίνω, κῦμα), to wave or bulge out, of a line of soldiers, 1. 8. 18.

Ἐκλέγω, λέξω, ἐξείλοχα, ἐξείλεγμαι, &c., to pick out, choose out, 3. 3. 19.

Ἐκλείπω, λείψω, &c. (ἐκ, λείπω), to leave out, pass over, forsake, 1. 2. 24 ; to fail, disappear, of snow, 4. 5. 15.

Ἐκμηρύομαι, ύσομαι (ἐκ, μηρύομαι), to unfold, make an army defile (explicare); intr. to defile, 6. 3. 22.

Ἐκπέμπω, ψω, &c. (ἐκ, πέμπω), to send out, off, away, 5. 2. 21.

Ἐκπεραίνω, ανῶ (ἐκ, περαίνω), to finish, bring to an end, 5. 1. 13.

Ἐκπηδάω, ήσομαι (ἐκ, πηδάω), to leap out, make sallies (excurrere), 7. 4. 16.

Ἐκπίμπλημι, πλήσω, &c. (ἐκ, πίμπλημι), to fill up, fulfil, accomplish, 3. 4. 22.

Ἐκπίνω, πίομαι, &c. (ἐκ, πίνω), to drink out or off, 1. 9. 25.

Ἐκπίπτω, πεσοῦμαι, ἐκπέπτωκα, 2 aor. ἐξέπεσον (ἐκ, πίπτω), to fall out, or off, or from, to be banished, 1. 1. 7 ; driven away, 5. 2. 1 ; rush out, 5. 2. 17, 18 ; to be cast ashore, suffer shipwreck, 6. 4. 2, 7. 5. 12, 13; to fall down, of trees, to lie on the ground, 2. 3. 10 ; to go away, slip out, ἐκ τῆς ὁδοῦ, 5. 2. 31.

Ἐκπλέω, πλεύσομαι, &c. (ἐκ, πλέω), to sail out or away, 2. 6. 2, 5. 6. 19.

Ἔκπλεως, ως, ων, Att. for ἔκπλεος, α, ον (ἐκ, πλέως), quite full, complete, 7. 5. 9.

Ἐκπλήττω, ξω, &c. (ἐκ, πλήττω), to strike out, drive away; Pass. 2 aor. ἐξεπλάγην, 1 aor. ἐξεπλήχθην, to be astonished, surprised, amazed, 1. 5. 13, 2. 2. 18.

Ἐκποδών, adv. ἐκ ποδῶν, out of the way, ποιεῖσθαί τινα, to put out of the way, get rid of, 1. 6. 9 ; ἐκποδὼν εἶναι, to be put out of the way, 2. 5. 29.

Ἐκπορεύομαι, εύσομαι, &c. (ἐκ, πορεύω), to go or march out, 5. 6. 33.

Ἐκπορίζω, ίσω, Att. ιῶ, &c. (ἐκ, πόρος), to invent, contrive, provide, furnish, procure, 5. 6. 19, 10. 4.

Ἔκπωμα, ατος, τό (ἐκ, πίνω), a drinking cup, beaker, 4. 3. 25.

Ἑκταῖος, αία, αῖον (ἕξ), on the sixth day, 6. 4. 38.

Ἐκτάττω, τάξω, &c., and ἐκτάττομαι, &c. (ἐκ, τάττω), to draw up in battle order, 5. 4. 12, 7. 1. 24.

Ἐκτείνω, τενῶ, &c. (ἐκ, τείνω), to stretch out; Mid. extend the line of an army, 2 aor. pass. ἐξετάθην, 5. 1. 2, 8. 14.

Ἐκτοξεύω, εύσω, &c. (ἐκ, τοξεύω), to shoot out from a place, 7. 8. 14.

Ἐκτρέπω, τρέψω, &c., to turn out of the course, turn aside; Pass. and 2 a. Mid. to get out of one's way, turn aside, 4. 5. 15, 5. 4. 17.

Ἐκτρέφω, θρέψω, &c., to bring up from childhood, to rear, 7. 2, 32.

Ἐκτρέχω, θρέξομαι, &c., 2 aor. ἐξέδραμον, to run out, make a sally, 5. 2. 17, 4. 16.

Ἐκφαίνω, φανῶ, &c., to show forth, bring to light, πόλεμον

τρός τινα, to declare war on one, 3. 1. 16.

Ἐκφέρω, ἐξοίσω, &c., to carry out, carry forth, accomplish; πόλεμον (bellum inferre), begin war; λόγον, to bring forward a statement, proclaim, 5. 6. 17, 29; εὐχήν τινος, to relate a prayer of one, 1. 9. 11.

Ἐκφεύγω, φεύξομαι, &c., to flee out, escape from, τὸ or τοῦ μή, with inf., 1. 3. 2.

Ἑκών, ἑκοῦσα, ἑκόν, g. ἑκόντος, &c., willing, of one's own accord, willingly, readily, 2. 4. 4.

Ἐλαία, ας, ἡ, the olive tree, the fruit of the olive, an olive, 6. 4. 6, 7. 1. 37.

Ἔλαιον, ον, τό, olive oil, oil, 5. 4. 28.

Ἐλάσσων, ων, ον, g. ονος, comp. of μικρός, smaller, less, worse, inferior, 6. 2 5, 7. 7. 35.

Ἐλαύνω, ἐλάσω or ἐλῶ, ἐλήλακα, ἐλήλαμαι, to drive, 5. 8. 5, sc. ἅρμα, ἵππον, ναῦν, drive, ride, sail; ἧκεν ἐλαύνων, he came riding, 1. 5. 15, 7. 3. 44; sc. στράτευμα, to march, 1. 2. 23, 1. 5. 7, 13, 1. 7. 14.

Ἐλάφειος, ος, ον (ἔλαφος), of or belonging to a stag; κρέα, venison, 1. 5. 2.

Ἔλαφος, ου, ὁ, ἡ, a deer, stag or hind, 5. 3. 10.

Ἐλαφρός, ά, όν, light in weight, opp. βαρύς, nimble, 3. 3. 6, 4. 2. 27; οἱ ἐ. light troops; adv. ἐλαφρῶς, quickly, 7. 3. 33.

Ἐλάχιστος, η, ον, superl. of μικρός, smallest, least, τοὐλάχιστον ἑκατόν, a hundred at least, 5. 7. 8.

Ἐλέγχω, ἐλέγξω, ἐλήλεγμαι, 1 a. act. ἤλεγξα, pass. ἠλέγχθην,

to examine, 3. 5. 14, 4. 1. 23; confute, disprove, reprove, reproach.

Ἐλεεινός, ή, όν (ἔλεος), finding pity, full of pity, piteous, pitiable, 4. 4. 11, better ἀλεεινόν.

Ἐλελίζω, ίξω, to raise the cry ἐλελεῦ, so, like ἀλαλάζω, to raise the war-cry, 1. 8. 18.

Ἐλευθερία, ας, ἡ (ἐλεύθερος), freedom, liberty, 1. 7. 3.

Ἐλευθέριος, ος, ον, speaking or acting like a free man, freespirited, frank, liberal, noble, 7. 4. 24, better ἐλευθέρων.

Ἐλεύθερος, α, ον (ἐλεύθω, root of ἐλεύσομαι, fut. of ἔρχομαι), free to come and go, free, independent, 7. 4. 24.

Ἐλισάρνη for Ἀλισάρνη, q. v.

Ἕλκω, ἕλξω and ἑλκύω, ύσω, εἵλκυκα, εἵλκυσμαι, to draw, 4. 2. 28; pull up, 5. 2. 15.

Ἑλλάς, άδος, ἡ, Hellas, the name for Greece amongst the Greeks; Greece and Greeks are words of Roman origin, 5. 6. 22.

Ἑλλάς, άδος, ἡ, Hellas, the mother of Gongylus, 7. 8. 8.

Ἕλλην, ηνος, ὁ, a Greek, 1. 1. 2; &c.

Ἑλληνίζω, to speak Greek, to imitate or favour the Greeks; Ἑλληνίζειν ἠπίστατο, he knew how to speak Greek, 7. 3. 25.

Ἑλληνικός, ή, όν, adj. Greek; Hellenic; τὸ Ἑλ. the Greek force, 1. 4. 13.

Ἑλληνικῶς, adv. in Greek, in the Greek language, opp. βαρβαρικῶς, 1. 8. 1.

Ἑλληνίς, ίδος, ἡ, a Greek woman; Greek-like, Ἑλληνικός, 5. 3. 2.

Ἑλληνιστί, adv. *in Greek fashion, in the Greek language*; Ἑλλ. ξυνιέναι, *to understand Greek*, 7. 6. 8.

Ἑλλησποντιακός, ή, όν. *of* or *belonging to the Hellespont, Hellespontine*, 1. 1. 9; from

Ἑλλήσποντος, ου, ὁ (ˊΕλλης πόντος), *the Hellespont* (sea of Helle), *the Dardanelles*, 1.1.9.

Ἐλπίζω, ίσω, Att. ιῶ (ἐλπίς), *to hope*, c. inf., 7. 6. 34; *expect*, 6. 3. 17.

Ἐλπίς, ίδος, ἡ, *hope*, ἐλπίδας λέγειν, *to excite hopes*, 1. 2. 11.

Ἐμαυτοῦ, ῆς, refl. pron. *of myself*, pl. ἡμῶν αὐτῶν, 5. 8. 15.

Ἐμβαίνω, βήσομαι, &c. (ἐν, βαίνω), *to go in, go on, go on board, embark*, εἰς πλοῖον, 1. 3. 17, 4. 7, 5. 6. 12.

Ἐμβάλλω, βαλῶ, &c., *to throw* or *bring in*, χιλόν, 1. 9. 27; *to put in*, μοχλόν, 7. 1. 12; *inflict*, πληγάς, 1. 5. 11; sc. ἑαυτόν, *to rush, enter in*, 3. 5. 17; sc. στρατόν, *to enter in a hostile way, invade*; of rivers, *to fall into*, 1. 2. 8, 4. 8. 2.

Ἐμβιβάζω, άσω, causative of ἐμβαίνω, *to cause to go in, to put on board*, εἰς τὰ πλοῖα, 5. 3. 1.

Ἐμβολή, ῆς, ἡ (ἐν, βάλλω), *a throwing in, an inroad, foray, raid*, 4. 1. 4.

Ἐμβρόντητος, ος, ον (ἐν, βροντή), *thunderstruck (attonitus)*, ἐμ. ποιεῖ, *strikes with terror*, 3. 4. 12.

Ἐμέω, ἐμέσω or ἐμῶ or ἐμοῦμαι, ἐμήμεκα, ἐμήμεσμαι, *to vomit*, 4. 8. 20.

Ἐμμένω, μενῶ, μεμένηκα, 1 aor. ἐνέμεινα (ἐν, μένω), *to remain*

in a place, 4. 7. 17; *abide by, stand by*, τοῖς νόμοις.

Ἐμός, ή, όν, poss. adj. *mine*, 7. 6. 33.

Ἔμπαλιν, adv. (ἐν, πάλιν), *back*, (εἰς) τοὔμπαλιν ἀπιέναι, *to go away back*, 1. 4. 15, 3. 5. 13, 4. 3. 21.

Ἐμπεδόω, ώσω (ἔμπεδος, *firm*, ἐν, πέδον), *to fix in the earth, to make firm, establish, ratify*, ὅρκους, νόμους, &c., 3. 2. 10.

Ἔμπειρος, ος, ον (ἐν, πεῖρα), *experienced* or *practised in a thing, skilful at it*, c. gen. or περί; adv. ἐμπείρως τινὸς ἔχειν, *to be acquainted with one*, 2. 6. 1.

Ἐμπίπλημι, ἐμπλήσω, ἐμπέπληκα, πέπλησμαι, impf. ἐνεπίμπλην, *to fill up*, τί τινος, ἀπάντων τὴν γνώμην, *to satisfy the expectations of all*, 1. 7. 8; c. part. ὑπισχνούμενος οὐκ ἐνεπίμπλασο, *you were not satisfied with promising*, 7. 7. 46.

Ἐμπίπρημι, ἐμπρήσω, ἐμπέπρηκα, πέπρημαι or πέπρησμαι, but aor. always ἐπρήσθην; impf. act. ἐνεπίμπρην, *to burn, kindle, set on fire*, οἰκίας, 4. 4. 14, 5. 2. 3.

Ἐμπίπτω, πεσοῦμαι, &c., *to fall on* or *in, to come upon, seize*, 5. 7. 26.

Ἔμπλεως, ως, ων (ἐν, πλέος), *full, quite full*, τινός, 1. 2. 22.

Ἐμποδίζω, ίσω (ἐν, πούς), *to put the feet in bonds, fetter, check, stop*, acc., gen. or dat., 4. 3. 29.

Ἐμπόδιος, ος, ον (ἐν, πούς), *in the way, an obstacle*, 7. 8. 3, 4.

Ἐμποδών, adv. like ἐκποδών (ἐν, ποσὶν ὤν), *among the feet, in*

. the way, ἐμ. εἶναί τινι, to be
in the way of, hinder, 4. 8. 14,
5. 7. 10; τί ἐμποδὼν μὴ οὐχί,
Lat. quid obstat quominus, 3.
1. 13.

Ἐμποιέω, ήσω, etc., to make in,
put in, cause, 2. 6. 19; produce an impression in one's
mind, 2. 6. 8.

Ἐμπολάω, ήσω (ἐμπολή, traffic,
πωλέω, to sell), to gain by
traffic, traffic, sell, 7. 5. 4.

Ἐμπόριον, ου, τό (ἔμπορος), a
trading-place, emporium, 1. 4.
6.

Ἔμπορος, ου, ὁ (ἐν, πόρος), a
traveller, merchant, 5. 6. 19.

Ἐμπρήθω, see ἐμπίπρημι.

Ἔμπροσθεν (ἐν, πρόσθεν), adv.
before (Lat. ante), PLACE, τὰ
ἔμπροσθεν, the places in front,
the front, 6. 3. 14; οἱ ἔμπροσθεν, the men in front, 4. 5.
20; TIME, ὁ ἔμπροσθεν λόγος,
the previous narrative, ἡ ἐμ.
προσβολή, 3. 4. 2.

Ἐμπωλέω, ήσω (ἐν, πωλέω), in
some edd. for ἐμπολάω.

Ἐμφαγεῖν, inf. of ἐνέφαγον, 2
aor. of ἐσθίω, to take some
food, 4. 2. 1, 5. 8.

Ἐμφανής, ής, ές (ἐν, φαίνω),
manifest, clear, plain; ἐν τῷ
ἐμφανεῖ=openly, publicly, 2. 5.
25; adv. ἐμφανῶς, 5. 4. 33.

Ἐν, prep. gov. dat. in, within,
on, upon; θάλαττα ἡ ἐν τῷ
Εὐξείνῳ Πόντῳ, 5. 1. 1; ἐν
τῷ δεξιῷ, 1. 8. 5; ἐν τρισὶν
ἡμέραις, 4. 8. 8; during, ἐν
ταῖς σπονδαῖς, 3. 1. 1; ἐν
τούτῳ τῷ χρόνῳ, 4. 2. 17; or
ἐν τούτῳ, 1. 5. 15, 8. 12; ἐν
ᾧ, during which time, while, 1.
2. 20, 2. 2. 15, 4. 2. 19.

Ἐναγκυλάω, ήσω (ἐν, ἀγκύλη, a

thong), to fit a thong to a
javelin, 4. 2. 28.

Ἐναντίος, α, ον (ἐν, ἀντί), opposite, 4. 3. 28; opposed to, gen.
or dat. 3. 2. 10, 7. 6. 25;
adverse, 4. 5. 3; τἀναντία
ποιεῖν τινα ἤ, to treat one in a
different way from, 5. 8. 24;
ἐναντίον τινός (coram aliquo),
in one's presence, 7. 6. 23; ἐκ
τοῦ ἐναντίου (ex adverso, e regione), over against, opposite,
1. 8. 23, 4. 7. 5.

Ἐναντιόω, ώσω, usually Mid.
(ἐναντίος), to set oneself
against, oppose, τινὶ περί τινος,
7. 6. 5.

Ἐνάπτω, ἅψω, ἦμμαι (ἐν, ἅπτω),
to fasten to, to kindle, set on
fire, 5. 2. 24.

Ἔνατος=ἔννατος.

Ἐναυλίζομαι, ίσομαι (ἐν, αὐλή),
to bivouac, encamp, 7. 7. 8.

Ἔνδεια, ας, ἡ (ἐν, δέω), want,
poverty, 1. 10. 18, 7. 8. 6.

Ἐνδείκνυμι, δείξω, etc., to mark,
point out, show forth, display,
5. 9. 19.

Ἐνδέκατος, η, ον, the eleventh, 1.
7. 18.

Ἐνδέω, δεήσω, etc., to be in want
of, to be deficient in; impers.
ἐνδεῖ, there is want or need;
πολλῶν ἐνέδει αὐτῷ, he was in
want of many things, 7. 1. 41,
5. 9. 31.

Ἔνδηλος, ος, ον (ἐν, δῆλος), manifest, certain, evident, c. part.
like φανερός, 2. 4. 2, 6. 23;
ἔνδηλον τοῦτο εἶχε ὅτι, this
was a settled thing with him
that, 2. 6. 18.

Ἔνδημος, ος, ον (ἐν, δῆμος),
dwelling among a people, home
revenue, 7. 1. 27.

Ἐνδίφριος, ος, ον (ἐν, δίφρος),

E

sitting on the same seat, a table companion, 7. 2. 33, 38.

Ἔνδοθεν (ἔνδον), from the inside, 5. 2. 22.

Ἔνδον (ἐν), inside, 7. 1. 17, 19.

Ἔνδοξος, ος, ον (ἐν, δόξα), of high repute, distinguished, glorious, 6. 1. 23.

Ἐνδύω, δύσω, &c., to put on another, ἐνδύομαι, δύσομαι, 2 aor. ἐνέδυν, to put on oneself, 1. 8. 3, 5. 4. 13.

Ἐνέδρα, ας, ἡ (ἐν, ἕδρα, a chair), a sitting in or on, an ambush (insidiæ), 4. 7. 22.

Ἐνεδρεύω, εύσω (ἐνέδρα), to lie in wait for, τινά, 1. 6. 2 ; to lie in ambush, 4. 6. 17.

Ἐνεῖδον, see ἐνοράω.

Ἔνειμι, ἔσομαι (ἐν, εἰμί), to be in, 1. 5. 1, 5. 3. 8.

Ἕνεκα, prep. gov. gen., on account of, by reason of, before the words governed, 5. 4. 19 ; between the adj. and subst., 1. 4. 5 ; and follows the gen., 1. 9. 21.

Ἕνεκεν = ἕνεκα, but stands before vowels, 2. 3. 20, 5. 4. 16.

Ἐνενήκοντα (ἐννέα), num. adj. indecl., ninety, 1. 5. 5.

Ἐνεός, ά, όν, also ἐννεός (ἄνεω, ἁ priv. αὔω, to cry), dumb, speechless, deaf and dumb, 4. 5. 33.

Ἐνετός, ή, όν (ἐνίημι), sent in privately, suborned, 7. 6. 41.

Ἐνέχυρον, ου, τό (ἐν, ἐχυρός), a pledge, surety, 7. 6. 23.

Ἐνέχω, ἐνέξω or ἐνοχήσω, &c., to hold or keep fast, entangle, catch, 7. 4. 17.

Ἔνθα (ἐν), adv. PLACE, there (ibi), 1. 9. 5, 7. 15, 2. 2. 11 ; TIME, ἔνθα δή, then, thereupon, 2. 1. 10, 4. 1. 16, 1. 8. 2 ;

where, 4. 1. 2 ; when, 5. 1. 1 ; ἔνθα καὶ ἔνθα, here and there, hither and thither (hic, illic ; huc, illuc).

Ἐνθάδε, thither, hither, or there, here, 2. 1. 4, 3. 21, 3. 3. 2, 5. 1. 10, 7. 18.

Ἔνθαπερ, stronger form of ἔνθα, there where, where, 4. 8. 25, 6. 4. 9.

Ἔνθεν (ἐν), adv. thence (inde), ἔνθεν μέν—ἔνθεν δέ, on this side — on that (hinc — illinc), on one side—on the other, 3. 5. 7, 2. 4. 22 ; ἔνθεν καὶ ἔνθεν, here and there, on both sides of the way (ab utraque parte), 4. 6. 12, 8. 13, 5. 2. 22.

Ἐνθένδε (ἔνθεν), hence (hinc), from you, 7. 7. 17.

Ἐνθυμέομαι, ήσομαι, ἐντεθύμημαι, 1 aor. ἐνεθυμήθην (ἐν, θυμός), to lay to heart, consider well, notice, ὅτι, 3. 1. 43.

Ἐνθύμημα, ατος, τό (ἐνθυμέομαι), a thought, argument, device, stratagem, 3. 5. 12.

Ἐνθωρακίζω, ίσω, p. p. ἐντεθωράκισμαι, 7. 4. 16 (ἐν, θωρακίζω), to arm, equip with armour.

Ἔνι for ἔνεστι, there is in, 5. 3. 11.

Ἐνιαυτός, οῦ, ὁ (ἔνος = annus), a year, 7. 8. 26.

Ἐνιδεῖν, see ἐνοράω.

Ἔνιοι, αι, α = ἔστιν οἱ, there are who, some, 2. 4. 1.

Ἐνίοτε = ἔστιν ὅτε, there is a time when, sometimes, 3. 1. 20.

Ἐνίσχω = ἐνέχω, q.v. 7. 4. 17.

Ἔννατος, η, ον, num. adj. ninth, 4. 5. 24.

Ἐννέα, num. adj. indecl., nine, 1. 4. 19.

Ἐννενήκοντα, num. adj. indecl., ninety, 1. 5. 5.

’Εννοέω——’Εννάλιος   51

’Εννοέω, ήσω, ἐννενόηκα, ημαι (ἐν, νοέω), to have in one's mind, to think, consider, 3. 1. 3; be anxious, μή, lest, 4. 2. 13; to find on reflection, 2. 2. 10, 3. 5. 3, 5. 9. 28.

῎Εννοια, ας, ἡ (ἐν, νοῦς), thought, notion, design, ἐνν. ἐμπίπτει τινί, a thought strikes one, 3. 1. 13.

’Ενοδίας, ου, ὁ, or Εὐοδεύς or ’Ενοκεύς, Enodias, a captain, 7. 4. 18.

’Ενοικέω, ήσω, &c. (ἐν, οἰκέω), to live in, dwell in, ἐν τόπῳ, 5. 6. 25, 1. 3. 4; ἐνοικοῦντες=οἱ ἔνοικοι, the in-dwellers, inhabitants, 1. 2. 24, 5. 5, 3. 4. 12.

’Ενόπλιος, ος, ον (ἐν, ὅπλον), under arms, ὁ ἐνόπ. (ῥυθμός), the music for the war-dance, the war-tune, 5. 9. 11.

’Ενοράω, ὄψομαι, ἑώρακα, ἑώραμαι, 2 aor. ἐνεῖδον, inf. ἐνιδεῖν, to see, remark, observe something in a person or thing, τί τινι, 7. 7. 45.

’Ενοχλέω, ήσω, ἐνώχληκα or ἠνώχ. ἐν or ἠνώχλημαι (ἐν, ὀχλέω, ὄχλος), to trouble, annoy, give trouble or annoyance to, τινί, 2. 5. 13.

’Εντάττω or τάσσω, τάξω, &c., to put in order; ἐν τῷ ἐντεταγμένῳ, in the place assigned to him, 3. 3. 18.

’Ενταῦθα (ἐν), adv. PLACE, there, 1. 4. 19; thither, 1. 2. 1, 10. 17; TIME, at the very time, past then, present now; ἐντ. δὴ, thereupon, 1. 10. 1; μέχρις ἐντ. up to this time (huc usque), 5. 5. 4.

’Εντείνω, τενῶ, &c., to stretch, strain; πληγάς τινι, to aim

blows at, 2. 4. 11; some say, to lay on blows (Lat. plagas intendere).

’Εντελής, ής, ἐς (ἐν, τέλος), full, complete, μισθός, 1. 4. 13.

’Εντέλλομαι, ἐντελοῦμαι, ἐντέταλμαι, 1 aor. ἐνετειλάμην, to enjoin, command, τινί τι, 5. 1. 13.

῎Εντερον, ου, τό (ἐντός), the intestines, bowels, usually pl., 2. 5. 33.

’Εντεῦθεν, adv. PLACE, thence or hence (hinc or illinc), 1. 2. 10; TIME, henceforth, thenceforth then, 4. 4. 15, 5. 4. 26, 6. 6. 1; CAUSE, therefore, hence, in consequence, 6. 4. 15.

’Εντίθημι, θήσω, &c., to put in; φόβον τινί, to inspire fear, 7. 4. 1; to put on board a ship, 1. 4. 7, 5. 7. 15.

῎Εντιμος, ος, ον (ἐν, τιμή), held in honour, honoured, prized, 5. 6, 32; adv. ἐντίμως, 2. 1. 7.

’Εντόνως (ἐν, τείνω), earnestly, eagerly, urgently, 7. 5. 7.

’Εντός, adv. (ἐν) with gen. inside, within, 2. 1. 11, 6. 4. 3, 6. 5. 7.

’Εντυγχάνω, τεύξομαι, τετύχηκα, 2 aor. ἐνέτυχον, to light upon, fall in with, meet with, τινί, 1. 8. 1, 2. 3. 10; τὸν ἀεὶ ὑμῶν ἐντυγχάνοντα σὺν τῷ ἄρχοντι κολάζειν, 3. 2. 31, that he among you, who at any time meets with such an one, should help the commander to punish him.

’Εννάλιος, ου, ὁ (’Εννώ, Bellona), Enyalius, an epithet of Mars, the warlike, 1. 8. 18, 5. 2. 14; hence a war-song or battle-cry.

E 2

'Ενύπνιον, ου, τό (ἐν, ὕπνος). a dream merely, ὄνειρος, a prophetic dream sent by the gods, 7. 8. 1.

'Ενωμοτία, ας, ἡ (ἐν, ὄμνυμι), any band of sworn soldiers, a division of the λόχος, containing from 24 to 32 men, 3. 4. 22, 4. 3. 26 ; the leader was called ἐνωμοτάρχης, ου, ὁ, 3. 4. 21.

'Ενώπια, ων, τά (ἐν, ὤψ), the inner wall fronting those who enter a building ; the wall next the street was called προνώπια, 7. 8. 1, al. ἐνύπνια.

'Εξ for ἐκ before vowels.

Ἑξ, num. adj., six, 1. 1. 10.

'Εξαγγέλλω, ελῶ, &c., to tell, make known, report, 2. 4. 24.

'Εξάγω, άξω, &c., to lead, bring out, lead out to battle, 6. 6. 36 ; Pass. to be led on to do a thing, c. inf. 1. 8. 21.

'Εξαίρετος, ος, ον (ἐξ, αἱρέω), taken out, picked, choice (eximius), selected portions, 7. 8. 23.

'Εξαιρέω, ήσω, &c., 2 aor. ἐξεῖλον, to take out, 5. 3. 4, 2. 1. 9 ; M. pick or choose out, 2. 5. 20 ; unlade, 5. 1. 16; remove, 2. 5. 4.

'Εξαιτέω, ήσω, &c. (ἐξ, αἰτέω), to demand or ask for anything from anybody, τί τινος or τινα ; M. to ask for oneself, to beg off, 1. 1. 3.

'Εξαίφνης, adv. (ἐξ, αἴφνης), on a sudden, suddenly, softer form ἐξαπίνης, 5. 6. 19, 7. 21.

'Εξακισχίλιοι, αι, α, num. adj. six thousand, 1. 7. 11.

'Εξακοντίζω, ίσω, Att. ιῶ (ἐξ, ἀκοντίζω), to dart or hurl forth, shoot, 5. 4. 25.

'Εξακόσιοι, αι, α, num. adj. six hundred, 1. 8. 6.

'Εξαλαπάζω, άξω (ἐξ, ἀλαπάζω), to sack, plunder, 7. 1. 29.

'Εξάλλομαι, αλοῦμαι, to leap out, jump forth, jump up, of a horse to rear, 7. 3. 33.

'Εξαμαρτάνω, αμαρτήσω, ἐξημάρτηκα, ἐξημάρτημαι, to err, do wrong, 5. 7. 33.

'Εξανίστημι, ἀναστήσω &c., to make to rise in pres. impf. fut. 1 aor., but elsewhere, to stand up, 6. 1. 30, 5. 2. 30.

'Εξαπατάω, ήσω,&c., strengthened for ἀπατάω, to deceive thoroughly, τινά τι, 5. 7. 6 ; fut. Mid. with Pass. signif. 7. 3. 3.

'Εξαπάτη, ης, ἡ, strengthened for ἀπάτη, deceit, 7. 1. 25.

'Εξάπηχυς, υς, υ (ἐξ, πῆχυς), six cubits long, 5. 4. 12.

'Εξαπίνης = ἐξαίφνης = αἴφνης, ἄφνω, suddenly, 3. 3. 7.

'Εξαρκέω, έσω, &c. to be quite enough, 7. 7. 54, al. ἐξικνῆται.

'Εξάρχω, άρξω, &c. to begin, c. gen. πετροβολίας, 6. 6. 15.

'Εξαναίνω, ανῶ, 1 aor. ἐξήνηνα= ἐξαύω, to dry up, wither up, 2. 3. 16.

'Εξαυλίζομαι, ισυμαι, to leave one's quarters, 7. 8. 21.

Ἔξειμι, to go out, march out, 6. 3. 3.

'Εξεῖναι, see ἔξεστι.

'Εξελαύνω, ελάσω (ἄ), &c. to drive out, sc. ἵππον, ἅρμα, πόδα, στρατόν, to ride, drive, walk, march out, 1. 2. 5, 10, 7. 7. 7, 11.

'Εξελέγχω, έγξω, strengthened for ἐλέγχω, to search out, convict, with part. 2. 5. 27.

'Εξεληλυθώς, pf. part. of ἐξέρχομαι.

Ἐξέρπω, 1 aor. ἐξείρπῦσα or ἐξείρψα, to creep out, 7. 1. 8.

Ἐξέρχομαι, ἐλεύσομαι, ἐλήλυθα, to go out, come out, go away; of Time, to come to an end, pass (praeterire), 7. 5. 4.

Ἔξεστι, it is allowed (licet), it is in one's power, it is possible, ἐξ. σοι ἀνδρὶ γενέσθαι, 7. 1. 21; part. ἐξόν, used absolutely, it being possible, allowed, since it is, &c., 2. 5. 22, 6. 6, 3. 1. 14; ἐξὸν τοῖς βαρβάροις φίλους εἶναι, 5. 6. 3.

Ἐξετάζω, ἄσω (ἐξ, ἐτάζω), to examine, review, 5. 4. 12, hence the subst.

Ἐξέτασις, εως, ἡ, an examination, inspection, review, ποιεῖν, to hold a review, 1. 2. 9, 7. 2; also ποιεῖσθαι, 1. 2. 14, 7. 1.

Ἐξευπορίζω, ίσω (ἐξ, εὖ, πορίζω), a barbarous form for ἐξευπορέω, 5. 6. 19, to contrive, devise, get ready.

Ἐξηγέομαι, ήσομαι, ημαι, to be leader of, to lead the way, show, point out, τινί τι, 4. 5. 28; to lead an army, 6. 6. 34.

Ἐξήκοντα, num. adj. indecl. sixty, 2. 2. 6.

Ἐξήκω, ήξω, to be come or gone out, pres. with pf. signif. 6. 3. 26.

Ἐξικνέομαι, ίξομαι, ἶγμαι, 2 aor. ἐξικόμην, to reach, arrive at, 7. 7. 54, 1. 8. 19, 3. 3. 7, 4. 4; ἐπὶ βραχὺ ἐξ. go, reach a short distance, 3. 3. 17; c. gen. 3. 3. 7.

Ἐξίστημι, ἐκστήσω, ἐξέστηκα, ἐξέσταμαι, to put out, change, intr. in pf. plp 2 aor., to stand aside from or out of the way,

ἐκ τοῦ μέσου, 1. 5. 14; retire from.

Ἔξοδος, ου, ἡ (ἐξ, ὁδός), a going or marching out, 7. 1. 9; a way or road out, 7. 4. 17; an expedition, a sally, 5. 2. 9, 6. 2. 9.

Ἐξόν, see ἔξεστι.

Ἐξοπλίζω, ίσω, &c. (ἐξ, ὁπλίζω), to arm; Mid. to arm oneself, to rush to arms, go forth armed, 1. 8. 3, 2. 1. 2, 3. 1. 28.

Ἐξοπλισία, ας, ἡ (ἐξ, ὁπλίζω), a being under arms, ἐν τῇ ἐξ. under arms (in procinctu), 1. 7. 10.

Ἐξορμάω, ήσω, &c. (ἐξ, ὁρμάω), to send forth, excite, stir up, rouse, ἐπὶ ἀρετήν, 3. 1. 24; Mid. to set out πεζῇ, 5. 7. 17, 2. 4.

Ἐξουσία, ας, ἡ (ἔξεστι), power, means, authority, 5. 8. 22.

Ἔξω (ἐξ), adv. without, outside (foris), 2. 5. 32, 7. 2. 29, c. gen. 1. 10. 6; out and away, 2. 6. 3; ἔξω βελῶν, out of shot, out of the reach of arrows, 3. 4. 15; ἐξωτέρω, ἐξωτάτω.

Ἔξωθεν (ἔξω), adv. from without, outside, c. gen. 3. 4. 21, 5. 7. 21.

Ἔοικα, 2 perf. of εἴκω, q. v.

Ἑορτή, ῆς, ἡ (Ion. ὁρτή, Æol. ἑορτή fr. ἔρος, love), a feast, a festival, 5. 3. 11.

Ἐπαγγέλλω, ελῶ, &c. to tell, command, τινί; Mid. to offer one's services, 7. 1. 33, to profess oneself willing, 4. 7. 20.

Ἐπάγω, άξω, &c. to bring on (adducere), lead on, induce; οὐ γάρ πω ψῆφος αὐτῷ ἐπῆκτο, for no vote or decree had yet been made against him, 7. 7. 57.

Ἐπαινέω, ἔσω better ἔσομαι, &c. to praise, commend, 1. 3. 7, 4. 16 ; τινὰ ἐπί τινι, 3. 1. 45; ἀλλὰ τὴν μὲν σὴν πρόνοιαν ἐπαινῶ, well, I am really much obliged to you for your considerate conduct, 7. 7. 52 ; to decline an offer with thanks.

Ἔπαινος, ου, ὁ, praise, 5. 7. 33.

Ἐπαίρω, αρῶ, &c. to lift up, raise, exalt, stir up, 5. 9. 21, 7. 7. 25.

Ἐπαίτιος, ος, ον (ἐπί, αἰτία), blameable, blameworthy, 3. 1. 5.

Ἐπακολουθέω, ήσω, &c. to follow close upon or after, τινί, to pursue, 3. 2. 35.

Ἐπακούω, ούσομαι, &c. to listen or hearken to, to hear, 7. 1. 14.

Ἐπάν (ᾰ) (= ἐπεί, ἄν), conjunc. whenever, as soon as, after, with conj. 1. 4. 13 ; ἐπὰν τάχιστα, as soon as, the moment that, 4. 6. 9.

Ἐπανατείνω, τενῶ, &c. (ἐπί, ἀνά, τείνω), to stretch out and hold up, τὸν τράχηλον, 7. 4. 9.

Ἐπαναχωρέω, ήσω, &c. to go back, retreat, retire, 3. 5. 13.

Ἐπανέρχομαι, ελεύσομαι, &c. (ἐπί, ἀνά, ἔρχομαι), to come or go back, 7. 3. 4.

Ἐπάνω (ᾰ) (ἐπί, ἄνω), above; ἐν τοῖς ἐπάνω εἴρηται, it has been previously stated, in the foregoing narrative (ut supra dictum est), 6. 1. 1.

Ἐπαπειλέω, ήσω (ἐπί, ἀπειλέω), to hold out as a threat, τί τινι; to threaten, τινί; to do, c. inf. 5. 10. 7.

Ἐπεγγελάω, άσομαι (ἐπί, ἐν, γελάω), to laugh at, insult, τινί (irridere), 2. 4. 27.

Ἐπεγείρω, εγερῶ, &c. to awaken, stir or rouse up, 4. 3. 10.

Ἐπεί (ἐπί), conjunc. when, since, whereas, usually with ind, ἐπάν takes conj., 1. 3. 6, 1. 9. 7, 4. 7. 2, 7. 6. 22, 3. 1. 31 ; in or. obl. opt. 5. 6. 30 ; ἐπεί τις διώκοι, whenever anyone pursued, as often as (quoties), 1. 5. 2. With particles ἐπειδή strengthened form of ἐπεί, usually ind. 7. 7. 18; opt. in or. obl. 3. 5. 18 ; to express repeated action, 4. 5. 8; ἐπειδή γε, since at least, 1. 9. 24 ; ἐπεί περ and ἐπειδή περ, since really, 2. 2. 10, 5. 38 ; ἐπεί γε, 1. 3. 9, 6. 4. 26 ; ἐπειδή becomes ἐπειδάν with conj. 2. 3. 29, 5. 6. 19, 7. 1. 6 ; ἐπεὶ τάχιστα, as soon as, = Lat. quum primum or simul ac.

Ἐπεῖδον, see ἐφοράω, 3. 1. 13, 7. 1. 30, 6. 31.

Ἔπειμι (ἐπί, εἰμί), to be on or upon, 1. 7. 15.

Ἔπειμι (ἐπί, εἶμι), to come upon, attack, 1. 2. 17, 7. 4, 10. 10 ; of things, to happen, 5. 7. 12 ; ἡμέρα ἐπιοῦσα, the following day, 1. 7. 2, 3. 4. 18 ; so νύξ, 5. 2. 23, 7. 4. 14, to come on the stage, 6. 1. 11.

Ἔπειτα (ἐπί, εἶτα), adv. afterwards, thereafter, thereupon, 2. 4. 5, 3. 1. 46; after εἰ, then surely, and emphatic, δὴ ἔπειτα, or καὶ δὴ ἐπ. or καὶ τότε ἐπ.; εἰς τὸν ἐπ. χρόνον, in after times, 2. 1. 17.

Ἐπέκεινα, adv. (ἐπ' ἐκεῖνα), on yonder side of, beyond (ultra), οἱ ἐπ. Εὐφράτου, those beyond the Euphrates, οἱ ἐκ τοῦ ἐπέκεινα, those beyond, 5. 4. 3.

Ἐπεισθέω, θεύσομαι = ἐπιτρέχω (ἐπί, ἐκ, θέω), to run out against, 5. 2. 22.

Ἐπέξειμι (ἐπί, ἐξ, εἶμι), to go out against, proceed against, 6. 3. 4.

Ἐπεξέρχομαι, ἐλεύσομαι, &c. to go out against, make a sally, 5. 2. 7.

Ἐπεξόδιος, ος, ον (ἐπί, ἐξ, ὁδὸς), of or belonging to a march or expedition; τὰ ἐπεξ. sc. ἱερά, sacrifices before marching, 6. 5. 2.

Ἐπέρομαι, ἐπερήσομαι, 2 aor. ἐπηρόμην, sometimes ἐπείρομαι, to ask, τινά τι, one about a thing, 3. 1. 6.

Ἐπέρχομαι, ἐλεύσομαι, &c. to come upon or to, 7. 8. 25.

Ἐπεύχομαι, εὔξομαι, εὖγμαι, to pray to, beseech, τινά; ἐπευξάμενος, calling the gods to witness, 5. 6. 3.

Ἐπέχω, ἐφέξω or ἐπισχήσω, &c. to hold, keep in, hold back, stop, τῆς πορείας, 3. 4. 36; 2 aor. ἐπέσχον.

Ἐπήκοος, ος, ον (ἐπί, ἀκούω), listening, giving ear to; within hearing, within ear-shot, 2. 5. 38, 3. 3. 1.

Ἐπήν = ἐπάν.

Ἐπί, prep., gov. gen., dat., acc., upon: 1. GEN. on, upon, ἐπὶ τῶν ἄκρων, 4. 6. 18; ἐπὶ τῆς γῆς, 3. 2. 19; ἐφ' ἵππων, on horseback, 3. 2. 19; ἐν Θράκῃ, in Thrace, ἐπὶ Θράκης, on the borders of Thrace; ἀπιέναι ἐπὶ Ἰωνίας, to go away towards Ionia, 2. 1. 3, 4. 7. 21, 6. 1. 24; with cardinal numbers, &c., ἐπὶ τεττάρων, four deep, 1. 2. 15; ἐφ' ἑνός, in single file, one by one, 5. 2. 6; ἐπὶ

ὀκτὼ πλίνθων, 7. 8. 14; ἐπὶ φάλαγγος παράγειν, 4. 3. 26; ἐφ' ἡμῶν, in our time, 1. 9. 12, but ἐφ' ἡμῖν, in our power, 1. 1. 4, 3. 1. 13, 5. 8. 17; ἐπὶ Κύρου, under Cyrus.

2. DAT. of place answering to where or whither, at, in, near, on, ἐπὶ τῇ τάφρῳ, 1. 7. 19; ἐπὶ τῷ ἄκρῳ, 3. 4. 49; ἐπὶ ταῖς πύλαις, 1. 4. 5; for an object or purpose, with a view to, ἐπὶ θανάτῳ, 1. 6. 10; ἐπὶ τούτοις θύεσθαι, with regard to this, in reference to this, 3. 5. 18; ἐπὶ τούτῳ ἐκπλήττεσθαι, to be surprised at this, 6. 1. 12; ἐπ' ἀγαθῷ κολάζειν, to punish for one's good, 5. 8. 18; TIME, in, on or at, about, ἥλιος ἦν ἐπὶ δυσμαῖς, the sun was close on setting, 7. 3. 34; ἐπὶ τῷ τρίτῳ, at the third time, 2. 2. 4; ἐφ' ᾧ and ἐφ' ᾧτε, c. inf. on condition that, 4. 4. 6, 6. 6. 22.

3. ACC. Motion to, to, upon, against, ἐπὶ τὴν Ἑλλάδα, 3. 2. 13; ἐπὶ τὰ ὅπλα, 3. 1. 40; ἐπὶ τὰ ὄρη, 4. 4. 15; ἐπί τινα, against a person, πορεύεσθαι, 2. 1. 4, 3. 21, χωρεῖν, 4. 2. 15, στρατεύεσθαι, 1. 2. 2, 4. 3, ἰέναι, 1. 3. 1; ἐπὶ τὸν λόφον, to the hill, on to, 3. 4. 41; ἐπὶ γήλοφον, 3. 4. 25; ἐπὶ πᾶν ἐλθεῖν, to venture on all, try every way, 3. 1. 18; TIME, for or during, ἐπὶ τρεῖς ἡμέρας, 6. 4. 36; ἐπὶ τὸ πολύ, generally, for the most part, 3. 1. 42, 43, 3. 4. 35; ἐπὶ δόρυ, towards the right, 4. 3. 29, for, ἐπὶ δεῖπνον ὕδωρ ἐφέροντο, 7. 4. 3; φρύγανα συλλέγειν ἐπὶ πῦρ, 4.

3. 11 ; *to, ἰέναι ἐπὶ τὸν ἀγῶνα,* 3. 1. 22.

Ἐπιβάλλω, βαλῶ, &c. *to throw or cast or put upon, ἐπιβεβλημένοι τοξόται, archers with their arrows on the string,* 4. 3. 28, 5. 2. 12.

Ἐπιβοηθέω, ήσω, &c. (ἐπί, βοή, θέω), *to come to help, to help, τινί,* 6. 5. 9.

Ἐπιβουλεύω, εύσω, *to plan or contrive against, τί τινι, to plot against, τινί, to form some plot, τι,* 1. 1. 3.

Ἐπιβουλή, ῆς, ἡ, *a plot, πρός τινα,* 1. 1. 8 ; ἐξ ἐπιβουλῆς, *from treachery,* 6. 4. 7.

Ἐπιγίγνομαι, γενήσομαι, &c. *to come into being after, to come after, to come upon, fall upon, to happen,* 3. 4. 25, 6. 4. 26.

Ἐπιγράφω, γράψω, &c. *to mark the surface, write upon, inscribe,* 5. 3. 5.

Ἐπιδείκνυμι, δείξω, &c. *to show, exhibit, display,* 1. 2. 14, 5. 4. 17, 6. 4. 4 ; *show* by words, 1. 3. 13, 7. 4. 23 ; by deeds, 3. 2. 26, 6. 4. 32. Mid. 1. 9. 10, 2. 6. 27, 4. 6. 15.

Ἐπιδεῖν, see ἐφοράω.

Ἐπιδιώκω, ώξω, &c. *to pursue after,* 1. 10. 11.

Ἐπιέσπομαι, poet. for ἐφέπομαι, *to follow after,* 4. 1. 6.

Ἐπιθαλάττιος, ος, ον (ἐπί, θάλαττα), *close on the sea,* 5. 5. 23.

Ἐπίθεσις, εως, ἡ (ἐπί, τίθημι), *a laying on, an attack,* 4. 4. 22, 7. 4. 23.

Ἐπιθυμέω, ήσω, &c. (ἐπί, θυμός), *to desire, long for, covet, τινός,* 1. 9. 21, 3, 2. 39, 4. 1. 14 ; with inf. 1. 9. 12, 2. 6. 21, 5. 9. 21.

Ἐπιθυμία, ας, ἡ, *desire,* 2. 6. 16.

Ἐπικαίριος, ος, ον (ἐπί, καιρός), *in season, seasonable, suitable (opportunus),* 7. 1. 6 ; οἱ ἐπικ. *the head men, chief men,* 7. 7. 15.

Ἐπικάμπτω, κάμψω, κέκαμμαι, *to bend in, wheel round, ὡς εἰς κύκλωσιν,* 1. 8. 23.

Ἐπικαταρρίπτέω, -ήσω, &c. and -ρίπτω, -ρίψω, &c. *to throw down upon,* 4. 7. 13.

Ἐπίκειμαι κείσομαι, *to lie upon, press upon* a friend, *urge,* an enemy, *attack, assault, τινί,* 4. 1. 16, 4. 3. 7, 5. 2. 5.

Ἐπικίνδυνος, ος, ον, *dangerous,* 1. 3. 19.

Ἐπικουρέω, ήσω, &c. (ἐπί, κοῦρος, *a boy*), *to help, aid, τινί,* 5. 8. 21 ; *to ward off from one, τινί τι,* 5. 8. 25.

Ἐπικούρημα, ατος, τό (ἐπικουρέω), *help, protection, χιόνος, against snow,* 4. 5. 13.

Ἐπικράτεια, ας, ἡ (ἐπικρατής), *mastery, protection, power,* 6. 4. 4, 7. 6. 42.

Ἐπικρύπτω, κρύψω, &c. also Mid. *to conceal, disguise,* 1. 1. 6.

Ἐπικύπτω, κύψω, κέκυφα, κέκυμμαι, *to bend or stoop over,* 4. 5. 32.

Ἐπικυρόω, ώσω, &c. (ἐπί, κυρόω, κῦρος, *power*), *to confirm, sanction, ratify,* 3. 2. 32.

Ἐπιλαμβάνω, λήψομαι, &c. *to lay hold of, seize, attain, reach,* 6. 5. 6 ; Mid. *to lay hold of, τινός,* 4. 7. 12, 13.

Ἐπιλανθάνω, λήσω, λέληθα, λέλησμαι, to *make to forget*; Mid. *to forget, τινός,* 3. 2. 25.

Ἐπιλέγω, λέξω, &c. *to say in addition, to add,* 1. 9. 26.

Ἐπιλείπω, λείψω, &c. *to leave*

behind, 1. 8. 18; *to fail, be
wanting* (deficere), 1. 5. 6, 4.
7. 1.

Ἐπίλεκτος, ος, ον, *chosen, picked*;
οἱ ἐπίλ., *picked men*, 3. 4. 43,
7. 4. 11.

Ἐπιμαρτύρομαι, Dep. Mid. *to call
on as witness, appeal to*, θεούς,
4. 8. 7.

Ἐπίμαχος, ος, ον, *assailable, open
to attack*, 5. 4. 14.

Ἐπιμέλεια, ας, ἡ (ἐπιμελής), *care,
attention, diligence*, 1. 9. 24.

Ἐπιμελέομαι, μελήσομαι, μεμέ-
λημαι, also ἐπιμέλομαι, *to take
care of, have charge of, attend
to, study, cultivate*, τινός, 1. 8.
21, 3. 2. 37, 5. 1. 7; *to take
care that*, acc. c. inf. or ὅπως
or ὡς, 1. 1. 5, *superintend*, 4.
8. 25.

Ἐπιμελής, ής, ές (ἐπί, μέλομαι),
careful, anxious, 3. 2. 30;
Comp. -έστερος, Sup.-έστατος.

Ἐπιμένω, μενῶ, &c. *to stay on,
wait*, ἔστε, 5. 5. 2.

Ἐπιμίγνυμι or νύω, μίξω, &c. *to
mix with*, τινί τι; Mid. *to have
intercourse with*, πρός, 3. 5.
16.

Ἐπινοέω, ήσω, &c. *to have in
one's mind, think on or of*, τι,
2. 5. 4, 3. 1. 6.

Ἐπιορκέω, ορκήσω, ὥρκηκα, *to
swear falsely by*, θεούς, 2. 4. 7;
forswear oneself, 2. 6. 22, 7.
6. 18, 3. 1. 22.

Ἐπιορκία, ας, ἡ (ἐπί, ὅρκος), *a
false oath, perjury*, 2. 5. 21,
3. 2. 4.

Ἐπίορκος, ος, ον (ἐπί, ὅρκος),
*swearing falsely, forsworn,
perjured*, 2. 6. 25.

Ἐπιπάρειμι (ἐπί, παρά, εἰμί), *to
be present in the neighbourhood*,
3. 4. 23.

Ἐπιπάρειμι (ἐπί, παρά, εἶμι), *to
march on high ground parallel
with one below*, 3. 4. 30, 6. 3.
19.

Ἐπιπίπτω, πεσοῦμαι, πέπτωκα,
2 aor. ἐπέπεσον, *to fall upon,
attack*, τινί, 1. 8. 2, 6. 3. 3;
of snow, *to fall*, 4. 4. 11.

Ἐπιπολύ, adv. for ἐπὶ πολύ, *very
far, for a long distance*, 1.
8. 8.

Ἐπίπονος, ος, ον (ἐπί, πόνος),
painful, toilsome, laborious, 1.
3. 19; of omens, *portending
suffering*, 6. 1. 23.

Ἐπιρρίπτω, ῥίψω, &c., some make
ἐπιρρἴπτέω, -ήσω, *to throw at*,
5. 2. 23.

Ἐπίρρῦτος, ος, ον (ἐπί, ῥέω),
*flowing, flowed· upon, well-
watered*, 1. 2. 22, Lat. *ir-
riguus*.

Ἐπισάττω, ξω, *to heap up, pile a
load upon*; ἵππον, *to saddle*,
3. 4. 35.

Ἐπισθένης, ους, ὁ (ἐπί, σθένος),
Episthenes, from Amphipolis
in Thrace, 1. 10. 7, 4. 6. 1;
also an Olynthian, 7. 4. 7.

Ἐπισιτίζομαι, ίσομαι or ιοῦμαι
(ἐπί, σῖτος), *to furnish oneself
with food, to procure provisions*, 1. 5. 4, 3. 4. 18, 1. 4.
19.

Ἐπισιτισμός, οῦ, ὁ (ἐπί, σῖτος), *a
furnishing oneself with provisions, foraging, a stock
of provisions*, 1. 5. 9, 7. 1.
9.

Ἐπισκέπτομαι, see ἐπισκοπέω.

Ἐπισκευάζω, άσω (ἐπί, σκευάζω,
σκεῦος), *to get ready, prepare,
repair*, ναόν, 5. 3. 13.

Ἐπισκοπέω, σκέψομαι, ἔσκεμμαι,
to look upon, inspect, 2. 3. 2,
consider, reflect.

'Επισπάω, σπάσω, &c. to draw, pull to, drag after, 4. 7. 14.

'Επίσταμαι, ἐπιστήσομαι (ἐπί, ἵσταμαι), impf. ἠπιστάμην, 1 aor. ἠπιστήθην and ἠπιστάσθην, to know, understand, 1. 3. 12.

'Επίστασις, εως, ἡ (ἐπί, ἵστημι), a stopping, halting, a halt, 2. 4. 26.

'Επιστατέω, to be an ἐπιστάτης, have charge or care of a thing, to exercise command, 2. 3. 11.

'Επιστέλλω, στελῶ, &c. to send to, send information, to enjoin, command, τινί τι, 5. 3. 6, 7. 6. 44.

'Επιστήμη, ης, ἡ (ἐπίσταμαι), acquaintance, knowledge, understanding.

'Επιστήμων, ων, ον, g. ονος (ἐπίσταμαι), wise, prudent, skilled in, acquainted with, τινός, 2. 1. 7.

'Επιστολή, ῆς, ἡ (ἐπιστέλλω), a letter, 1. 6. 3.

'Επιστρατεία, ας, ἡ (ἐπί, στρατεία), a march or expedition against one, 2. 4. 1.

'Επιστρατεύω, εύσω, &c. to march against, make war on, τινί or ἐπί τινα, 2. 3. 19.

'Επισφάττω, ξω, or ἐπισφάζω, ξω, to kill, put to death, slaughter over or upon, τινά τινι, 1. 8. 29.

'Επιτάττω or τάσσω, τάξω, &c. to set over, enjoin, order, τί τινι, order, τινί, c. inf. one to do, 2. 3. 6, 7. 6. 14; to place behind or next, τινά τινι, 6. 5. 9.

'Επιτελέω, έσω, &c. (ἐπί, τελέω), to complete, finish, accomplish, fulfil, perform, 4. 3. 13.

'Επιτήδειος, α, ον (ἐπιτηδές, adv.

fittingly, ἐπὶ τάδε, like idoneus, fr. ideo, Butt.), suitable, proper, 2. 3. 11, 7. 7. 2, 2. 5. 18; necessary, τὰ ἐπιτ. the necessaries of life, provisions, 2. 3. 26, 27, 7. 6. 29.

'Επιτίθημι, θήσω, &c. to put, lay, place on or by, to impose, inflict, δίκην τινί, 1. 3. 20, 5. 6. 34; Mid. to fall upon, attack, τινί, 2. 4. 3, 3. 4. 1.

'Επιτοπολύ, adv. for ἐπὶ τὸ πολύ, in general, for the most part, commonly, 3. 1. 42.

'Επιτρέπω, τρέψω, &c. to entrust to, τινί τι, 5. 9. 31, 1. 9. 8; (ἐπιτρέπομαί τι, I am entrusted with a thing) to command, τινὰ ποιεῖν τι, 6. 5. 11; permit, suffer, οὐδενὶ εἶναι κακῷ, 3. 2. 31; to give up, τί τινι c. inf. 1. 2. 19, 2. 4. 27.

'Επιτρέχω, θρέξομαι, &c. to run to, at, upon, to make a sudden attack, 4. 3. 31.

'Επιτυγχάνω, τεύξομαι, &c. to light or fall upon, meet with, τινί, 1. 9. 25, 3. 4. 18; τινός, to hit, reach, gain; ὁ ἐπιτυχών, the first one meets, anyone.

'Επιφαίνομαι, φανοῦμαι, &c. to appear, 3. 3. 6, 4. 13.

'Επιφέρω, ἐποίσω, &c., to bring, put, lay upon; Mid. to rush upon, attack, τινί, 1. 9. 6; ὅταν θάλαττα μεγάλη ἐπιφέρηται, whenever a great sea strikes against the ship, 5. 8. 20.

'Επιφθέγγομαι, γξομαι, &c. to sound the charge, 4. 2. 7, proper reading is ἐφθέγξατο.

'Επιφορέω, ήσω, &c. to put upon, γῆν ἐπιφ., 3. 5. 10.

'Επίχαρις, ις, ι, gen. -ιτος (ἐπί,

χάρις), *pleasing, agreeable*, τὸ
ἐπίχαρι (*suavitas*), *suavity,
pleasantness of manner*, 2. 6.
12 ; Comp. ἐπιχαριτώτερος,
Superl. ἐπιχαριτώτατος.
Ἐπιχειρέω, ήσω, &c. (ἐπί, χείρ),
to put one's hand to, attempt,
καίειν, 3. 5. 3 ; βάλλειν, 6. 4.
7 ; διορύττειν, 7. 8. 13 ; ἀπιέναι, 5. 2. 5 ; διώκειν, 3. 4. 27,
4. 3. 25 ; λέγειν, 5. 6. 34 ;
ἁρπάζειν, 6. 4. 6 ; ἐλεύθεροι
γίγνεσθαι, 7. 7. 29.
Ἐπιχέω, χέω, &c. *to pour in,*
4. 5. 27.
Ἐπιχωρέω, ήσω, &c. *to advance,*
· 1. 2. 17.
Ἐπιψηφίζω, ίσω Att. ιῶ, *to put
to the vote* (*in suffragia mittere*),
· 5. 1. 14, 5. 6. 35 ; Mid. *to
decree, confirm by vote,* ταῦτα,
· 7. 6. 14.
Ἐποικοδομέω, ήσω, &c. (ἐπί, οἶκος,
δέμω), *to build upon,* 3. 4. 11.
Ἐπόμνυμι and ύω, ομοῦμαι, &c.
to swear; ἐπο μόσαςεἶπε, *he
said upon oath,* 7. 8. 2.
Ἑπτά, *seven;* ἑπτακαίδεκα, *seventeen;* ἑπτακόσιοι, *seven hundred.*
Ἐπύαξα, ης, ἡ, *Epyaxa,* queen
of Cilicia, wife of Syennesis, 1.
2. 12.
Ἔραμαι, poet. for ἐράω, ἐρασθή-
σομαι, ἤρασμαι, *to love, be fond
of,* παιδός, 4. 6. 3.
Ἐργάζομαι, άσομαι, εἴργασμαι
(ἔργον), *to work, till,* 2. 4.
22, *to do,* χώραν κακόν, 5. 6.
11, two acc.
Ἔργον, ου, τό, *a work,* ἔργῳ
ἐπεδείκνυτο καὶ ἔλεγεν, *he
showed both in deed and in
word,* 1. 9. 10.
Ἐρεῖν, see εἴρω.
Ἐρετριεύς, έως, ὁ, *a native of*

Eretria, a city in Eubœa, 7.
8. 8.
Ἐρημία, ας, ἡ (ἔρημος), *a desert,
solitude,* 2. 5. 9.
Ἔρημος, ος, ον and η, ον, *lonely,
desert, desolate;* οἰκιῶν, *without houses,* 7. 1. 24, hence
Eng. *eremite, hermit.*
Ἐρημόω, ώσω (ἔρημος), *to deprive,* 1. 3. 6.
Ἐρίζω, ἐρίσω, ἤρικα, ἐρήρισμαι,
to strive, dispute, quarrel, 1. 2.
8, 4. 7. 12.
Ἐρίφειος, ος, ον, *of a kid,* ἔριφος,
4. 5. 31.
Ἑρμηνεύς, έως, ὁ (Ἑρμῆς, *Mer-
cury*), *an interpreter,* 4. 5. 34,
2. 3. 17, 4. 2. 18.
Ἑρμηνεύω, εύσω (Ἑρμῆς, *Mer-
cury*), *to interpret,* 5. 4. 4.
Ἔρομαι, ήσομαι, 2 aor. ἠρόμην,
to ask, 5. 9. 13, 7. 2. 19, 3. 1. 7.
Ἐρρωμένος, η, ον, p. p. from
ῥώννυμι, *in good health, stout,*
Comp. -έστερος Sup. -έστατος,
resolute, 3. 1. 42; adv. ἐρρω-
μένως, *in great strength,* 6. 1.
6.
Ἐρύκω, ύξω, *to hold back, ward
off, impede,* 3. 1. 25.
Ἔρυμα, ατος, τό (ἐρύομαι), *a defence, fortification, stronghold,*
1. 7. 16, 2. 4. 22, 4. 5. 9.
Ἐρύμαχος, or Εὐρύμαχος, *Eurymachus,* a Dardanian, 5. 6. 21.
Ἐρυμνός, ή, όν (ἐρύομαι), *forti-
fied,* τὰ ἐρυμνά, *strong positions,*
5. 7. 31.
Ἔρχομαι, ἐλεύσομαι, ἐλήλυθα, 2
aor. ἤλυθον contr. ἦλθον, *to
go, come,* εἰς λόγους, 2, 5. 4 ;
ἐπὶ βωμόν, 1. 6. 7 ; παρά τινα,
1. 4. 3 ; πρός τινα, 1. 1. 10 ;
ὁδόν, 2. 2. 10 ; σταθμούς, 4. 7.
19 ; ἀφαιρησόμενοι, 7. 1. 28 ; ὡς
ἀφανιοῦντες, 3. 2. 11.

Ἔρως, ωτος, ὁ (ἐράω), love, 2. 5. 22.

Ἐρωτάω, ήσω, &c. to ask, τινά τι, 3. 1. 7, 4. 4. 17.

Ἐς = εἰς.

Ἐσθής, ῆτος, ἡ (ἕννυμι), dress, clothing, 3. 1. 19, 4. 3. 25, 7. 4. 18.

Ἐσθίω, ἔσομαι, ἐδήδοκα, ἐδήδομαι and ἐδήδεσμαι, 2 aor. ἔφαγον, to eat, ὀλίγον, 4. 8. 20.

Ἑσπέρα, ας, ἡ, evening (Lat. vespera), ἀπὸ ἑσπέρας, after evening, at nightfall, εἰς, πρὸς ἑσπέραν, towards evening, westwards, 3. 5. 15; hence

Ἑσπερῖται, ῶν, οἱ, the Hesperitæ, a people in Armenia, 7. 8. 25.

Ἔστε (ἐς, ὅτε) Lat. usque, even to, 4. 5. 6. Conj. until with ind. 2. 5. 30, 3. 1. 28; with opt. 1. 9. 11, 5. 5. 2, ἔστ᾽ ἄν with conj. 4. 5. 28, 5. 1. 4; so long as, with ind. 3. 1. 19; opt. 3. 3. 5.

Ἔσχατος, ος, ον and η, ον (ἐξ = outermost), last, 1. 2. 10; severest, δίκη, 6. 4. 15; τὰ ἔσχατα πάσχειν, the severest punishment, 2. 5. 24; αἰκίζεσθαι, 3. 1. 18; adv. ἐσχάτως, exceedingly, 2. 6. 1.

Ἔσωθεν, from within, τὸ ἔ. the inner wall, 1. 4. 4.

Ἑταίρα, ας, ἡ, a female companion, a harlot, 4. 3. 19, 30, 5. 4. 33.

Ἑταῖρος, ου, ὁ, a companion, 4. 8. 27.

Ἐτεόνικος, ου, ὁ (ἐτεός, true, νίκη, victory), Eteonicus, a Lacedæmonian, 7. 1. 12, 20.

Ἕτερος, α, ον (comp. of εἷς), Lat. alter, the other, one of two, ὁ ἕτερος τὸν ἕτερον παίει, the one strikes the other, 5. 9. 5; ὁ μὲν ἕτερος—ὁ δὲ λοιπός, 4. 1. 23.

Ἔτι, adv. still, yet, as yet, πρὸς δ᾽ ἔτι, besides, further, 3. 2. 2; ἔτι δὲ, 3. 1. 23, 6. 4. 13, οὐκ ἔτι, no more, not at all, 1. 7. 18.

Ἕτοιμος, η, ον and ος, ον, ready, prepared; χρήματα, ready money, 7. 8. 11, ἐστὶν ἀδικεῖν, 5. 9. 2; adv. ἑτοίμως, 2. 5. 2, 5. 7. 4.

Ἔτος, εος, τό, a year, ἑκάστου ἔτους, every year, 5. 3. 13; pl. ἔτη, years.

Εὖ, adv. well, opp. to κακῶς.

Εὐδαιμονία, ας, ἡ, prosperity, good fortune, 2. 5. 13.

Εὐδαιμονίζω, ίσω, to call or reckon happy, 2. 5. 7, 1. 7. 3.

Εὐδαιμόνως, adv. from

Εὐδαίμων, ων, ον, gen. ονος (εὖ, δαίμων), happy, fortunate, prosperous, wealthy, 1. 2. 6, 5. 7, 5. 6. 25, 4. 32.

Εὔδηλος, ος, ον (εὖ, δῆλος), quite clear, εὔδηλον ἦν ὅτι, 3. 1. 2, 5. 6. 13.

Εὐδία, ας, ἡ (εὖ, Διός), gen. of Ζεύς), fair weather, a calm, 5. 8. 19.

Εὐειδής, ής, ές (εὖ, εἶδον, 2 aor. of ὁράω), handsome, good-looking, 2. 3. 3.

Εὔελπις, ις, ι, gen. ιδος (εὖ, ἐλπίς), of good hope, hopeful, 2. 1. 18.

Εὐεπίθετος, ος, ον (εὖ, ἐπί, τίθημι), easy to set upon or attack, exposed, ἦν τοῖς πολεμίοις, the enemy could easily attack them, 3. 4. 20.

Εὐεργεσία, ας, ἡ (εὖ, ἔργον), good service, kindness, προΐεσθαι, 7. 7. 47, 2. 6. 27.

Εὐεργετέω, ήσω (εὖ, ἔργον), to do

good, show kindness to, 2. 6. 17, hence

Εὐεργέτης, ου, ὁ, a benefactor, 2. 5. 10, 7. 7. 11.

Εὔζωνος, ος, ον (εὖ, ζώνη), well-girdled, active, Lat. expeditus, light-armed, 4. 2. 7, &c.

Εὐήθεια, ας, ἡ, silliness, absurdity, 1. 3. 16, from

Εὐήθης, ης, ες (εὖ, ἦθος), silly.

Εὐθέως, adv. from εὐθύς, directly, immediately.

Εὐθυμέομαι, ήσομαι (εὔθυμος), to be cheerful, enjoy oneself, 4. 5. 30.

Εὔθυμος, ος, ον (εὖ, θυμός), kind, cheerful, in good spirits, 3. 1. 41.

Εὐθύς, adv. immediately of time, εὐθύ, of place, straight, εὐθὺς παῖδες ὄντες, even from boyhood, 1. 9. 4, Lat. a pueris, so ἐκ παίδων, 4. 6. 14.

Εὐθύωρον (εὐθύς), adv. straight on, 2. 2. 16.

Εὔκλεια, ας, ἡ (εὖ, κλέος, glory), good fame, glory, 7. 6. 32.

Εὐκλείδης, ου, ὁ (εὖ, κλέος), Euclides, a seer, son of Cleagoras from Phlius, 7. 8. 1.

Εὐκλεῶς, adv. fr. εὐκλεής, famous, glorious, 6. 1. 17.

Εὐμενής, ής, ές (εὖ, μένος, εος, τό, force), well-disposed, favourable, friendly, 4. 6. 12.

Εὐμεταχείριστος, ος, ον (εὖ, μετά, χείρ), manageable, 2. 6. 20.

Εὔνοια, ας, ἡ (εὖ, νοῦς), good-will, kindness; τῶν Ἑλλήνων εὔνοια, good-will to the Greeks, 4. 7. 20.

Εὐνοϊκῶς, adv. ἔχοιεν αὐτῷ, might be well disposed towards him, 1. 1. 5.

Εὔνοος, ος, ον, contr. εὔνους,

well-disposed, kind, τινί, 2. 4. 16, 3. 3. 2, 7. 2. 31.

Εὔξεινος, ος, ον (εὖ, ξένος), hospitable, Πόντος, the Pontus Euxinus, the Euxine or Black Sea, formerly called Ἄξεινος or Ἄξεινος (ἀ priv. ξένος), inhospitable, 4. 8. 22.

Εὐοδεύς, έως, ὁ (εὖ, ὁδός), Euodeus, a captain, 7. 4. 18, sometimes Εὐοδίας or Ἐνοδίας.

Εὔοδος, ος, ον (εὖ, ὁδός), easy to travel through, practicable, 4. 2. 9, 4. 8. 10; ᾗ τε ἂν εὔοδον ᾖ, wherever it is easy to ascend, 4. 8. 12, 10.

Εὔοπλος, ος, ον (εὖ, ὅπλον), well-armed, 2. 3. 3.

Εὐπετῶς, adv. (εὖ, πίπτω), easily, without trouble, 2. 5. 23.

Εὐπορία, ας, ἡ, an easy way, facility for going, 7. 6. 37.

Εὔπορος, ος, ον (εὖ, πόρος), easy to pass, 3. 5. 17, easy, 6. 3. 18, ὁδός, 2. 5. 9.

Εὔπρακτος, ος, ον (εὖ, πράσσω), easy to be done, 2. 3. 20.

Εὐπρεπής, ής, ές (εὖ, πρέπει), good-looking, beautiful, 4. 1. 14.

Εὐπρόσοδος, ος, ον (εὖ, πρός, ὁδός), accessible, 5. 4. 30.

Εὕρημα, ατος, τό (εὑρίσκω), a piece of good luck, a godsend, windfall; ἐποιησάμην, I considered it a piece of good luck, 2. 3. 18.

Εὑρίσκω, εὑρήσω, εὕρηκα, εὕρημαι, 2 aor. εὗρον, 1 aor. pass. εὑρέθην, to find, find out, 4. 4. 13, 5. 8. 22, 2. 3. 21; Mid. to find for themselves, 2. 1. 8, 7. 1. 31.

Εὖρος, εος, τό (εὐρύς), breadth, δύο πλέθρα, 1. 2. 5; πλέθρον, 1. 4. 10; without the art.

ποταμὸς εὖρος πλέθρου, 1. 4. 4,
2. 23, 2. 4. 12; with the art.
διώρυχες, 1. 7. 15; τάφρος, 1.
7. 14; τεῖχος, 3. 4. 11, 2. 4.
. 25, 7. 8. 14.

Εὐρύλοχος, ου, ὁ (εὐρύς, λόχος),
Eurylochus, a hoplite from
Lusi, a town in Arcadia, 4. 2.
21, 7. 11, 7. 1. 32, 6. 40.

Εὐρύμαχης, ου, ὁ (εὐρύς, μάχη),
Eurymachus or Erymachus,
5. 6. 21.

Εὐρύς, εῖα, ύ, adj. wide, broad, 4.
5. 25.

Εὐρώπη, ης, ἡ (εὐρύς, ὤψ),
Europe, 7. 1. 27.

Εὔτακτος, ος, ον (εὖ, τάσσω),
well-arranged, in good order;
Comp. εὐτακτοτέοους, more
orderly, 3. 2. 30; adv. εὐ-
τάκτως, 6. 4. 35.

Εὐταξία, ας, ἡ (εὖ, τάσσω), good
order, discipline, 1. 5. 8, 3. 1.
38.

Εὔτολμος, ος, ον (εὖ, τόλμα,
daring), brave, courageous, 1.
7. 4.

Εὐτυχέω, ήσω, εὐτύχηκα, εὐτύ-
χημαι, aor. εὐτύχησα (εὖ,
τύχη), to be fortunate, suc-
cessful, 1. 4. 17; εὐτύχημα,
they luckily met with this piece
of good fortune, 6. 1. 3.

Εὐτυχία, ας, ἡ (εὖ, τύχη), good
fortune.

Εὐφράτης, ου, ὁ, the river Euphrates, 1.4. 11, 4.1.3, 1.7.15.

Εὐχή, ῆς, ἡ, a prayer, a wish, 1.
9. 11.

Εὔχομαι, εὔξομαι, ηὖγμαι, impf.
ηὐχόμην, to pray, ζῆν, 1. 9. 11;
αὐτὸν εὐτυχῆσαι, 1. 4. 17; to
vow, 3. 2. 9, 4. 8. 16, 4. 3. 13.

Εὐώδης, ης, ες (εὖ, ὄζω), sweet-
smelling, fragrant, οἶνος, 4. 4.
9, 5. 4. 29.

Εὐώνυμος, ος, ον (εὖ, ὄνομα),
of good name, lucky, euphe-
mistic term for ἀριστερά, on
the left hand: the left, being
unlucky, was avoided in
writing and speaking, 1. 8. 4,
9, 23.

Εὐωχέω, ήσω, &c. (εὖ, ἔχω), to
entertain, feast, 4.5.30, 5.3.11.

Εὐωχία, ας, ἡ (εὖ, ἔχω), a feast
or entertainment, 5. 9. 4.

Ἔφεδρος, ου, ὁ (ἐπί, ἕδρα, a seat),
a third combatant who sits by
to fight the conqueror, an
avenger, 2. 5. 10.

Ἐφέπομαι, -έψομαι, &c., to follow, pursue, 3. 4. 3, 6. 3. 11,
4. 6. 25, 1. 6, 2. 2. 12.

Ἐφέσιος, α, ον, of or belonging to
Ἔφεσος, ου, ἡ, Ephesus in Asia
Minor, 2. 2. 6, 5. 3. 4, 6, 8.

Ἐφθός, ή, όν (ἕψω), boiled, 5.4. 32.

Ἐφίημι, ήσω, &c. Mid. ἐφίεμαι, to
allow, 6. 4. 31, al. ὑφεῖτο.

Ἐφίστημι, ἐπιστήσω, ἐφέστηκα,
ἐφέσταμαι (ἐπί, ἵστημι), to stop,
to make to halt, 1. 8. 15, ἵππον
to be supplied: to set over, appoint, 3. 3. 20, 4. 21; τριήρει
τινά, 5. 1. 15, 16; Pass. to
stand by or near, 4. 7. 9, 5. 8.
9, 1. 4. 4; to stop or halt, 1.
5. 7, 2. 4. 26, 5. 4. 34, ἐφεσ-
τήκει, plp. as pass. was set
over, 6. 3. 11.

Ἐφόδιον, ου, τό (ἐπί, ὁδός), supplies for travelling, travelling
expenses, 7. 3. 20, 8. 2; Lat.
viaticum.

Ἔφοδος, ου, ἡ (ἐπί, ὁδός), approach, ἐπὶ τὸν λόφον, 3. 4.
41, 4. 2. 6, 2. 2. 18, 3. 1.

Ἐφοράω, ἐπόψομαι, ἐφεώρακα, 2
aor. ἐπεῖδον, to oversee, or
simply to look upon, to behold,
6. 1. 14, 7. 6. 31, 3. 1. 13.

Ἐφορμέω, ήσω, &c. to lie at anchor opposite a place, 7. 6. 25.

Ἐφορος, ου, ὁ (ἐπί, ὁράω), an overseer; at Sparta οἱ ἔφοροι, the Ephors, five men who controlled even the kings, 2. 6. 3.

Ἔχθρα, ας, ἡ (ἔχθος), enmity, ill-will, 2. 4. 11.

Ἐχθρός, ρά, ρόν (ἔχθος, hatred, ἔξ), hostile; subst. an enemy (Lat. inimicus), 1. 3. 12, 20; οἱ ἐκείνου ἔχθιστοι, his bitterest enemies, 3. 2. 5.

Ἐχυρός, ά, όν (ἔχω), strong, 2. 5. 7, 7. 4. 12.

Ἔχω, ἕξω or σχήσω, ἔσχηκα, ἔσχημαι, impf. εἶχον, 2 aor. ἔσχον (σχῶ, σχοίην, σχές, σχεῖν, σχών), 1 aor. pass. ἐσχέθην, to have, hold, possess, 5. 4. 15, &c.; θυγατέρα, to have for a wife, 3. 4. 13, ἔχων, with, 1. 1. 2, 2. 3, &c. pl. 1. 5. 8; ἔχομεν θάλατταν, we have reached the sea, 5. 1. 2; ἔχονται οἱ ἄνθρωποι, the inhabitants are kept prisoners, 7. 3. 47; ἀνάγκη ἔχεσθαι, to be held down by necessity, 2. 5. 21; to restrain, 7. 1. 20; to prevent, τοῦ μὴ καταδῦναι, 3. 5. 11; lying, 7. 8. 21; οὐκ εἶχον εὑρεῖν, they could not find, 3. 2. 12, 2. 2. 11, 7. 6. 39; with adverbs ἄλλως ἐχέτω, let it be settled otherwise, 3. 2. 37; καλῶς, it is well, 4. 3. 16; κακῶς, 1. 5. 16, our affairs proving adverse; ἀσφαλῶς, all is safe, 4. 3. 27; εὐνοϊκῶς, 1. 1. 5; ἐντίμως, 2. 1. 7; θαρραλέως, 2. 6. 14; ἀθύμως, 3. 1. 3; πολεμικῶς, 5. 9. 1; ταῦτα οὕτως ἔχει, these things

stand in this position, this is the position of affairs, 1. 3. 9, 6. 3. 15, &c.; ἧπερ εἶχον, in which they were, lit. in which they had themselves, 2. 2. 21; ὥσπερ εἶχεν, just as he was, 4. 1. 19; ἀμφί τι ἔχειν, to be engaged in anything, 7. 2. 16; ἔχομεν ἡρπακότες, 1. 3. 14, 3. 4. 14, 4. 7. 1, 7. 7. 27; ἐχόμενος, next, 1. 8. 4, 9; ἔχομαι τινός, to lay hold of, 7. 6. 41; τῆς σωτηρίας, to be taken up with the common safety, 6. 1. 17.

Ἑψητός, ή, όν, boiled, 2. 3. 14. from

Ἕψω, ἑψήσω, ἕψηκα (lenis), ἥψημαι, and ἕψημαι, to boil.

Ἕωθεν (ἕως), in the morning, 4. 4. 8, 6. 1. 23.

Ἕως, ἕω, acc. ἕω or ἕων, ἡ, morning, 2. 4. 24, 4. 3. 9, 1. 7. 1; πρὸς ἕω, towards the east, 3. 5. 15, 5. 7. 6.

Ἕως, conj. so long as, while, until, with ind. 1. 3. 11, 2. 6. 2, 3. 4. 49, 4. 8. 8, with subj. and ἄν, 1. 4. 8, 3. 1. 43, 6. 1. 14, with opt. 2. 1. 2, 6. 3. 25.

Z

Ζάβατος, ου, ὁ, the river Zab in Assyria, flowing into the Tigris, 2. 5. 1.

Ζάω, ζήσω, ἔζηκα, to live, inf. ζῆν, 3. 2. 39, 5. 9. 1.

Ζειά, ᾶς, ἡ, spelt, Lat. far, a kind of grain, 5. 4. 27.

Ζειρά, ᾶς, ἡ, a mantle, 7. 4. 4.

Ζευγηλατέω, ήσω (ζεῦγος, a yoke, ἐλαύνω), to drive a yoke of

oxen, 5. 9. 8 ; ζευγηλάτης, ου,
ὁ, the driver, 5. 9. 8.
Ζεύγνυμι, ζεύξω, ἔζευγμαι, 2 aor.
pass. ἐζύγην, to join, attach, 3.
5. 10, 5. 9. 8; γέφυρα ἐζευγμένη πλοίοις, a bridge made of
boats, 1. 2. 5, 2. 4. 24, 2. 4. 13.
Ζεῦγος, εος, τό (ζεύγνυμι), a yoke
of oxen, horses, or mules, 5.
9. 8, 7. 5. 2, 4, 3. 2. 27.
Ζεύς, Διός, ὁ, Jupiter, σωτήρ, 3.
2. 9, 4. 8. 25 ; ξένιος, 3. 2. 4;
βασιλεύς, 5. 9. 22, 7. 6. 44 ;
μειλίχιος, 7. 8. 4 ; acc. Δία,
voc. Ζεῦ, hence Jupiter=Ζεὺς
πατήρ.
Ζηλαρχος, ου, ὁ (ζῆλος, ἀρχή),
Zelarchus, a market superin-
tendent, 5. 7. 24.
Ζηλωτός, ή, όν (ζηλόω, ζῆλος,
zeal, ζέω, to boil), enviable;
τοῖς οἴκοι, envied by those at
home, 1. 7. 4.
Ζημιόω, ώσω, &c. (ζημία, loss),
to punish, 6. 2. 11.
Ζητέω, ήσω, &c. to seek, ask for,
2. 3. 2, inf. 5. 4. 33.
Ζυμίτης ἄρτος (ζύμη, leaven, ζέω,
to boil), leavened bread, 7. 3.
21.
Ζωγρέω, ήσω, &c. (ζωός,- ἄγρα,
booty), to take alive, take
prisoner, 4. 7. 22.
Ζώνη, ης, ἡ (ζώννυμι), a girdle,
1. 6. 10 ; εἰς ζώνην, for girdle
money, pin-money, 1. 4. 9.
Ζωός, ή, όν (ζάω), alive, living,
3. 4. 5.

II

Ἤ, or, Lat. aut, interrog. an,
and after comp. quam : ἤ, (1)
adv. truly, Lat. vero ; (2) interrog., Lat. an or num ; (3)

for ἔφη, from ἠμί ; (4) for ἔα, 1
sing. impf. of εἰμί ; ἦ, 3 sing.
pres. conj. of εἰμί ; ἥ, fem. of
art. ὁ, ἡ, τό ; ἥ, fem. of rel. ὅς, ἥ,
ὅ ; ᾖ, dat. sing. fem. of rel. or
poss. pron. ὅς, ἥ, ὅν, his,
usually adv. where, 3. 4. 37,
&c.; with superl. ᾖ ἐδύνατό
τάχιστα, as quickly as possible,
1. 2. 4, &c. ; so ᾖ δυνατὸν
μάλιστα, 1. 3. 15 ; ᾖ τάχιστα,
6. 3. 13.
Ἡβάσκω, ἡβήσω (ἥβη, youth), to
come to man's estate, be a man,
4. 6. 1.
Ἡγεμονία, ας, ἡ (ἡγεμών), command, 4. 7. 8.
Ἡγεμόσυνος, η, ον (ἡγεμών), τὰ
ἡγεμόσυνα, thank-offerings for
safe conduct, 4. 8. 25.
Ἡγεμών, όνος, ὁ (ἡγέομαι), a
leader, guide, 1. 3. 14, 16, 17;
τῆς ὁδοῦ, 3. 1. 2.
Ἡγέομαι, -ήσομαι, ἥγημαι (ἄγω),
to lead the way, τινί, 4. 6. 2, 5.
4. 20; τινὶ τὴν ὁδόν, 5. 4. 10; εἰς,
6. 3. 1, 7. 1. 33; πρὸς, 4. 2. 2. ὁ
ἡγησόμενος οὐδεὶς ἔσται, there
will be no one to guide, 2. 4. 5,
τὸ ἡγούμενον, the van, 2. 4.
26 ; to suppose, believe, consider, πῶς μέγα ἡγοῦ, how
important you considered it,
with inf. 7. 7. 27, 5. 4. 20,
1. 2. 4, 5. 9. 18.
Ἡγήσανδρος, ου, ὁ (ἡγέομαι,
ἀνήρ), Hegesander, a captain,
6. 1. 5.
Ἡδέως, adv. from ἡδύς, gladly,
cheerfully, with pleasure,
agreeably, 4. 3. 2, 1. 9. 19, 2.
5. 15. C. ἥδιον, S. ἥδιστα.
Ἤδη, adv. now, already, Lat.
jam (ᾔδη, plp. of οἶδα), τὰς ἤδη
κολάσεις, the ready chastise-
ments, 7. 7. 24.

Ἥδομαι, ἡσθήσομαι, 1 aor. ἥσθην (ἧδος, ἡδύς), take delight in, be pleased with, τούτοις, 1. 9. 26, ἵππῳ, 7. 8. 6; ἥσθη ἰδών, 1. 2. 18.

Ἡδονή, ῆς, ἡ (ἡδύς), sweetness, pleasure, 2. 3. 16, 4. 4. 14.

Ἡδύοινος, ος, ον (ἡδύς, οἶνος), producing sweet wine, 6. 2. 6.

Ἡδύς, εῖα, ύ, Comp. ἡδίων, Superl. ἥδιστος, late ἡδύτερος, sweet, pleasant, agreeable, κρέα, 1. 5. 3; οἶνος, 1. 9. 25, 6. 2. 4, 5. 8. 26.

Ἧιπερ, where, by the same road as, 4. 2. 9.

Ἥκιστα, adv. from ἧκα, by no means, not in the least, 1. 9. 19.

Ἥκω, ἥξω, I am come, perf., Lat. veni; ἔρχομαι is the pres. I am coming; imp. ἧκον, used as aor. 2. 5. 6, 1. 2. 6, 2. 1. 9, 15, 3.

Ἠλεῖος, α, ον, of or belonging to Elis in the Peloponnesus, Elean, 3. 1. 34.

Ἤλεκτρον, ου, τό (ἕλκω, to attract), amber, in 2. 3. 15, probably the metal compound of gold and silver called electrum, because yellow like amber.

Ἠλίβατος, ος, ον (ἥλιος, βαίνω; Butt. for ἡλιτόβατος, ἀλιτεῖν, to slip, and βαίνω), high, steep, 1. 4. 4.

Ἠλίθιος, α, ον (ἠλεός), idle, silly, foolish, 2. 6. 22, 5. 7. 10.

Ἡλικία, ας, ἡ (ἧλιξ, of the same age), age; ἡλικιώτης, ου, ὁ, an equal in age, 1. 9. 5.

Ἥλιος, ου, ὁ (ἕλη, heat, Lat. sol),

the sun, δύεσθαι, 1. 10. 15; δυσμαί, 6. 2. 26; ἀνίσχων, 2. 1. 3; ἀνατέλλων, 2. 3. 1.

Ἠμελημένως, adv. from ἀμελέω, carelessly, 1. 7. 19.

Ἡμέρα, ας, ἡ (διά, μέρος; Don.*), a day; ἡμέρας, by day, 2. 6. 7; ἡμέραν, during the day, for a day, 1. 2. 21, &c.; ἅμα τῇ ἡμέρᾳ, at dawn of day, at daybreak, 6. 3. 6.

Ἥμερος, ος, ον, and α, ον, tame, cultivated, δένδρα, not wild, 5. 3. 12.

Ἡμέτερος, α, ον, our, ἡ ἡμετέρα (χώρα), our country, 4. 8. 6.

Ἡμίβρωτος, ος, ον (ἡμι, βιβρώσκω), half-eaten, 1. 9. 26.

Ἡμιδαρεικόν, ου, τό (ἡμι, δαρεικός, sc. νόμισμα, a coin), a half-daric, 1. 3. 21, about half-a-sovereign.

Ἡμιδεής, ής, ές (ἡμι, δέω), wanting half, half-full, half-empty, 1. 9. 25.

Ἡμιοβόλιον, ου, τό, also ἡμιωβόλιον (ἡμι, ὀβολός, sc. νόμισμα, a coin), half an obol, 1. 5. 6, about three farthings of our money.

Ἡμιόλιος, ος, ον, and α, ον (ἡμι, ὅλος), half as much again; οὗ πρότερον, one half more than before, 1. 3. 21.

Ἡμιονικός, ή, όν = ἡμιόνειος, α, ον, of or belonging to a mule, 7. 5. 2, from

Ἡμίονος, ου, ὁ (ἡμι, ὄνος), a half-ass, a mule.

Ἡμίπλεθρον, ου, τό, half a plethron, fifty feet, 4. 7. 6.

Ἥμισυς, εια, υ (ἡμι, or δία, μέσος), half, 1. 8. 22, 4. 2. 9;

---

* Don. makes ἡμέρα=διά, μέρος, 'the light,' 'the day part;' and he considers ἥμερος as originally applicable to a country (διάμεσος) 'divided' by roads, and therefore civilised, (pp. to ἄγριος, with nothing but fields (ἀγροί).—Cratylus, § 150.

F

ἄρτων ἡμίσεα, half-loaves, 1. 9. 26; ὑπὲρ ἥμισυ, more than half, 5. 10. 10.

*Ην for ἐάν, conj. if, Lat. si, εἰ μή, ἐὰν μή, ἢν μή=nisi, unless, takes conj., 4. 6. 11, 7. 5; ἤν που, 1. 2. 27; ἤν—ἤν, 3. 2. 31; ἤν—ἤν τε—ἤν τε, 7. 7. 24; ἢν μέν—εἰ δέ, 7. 1. 31, 5. 3. 6. ἤν=en, ecce, lo! ἦν impf. of εἰμί; ἤν, acc. sing. fem. of rel. or poss. pron.

'Ηνίκα, adv. when, takes ind. 1. 8. 1; ἡνίκ' ἄν, with conj. 3. 5. 18.

'Ηνίοχος, ου, ὁ (ἡνία, ἔχω), a charioteer, 1. 8. 20.

*Ηνπερ or ἐάνπερ, even if, 4. 6. 17.

'Ηράκλεια, ας, ἡ, Heraclēa, a city in Bithynia, on the Black Sea, 5. 6. 10,

'Ηρακλείδης, ου, ὁ, Heraclīdes, a native of Maronēa in Thrace, 7. 5. 4, 5, 6, 8, &c.

'Ηρακλεώτης, ου, ὁ, an inhabitant of Heraclēa, 5. 6. 11, 10. 3,

'Ηρακλεῶτις, ιδος, ἡ, sc. γῆ, the district of Heraclēa, 5. 10. 19, all from

'Ηρακλῆς, έους, ὁ ("Ηρη, κλέος, Hera's glory), Hercules, son of Jupiter and Alcmena, 4. 8. 25, 6. 3. 25.

'Ησυχάζω, to be quiet, 5. 4. 16, and 'Ησυχῇ, quietly, 1. 8. 11, and 'Ησυχία, ας, ἡ, quietness; ἡσυχίαν ἄγειν, ἔχειν, to keep quiet, be at rest, 3. 1. 14, 4. 5. 13, 5. 8. 15; καθ' ἡσυχίαν, undisturbed, 2. 3. 8, from

'Ησυχος, ος, ον (ἧκα, gently), still, quiet, 6. 3. 11.

*Ητρον, ου, τό (ἦτορ), the belly, 4. 7. 15.

'Ηττάομαι, ἡσομαι, ἥττημαι (ἥσσων, inferior, Eng. to be worsted), to be conquered, 2. 4. 6, 19, 3. 1. 2, &c.; οὐχ ἡττησόμεθα εὖ ποιοῦντες, we shall not be beaten in doing good, 2. 3. 23.

'Ηττων, ων, ον, or ἥσσων (ἧκα), inferior, weaker, acc. pl. ἥττονας, contr. ἥττους τῶν πολεμίων, inferior to our enemies, 5. 6. 13. Adv. ἧττον, less; οὐδὲν ἧσσον, not less effectively, 7. 5. 9.

Θ.

Θάλαττα, ης, ἡ (ἅλς, sal, salt), the sea, 4. 7. 24, 5. 10. 4.

Θάλπος, εος, τό, warmth, heat; pl. θάλπη, 3. 1. 23.

Θαμῑνά, adv. (ἅμα), frequently, 4. 1. 16.

Θάνατος, ου, ὁ (θνήσκω=θανή-σκω), death, 2. 6. 29.

Θανατόω, ώσω, to condemn to death, 2. 6. 4.

Θάπτω, ψω, τέθαμμαι, 1 a. pass. ἐθάφθην, 2 a. ἐτάφην, to bury, 4. 1. 19, 5. 7. 20.

Θαρραλέως (θάρρος), adv. boldly, 1. 9. 19.

Θαρρέω, ήσω, &c. (θάρρος), to be of good courage, 1. 3. 8, 7. 4. 13; μάχην, to venture on fighting, 3. 2. 20.

Θάρρος, εος, τό, boldness, 6. 3. 17.

Θαρρύνω, ὐνῶ, causal of θαρρέω, to encourage, τινά, 1. 7. 2.

Θαρύπας, ου, ὁ, Tharypas, a favourite of Menon's, 2. 6. 28.

Θάτερον for τὸ ἕτερον, ἐκ τοῦ ἐπὶ θάτερα, from the other side, 5. 4. 10.

Θᾶττον or θᾶσσον, from ταχύς,

more quickly, ἢν θᾶττον ἐκεῖ γενώμεθα, the sooner we get there, 6. 3. 20.

Θαῦμα, ατος, τό (θάω, θάομαι, to wonder at), a wonder, 6. 1. 23.

Θαυμάζω, άσω, τεθαύμᾶκα, τεθαύμασμαι (θαῦμα), to wonder, be surprised at, τι, 2. 5. 33; ὅτι 1. 10. 16, 2. 1. 2; τῶν στρατηγῶν, 5. 10. 4 ; εἰ, 3. 2. 35 ; πότερα—ἢ, 2. 1. 10; τίς, 1. 8. 16 ; ὅ, τι, 5. 7. 13; ὅπωι, 3. 5. 13.

Θαυμάσιος, α, ον (θαυμάζω), wonderful, marvellous, τὸ κάλλος, for beauty, 2. 3. 15.

Θαυμαστός, ή, όν (θαυμάζω), wonderful, surprising, 1. 9. 24, 7. 7. 10.

Θάψακος, ου, ἡ, Thapsacus, a town in Syria, 1. 4. 11; inhabitants are Θαψακηνοί.

Θέα, ας, ἡ, a view, a sight, 4. 8. 27.

Θεά, ᾶς, ἡ, fem. of θεός, a goddess, 6. 4. 17.

Θεαγένης, εος, ὁ (θεά, γίγνομαι), Theagenes, a captain from Locris, 7. 4. 18, al. Θεογένης.

Θέαμα, ατος, τό (θεάομαι), a sight, 4. 7. 13.

Θεάομαι, άσομαι, τεθέαμαι (θέα), to see, behold, 3. 5. 13, 4. 8. 27, 6. 3. 16.

Θεῖος, α, ον (θεός), of or belonging to the gods, divine ; θεῖον, a divine intervention, 1. 4. 18.

Θέλω, θελήσω, τεθέληκα, to wish, 4. 4. 5, 7. 3. 31; inf. 3. 2. 16.

Θεόπομπος, ου, ὁ (θεός, πέμπω), Theopompus, an Athenian, 2. 1. 12.

Θεός, οῦ, ὁ and ἡ (Lat. deus, τίθημι, Hdt. 2. 52 ; θέω, to run, because the planets were at a very early time considered

gods, Plat. Crat.), God, without the art. 7. 3. 43, 2. 5. 7, 5. 2. 24, &c.; with the art. 3. 1. 5, 5. 3. 7, 2. 5. 7, 3. 2. 3; ἡ θεός, the goddess, 3. 2. 12, 5. 3. 6; σὺν τοῖς θεοῖς, with the help of the gods (dis juvantibus), 3. 1. 23, 42, 2. 8, 11.

Θεοσέβεια, ας, ἡ (θεός, σέβομαι), the fear of God, 2. 6. 26.

Θεραπεύω, εύσω, τεθεράπευκα, τεθεράπευμαι (θεράπων), to serve, attend, wait upon, 7. 2. 6; φίλους, 1. 9. 20, 2. 6. 27.

Θεράπων, οντος, ὁ (θέρω), an attendant, servant, 1. 8. 28, 3. 3. 2.

Θερίζω, ίσω, &c. (θέρος), to pass the summer, 3. 5. 15.

Θερμασία, ας, ἡ (θέρω), warmth, heat, 5. 8. 15.

Θερμώδων, οντος, ὁ, The Thermödon, a river in Cappadocia, flowing into the Black Sea (the Amazons lived beside it), 5. 6. 9.

Θεσσαλία, ας, ἡ (θέω for τίθημι, ἥλιος, sunset, the western land; or θάλασσα, as being once a lake), Thessaly in Northern Greece; the people Θεσσᾶλοί, 1. 1. 10.

Θέω, θεύσομαι, to run, εἰς, 2. 2. 14, 4. 3. 21, 29.

Θεωρέω, ήσω, &c. (θέα, a sight), to view, behold, τὸν ἀγῶνα, 1. 2. 10 ; to review, inspect, τοὺς βαρβάρους, 1. 2. 16, 2. 4. 25.

Θῆβαι, ῶν, αἱ, Thebes, the capital of Bœotia; adj. Θηβαῖος, Theban.

Θήβη, ης, ἡ, Thebé, a town in Mysia, 7. 8. 7.

Θήρα, ας, ἡ, a hunt, 5. 3. 8, 10.

Θηράω, άσω, &c. (θήρα), to hunt, λαγώς, 4. 5. 24, 5. 1. 9.

Θηρεύω, εύσω, &c. (θήρα), to hunt, 1. 2. 7; to catch, 1. 2. 13.

Θηρίον, ου, τό (dim. from θήρ), a wild beast, 1. 2. 7, 5. 3. 8.

Θησαυρός, οῦ, ὁ (τίθημι), a treasure, treasure-house, treasury, 5. 4. 27, 5. 3. 5.

Θήχης, ου, ὁ, Theches, a mountain near Trebisond, 4. 7. 21.

Θίμβρων, ωνος, ὁ, or Θίβρων Thimbron, a Lacedæmonian general, 7. 6. 1.

Θνήσκω, θανοῦμαι, τέθνηκα, 2 aor. ἔθανον, to die, τέθνατον, 4. 1. 19; τεθνᾶσι, 4. 2. 17, 6. 1. 12; τεθνηκώς, 1. 10. 16; τεθνιώς, 7. 4. 19; τεθνάναι, 4. 7. 20.

Θνητός, ή, όν (θνήσκω), liable to death, mortal; Lat. mortalis, 3. 1. 23.

Θόρυβος, ου, ὁ (θρόος, θρέω), noise, uproar, confusion, 2. 2. 19, 4. 2. 20, 1. 8. 16.

Θούριος, α, ον, Thurian, from Thurii, a town in Lucania in Italy, 5. 1. 2.

Θράκη, ης, ἡ (τραχύς, rough), Thrace, west of the Black Sea (also a district in Bithynia, 6. 4. 1), adj. Θράκιος, Thracian, 7. 1. 13, 24.

Θρανίψαι, ῶν, οἱ, The Thranipsæ, a people in Thrace, 7. 2. 32, al. Τρανίψαι.

Θρᾷξ, Θρᾳκός, ὁ, a Thracian, pl. Θρᾷκες, 7. 1. 5.

Θρασέως, adv. boldly, 4. 3. 30, from

Θρασύς, εῖα, ύ, bold, 5. 8. 19.

Θρόνος, ου, ὁ (θρέω, to set), a throne, 2. 1. 4.

Θυγάτηρ, τρός, ἡ, a daughter, 2. 4. 8.

Θύλακος, ου, ὁ, a bag, 6. 2. 23.

Θῦμα, ατος, τό (θύω), a victim, a sacrifice, 6. 2. 20, 7. 8. 19.

Θύμβριον, ου, τό, Thymbrium, a town in Mysia, 1. 2. 13.

Θυμοειδής, ής, ές (θυμός, εἶδος), high-spirited, courageous, 4. 5. 36.

Θυμόω, ώσω, &c., to make angry, θυμοῦσθαι, to be angry, τινί, 2. 5. 13.

Θυνοί, ῶν, οἱ, The Thyni, a people in Thrace, 7. 2. 22.

Θύρα, ας, ἡ, a door; ἐπὶ ταῖς βασιλέως θύραις, at the court of the king, 1. 9. 3, from the practice in the East of receiving petitions at the gate, hence in Turkey, the Sublime Porte; ἐπὶ ταῖς θύραις Ἑλλάδος, at the door of Greece, close to Greece, 6. 5. 23.

Θύρετρον, ου, τό=θύρα, a door, 5. 2. 17.

Θυσία, ας, ἡ (θύω), a sacrifice, 4. 8. 25, 6. 2. 15; ποιεῖν, to offer, 5. 3. 9.

Θύω, θύσω, τέθυκα, τέθυμαι, to sacrifice; Mid. to take the auspices, σωτήρια, 3. 2. 9; θεῷ, 3. 1. 6, 5. 5. 5; θύομαι ἰέναι, I consult the auspices about going, 2. 2. 3; ὑπὲρ, 5. 6. 27, 28; περὶ, 6. 2. 17; ἐπὶ, 6. 2. 13; εἰ βέλτιον εἴη, I sacrificed (to learn) if it were better, 5. 9. 31, 6. 28; πότερον—ἤ, 7. 6. 44; τῷ Κύρῳ θυόμενος, consulting the auspices for Cyrus; ἐθύετο τῷ Διί, he sacrificed to Jupiter, and inspected the entrails.

Θωρακίζω, ίσω, &c., to put on the θώραξ; Mid. to arm oneself, 2. 2. 14, 7. 3. 40, 3. 4. 35.

Θώραξ, ακος, ὁ, the breastplate,

I.

corslet, cuirass, 1. 8. 26; λινοῦς, 4. 7. 15; ἱππικός, 3. 4. 48, 1. 8. 6, 3. 3. 20.

Ἰάομαι, ἰάσομαι (ἴαμαι), to heal, 1. 8. 26.

Ἰασονία ἀκτή, Jasonium promontorium, Jason's Cape in Pontus, Cape Bona, 6. 2. 1.

Ἰατρός, οῦ, ὁ (ἰάομαι), a physician, 1. 8. 26, 3. 4. 30.

Ἴδη, ης, ἡ, Ida, a mountain in the Troad, 7. 8. 7.

Ἴδιος, α, ον, and ος, ον, private, εἰς τὸ ἴδιον, for my own use, 1. 3. 3, 7. 7. 39; ἰδίᾳ, adv. on one's own account, privately, 5. 6. 27, 6. 4. 27.

Ἰδιώτης, τητος, ἡ (ἴδιος), peculiarity, 2. 3. 16.

Ἰδιώτης, ου, ὁ (ἴδιος), a private person, opp. to βασιλεύς, 7. 7. 28; a private soldier, opp. to στρατηγός, 1. 3. 11, 3. 2. 32; a layman, opp. to μάντις, 5. 9. 31. (Eng. idiot, originally one who could not take part in public affairs.)

Ἰδιωτικός, ή, όν, private, what belongs to the ἰδιώτης, 5. 9. 23.

Ἰδρόω, ώσω (ἱδρώς, ὕδωρ), to sweat—contracts usually with ω, ῳ instead of ου, οι; so also its opp. ῥιγόω, to shiver with cold, but ου in 1. 8. 1.

Ἰέναι, inf. of ἵημι, to send, throw; ἰέναι, inf. pres. of εἶμι, to go.

Ἰερεῖον, ου, τό, a victim, 5. 9. 4, 6. 3: 2, without ἱερείου, 4. 3. 9, 6. 3. 8, 4. 4. 9.

Ἰερός, ά, όν, sacred, holy, 5. 3. 9, 10, 11; ἡ ἱερὰ συμβουλή

λεγομένη, counsel which is called sacred, alluding to the proverb ἱερὸν ἡ συμβουλή, Plat. Theag. 5. 6. 4; ἱερὸν τό, a temple, 5. 3. 11; τὰ ἱερὰ καλὰ ἦν, the entrails were favourable, 4. 3. 9, 5. 6. 29, &c.; κάλλιστα, 7. 8. 10.

Ἱερὸν Ὄρος, the Sacred Mount in Thrace, 7. 1. 14.

Ἱερώνυμος, ου, ὁ (ἱερός, ὄνομα), Hieronymus (Jerome), one of the oldest captains, from Elis, 3. 1. 34, 6. 2. 10.

Ἵημι, ἥσω, εἷκα, εἷμαι, 1 aor. ἧκα, 2 aor. ἧν (sing. wanting), 1 aor. pass. εἵθην, fut. ἐθήσομαι, to send; τινὰ τῇ ἀξίνῃ, to throw an axe at one, 1. 5. 12; Mid. to rush, 4. 2. 20; ἄνω, 4. 2. 8; εἴσω, 5. 2. 18; κατὰ γηλόφου, 1. 5. 8; ἐπὶ τὸ ἄκρον, 3. 4. 41; ἐπί τινα, 1. 8. 26, 5. 7. 24; εἰς τοὺς ἀνθρώπους, 4. 2. 7.

Ἱκανός, ή, όν (ἵκω), fit, suitable, ἱκανόν, sufficiently far, 5. 2. 30, with inf. 1. 2. 1, 5. 8. 20, 7. 1. 20, &c.; efficient, 5. 6. 15; fully qualified, 2. 3. 4; able, 1. 3. 6, 2. 6. 8, with inf. 3. 1. 23; a sufficient number, 1. 7. 7, 3. 2. 12, 4. 8. 25. Adv. ἱκανῶς, well enough, 4. 3. 31.

Ἱκετεύω, εύσω, &c. (ἱκέτης), to supplicate, entreat, with inf. 7. 4. 7, 10, 22.

Ἱκέτης, ου, ὁ (ἵκω), a suppliant, 7. 2. 33.

Ἰκόνιον, ου, τό Iconium, the capital of Lycaonia, fr. εἰκόνιον, an image of Medusa that Perseus set up, 1. 2. 19.

Ἴλεως, ως, ων, Att. for ἵλαος, propitious, 6. 4. 32.

Ἴλη, ης, ἡ (εἴλω, to gather; cf.

legio, lego), a troop of horse, Lat. turma (sixty-four men, eight front, eight deep); κατ' ἴλας=ἰλαδόν, by troops, opp. to κατὰ τάξεις, by companies (infantry), 1. 2. 16.

'Ιμάς, άντος, ὁ, a strap, thong, 4. 5. 14.

'Ιμάτιον, ου, τό (εἶμα, ἕννυμι), a cloak, pl. clothes, 7. 5. 5.

"Ινα, in order that, with conj. after a pres. 1. 3. 15, 2. 2. 12, 3. 2. 27, &c.; after a past, 2. 5. 36, 1. 4. 18, 4. 6. 6; with opt. after a past, 2. 3. 13, 21, 2. 6. 21, 1. 10 18, 7. 4. 11.▪

"Ιππαρχος, ου, ὁ (ἵππος, ἄρχω), a general ,of cavalry, 3. 3. 20.

'Ιππᾶσία, ας, ἡ, riding about, horse-exercise, 2. 5. 33.

'Ιππεία, ας, ἡ, cavalry, 5. 6. 8. .

'Ιππεύς, έως, ὁ, a horseman, pl. ἱππεῖς, cavalry, 3. 3. 20, 4. 3. 20, 1. 5. 13, &c.

'Ιππικός, ή, όν, of or belonging to a horse, τὸ ἱππικόν, the cavalry, 6. 3. 29, 30, 7. 3. 37 ; δύναμις, 1. 3. 12.

'Ιππόδρομος, ου, ὁ (ἵππος, δρόμος), a race-course, 1. 8. 20.

"Ιππος, ου, ὁ, a horse, 1. 9. 5, 7. 2. 8 ; ἐφ' ἵππου, on horseback, 3. 4. 47, 49, 7. 4. 4.

'Ιρις, ιος and ιδος, ὁ, a river in Pontus, 5. 6. 9.

'Ισθμός, οῦ, ὁ (εἰς, ἴθμα, εἶμι), an isthmus, ὁ Κορινθιακός, the isthmus of Corinth, 2. 6. 3.

'Ισόπλευρος, ος, ον (ἴσος, πλευρά), equal-sided, πλαίσιον, a square, 3. 4. 19.

Ἴσος, η, ον, equal, τὸ μῆκος, 5. 4. 32 ; εἰς τὸ ἴσον, to equal terms, 4. 6. 18 ; ἐν ἴσῳ, with equal step, 1. 8. 11; ἐξ ἴσου,

on equal terms, 3. 4. 47; ἴσον, equally, 2. 5. 7.

'Ισοχειλής, ής, ές (ἴσος, χεῖλος), κριθαί, barley on a level with the lips, malt up to the brim, 4. 5. 26.

'Ισσοί, ῶν, οἱ, and 'Ισσός, οῦ, ὁ, Issus, a town in Cilicia, 1. 2. 24.

"Ιστημι, στήσω, ἕστηκα, ἕσταμαι, 1 aor. ἕστησα, 2 aor. ἕστην, pres. impf. fut. and 1 aor. are trans.; 2 aor. perf. plp. are intrans., to make to stand, stop, 1. 2. 17, 10. 14; Mid. to stand, make a stand, 1. 10. 1, 4. 2. 19; τρόπαιον, to erect, 4. 6. 27.

'Ιστίον, ου, τό (ἵστημι), a sail, 1. 5. 3.

'Ισχυρός, ά, όν (ἰσχύς), strong, 2. 5. 22, 1. 5. 9; severe, χειμών, 5. 8. 14 ; a stronghold, 4. 6. 11, 5. 2. 7; adv. ἰσχυρῶς, severely, 4. 1. 16; κολάζειν, 2. 6. 9; very, exceedingly, ὠργίζοντο, 1. 5. 11; ἐπιθυμεῖν, 2. 6. 21 ; βαθύς, 1. 7. 15; ὄρθιος, 1. 2. 21, 4. 8. 28 ; vehemently, κατέτεινεν, 2. 5. 30; ἰσχυρῶς ἀλλήλων ἐπεμέλοντο, they took great care of each other, 4. 2. 26; strongly, 6. 1. 11.

'Ισχύς, ύος, ἡ (ἴς, Lat. vis, ἴσχω, ἔχω), strength, force, 1. 8. 22, 5. 7. 30.

"Ισχω, a form of ἔχω, hence 2 aor. ἔσχον, τὸ ἴσχον, the hindrance, 6. 3. 13; ἴσχετο ἐν τούτῳ, here there was a stoppage, a hitch, 6. 1. 9.

"Ισως, adv. perhaps, 2. 4. 4, 3. 2. 36, 3. 1. 37.

'Ιταβέλις, ιος, ὁ, or 'Ιταμβέλεσις, ιος, ὁ, Itabelis, a Persian commander in Comania, 7. 8. 15.

Ἴτυς, υος, ἡ (ἰέναι), the rim of the shield, 4. 7. 12.

Ἴχνιον, ου, τό (ἴχνος), a trace, 1. 6. 1.

Ἴχνος, εος, τό (ἴκω, ἱκνέομαι), a trace, φανερὰ ἦσαν, 1. 7. 17 ; pl. therefore, scattered, εἰ εἴη ἴχνη, 7. 3. 42.

Ἰωνία, ας, ἡ (ἠϊών, the coast), Ionia, in Asia Minor, adj. Ἰωνικός, ή, όν, Ionian, 1. 1. 6, 4. 13.

K.

Καθαίρω, ἀρῶ, κεκάθαρμαι (καθαρός), to make clean, to purify, 5. 7. 35, hence proper name Catharine, the pure one.

Καθάπερ (καθ᾽ ἅ περ), just as, 5. 4. 28.

Καθαρμός, οῦ, ὁ (καθαίρω), purification, 5. 7. 35.

Καθέζομαι, καθεδοῦμαι (κατά, ἕζομαι), to sit down, halt, 3. 1. 33, 5. 8. 14, 1. 5. 9.

Καθέλκω, έλξω, εἵλκῦκα, εἵλκυσμαι (κατά, ἕλκω), to draw down, 7. 1. 19.

Καθεύδω, ήσω (κατά, εὕδω), to sleep, 1. 3. 11.

Καθηγέομαι, ήσομαι, &c., to point out, 7. 8. 9.

Καθηδυπαθέω, ήσω (κατά, ἡδύς, πάθος), to squander in pleasures, 1. 3. 3.

Καθήκω, ήξω (κατά, ἥκω), to reach down, ἀπὸ τοῦ ὄρους, 3. 4. 24; ἐπὶ τὸν ποταμόν, 4. 3. 11; εἰς τὴν θάλατταν, 1. 4. 4, 6. 2. 3; impers. οἷς καθήκει, whose duty it is, 1. 9. 7.

Κάθημαι, ήσομαι (κατά, ἧμαι),

to sit, sit down, 4. 2. 5, 6, 5. 15, &c.; in council, 5. 10. 5, 7. 1. 33; to be encamped, 1. 3. 12.

Καθίζω, καθίσω and καθιῶ (κατά, ἴζω), to set, place, 2. 1. 4, 3. 5. 17.

Καθίημι, ήσω, &c. (κατά, ἵημι), to send down, let fall, εἰς προβολὴν δόρατα, having couched their spears, 6. 5. 25.

Καθίστημι, καταστήσω, καθέστηκα, καθέσταμαι (κατά, ἵστημι), to set in order, 1. 10. 10, 2. 3. 3; to set as guards, 3. 2. 1, 5. 1. 16; to bring, 1. 4. 13, 4. 8. 8, 5. 7. 34; to appoint, 3. 2. 5, 3. 1. 39; to make, 6. 1. 18, 7. 7. 23; ὡς καταστησομένων τούτων εἰς τὸ δέον, since these things would turn out well, 1. 3. 8; κατέστη εἰς τὴν βασιλείαν, was settled on the throne, 1. 1. 3; Mid. to set or place oneself, 1. 8. 3, 5. 9. 22.

Καθοράω, κατόψομαι, καθεώρακα, καθεώραμαι (κατά, ὁράω), to look down upon, behold, 4. 4. 15, 1. 8. 26, 1. 10. 14, 4. 3. 11, &c.

Καί, and, Lat. et; καί—καί, both—and, not only—but also; Lat. et—et, quum—tum, 1. 8. 1, 8, &c.; also, πολλαὶ δὲ καὶ πέλται, 2. 1. 6, &c.; although, with part. 1. 6. 1; even, 3. 1. 34, 2. 1. 22; καὶ γάρ (etenim), for, for truly; καὶ γὰρ οὖν, wherefore; καὶ δέ, and yet; καὶ δή, and even, even then, 1. 10. 10; καὶ εἰ, even if, although, 3. 2. 24; κἄν, 3. 2. 10; εἰ καί, 3. 2. 22.

Κάϊκος, ου, ὁ, The Caïcus, a river in Mysia, 7. 8. 8.

Καιναί, ῶν, αἱ, Cænæ, a town in Mesopotamia, 2. 4. 28.

Καίπερ, although, with part. 1. 6. 10, 2. 3. 25, 5. 5. 17, 18.

Καιρός, οῦ, ὁ, a fit time, opportunity, Lat. occasio, χρόνος = tempus, βοηθῆσαι, 5. 1. 8; ἐν καιρῷ, in season, 3. 1. 39; μέγιστον ἔχετε καιρόν, ye have a very great responsibility, 3. 1. 36; critical juncture, 3. 1. 44.

Καίτοι, and yet, yet, 7. 7. 45, 1. 4. 8.

Καίω, καύσω, κέκαυκα, κέκαυμαι, 1 aor. ἔκαυσα, poet. ἔκεα, to burn, 1. 6. 2; χιλόν, 1. 6. 1; κώμας, 3. 5. 3; χώραν, 3. 5. 5; πῦρ, 4. 4. 13, pl. 4. 1. 11, 6. 1. 20.

Κακόνοια, ας, ἡ, ill-will, 7. 7. 45, from

Κακόνους, ους, ουν (κακός, νόος), ill-disposed, 2. 5. 16, 27.

Κακοποιέω, ήσω, &c., to do ill to, lay waste, 2. 5. 4.

Κακός, ή, όν, bad, wicked; Comp. κακίων, Sup. κάκιστος, cowardly, 6. 4. 23, 1. 3. 18, 2. 6. 30; τὸ κακόν, evil, misfortune, 4. 8. 11; πάσχειν, 4. 3. 2, 14; ποιεῖν, 7. 4. 24; τί τινα, 7. 2. 33; τι χώραν κακὸν ἐργάζεσθαι, 5. 6. 11.

Κακουργέω, ήσω, to do evil, τινά, 5. 9. 1.

Κακουργός, οῦ, ὁ (κακός, ἔργον), a villain, 1. 9. 13.

Κακόω, ώσω, to treat badly, 4. 5. 35.

Κακῶς, adv. fr. κακός, ill, ἔχειν, 1. 5. 16; ἀποθνήσκειν, to die miserably, 3. 1. 43; ποιεῖν, to treat ill, 4. 8. 6; τινά, 1. 4. 8; πάσχειν, to be treated ill, 3. 3. 12, 7. 7. 16.

Κάκωσις, εως, ἡ (κακόω), ill-treatment, 4. 6. 3.

Καλάμη, ης, ἡ, straw, 5. 4. 27.

Κάλαμος, ου, ὁ, a reed, 1. 5. 1, 4. 5. 26; Lat. calamus.

Καλέω, ἔσω, κέκληκα, κέκλημαι, to call, summon, 1. 7. 18, 4. 1. 9, 1. 2. 2; to invite, ἐπὶ δεῖπνον, 7. 3. 15, ἐπὶ ξένια, 7. 6. 3.

Καλλιερέω, ήσω (καλός, ἱερόν), to have favourable signs in a sacrifice, obtain good omens, 7. 1. 40, 5. 4. 22.

Καλλίμαχος, ου, ὁ (καλός, μάχη), Callimachus, a Parrhasian captain, 4. 1. 27, 4. 7. 8, 10, 5. 10. 7, 9, 5. 6. 14.

Καλλωπισμός, οῦ, ὁ (καλός, ὤψ), adornment, 1. 9. 23.

Καλός, ή, όν, Comp. καλλίων, Sup. κάλλιστος, beautiful, noble, good, 7. 4. 7, 2. 6. 19, 2. 1. 9, &c.; εἰς καλόν, at the right time, 4. 7. 3; οὐδενὶ καλῷ ἔοικε, looks like nothing honourable, 6. 3. 17; τὸ. καλόν, honour, 2. 6. 18. Adv. καλῶς, beautifully, well, rightly, nobly, ἔχειν, to be or go well, 1. 8. 13; ἔχειν ὁρᾶσθαι, it was beautifully disposed to view, 2. 3. 3; τὰ τῶν θεῶν καλῶς εἶχεν, the rites of the gods were duly celebrated, 3. 2. 9.

Κάλπη, ης, ἡ, Calpe, a river and town in Bithynia, 6. 2. 1.

Καλχηδών, όνος, ἡ, Calchedon, a town in Bithynia, 7. 1. 20; Calchedonia, the district, 6. 4. 38.

Κάμνω, καμοῦμαι, κέκμηκα, 2 aor. ἔκαμον, to labour, be weary, sick, 3. 4. 47, 4. 5. 17, 5. 5. 20.

Κάν for καὶ ἐν, 6. 4. 5; κἄν for καὶ ἐάν, 1. 8. 12.

Κάνδυς, υος, ὁ, a cape, a Median upper garment with sleeves, 1. 5. 8.

Καπηλεῖον, ου, τό (κάπηλος, κάπτω, to eat), a tavern or shop, 1. 2. 24; ἔμπορος is the wholesale merchant, Lat. mercator; κάπηλος, the retailer.

Καπίθη, ης, ἡ, a measure=two choenices or half a gallon, 1. 5. 6.

Καπνός, οῦ, ὁ, smoke, 2. 2. 15.

Καππαδοκία, ας, ἡ, Cappadocia, a district in Asia Minor, 1.2.20.

Καππάδοξ, οκος, ὁ, a Cappadocian, an inhabitant of Cappadocia.

Κάπρος, ου, ὁ, a boar, 2. 2. 9.

Καρβάτιναι, ῶν, αἱ, shoes of undressed leather, brogues, 4. 5. 14.

Καρδία, ας, ἡ (κέαρ, κῆρ, Lat. cor), the heart, 2. 5. 23.

Καρδοῦχος, ου, ὁ, a Carduchian; οἱ Καρδοῦχοι, a hill tribe in Armenia; adj. Καρδούχιος, modern Kurds, Kurdistan, 4. 1. 2, 3, &c.

Καρπαία, ας, ἡ, a mimic dance among the Thessalians, 5. 9. 7.

Καρπός, οῦ, ὁ, fruit, 2. 5. 19, hence

Καρπόω, ώσω, to bear fruit; Mid. to gather in fruit, 5. 3. 13; τὴν χώραν, from the land, 3. 2. 23.

Κάρυον, ου, τό, a nut, τὰ πλατέα, the chestnut, 5. 4. 29, 32.

Κάρφη, ης, ἡ, hay=κάρφος, εος, τό, a dry stalk (κάρφω), 1. 5. 10.

Καστωλός, οῦ, ἡ, Castolus, a town in Lydia, 1. 1. 2, 1, 9. 7.

Κατά, a prep. gov. gen. and acc. with gen. down, 1. 5. 8, 4. 8. 28, 2. 17; under, 7. 7. 11; with acc. near, 5. 2. 16, 19, 4. 3. 17, 7. 2. 1, down to, to, 1. 8. 12, 5. 2. 23; on, 1. 8. 26, 5. 7. 25; καθ' ἁρπαγήν, for plunder, 3. 5. 2; καὶ κατὰ γῆν καὶ κατὰ θάλατταν, Lat. terra marique, by sea and land, 1. 1. 7; τὸ καθ' αὑτοὺς, on their own ground, 1. 8. 21, 7. 5. 13; in accordance with, according to, νόμον, 7. 2. 23; κατὰ σπουδήν, in haste, 7. 6. 28; τὸ κατὰ τοῦτον εἶναι, as far as this man is concerned, 1. 6. 9; καθ' ἑαυτούς, by themselves, 5. 10. 11; καθ' ἕνα, one by one, 4. 7. 8; ὀλίγους, 7. 6. 29; λόχους, 3. 4. 22; ἔθνη, 1. 8. 9; μῆνα, monthly, 1. 9. 17; ἐνιαυτόν, yearly, 3. 2. 12, &c.

Καταβαίνω, βήσομαι, βέβηκα, 2 aor. κατέβην, to go or come down, descend; κατὰ κλίμακος, 4. 5. 25; ἀπὸ μαστοῦ, 4. 2. 20; to enter the lists, in certamen descendere, 4. 8. 27; to go from the interior of a country to the sea, 2. 5. 22, 7. 4. 21.

Κατάβασις, εως, ἡ, descent, the march down, opp. to ἀνάβασις, 3. 4. 37, 5. 2. 28, 5. 5. 4, &c.

Καταβλακεύω, εύσω (κατά, βλακεύω, βλάξ, adj. slack), to mismanage, 7. 6. 22.

Καταγγέλλω, ελῶ, &c., to denounce, condemn, 2. 5. 38.

Κατάγειος, ος, ον (κατά, γῆ), underground, subterranean, 4. 5. 25.

Καταγελάω, άσομαι, γεγέλασμαι (κατά γελάω), to laugh at,

τινός, 2. 6. 23, 30, 1. 9. 13, 2. 4. 4.

Κατάγνυμι, άξω, ίᾶγα, έαγμαι (κατά, ἄγνυμι), to break, 4. 2. 20.

Καταγοητεύω, εύσω (κατά, γόης, a wizard), to cheat, to trick, 5. 7. 9.

Κατάγω, άξω, ῆχα, ῆγμαι (κατά, ἄγω), to bring in ships, 5. 1. 11; to restore, 1. 1. 7, 2. 2, arrive at, 3. 4. 36.

Καταδαπανάω,ήσω(κατά, δαπάνη, δάπτω), to waste, squander, 2. 2. 11.

Καταδειλιάω, άσω (κατά, δειλός, δέος), to show fear or cowardice, 7. 6. 22.

Καταδικάζω, άσω (κατά, δικάζω, δίκη), to give in judgment, 5. 8. 21; condemn, c. gen. ἐμαυτοῦ, 6. 4. 15; τινός θάνατον, to condemn to death, Lat. capitis damnare.

Καταδιώκω, ξω (κατά, διώκω), to pursue close, 4. 2. 5.

Καταδοξάζω, άσω=καταδοκέω, to form an opinion against one, τινός, 7. 7. 30.

Καταδύω, δύσω, δέδυκα, δέδυμαι, to sink, Act. 1. 3. 17, 7. 2. 13; Mid. and 2 aor. κατέδυν, p. and plp. Neut. to sink, 3. 5. 11, 4. 5. 36; κατὰ τῆς γῆς, 7. 7. 11.

Καταθεάομαι, άσομαι, &c., to look down upon, watch from above, 6. 3. 30, εἴς τι, 1. 8. 14.

Καταθέω, θεύσομαι, to run down, 7. 3. 44.

Καταθύω, θύσω, &c., to sacrifice, 3. 2. 12, 4. 5. 35, 5. 5. 3; τὴν δεκάτην, to dedicate, 5. 3. 13.

Καταισχύνω, ὐνῶ, &c., to disgrace, be a disgrace to, τὴν πατρίδα, 3. 1. 30, 2. 14.

Κατακαίνω, κᾰνῶ, 2 aor. κατέκανον (κατά, καίνω), to kill, 3. 1. 2, &c.

Κατακαίω, καύσω, &c., to burn down or up, ἁμάξας, 3. 3. 1; βασίλεια, 1. 4. 10; κώμας, 7. 4. 1; γῆν, 7. 7. 5; 1 a. p. κατεκαύθην, 5. 2. 27, 4. 26, 7. 4. 18.

Κατάκειμαι, κείσομαι, to lie down, 3. 1. 15, 4. 4. 11, 3. 1. 13, 14.

Κατακηρύττω, ξω, &c., to proclaim by herald, σιγήν, 2. 2. 20.

Κατακλείω, κλείσω, &c., or κατακλήω, κλήσω, &c., to shut in, 3. 4. 26, plp. p. κατεκεκλήμην, 3. 3. 7; 1 a. p. κατεκλήσθην, 7. 2. 15.

Κατακοντίζω, ίσω (κατά, ἀκοντίζω), to shoot down with darts, 7. 4. 6.

Κατακύπτω, κόψω, &c., to cut down, or cut up, 1. 8. 24, 1. 5. 16, &c.

Κατακτείνω, κτενῶ, ἔκτονα, 2 aor. κατέκτανον, to kill, slay, 2. 5. 10, 4. 8. 25.

Κατακωλύω, ύσω, &c., to keep back, ἔξω, 5. 2. 16.

Καταλαμβάνω, λήψομαι, εἴληφα, εἴλημμαι, 2 aor. κατέλαβον, to seize upon, 1. 3. 14, 4. 1. 4; to find, 3. 1. 8; with part. 1. 10. 18, &c., κατελήφθη, was caught, 1. 8. 20, 4. 2. 14, 4. 7. 4; to reach, Πέργαμον, 7. 8. 8; to overtake, 2. 2. 12, 3. 3. 8, 9, 15, &c.

Καταλέγω, λέξω, &c., to reckon, 2. 6. 27.

Καταλείπω, λείψω, λέλοιπα, λέλειμμαι, 2 aor. κατέλιπον, to leave (behind), τὴν ὁδόν, 4. 2. 7, 4. 2. 13, 3. 1. 2, 5. 3. 6, 3. 3. 19, &c.

Καταλεύω, λεύσω, 1 aor. p. κατελεύσθην (κατά, λεύω), to stone to death, 1. 5. 14, 5. 7. 2, 19, 7. 6. 10.

Καταλλάττω, άξω, &c., pass., to become reconciled, τινί, 1. 6. 1.

Καταλογίζομαι, ίσομαι, to reckon, 5. 6. 16.

Καταλύω, λύσω, &c., to put down, destroy, ἀρχήν, 5. 10. 12, 6. 1. 1; to end (τὸν πόλεμον), 1. 1. 10, 5. 7. 27; to halt (to unloose the horses, &c.), 1. 8. 1; πρὸς ἄριστον, 1. 10. 19.

Καταμανθάνω, μαθήσομαι, &c., 2 aor. κατέμαθον, to learn thoroughly, σωφροσύνην, 1. 9. 3; to learn, know, find, τι, 3. 1. 44; ὅτι, 7. 2. 18, 7. 43; τὸ χωρίον ὅτι μικρὸν εἴη, 5. 7. 14, 2. 3. 11; κατέμαθον ἀνασστὰς μόλις or μόγις, I found I could hardly rise, 5. 8. 14.

Καταμελέω, ήσω, to be careless, neglect one's duty, 5. 8. 1.

Καταμένω, μενῶ, μεμένηκα, to stay behind, 6. 4. 2, 28, 7. 3. 47; παρ' ἑαυτῷ, 7. 6. 43, 5. 6. 17, 19.

Καταμερίζω, ίσω, or ιῶ (κατά, μερίζω, μέρος), to distribute, 7. 5. 4.

Καταμίγνυμι, μίξω, &c., to mix, mingle, 7. 2. 3.

Κατανοέω, ήσω, &c., to observe, notice, 7. 7. 43, 1. 2. 4, 7. 7. 45.

Καταντιπέρας, adv. (κατά, ἀντί, πέρας), right opposite, Lat. e regione, 1. 1. 9, 4. 8. 3.

Καταπέμπω, πέμψω, &c., to send down from the interior to the coast, 1. 9. 7.

Καταπετρόω, ώσω, =καταλεύω, to stone to death, 1. 3. 2.

Καταπηδάω, ήσω, to leap down

from, ἐκ τοῦ ἅρματος, 1. 8. 3; ἀπὸ τοῦ ἵππου, 1. 8. 28, 3. 4. 48.

Καταπίπτω, πεσοῦμαι, πέπτωκα, 2 aor. κατέπεσον, to fall down, 3. 2. 19.

Καταπολεμέω, ήσω, &c., pass., to be reduced by war, 7. 1. 27.

Καταπράττω, άξω, &c., to accomplish, achieve, τι, 1. 2. 2, 7. 7. 46; τινί τι, 7. 7. 17.

Καταράομαι, άσομαι, κατήραμαι (κατά, ἀράομαι), to call down curses on, 5. 6. 4; τινί, 7. 7. 48.

Κατασβέννυμι, σβέσω, ἔσβηκα, ἔσβεσμαι, to extinguish, πυρά, 6. 1. 21.

Κατασκεδάννυμι, σκεδάσω, &c., to scatter, sprinkle about, 7. 3. 32.

Κατασκέπτομαι, better κατασκοπέω, σκέψομαι, κατέσκεμμαι, to take a view of, 1. 5. 12.

Κατασκευάζω, άσω, &c., to prepare, furnish, 1. 9. 19; ὡς with gen. 3. 2. 24, 3. 3. 19.

Κατασκηνέω, ήσω, &c., to pitch one's tent, to encamp, 3. 4. 32, 7. 4. 11, the same as

Κατασκηνόω, ώσω, &c., 2. 2. 16.

Κατασκοπή, ῆς, ἡ (κατά, σκοπέω), watching, reconnoitring, 7. 4. 13.

Κατασπάω, σπάσω, &c., to draw or pull down, 1. 9. 6.

Κατάστασις, εως, ἡ (καθίστημι), condition, constitution, 5. 7. 26.

Καταστρατοπεδεύω, εύσω, &c., to encamp, 3. 4. 18, 4. 5. 1, &c.

Καταστρέφω, στρέψω, &c., to conquer, subdue, 1. 9. 14.

Κατασφάττω, άξω, and also

Κατασφάζω, to kill, murder, Lat. contrucidare, 4. 1. 23.

Κατασχίζω, σχίσω, to cleave asunder, burst open, Lat. perfringere, 7. 1. 16.

Καρατείνω, τενῶ, τέτἄκα, τέτᾰμαι, to stretch tight, strain one's self, strive earnestly, Lat. contendere, 2. 5. 30.

Καρατέμνω, τεμῶ, τέτμηκα, τέτμημαι, plp. 3 pl. κατετέτμηντο, to cut, 2. 4. 13 ; to cut in pieces, 4. 7. 26.

Καρατίθημι, θήσω, &c., to lay or put down, 7. 1. 37 ; ὅπλα, 5. 2. 15 ; μαρσίπους ἐν πέτρᾳ, 4. 3. 11 ; τὴν φιλίαν παρὰ τοῖς θεοῖς, to deposit, 2. 5. 8 ; χρήματα, to lay up or by, 1. 3. 3 ; ἀποστροφήν, to establish, 7. 6. 34.

Καρατιτρώσκω, τρώσω, to cover with wounds, wound severely, 3. 4. 26, 4. 1. 10.

Καταρρέχω, θρέξω, better δραμοῦμαι, δεδράμηκα, to run down, 5. 4. 23, 7. 1. 20.

Καταυλίζομαι, ίσομαι, to encamp, 7. 5. 15, castra locare.

Καταφαγεῖν, see κατεσθίω.

Καταφανής, ής, ές (κατά, φαίνω), in sight, clearly seen, 1. 8. 8, 2. 3. 3, &c.

Καταφεύγω, φεύξομαι, &c., to flee for refuge, Lat. confugere, 1. 5. 13, 3. 4. 11 ; εἰς, 5. 7. 2.

Καταφρονέω, ήσω, &c., to despise, τινός and τινά, 3. 4. 2, 5. 7. 12.

Καταχωρίζω, ίσω, Att. ιῶ, to bring to a place, station, 6. 3. 10.

Κατεῖδον, see καθοράω.

Κάτειμι, to go or come down, 5. 7. 13.

Κατεργάζομαι, άσομαι, εἰργασμαι, to work out, effect, gain, 1. 9. 20, 5. 10. 10, 7. 7. 26.

Κατέρχομαι, ελεύσομαι, ελήλυθα, to go or come down, 7. 2. 2.

Κατεσθίω, έδομαι, &c., 2 aor. κατέφαγον, to eat up, devour, τινὰ ὠμόν, 4. 8. 14.

Κατέχω, καθέξω or κατασχήσω, κατέσχηκα, κατέσχημαι, 2 aor. κάτεσχον, to have, hold, Lat. retinere, 4. 2. 1, 5, 6, 12, 5. 6. 7 ; keep, Lat. continere, 4. 8. 12 ; maintain, 7. 7. 28 ; restrain, 7. 7. 29, 3. 1. 20 ; compel, 2. 6. 13 ; reach, 5. 6. 20, 9. 33.

Κατηγορέω, ήσω (κατά, ἀγορεύω), to speak against, charge, accuse, τινός, 5. 7. 4, 8. 1, 7. 7. 44.

Κατηρεμίζω, ίσω, &c. (κατά, ἠρεμέω, ἠρέμα), to calm, appease, 7. 1. 24. So κατηρεμέω, ήσω, 7. 1. 22.

Κατιδεῖν, see καθοράω.

Κατοικέω, ήσω, &c. (κατά, οἶκος), to dwell in, inhabit, 5. 3. 7.

Κατοικίζω, ίσω, Att. ιῶ, &c., to found, πόλιν, 5. 6. 15, 6. 2. 7.

Κατορύττω, ύξω, ορώρυχα, ορώρυγμαι, and ὥρυγμαι, to bury, οἶνον, 4. 5. 29 ; ἄνθρωπον, 5. 8. 9, 11.

Κάτω, adv. down, below, πρὸς τὸ κάτω, to the lower part, 4. 2. 28, 4. 8. 28.

Καῦμα, ατος, τό (καίω), heat, 1. 7, 6.

Καύσιμος, ος, ον (καίω), fit for burning, 6. 1. 15, 19.

Κάϋστρος, ου, ὁ, the Caÿster, a river in Lydia, hence adj. Καύστριος, α, ον, 1. 2. 11.

Κέγχρος, ου, ὁ, millet, a kind of grain, Lat. milium, 1. 2. 22.

Κεῖμαι, κείσομαι, to lie, 2. 4. 12, 3. 4. 10, 1. 8. 27 ; ὅπλα, 4. 2. 20 ; τράπεζαι, 7. 3. 23.

Κελαιναί, ῶν, αἱ, Celænæ, a town in Phrygia, 1. 2. 7.

Κελεύω, εύσω, κεκέλευκα, κεκέλευσμαι (κέλομαι), to order, 2. 3. 1; with acc. and inf. 1. 5. 8, 13, 2. 1. 8. &c.

Κενός, ή, όν, empty, 3. 4. 20; ἅρμα, 1. 8. 20; φόβος, groundless, 2. 2. 21. Comp. κενότερος, Sup. κενότατος, from poet. κεινός.

Κενοτάφιον, ου, τό (κενός, τάφος, θάπτω), an empty tomb, cenotaph, 6. 2. 9.

Κεντέω, ήσω, Ep. κένσω, κεκέντημαι, to prick, goad, torment, 3. 1. 29.

Κεντρίτης, ου ὁ, the Centrites, a river in Armenia, 4. 3. 1.

Κεράμιον, ου, τό (κέραμος, clay), an earthenware vessel, a jar, containing 5⅞ gall. liquid measure, 5. 9. 15, 10. 3.

Κεράμιος, α, ον, made of clay, 3. 4. 7.

Κεραμῶν ἀγορά, the Ceramian forum, a town in Mysia, 1. 2. 10.

Κεράννυμι, κεράσω, κεκέρακα late, κεκέρασμαι, and κέκραμαι, to mix, 1. 2. 13, 5. 4. 29.

Κέρας, ἄτος, τό, a horn for blowing, 2. 2. 4; to drink with, 7. 2. 23; the wing of an army, ἐπὶ κέρας ἄγειν, to lead in column, i.e. with few men in front, Lat. longo agmine, opp. ἐπὶ φάλαγγος, in phalanx, i.e. with a broad front, Lat. quadrato agmine, κατά, 4. 6. 6, 6. 3. 5; a mountain peak, Lat. jugum, 5. 6. 7.

Κερασοῦς, οῦντος, ἡ, Cerasus, a town in Pontus, the inh. Κερασούντιοι, 5. 7. 13, 16: hence cherry, because first

brought from Cerasus to Rome by Lucullus, 73 B.C.

Κεράτινος, η, ον, adj. from κέρας, made of horn, ποτήρια, 5. 9. 4.

Κέρβερος, ου, ὁ, Cerberus (κέρω, to cut, βέρω, to devour; prob. onomat. like βάρβαρος, Τάρταρος, &c.), the three-headed dog that guards the entrance to Hades, 5. 10. 2.

Κερδαίνω, κερδανῶ, (κεκέρδηκα) (κέρδος), to gain, 2. 6. 21.

Κερδαλέος, α, ον (κέρδος), profitable, 1. 9. 17.

Κέρδος, εος, τό, gain, 1. 9. 17.

Κέρσος, ου, ὁ, Cersus, a river in Cilicia, 1. 4. 4, al. Κάρσος.

Κερτόνιον, ου, τό, Certonium, a town in Mysia, 7. 8. 8, al. Κυτώνιον, Κερτωνόν.

Κεφαλαλγής, ής, ές (κεφαλή, ἄλγος), causing headaches, 2. 3. 15.

Κεφαλή, ῆς, ἡ, the head, 7. 4. 4, 3. 1. 17.

Κηδεμών, όνος, ὁ (κήδω), one who cares for another, a friend, 3. 1. 17.

Κήδω, κηδήσω, κέκηδα, Act. to trouble; Mid. to care for, with gen. 7. 5. 5.

Κηρίον, ου, τό (κηρός), a honeycomb, 4. 8. 20.

Κηρύκιον, ου, τό (κῆρυξ), a herald's wand, Lat. caduceus, usually represented with two serpents twisted round it, 5. 7. 30.

Κῆρυξ, ῦκος, ὁ, a herald, 2. 2. 20, 3. 1. 46, &c.

Κηρύττω or κηρύσσω, ύξω, κεκήρυχα, κεκήρυγμαι, to proclaim, announce, impers. sc. κῆρυξ, proclamation is made, 3. 4. 36; inf. 4. 1. 13, 6. 2. 15.

Κηφισόδωρος, ου, ὁ (Κηφισός, δῶρον), *Cephisodorus*, a Greek captain, 4. 2. 13.

Κηφισοφῶν, ῶντος, ὁ (Κηφισός), *Cephisophon*, an Athenian, 4. 2. 13.

Κιβώτιον, ου, τό, a box, chest, 7. 5. 14, diui. fr. κιβωτός.

Κιλικία, ας, ἡ, *Cilicia*, a district in Asia Minor, divided into ἡ ὀρεινή or τραχεῖα, *Cilicia trachœa*, rocky *Cilicia*, and ἡ Κ. πεδιάς, *Cilicia campestris*, the flat *Cilicia*, 1. 2. 21. Κίλιξ, ικος, ὁ, a *Cilician*, fem. Κίλισσα, 1. 2. 16.

Κινδυνεύω, εύσω, &c. (κίνδυνος), to incur danger, run a risk, 1. 1. 4; acc and inf. 5. 6. 19.

Κίνδυνος, ου, ὁ, danger, risk, κίνδυνός ἐστι, with inf., 2. 5. 17, 5. 1. 6, 9. 21; with μή and conj., 7. 7. 31.

Κινέω, ήσω, &c. (κίω), to move, 3. 4. 28, 6. 2. 27, 4. 5. 13.

Κιττός, οῦ, ὁ, ivy, Lat. *hedera*, 5. 4. 12.

Κλεαγόρας, ου, ὁ (κλέος, glory, ἀγορά), *Cleagoras*, a painter in Athens, 7. 8. 1.

Κλεαίνετος, ου, ὁ (κλέος, αἰνέω), *Clecenetus*, 5. 1. 17.

Κλέανδρος, ου, ὁ (κλέος, ἀνήρ), *Cleander*, a Spartan harmost, 6. 4. 5, 7. 2. 6, 1. 8.

Κλεάνωρ, ορος, ὁ (κλέος, ἀνήρ), *Cleanor*, a Greek general, 3. 1. 47, 2. 4, 7. 5. 10.

Κλεάρετος, ου, ὁ (κλέος, ἀρετή), or Κλεάρατος, *Clearetus*, 5. 7. 14, 16.

Κλέαρχος, ου, ὁ (κλέος, ἀρχή), *Clearchus*, the most famous of the Greek generals, 1. 1. 9, 2. 6. 1, 2. 5. 32.

Κλεῖθρον, ου, τό (κλείω), a bolt or bar, 7. 1. 17.

Κλείω, κλείσω, κέκλεικα, κέκλειμαι and -σμαι, to shut, 7. 1. 36.

Κλέπτω, κλέψω, κέκλοφα, κέκλεμμαι, to steal, 4. 6. 14, 15, 16, &c.

Κλεώνυμος, ου, ὁ (κλέος, ὄνομα), *Cleonymus*, a Spartan, 4.1.18.

Κλῖμαξ, ακος, ἡ (κλίνω), a ladder, 4. 5. 25.

Κλίνη, ης, ἡ (κλίνω), a couch, bed, 4. 4. 21.

Κλοπή, ῆς, ἡ (κλέπτω), a theft, 4. 6. 14.

Κλωπεύω, εύσω, to steal, 5. 9. 1, from

Κλώψ, κλωπός, ὁ (κλέπτω), a thief, 4. 6. 17.

Κνέφας, αος and ους, τό (νέφος, a cloud), twilight, dawn, 4. 5. 9.

Κνημίς, ῖδος, ἡ (κνήμη, the shin-bone), a greave, legging, 1. 2. 16, &c.

Κόγχη, ης, ἡ, concha, a mussel, 5. 3. 8.

Κογχυλιάτης, ου, ὁ, sc. λίθος, shelly-marble, 3. 4. 10.

Κοῖλος, η, ον, hollow, 5. 4. 31.

Κοιμάω, ήσω, &c. (κεῖμαι), to put to sleep; Mid. to fall asleep, 4. 3. 2.

Κοινός, ή, όν (σύν), common; τό κοινόν, the community, 5. 6. 27; ἀπὸ κοινοῦ, at the public expense, 4. 7. 27, 5. 1. 12; the public council, 5. 7. 17, 18.

Κοινόω, ώσω, &c. (κοινός), to make common; Mid. to consult, 5. 10. 15, 5. 6. 27; to communicate, 5. 6. 36.

Κοινωνέω, ήσω, &c. (κοινωνός), to take part, share, τινός, in anything; τινί, with a person, 7. 6. 28.

Κοινωνός, οῦ, ὁ (κοινός), a sharer, partner, 7. 2. 38.

Κοιρατάδης, ου, ὁ, Cæratades, a Theban, 7. 1. 33.

Κοῖτοι, ων, οἱ, the Cætæ, a people in Pontus, 7. 8. 25.

Κολάζω, άσω, κεκόλασμαι (κολάω), to punish, 2. 6. 9, 5.'13.

Κόλασις, εως, ἡ (κολάζω), punishment, 7. 7. 24.

Κολοσσαί, ῶν, αἱ, Colossæ, a town in Phrygia, 1. 2. 6.

Κολχίς, ίδος, ἡ, Colchis, a country at the eastern extremity of the Black Sea, 4. 8. 23, 5. 3. 2. Κόλχοι, the people, the Colchians, 4. 8. 8.

Κολωνός, οῦ, ὁ=κολώνη, collis, a mound, cairn, 4. 7. 25.

Κομανία, ας, ἡ, Comania, a castle in Mysia, 7. 8. 15.

Κομιδή, ῆς, ἡ (κομίζω), conveyance, 5. 1. 11.

Κομίζω, ίσω, Att. ιῶ, &c. (κομέω), to fetch, bring, convey; Mid. to come, return, 3. 2. 26, 5. 4. 1, 5. 20.

Κονιᾱτός, ή, όν (κονία, dust), plastered, 4. 2. 22.

Κονιορτός, οῦ, ὁ (κόνις, ὄρνυμι), a cloud of dust, 1. 8. 8.

Κόπος,ου,ὁ(κόπτω),fatigue,5.8.3.

Κόπρος, ου, ὁ, dung, 1. 6. 1.

Κόπτω, κόψω, κέκοφα, κέκομμαι, to cut down, δένδρα, 4. 8. 2; to knock at (from the outside), ψοφέω, from the inside, πύλας, 7. 1. 16; to slaughter, 2. 1. 6.

Κόρη, ης, ἡ, a maiden, 4. 5. 9.

Κορσωτή, ῆς, ἡ, Corsote, a town in Mesopotamia, 1. 5. 4.

Κορύλας, α, ὁ, Corylas, a Paphlagonian, 5. 5. 12, 22.

Κορυφή, ῆς, ἡ (κόρυς), top, summit, 4. 2. 20.

Κορώνεια, ας, ἡ, Coronēa, a town in Bœotia, where Agesilaus defeated the allied Greeks, B.C. 394, 5. 3. 6.

Κυσμέω, ήσω, &c. (κόσμος), to order, arrange, 3. 2. 36; to dress, adorn, 1. 9. 23.

Κόσμιος, ος, ον, or a, ον (κόσμος), orderly, under good discipline, 6. 4. 32.

Κόσμος, ου, ὁ, order, an ornament, 1. 9. 3; hence, the world.

Κοτύωρα, ων, τά, Cotyora, a town in Pontus, 5. 5. 3; Κοτυωρίτης, an inhabitant, 5. 5. 6.

Κοῦφος, η, ον, light, not heavy, 1. 5. 10; adv. κούφως, 6. 1. 5.

Κράζω, κεκράξομαι, κέκρᾱγα, to cry out, 2 aor. ἔκρᾱγον, 7.8.15.

Κράνος, εος, τό (κράς, κάρα, the head), a helmet, 1. 2. 16.

Κρατέω, ήσω, &c. (κράτος), to rule, prevail over, conquer, 3. 2. 26, 2. 1. 10; τινός, 2. 5. 7, 7. 2. 25; get possession of, 7. 3. 3; to hold, 5. 6. 7, with acc.

Κρατήρ, ῆρος, ὁ (κεράννυμι), a goblet, a large bowl, 4. 5. 26.

Κράτιστος, η, ον, superl. from κρατύς, used as superl. of ἀγαθός, the strongest, best, noblest, 1. 9. 2, 18, &c.; κράτιστον ἡμῖν, most for our benefit, 3. 4. 41, 6. 1. 13; adv. κράτιστα, 5. 2. 11, 3. 2. 6.

Κράτος, εος, τό (κράς), strength, κατὰ κράτος, with all one's might, 1.9.18, 7. 7. 7; so ἀνὰ κράτος, 1. 10. 15; ἐλαύνειν, to ride at full gallop, 1. 8. 1.

Κραυγή, ῆς, ἡ (κράζω), a shout, 1. 5. 12.

Κρέας, ἄτος or ως, τό, flesh, often pl. τὰ κρέα, 1. 5. 2.

Κρείττων, ων, ον, or κρείσσων, comp. of κρατύς used as comp. of ἀγαθός, *better, stronger, nobler, more powerful*; acc. m. or f. κρείττονα, κρείττω, 2. 2. 10, &c.

Κρεμάννυμι, άσω, κεκρέμασμαι, *to hang up*; Mid. *to hang*, and κρέμαμαι, κρεμήσομαι, ἐφ' ἵππων, *on horses*, 3. 2. 19; ὄρη (*impendebant*), 4. 1. 2.

Κρήνη, ης, ἡ (ἐκ, ῥέω), *a fountain*, 1. 2. 13, 6. 4. 4.

Κρηπίς, ῖδος, ἡ, Lat. *crepido, foundation, basement*, 3. 4. 7.

Κρής, Κρητός, ὁ, *a Cretan*. The Cretans were famous archers, 1. 2. 9, 3. 3. 7.

Κριθή, ῆς, ἡ, *barley*, often pl., 1. 2. 22, 3. 4. 31; adj. is

Κρίθινος, η, ον, *made of barley*, 4. 5. 31; οἶνος, *beer*, or, as some think, *whisky*, 4. 5. 26.

Κρίνω, κρινῶ, κέκρικα, κέκρῐμαι, *to judge, try*, 6. 4. 16; *distinguish*, 1. 9. 30; *consider*, with acc. and inf., 1. 9. 5, 20, 28, etc.

Κριός, οῦ, ὁ, *a ram*, 2. 2. 9.

Κρίσις, εως, ἡ (κρίνω), *a trial*, 1. 6. 5, 6. 4. 20.

Κρόμμυον, ου, τό, or κρόμυον (κόρη, *the pupil of the eye*, and μύω, *to close?*), *an onion*, 7. 1. 37.

Κροτέω, ήσω, etc. (κρότος, κρούω), *to strike* = κρούω, κρούσω, etc., 5. 9. 10, 4. 5. 18.

Κρότος, ου, ὁ, *a noise* produced by striking, 5. 9. 13.

Κρύπτω, κρύψω, κέκρυφα, κέκρυμμαι, 2 aor. pass. ἐκρύβην, *to conceal*, τινά τι, 1. 9. 19, 1. 4. 12, 5. 9. 18.

Κρωβύλος, ου, ὁ, *a knot of hair* on a helmet, 5. 4. 13.

Κτάομαι, κτήσομαι, κέκτημαι and ἕκτημαι, *to acquire, possess*, 1. 7. 3, &c.; *get, make*, 2. 6. 26, 5. 5. 17.

Κτείνω, κτενῶ, ἕκτονα, ἕκτᾰκα and ἕκταγκα, 2 aor. ἕκτᾰνον, *to kill, slay*, 2. 5. 32.

Κτῆμα, ατος, τό (κτάομαι), *property*, 7. 7. 41.

Κτῆνος, εος, τό (κτάομαι), pl. *cattle, beasts of burden*, 4. 5. 25.

Κτησίας, ου, ὁ (κτάομαι), *Ctesias*, Artaxerxes' physician, 1. 8. 26.

Κυβερνήτης, ου, ὁ (κυβερνάω), *a steersman*, Lat. *gubernator*, 5. 8. 20.

Κυβιστάω, ήσω (κύπτω), *to turn a somerset*, 6. 1. 9.

Κύδνος, ου, ὁ, *Cydnus*, a river in Cilicia, 1. 2. 23.

Κυζικηνός, ή, όν, *of* or *from Cyzicus* (Κύζικος, ου, ἡ, a town in Arctonnesus in the Propontis). ὁ Κυζικηνός (στατήρ) was a gold coin equal to 28 Attic drachmæ, or £1 2s. 9d., 5. 6. 23, 10. 4, 7. 3. 10.

Κύκλος, ου, ὁ, *a circle, a ring*, 3. 4. 7, 5. 7. 2; κύκλῳ, *in a circle*, 7. 8. 18; *round about*, 3. 1. 12; ἡ κύκλῳ χώρα, *the country round*, 5. 6. 20, 3. 5. 14; hence

Κυκλόω, ώσω, &c., *to surround*, 1. 8. 13, 4. 2. 15, 6. 2. 20; and

Κύκλωσις, εως, ἡ, *a surrounding, encircling*, 1. 8. 23.

Κυλίνδω, and κυλινδέω, and κυλίω, κυλινδήσω, and κυλίσω, κεκύλισμαι, *to roll*, 4. 2. 20, 8. 28, 5. 2. 31.

Κῦμα, ατος, τό (κύω, *to swell*), *a wave*.

Κυνίσκος, ου, ὁ (κύων), *Cyniscus*, a Spartan, 7. 1. 13.

Κυπαρίσσϊνος or ίττινος, η, ον, *of cypress* (κυπάρισσος), 5. 3. 12.

Κύπτω, κύψω, κέκυφα, *to stoop*, compd. with ἐπὶ, 4. 5. 32.

Κύρως, α, ον, and ος, ον (κῦρος, *power*), *having power*, 5. 7. 27.

Κῦρος, ου, ὁ (from *kohr*, Persian for *the sun*), *Cyrus* ὁ νεώτερος, *the Younger*, the second of the two sons of Darius Nothus and Parysatis, died at Cunaxa B.C. 401, Sept. 7th, 1. 8. 27, etc. Cyrus the Elder, ὁ παλαιός or ἀρχαῖος, defeated Astyages, and became king of the Medes and Persians 559 B.C.; conquered Crœsus, king of Lydia, 546 B.C., and was killed 529, 1. 9. 1. Adj.

Κυρεῖος, α, ον, *of or belonging to Cyrus*; οἱ Κυρεῖοι, *the followers of Cyrus*, 1. 10. 1, 3. 2. 17, 7. 2. 7.

Κύων, κυνός, ὁ, and ἡ, *a dog*, 3. 2. 35.

Κωλύω(ῠ), ύσω, κεκώλυκα, κεκώλυμαι, *to hinder*, τινά τινος, 1. 6. 2, 4. 8. 5, &c., with inf. 1. 7. 19, 4. 3. 3, 7, 4. 7. 5.

Κωμάρχης, ου, ὁ (κώμη, ἄρχω), *a village chief*, 4. 5. 10.

Κώμη, ης, ἡ (κεῖμαι), *a village*; κωμήτης, ου, ὁ, *a villager*, 4. 5. 24.

Κώπη, ης, ἡ (κύπτω or κάπτω, *capio*), *an oar*, 6. 2. 2.

Λ

Λαγχάνω, λήξομαι, εἴληχα, εἴληγμαι, 2 aor. ἔλαχον (λάχω), *to*

obtain by lot, 4. 5. 24, *to get*, 3. 1. 11.

Λαγώς, ώ, ὁ, *a hare*, 4. 5. 24.

Λάθρᾳ, adv. (λάθω, λανθάνω), *secretly, without the knowledge of*, τινός, 1. 3. 8, al. λάθρᾱ.

Λακεδαιμόνιος, α, ον, adj. from

Λακεδαίμων, ονος, ἡ (λάκκος " a hollow "), *Lacedæmon*, or *Sparta*, in the Peloponnesus, 1. 1. 9, 4. 3, 7. 1. 25.

Λάκκος, ου, ὁ, *a hole, pit, vat*, Lat, *lacus*, 4. 2. 22.

Λακτίζω, ίσω (λάξ, adv. *with the heels*), *to kick*, 3. 2. 18.

Λάκων, ωνος, ὁ, *a Laconian*, Spartan, 5. 1. 15; and the adj. is

Λακωνικός, ή, όν, *Laconian*, 4. 1. 18.

Λαμβάνω, λήψομαι, εἴληφα, εἴλημμαι, 2 aor. ἔλαβον, *to take, seize*, 2. 1. 10, 3. 4. 49, &c.; *find, catch*, 1. 1. 6, 2. 3. 21, &c.; *receive*, 1. 9. 22, 3. 4. 8; Mid. *take hold of*, τινὰ τῆς ζώνης, 1. 6. 10.

Λαμπρός, ά, όν (λάμπω), *bright, illustrious*, 7. 7. 41, hence

Λαμπρότης, τητος, ἡ, *brightness*, 1. 2. 18.

Λάμπω, λάμψω. λέλαμπα, *to shine*, 3. 1. 11, 12.

Λαμψακηνός, ή, όν, adj. from

Λάμψακος, ου, ἡ, *Lampsacus*, a town in Mysia, 7. 8. 1, 3.

Λανθάνω, λήσω, λέληθα, λέλησμαι, 2 aor. ἔλαθον, *to lie hid, escape notice*; Mid. *to forget*; 5. 9. 18, 4. 1. 3; with part. τρεφόμενον ἐλάνθανε, *was secretly supported*, 1. 1. 9, 10, 1. 3. 17, 4. 2. 7; λήσομεν ἐπιπεσόντες, *we shall fall on them unawares*, 7. 3. 43, 6. 1. 22.

G

Λάρισσα, ης, ἡ,* *Larissa*, a town in Assyria, 3. 4. 7.

Λάσιος, α, ον (cf. δασύς), *rough, bushy*, 5. 2. 29, 6. 2. 26.

Λάφυρον, ου, τό (λάπτω, λαπάζω, *to plunder*), *spoils*, 6. 4. 38, seldom sing. ; hence

Λαφυροπωλέω, ήσω, *to sell booty*, 6. 4. 38.

Λαφυροπώλης, ου, ὁ, *a seller of booty*, 7. 7. 56.

Λάχος, εος, τό (λαγχάνω), *a lot or share*, 5. 3. 9, 6. 1. 2.

Λέγω, λέξω, λέλεγμαι, *to say*, perf. *I have said*, εἴρηκα, 2 aor. εἶπον (but εἴλοχα, εἴλεγμαι, *to gather*), πρός, 2. 5. 25, 7. 7. 15; εἰς, 5. 6. 28; ἐν, 5. 7.10; διά, 2. 3. 17; ὅτι, 1. 2. 21, 5. 9. 23 ; acc. and inf. 5. 7. 34, 1. 8. 6, 4. 1. 3, 1. 3. 8; *to speak, speak of, to mention*, 1. 2. 11, 1. 5. 15, 3. 1. 26; λεγόμενος, *said to be, considered*, 1. 10. 2, 5. 6. 4, 1. 6. 1.

Λεία, ας, ἡ (λάω, *to take*), *booty, plunder*, 7. 4. 2.

Λειμών, ῶνος, ὁ (λείβω, *to water*), *a meadow*, 5. 3. 11.

Λεῖος, α, ον, *smooth, free from stones and bushes*, 4. 4. 1, with dig.=Lat. *lēvis*.

Λείπω, λείψω, λέλοιπα, λέλειμμαι, 2 aor. ἔλιπον, *to leave*, 1. 2. 21, 1. 10. 13, 4. 2. 7, &c.; οὐδὲ πλήθει ἡμῶν λειφθέντες, *not being inferior to us in numbers*, 7. 7. 31; *to leave behind*, 4. 5. 12, 7. 3. 43.

Λεκτέος, α, ον, verbal fr. λέγω, 5. 6. 6.

Λεοντῖνοι, ων, οἱ, *Leontini*, a town in Sicily ; adj. Λεοντῖνος, η, ον, 2. 6. 16.

Λευκοθώραξ, ᾱκος, ὁ, ἡ, *wearing a white corselet*, 1. 8. 9.

Λευκός, ή, όν (λάω, λεύσσω, *to see*), *white*; Lat. *lux, luceo*, 7. 3. 26.

Λήγω, λήξω (λέγω), *to end*, 7. 6. 6 ; *cease*, 3. 1. 9, 4. 5. 4.

Ληΐζω, better ληΐζομαι, ἴσομαι, λελήϊσμαι (λεία), *to plunder, ravage*, 6. 4. 27, 5. 9. 1, 5. 1. 9, 7. 3. 31, 4. 8. 23.

Λῆρος, ου, ὁ, *silly talk, nonsense*, 7. 7. 41.

Λῃστεία, ας, ἡ (λεία), *plundering, robbery*, 7. 7. 9, from

Λῃστής, οῦ, ὁ (λεία), *a robber, plunderer*, 5. 9. 8.

Λίαν, adv. *too much*, 5. 9. 28, 7. 6. 23.

Λίθϊνος, η, ον (λίθος), *made of stone*, 3. 4. 7.

Λίθυς, ου, ὁ (λάω, *to take*), *a stone*, 3. 4. 10, 5. 4. 23, 4. 2. 4, 5. 2. 14.

Λιμήν, ένος, ὁ, *a harbour*, 6. 2. 1.

Λιμός, οῦ, ὁ (λίπτω, *to be eager* or λείπω), *hunger*, 2. 5. 19, 7. 4. 5, 1. 5. 5, 2. 2. 11.

Λινοῦς, ῆ, οῦν, contr. for λίνεος, *made of linen*, λίνον, 4. 7. 15.

Λογίζομαι, ἴσομαι, and ιοῦμαι, λελόγισμαι (λόγος), *to count, consider*, 2. 2. 13.

Λόγος, ου, ὁ (λέγω), *a word*, 2. 5. 16, 2. 6. 4, 5. 10. 10 ; εἰς λόγους, *to a conference*, 2. 5. 4, 3. 1. 29, *a report*, 1. 4. 7, 6. 4. 13, *narrative*, 2. 1. 1, 3. 1. 1, &c.

Λόγχη, ης, ἡ, a spear-head, lance, 1. 8. 8, 2. 2. 9, &c.

Λοιδορέω; ήσω (λοίδορος), to rail at, abuse, Act. acc. 7. 5. 11; Mid. dat.

Λοιπός, ή, όν (λείπω), remaining, the rest, Lat. reliquus, 4. 2. 14; πορεία, 5. 1. 2; ἡ λοιπή (ὁδός), 3. 4. 46; τὸ λοιπόν, the remaining part, 4. 7. 6; οἱ λοιποί, 4. 3. 30, 6. 2. 26; λοιπόν μοι εἰπεῖν, it remains for me to say, 3. 2. 29; τὸ λοιπόν, the rest, 3. 4. 6, 16; henceforward, 3. 2. 8, 38, 5. 1. 2, 2. 2. 5, &c., so also gen. τοῦ λοιποῦ, 5. 7. 34, 6. 2. 11.

Λοκρός, οῦ, ὁ, a Locrian; the Locrians were divided into, (1) οἱ Ἐπικνημίδιοι, on the Malic Gulf round Mount Knemis; (2) οἱ Ὀπούντιοι, on the Euboean Sea, chief town Opus; (3) οἱ Ὀζόλαι (ὄζειν, to smell from mephitic exhalations, or ὄζοι, branches of the vine), bordering on Ætolia; Λοκροὶ οἱ Ἐπιζεφύριοι, a colony in Italy on Mount Zephyrion.

Λουσιάτης, ου, ὁ, an inhabitant of

Λουσοί, ῶν, οἱ, Lusi, a town in N. Arcadia, 7. 6. 40.

Λόφος, ου, ὁ (λέπω, I peel = the back of the neck peeled by the yoke), a hill, = γήλοφος, 1. 10. 12, = ἀκρωνυχία ὄρους, 3. 4. 38, 39, = μαστός, 4. 2. 10, 14.

Λοχαγέω, ήσω (λόχος, ἄγω), to lead a λόχος or company, 5. 9. 30, and

Λοχαγία, ας, ἡ, the rank or office of λοχαγός, 1. 4. 15, 3. 1. 30, from

Λοχαγός, οῦ, ὁ (λόχος, ἄγω), a captain; below him were the

πεντηκοστῆρες and ἐνωμότάρχοι, above him the στρατηγοί and ταξίαρχοι, 7. 2. 36, 4. 1. 26, &c.

Λοχίτης, ου, ὁ (λόχος), one of the same λόχος, a comrade, fellow soldier, 6. 4. 7, 17.

Λόχος, ου, ὁ (λέγω, to gather), a company (Lat. centuria) of about one hundred men, 1. 2. 25, 3. 4. 21; λόχοι φύλακες, companies on guard, 6. 3. 9.

Λυδία, ας, ἡ, Lydia in Asia Minor, capital Sardis, 1. 9. 7, 7. 8. 7; adj. Λύδιος, α, ον, Lydian, 1. 5. 6; subst. Λυδός, οῦ, ὁ, a Lydian, 3. 1. 31.

Λυκαῖος, α, ον, Lycæan, from Mount Lycæus in Arcadia; τὰ Λυκαῖα ἔθυσε, celebrated the festival of the Lycæan Jove, 1. 2. 10, from λύκος, Lat. lupus, Lupercalia.

Λυκάονες, ων, οἱ, the inhabitants of

Λυκαονία, ας, ἡ (Λυκάων), Lycaonia in Asia Minor, 1. 2. 19.

Λύκειον, ου, τό (λύκειος, epithet of Apollo, λύκη = lux), the Lyceum, a place of public resort in Athens, where Aristotle taught, 7. 8. 1.

Λύκιος, ου, ὁ (λύκος), Lycius, (1) an Athenian, 3. 3. 20, 4. 3. 22; (2) a Syracusan, 1. 10. 14.

Λύκος, ου, ὁ, the Lycus, a river in Bithynia, 5. 10. 3.

Λύκος, ου, ὁ, a wolf, 2. 2. 9.

Λύκων, ωνος, ὁ, Lycon, an Achæan, 5. 6. 27, 4. 7. 8.

Λυμαίνομαι, λυμανοῦμαι, λελύμασμαι, 1 aor. ἐλυμάνθην, to injure, mar, 1. 3. 16.

Λυπέω, ήσω, &c. (λύπη), to pain, distress, grieve, hurt, 2. 3. 23, 5. 2. 26; Mid. 1. 3. 8.

Λύπη, ης, ἡ, grief, sorrow, 3. 1. 3.

Λυπηρός, ά, όν (λύπη), painful, troublesome, 2. 5. 13, 7. 7. 28.

Λυσιτελέω, freq. impers. λυσιτελεῖ (λύω, τέλος), it is profitable, better, 3. 4. 36.

Λύσσα, ης, ἡ, Att. λύττα, rage, fury, madness, 5. 7. 26.

Λύω, λύσω, λέλῠκα, λέλῠμαι, to loose, release, Lat. solvere, 4. 3. 8, 4. 6. 2, &c.; to break down, Lat. rescindere, γέφυραν, 2. 4. 17 ; to break, ὅρκους, 3. 2. 10 : σπονδάς, ὕβριν, ὑπο-ψίαν, 3. 1. 21 ; Mid. to ransom, redeem, 7. 8. 6.

Λώων, λώων, λῷον (λῶ, I wish), better, 3. 1. 7, &c.; cf. Lat. optimus, opto.

Λωτοφάγοι, ων, οἱ (λωτός, ἔφαγον), Lotus-eaters—the lotus was a shrub that grew on the coast of Libya, the fruit of which was so pleasant to the taste that those who ate of it had no desire to return home=the jujube, Hom. Od. 9. 94, 3. 2. 25.

Λωφάω, ήσω (λόφος, the neck freed from the yoke), to slacken, abate, 4. 7. 6, ubi lapides non amplius dejicientur.

M

Μά, one of the particles of adjuration, neither affirmative nor neg. in itself, gov. the acc. μὰ τοὺς θεούς, by the gods, 1. 4. 8 ; ναὶ μή, yes, by, 5. 8. 6.

Μαγάδις, ιδος, or ις, εως, ἡ, a magadis, a harp with twenty strings, 7. 3. 32.

Μάγνης, νητος, ὁ, a Magnesian ; Magnesia was in Thessaly, hence magnet, 5. 9. 7.

Μαίανδρος, ου, ὁ, the Mœander, a river in Ionia and Phrygia, 1. 2. 5, 7, hence meander.

Μαίρομαι, μανοῦμαι, μέμηνα, with pres. meaning, 1 aor. act. ἔμηνα, 2 aor. pass. ἐμάνην, to be mad, rage, 2. 5. 10.

Μαισάδης, ου, ὁ, Mœsades, king of Thrace, father of Seuthes, 7. 2. 32, 5. 1.

Μακαρίζω, ίσω (μάκαρ, happy), to regard as happy, 3. 1. 19.

Μακαριστός, ή, όν, envied, πολλοῖς, by many, 1. 9. 6.

Μακέστιος and Μακίστιος, ου, ὁ, an inhabitant of Macestus, a town in Elis, 7. 4. 16.

Μακρός, ά, όν, comp. μακρότερος and μάσσων, sup. μακρότατος and μήκιστος (μᾶκος or μῆκος, length), large, great, long, ὁδός, 2. 2. 11 ; ἡμέρα, 6. 2. 2 ; μακρότερον, farther, 3. 4. 16 ; ὅτι μακροτάτην, sc. ὁδόν, as far as possible, 7. 8. 20 ; μακράν, a long way, 3. 4. 17, 42.

Μάλα, μᾶλλον, μάλιστα, much, more, most, μάλα συχνοί, very, 5. 4. 18, 3. 4. 15 ; οὐ μάλα τι, by no means, 2. 6. 15 ; μᾶλλον ἐμοῦ, more than myself, 7. 3. 30, with comp. 4. 6. 11, 7. 4. 12, ἑκατὸν μάλιστα, about one hundred, 5. 4. 12, 6. 2. 3 ; μάλιστα, with superl. 7. 2. 22.

Μαλακίζομαι, ίσομαι (μαλακός, soft), to be soft, become indolent, 5. 8. 14.

Μανθάνω, μαθήσομαι, μεμάθηκα, 2 aor. ἔμαθον (μήθω), to learn, 5. 2. 25, 3. 2. 25, 2. 5. 37, 4. 8. 5.

Μαντεία, ας, ἡ (μάντις), a prediction, an oracle, 3. 1. 7.

Μαντεύομαι, εύσομαι, μεμάντευμαι (μάντις), to prophesy, consult an oracle ; hence

Μαντευτός, ή, όν, advised by the oracle, 5. 9. 22.

Μαντινεῖς, ῶν, οἱ, Mantineans, natives of Mantinéa, a town in Arcadia, where Epaminondas died victorious, 5. 9. 11.

Μάντις, εως, ὁ (μαίνομαι, to rage), a priest, a soothsayer, seer, 1. 7. 18, &c.

Μαρδόνιοι, ων, οἱ, the Mardonians, or Mardi, Μάρδοι, a people in Armenia, 4. 3. 4.

Μαριανδῦνοί, ῶν, οἱ, the Mariandyni, a people in Bithynia, 5. 10. 1.

Μάρσιπος, ου, ὁ, or μάρσιππος, or μάρσυπος, a bag ; Lat. marsupium ; Eng. marsupial, 4. 3. 11.

Μαρσύας, ου, ὁ, Marsyas, a Satyr, who was killed by Apollo, after being beaten in a musical contest, 1. 2. 8 ; a river in Phrygia, 1. 2. 8.

Μαρτυρέω, ήσω (μάρτυς), &c. to be a witness, bear witness, testify, 7. 6. 39, 3. 3. 12.

Μαρτύριον, ου, το (μάρτυς), a testimony, proof, 3. 2. 13.

Μάρτυς, υρος, ὁ (μάρη, a hand?), a witness ; Eng. martyr, 7. 7. 39.

Μαρωνείτης, ου, ὁ, a Maronite, a native of Μαρώνεια, Maronéa, a town in Thrace, 7. 3. 16.

Μασκάς, ᾱ, ὁ, Mascas, a river in Mesopotamia, 1. 5. 4.

Μαστεύω, εύσω (μάω), to seek, strive, with inf. 3. 1. 43.

Μαστιγόω, ώσω (μάστιξ), to inflict stripes, flog, 4. 6. 15.

Μάστιξ, ιγος, ἡ (μάω, μάσσω, to strike), a whip, ὑπὸ μαστίγων, under the lash, 3. 4. 25.

Μαστός, οῦ, ὁ (μάσσω, to touch), the breast, 1. 4. 17, 4. 3. 6 ; a round hill, Eng. pap, 4. 2. 6, &c.

Μάταιος, α, ον, and ος, ον (μάτην), foolish, vain, 7. 6. 17.

Μάχαιρα, ας, ἡ (μάχη), a curved sword, a sabre, 1. 8. 7, 4. 6. 26, 7. 2. 30 ; the straight sword was ξίφος.

Μαχαίριον, ου, τό, dim. of μάχαιρα, a short sabre, knife, 4. 7. 16.

Μάχη, ης, ἡ, a fight, battle, τὴν μάχην νικᾶν, 2. 1. 4, the battle-field, 2. 2. 6, 5. 5. 4.

Μάχιμος, η, ον (μάχη), fit for battle, warlike, 7. 8. 13.

Μάχομαι, μαχέσομαι or ἤσομαι or μαχοῦμαι, μεμάχημαι, to fight, τινί, with one, 1. 5. 9, 5. 5. 13 ; σύν τινι, in company with one, 6. 1. 13.

Μεγάβυζος, ου, ὁ, Megabyzus, the guardian of the temple of Diana at Ephesus, 5. 3. 6.

Μεγαληγορέω, ήσω (μέγας, ἀγορεύω), to boast, talk big, 6. 1. 18.

Μεγαλοπρεπής, ής, ές (μέγας, πρέπει), magnificent, adv. μεγαλοπρεπῶς, ἕστερον, ἕστατα, supl. 7. 3. 19, in the most splendid manner ; ξενίζειν, 7. 6. 3.

Μεγάλως, adv. from μέγας, 3. 2. 22.

Μεγαρεύς, έως, ὁ, a Megarian, a native of Megara, the capital of Megaris in Central Greece, 1. 2. 3.

Μέγας, μεγάλη, μέγα, gen. μεγάλου, ης, ον, comp. μείζων,

sup. μέγιστος, *great, vast,
large*, 2. 6. 17; *loud,* βοή, 4.
7. 23; *towering,* θάλαττα, 5.
8. 20; μέγιστα, *of the greatest
importance,* 5. 7. 33; τὸ μὲν
μέγιστον, *chiefly, what is most
important,* 1. 3. 10, 5. 6. 29;
most valuable, powerful, 2. 5.
14, 3. 2. 10, 7. 1. 21.

Μεγαφέρνης, ου, ὁ, *Megaphernes,*
a Persian, 1. 2. 20.

Μέγεθος, εος, τό (μέγας), *size,
greatness,* 2. 3. 15.

Μέδιμνος, ου, ὁ (μέδομαι, *to be
careful*), *a medimnus,* the Attic
corn-measure, about twelve
English   gallons=forty-eight
χοίνικες, 5. 9. 15, 10. 3.

Μεθίημι, ήσω, εἶκα, εἶμαι, 1 aor.
μεθῆκα, *to send away* (μετά,
ἵημι), 7. 4. 10.

Μεθίστημι, μεταστήσω, μεθέστηκα,
μεθέσταμαι, 2 aor. μετέστην
(μετά, ἵστημι), Act. *to remove,*
2. 3. 8; Neut. *to stand apart,*
2. 3. 21.

Μεθυδριεύς, έως, ὁ (μέτα, ὕδωρ),
a Methydrian, an inhabitant
of Methydrium, a town in
Arcadia, 4. 1. 27.

Μεθύω, ύσω (μέθυ, *pure wine,*
Lat. *merum*), *to be drunk,* 4.
8. 20, 7. 3. 35.

Μείζων, *greater,* comp. of μέγας.

Μειλίχιος, α, ον (μέλι, *honey*),
mild, gentle, gracious, Ζεύς, 7.
8. 4.

Μειράκιον, ου, τό (μεῖραξ), *a
young man,* a boy about four-
teen, 2. 6. 16.

Μείωμα, ατος, τό (μειόω, μείων,
less), *a lessening, a fine,* 5. 8. 1.

Μείων, ων, ον, comp. of μικρός,
smaller, less, worse, inferior,
3. 2. 17; μεῖον ἔχειν, *to have
the disadvantage, have the*

worst of it, 1. 10. 8, 3. 4.
18.

Μελανδέπται, ῶν, οἱ, *the Melan-
deptæ,* more frequently Μελαν-
δῖται, *the Melanditæ,* the inhabitants   of   Melandia   in
Thrace, 7. 2. 32.

Μελανία, ας, ἡ (μέλας), *a blackness,* 1. 8. 8.

Μέλας, μέλαινα, μέλαν, comp.
μελάντερος, sup. μελάντατος;
black, 4. 5. 13, 15.

Μέλει, μελήσει, μεμέληκε, Impers.
it concerns, it is a care to,
ἐμοί, 1. 4. 16; θεῷ, 5. 3. 13;
ὅπως, 1. 4. 16, 1. 8. 13, 7. 7. 44.

Μελετάω, ήσω, &c. (μέλει), *to
practise;* τοξεύειν, *shooting,* 3.
4. 17.

Μελετηρός, ά, όν (μελετάω), *prac-
tising diligently,* 1. 9. 5.

Μελίνη, ης, ἡ, *millet, panicum,*
Pl. 6. 2. 6, 2. 4. 13.

Μελινοφάγοι, ων, οἱ (μελίνη,
φάγω), *millet-eaters,* a people
in Thrace, 7. 5. 12.

Μέλλω, μελλήσω (μέλει), *to be
about, intend, delay;* ὁρμᾶν, 3.
1. 8; ἄγειν, 5. 7. 5, 1. 8. 1,
7. 4. 9, 3. 3. 16, 2. 1. 3, 3. 4.
37, with fut. inf. 2. 4. 24,
7. 8. 3, 5. 6. 12, 1. 9. 28, 4.
7. 16, 3. 1. 2, 2. 6. 10, 7. 7.
1; τὸ μέλλον, *the future,* 5. 9.
21.

Μέμφομαι, μέμψομαι, *to blame,
find fault with,* τινά, 7. 6. 39,
2. 6. 30.

Μέν (neut. of εἷς, ἕν=μέν), *in
the first place, on the one hand,*
correlative of δέ (δύο, δέω),
*in the second place, on the
other hand,* 3. 3. 7, 4. 3. 14,
&c.; καλὸς μὲν μέγας δ᾽ οὔ,
4. 4. 3; μέν—ὅμως δέ, 1. 3.
21; ὁ μέν—ὁ δέ, *the one—the*

other, pl. some—others, 1. 10. 4,
5. 4. 12; μέν—μέν—δέ—δέ,
3. 1. 43, with μέντοι following,
2. 3. 9, 2. 1. 13, 19, with ἀλλά,
4. 8. 10, 12; τοίνυν; 5. 1. 6, 8,
7. 7. 16; μὲν οὖν, 1. 10. 19, 1.
9. 1, &c.; μὲν δή, 1. 1. 4, &c.

Μέντοι (μέν, τοι), certainly, now,
yet, still, however, 2. 3. 22.

Μένω, μενῶ, μεμένηκα, 1 aor.
ἔμεινα, 2 perf. μέμονα, to remain, 1. 3. 11, 2. 1. 21; to
wait for, τινά, 4. 4. 20.

Μένων, ωνος, ὁ, Menon, one of
the Greek generals, a Thessalian, 1. 4. 13, 2. 6. 21.

Μερίζω, ίσω, μεμέρισμαι (μέρος),
to divide, 5. 1. 9.

Μέρος, εος, τό, a part, portion,
share, 7. 8. 11, 5. 3. 4, 6. 4.
28; ἐν τῷ μέρει, in succes-
sion, one after another, 3. 4.
23; καὶ ἐν τῷ μέρει καὶ παρὰ τὸ
μέρος, both in his share and
beyond his share, 7. 6. 36;
κατὰ μέρος, into portions, 5. 1. 9.

Μεσημβρία, ας, ἡ (μέσος, ἡμέρα),
mid-day, 1. 7. 6, Lat. meridies
=medius dies.

Μεσόγαιος, α, ον, and ος, ον
(μέσος, γῆ), inland, the interior, 5. 10. 19, 6. 2. 5.

Μέσος, η, ον (μετά), Lat. medius,
middle; ἐν μέσῃ τῇ πόλει, in the
middle (heart) of the city, 1. 2.
23, 2. 1. 11; τῆς φάλαγγος
μέσης, 1. 2. 17; μέσαι νύκτες,
mid-night, 7. 8. 12; μέσον
ἡμέρας, 1. 8. 8, 7. 3. 44; τὸ
μέσον, the centre, 1. 2. 15, 4.
8. 17; τὰ ἐν μέσῳ τούτων, the
parts between these, 1. 7. 6;
ἐν μέσῳ τῆς οἴκαδε ὁδοῦ, intervening in their homeward journey, 3. 1. 2, 3. 4. 43. Comp.
μεσαίτερος, Sup. αίτατος.

Μεσόω, ώσω (μέσος), to be in the
middle; μεσοῦσα ἡμέρα, mid-
day, 6. 3. 7.

Μέσπιλα, ης, ἡ, Mespila (prob.
Kouyounjik, opp. Mosul), a
town in Assyria on the Tigris,
3. 4. 10.

Μεστός, ή, όν (ἔδω, to eat), full,
τινός, 1. 4. 19, 3. 5. 1.

Μετά, a prep. gov. gen. and acc.
with gen. with Σεύθου, 7. 3.
13; μεθ' ὑμῶν, 7. 6. 34, 1. 3.
5; μετ' ἀδικίας, with injustice,
2. 6. 18; with acc. after, μετὰ
τοῦτο, 4. 6. 4, 5. 7. 17, &c.;
μετὰ ταῦτα, 1. 4. 9, 2. 4. 23;
τὰ πιστά, 4. 8. 8; τοῦτον, 1.
3. 16, 2. 1. 12, &c.; μεθ'
ἡμέραν, by day, 4. 6. 12.

Μεταβάλλω, βαλῶ, &c., to throw
round, over their shoulders,
opp. προβάλλω, 5. 3. 16.

Μεταγιγνώσκω, γνώσομαι, &c.,
2 aor. μετέγνων, to change
their minds, 2. 6. 3.

Μεταδίδωμι, δώσω, &c., to share,
7. 8. 11; τινί, 3. 3. 1; τινί
τινος, 4. 5. 6.

Μεταμέλει, μελήσει, to repent,
with dat. 1. 6. 7.

Μεταξύ, adv. (μετά), between,
gen. 1. 7. 16; μεταξὺ γενο-
μένου, intervening, 5. 2. 17;
in the midst, 3. 1. 27.

Μεταπέμπω, πέμψω, &c., to send
for, summon, 1. 2. 26, 3. 8.

Μετάπεμπτος, ος, ον, sent for,
1. 4. 3.

Μεταστρέφω, στρέψω, &c., to turn
round, 5. 9. 8.

Μεταχωρέω, ήσω, &c., to go to
another place, retire, 7. 2. 18.

Μέτειμι (μετά, εἰμί), to be among,
have a share in, ἐμοὶ τινος, 3.
1. 20.

Μετέχω, μεθέξω or μετασχήσω,

μετέσχηκα, μετέσχημαι, *to share in, partake of, τινός*, 5. 10. 14, 5. 3. 9, 7. 6. 28.

Μετέωρος, ος, ον (μετά, ἐώρα, *raised off the ground*), *high*, 1. 5. 8; Eng. *meteor.*

Μετρέω, ήσω, &c. (μέτρον), *to measure*, 4. 5. 6.

Μετρίως, adv. from μέτριος, *moderately*, 2. 3. 20.

Μέτρον, ου, τό, *a measure*, 3. 2. 21.

Μέχρι, before a vowel often μέχρις, yet μέχρι εἰς, 6. 2. 26, μέχρις ἐπί, 5. 1. 1, *until, as far as*; μέχρις ἐνταῦθα, *so far*, 5. 5. 4; μέχρι τοῦ τείχους, *up to*, 1. 7. 15, 2. 2. 6, 6. 2. 1; μέχρι οὗ, *unto where*, 1. 7. 6; of TIME, 6. 2. 25; also conj. *until*, with ind. 3. 4. 8, 4. 2. 4, &c.; μέχρι οὗ, 2. 6. 5, 5. 4. 16; with ἄν and conj., 2. 3. 7, 1. 4. 13.

Μή, conj. *lest*, Lat. *ne*, with part. *not*, 4. 4. 15, 6. 2. 19; with inf. 1. 1. 10, 2. 3. 13, 5. 7. 3; after ἀντιλέγειν, 2. 5. 29; ἀπειπεῖν, 7. 2. 12; ἀποκωλῦσαι, 6. 2. 24; τὸ μή, 1. 3. 2, 4. 8. 14, 3. 5. 11; with imp. pres., 1. 3. 3, 2. 1. 12; with conj., 7. 1. 29, 6. 4. 18, 7. 1. 8; μηδέν, 3. 2. 17, 5. 4. 19; after pres. or fut., 1. 3. 10, 2. 3. 9, 3. 2. 25, &c.; after a historical tense, 1. 8. 24, 3. 4. 34, and a historical pres. 4. 5. 35, 5. 6. 17; with opt. after a historical tense, 1. 8. 13, 2. 4. 22, 3. 4. 29, &c.; after a pres. 5. 9. 28, 6. 4. 5; after ὑποπτεύω, 3. 1. 5; ἐννοέω, 4. 2. 13, 5. 9. 28, 3. 5. 3; μὴ οὐ, *ne non*, after δέδοικα, 1. 7. 7, 4. 7. 11; *quominus* after τί ἐμποδών, 3. 1. 13; αἰσχύνη, 2. 3. 11.

Μηδαμῇ (μηδαμός), adv. *nowhere*, 7. 6. 29, al. μηδαμῆ.

Μηδαμῶς, adv. *in no way*, 7. 7. 23.

Μηδέ (μή, δέ), adv. *nor*, Lat. *nec, neque*, and *ne-quidem, not even*, 6. 4. 17, 7. 7. 40, &c.

Μήδεια, ας, ἡ, sometimes Μηδία, *Media*, a country in Asia, south of Armenia, 2. 4. 12, 27, 1. 7. 15.

Μηδείς, εμία, ἐν (μηδέ, εἷς), *not even one, none, nobody*, μηδέν, *not by any means*, 5. 4. 19.

Μηδέποτε (μηδέ, ποτέ), adv. *never*, 3. 2. 3.

Μηδέτερος, α, ον (comp. of μηδείς), *neither of two*, Lat. *neuter*, 7. 4. 10.

Μῆδοι, ων, οἱ, *the Medes*, 3. 2. 25.

Μήδοκος, ου, ὁ, *Medocus*, king of the Odrysi in Thrace, 7. 2. 32.

Μηδοσάδης, ου, ὁ, *Medosades*, a Thracian, 7. 2. 23, &c.

Μηκέτι (μή, ἔτι), *no longer*, 1. 4. 16, 1. 6. 9, 5. 7. 15.

Μῆκος, εος, τό, *length*, 2. 4. 12, 5. 4. 32; τὰ μήκη τῶν ὁδῶν, 1. 5. 9.

Μήν ' (μέν), Lat. *vero, truly, assuredly*, 2. 5. 12, 3. 2. 16; καὶ μήν, *et vero, besides, moreover*, 1. 7. 5, 3. 1. 17, 7. 7. 51; οὔτε μήν, *neque vero, nor indeed*, 7. 6. 22; οὐδὲ μήν, 2. 4. 20.

Μήν, μηνός, ὁ (ἕν neut. of εἷς), *a month*, τοῦ μηνός, *monthly, per month*, 1. 3. 21, 5. 6. 23, 7. 3. 10.

Μηνοειδής, ής, ές (μήνη, εἶδος), *moon-shaped, like a crescent*, 5. 2. 13.

Μηνύω, ύσω, μεμήνυκα, μεμήνυμαι, *to declare*, 2. 2. 20.

Μήποτε (μή, ποτέ), *never*; μήποτε ἔτι, *no longer*, 1. 1. 4.

Μήπω (μή, πω), not yet, Lat. nondum, 3. 2. 24, &c.

Μηρός, οῦ, ὁ, the thigh, 7. 4. 4.

Μήτε (μή, τε), neither—nor, 6. 4. 17; μήτε—τε, · not only not—but, 2. 2. 8, 3. 1. 30; μήτε—τε μηδείς, 3. 2. 23.

Μήτηρ, τρός, ἡ, a mother, 1. 1. 4.

Μητρόπολις, εως, ἡ, the mother-state, chief-city, capital, 5. 2. 3, 4. 15.

Μηχανάομαι, ήσομαι, μεμηχάνημαι (μηχανή), to contrive, 2. 6. 27, 4. 7. 10.

Μηχανή, ῆς, ἡ (μῆχος, a means), Lat. machina, means, σωτηρίας, 5. 2. 24, contrivance, 4. 5. 16, 7. 2. 8.

Μία, fem. of εἷς, one.

Μίδας, a and ου, ὁ, Midas, son of Gordius and Cybele, king of Thrace, 1. 2. 13.

Μιθριδάτης, ου, ὁ (Pers. mithra, the sun, da, to give), or Μιθραδάτης, Mithridates, a Persian satrap, 2. 5. 35, 3. 3. 1, 4, 6.

Μικρός, ά, όν, small, little, μικρότερος, μικρότατος, and ἐλάσσων or μείων, ἐλάχιστος, 3. 2. 10; μικρόν τι, some little distance, 4. 7. 7; very little money, 7. 7. 53; μικρόν, narrowly, 1. 3. 2; κατὰ μικρόν, in small pieces, 7. 3. 22; κατὰ μικρά, 5. 6. 32.

Μιλήσιος, a, ον, Milesian, an inhabitant of

Μίλητος, ου, ἡ, Miletus, a town in Asia near Ephesus and Smyrna, 1. 9. 9.

Μιλτοκύθης, ου, ὁ (μίλτος, red earth), Miltocythes, a Thracian, 2. 2. 7.

Μιμέομαι, ήσομαι, μεμίμημαι (μῖμος), to mimic, imitate, 5. 9. 9.

Μιμνήσκω, μνήσω, μέμνημαι, as pres. to remind; Mid. to remember, 1. 7. 5, 7. 6. 38; τινός, 5. 8. 25; with inf. 3. 2. 39, to mention, ὡς, 7. 5. 8; δίχα ποιεῖν, 6. 2. 11.

Μισέω, ήσω, μεμίσηκα (μῖσος), to hate, 7. 6. 15.

Μισθοδοσία, ας, ἡ (μισθός, δίδωμι), the giving of pay, 2. 5. 22.

Μισθοδοτέω, ήσω, to give pay, 7. 1. 13.

Μισθυδότης, ου, ὁ, a giver of pay, a paymaster, 1. 3. 9.

Μισθός, οῦ, ὁ, pay, 1. 1. 10, 1. 2. 11, &c.; reward, 2. 2. 20, 3. 5. 8.

Μισθόω, ώσω, &c. (μισθός), to let out for hire; Lat. collocare; Mid. to hire; ἐπί τινι, 1. 3. 1; Lat. conducere, 7. 7. 34.

Μισθοφορά, ᾶς, ἡ (μισθός, φέρω), receipt of wages, pay, 5. 6. 26.

Μισθοφορία, ας, ἡ=μισθοφορά,

Μισθοφόρος, ου, ὁ, serving for hire, pl. mercenaries, 1. 4. 3, 4. 4. 18.

Μνᾶ, μνᾶς, ἡ, for μνάα, Lat. mina =100 drachmæ=4l. 1s. 3d., 60 minæ made a talent, 1. 4. 13.

Μνήμη, ης, ἡ (μιμνήσω, μνάω), remembrance, 6. 3. 24.

Μνημονεύω, εύσω, ἐμνημόνευκα (μνήμων), to remember, 4. 3. 2.

Μνημονικός, ή, όν (μνήμων), having a good memory, ὦ μνημονικώτατοι, ye men with most excellent memories, 7. 6. 38.

Μνησικακέω, ήσω (μιμνήσκω, κακός), to remember injuries, to bear a grudge, τινί τινος, 2. 4. 1.

Μόγις, adv. with difficulty, 3. 4. 48, 4. 8. 28, 5. 2. 27, &c.

Μολεῖν, 2 aor. of βλώσκω, 7. 1. 33.

Μόλις = μόγις, 7. 1. 39.

Μολυβδίς, ίδος, ἡ, a leaden ball or bullet, 3. 3. 17, from

Μόλυβδος, ου, ὁ, lead, Lat. plumbum, 3. 4. 17.

Μοναρχία, ας, ἡ (μόνος, ἄρχω), single rule, 5. 9. 31; Eng. monarchy.

Μοναχῇ, alone, only, 4. 4. 18.

Μονή, ῆς, ἡ (μένω), a staying, stay, 5. 1. 5, 5. 6. 22, 27. .

Μονόξυλος, ος, ον (μόνος, ξύλον), made from a solid trunk, πλοῖα, canoes, 5. 4. 11.

Μόνος, η, ον (μένω, or rather μέν, ἕν fr. εἷς, one), alone, only, 5. 2. 26, 7. 7. 50, 5. 8. 20, 7. 3. 45; μόνον, adv. only, 5. 2. 15, 5. 7. 10.

Μόσυν or μόσσυν, υνος, ὁ, a wooden house, d. pl. μοσσύνοις, 5. 4. 26.

Μοσύνοικος, ου, ὁ (μόσυν, οἰκέω), one of the Mosynœci, a people in Asia Minor on the Black Sea, 5. 4. 2.

Μόσχειος, ος, ον (μόσχος, a calf), κρέα μόσχεια, veal, 4. 5. 31.

Μοχθέω, ήσω (μόχθος, trouble), to be distressed, περί τινα, 6. 6. 31.

Μοχλός, οῦ, ὁ, a lever, crowbar, bolt, 7. 1. 12, 15.

Μυγδόνιοι, ων, οἱ, the Mygdonians, in Mesopotamia.

Μύζω and μυζέω, μυζήσω (μύω), to suck in, 4. 5. 27.

Μυρίανδρος, ου, ἡ (μύριοι, ἄνδρες), Myriander, a town in Seleucia on the Gulf of Issus, 1. 4. 6.

Μυριάς, άδος, ἡ (μύριοι) = 10,000, a myriad, 1. 4. 5, 5. 6. 9.

Μύριοι, αι, α (μύρω, to drop), ten thousand, 1. 2. 9, 5. 3. 3;

μυρίοι, αι, α, countless, numberless, ἐλπίδες, 2. 1. 19, 3. 2. 18, 31, 7. 1. 30, 3. 48.

Μύρον, ου, τό, oil, an ointment, a perfume, 4. 4. 13.

Μυσία, ας. ἡ, Mysia, a district in Asia Minor; adj. Μύσιος, α, ον ; subst. Μυσός, οῦ, ὁ, a Mysian, 1. 6. 7.

Μυχός, οῦ, ὁ (μύω), the innermost place, nook or corner, 4. 1. 7.

Μωρός, ά, όν, foolish, silly, 3. 2. 22 ; μωρῶς, adv. 7. 6. 21.

N

Ναί, adv. yes ; Lat. næ, 5. 8. 6.

Ναός, οῦ, ὁ (ναίω, to dwell), a temple ; Att. νεώς; ἱερόν, the whole temple, ναός, the shrine, where the god dwells, 5. 3. 9.

Νάπη, ης, ἡ, a woody dell or glen ; Lat. saltus, 4. 5. 15, 5. 2. 31.

Νάπος, εος, τό = νάπη, 6. 3. 12.

Ναυαρχέω, ήσω (ναῦς, ἄρχω), to command a fleet, 5. 1. 4, 7. 2. 7.

Ναύαρχος, ου, ὁ (ναῦς, ἄρχω), the commander of a fleet, an admiral, 1. 4. 2, 5. 9. 16, 6. 4. 13, 7. 1. 2.

Ναύκληρος, ου, ὁ (ναῦς, κλῆρος, a lot), a shipowner, captain, 7. 2. 12, 5. 14.

Ναῦλος, ου, ὁ (ναῦς), passage-money, fare, 5. 1. 12.

Ναυπηγήσιμος, ος, ον, or η, ον (ναῦς, πήγνυμι), useful in shipbuilding, 6. 2. 4.

Ναῦς, νεώς, ἡ (νέω, to swim), a ship, 7. 5. 12 ; Lat. navis.

Ναυσίπορος, ος, ον (ναῦς, πόρος), traversed by ships, navigable,

2. 2. 3 ; but ναυσιπόρος, passing in a ship, causing a ship to pass.

Ναυτικός, ή, όν (ναῦς), nautical, naval ἕύναμις, 1. 3. 12.

Νεανίσκος, ου, ὁ (νέος), a young man, until forty, 7. 2. 33; applied to Xenophon, 2. 1. 13.

Νεκρός, οῦ, ὁ (νέκυς), a dead body, corpse, 4. 2. 18, 5. 2. 9.

Νέμω, νεμῶ, νενέμηκα, νενέμημαι, 1 aor. ἔνειμα, to distribute, pasture, consider; Pass. to be grazed, 4. 6. 17; heaped up, 7. 3. 21.

Νεόδαρτος, ος, ον (νέος, δέρω), newly flayed, βόες, 4. 5. 14.

Νέον τεῖχος, τό, New Wall, a town in Thracia, 7. 5. 8.

Νέος, α, ον, new, fresh, young, with dig. Lat. novus, 1. 1. 1, 3. 2. 37; νεώτερος, younger; νεώτατος, youngest.

Νεῦμα, ατος, τό (νεύω), a nod or sign, 5. 8. 20.

Νευρά, ᾶς, ἡ (νεύω), a sinew, cord, bow-string, 4. 2. 28, 5. 2. 12.

Νεῦρον, ου, τό (νεύω), a sinew, cord for a sling, 3. 4. 17.

Νεφέλη, ης, ἡ (νέφος), a cloud, 1. 8. 8, 3. 4. 8.

Νέω, νήσω, νένημαι and νένησμαι, to heap up, 5. 4. 27.

Νέω, νεύσομαι and νευσοῦμαι, νένευκα, to swim, 4. 3. 12, 5. 7. 25.

Νεωκόρος, ου, ὁ (νεώς, κορέω), a temple-sweeper, a warden or guardian of a temple, 5. 3. 6.

Νέων, ωνος, ὁ, Neon, a native of Asine, 5. 7. 1, 6. 2. 11, 23.

Νεώριον, ου, τό (νεώς, ὥρα, care), a dockyard, 7. 1. 27.

Νεώς, ώ, Attic for ναός, 5. 3. 8.

Νεωστί (νέος), adv. recently, 4. 1. 12.

Νή, particle of adjuration, νὴ Δία, yea by Jove, 1. 7. 9, 5. 7. 22. The other particles are ναί and μά.

Νῆσος, ου, ἡ (νέω), an island, 2. 4. 22.

Νίκανδρος, ου, ὁ (νίκη, ἀνήρ), Nicander, a Spartan, 5. 1. 15.

Νίκαρχος, ου, ὁ (νίκη, ἄρχω), Nicarchus, an Arcadian, 3. 3. 5.

Νικάω, ήσω, &c. to conquer, μάχας, 6. 3. 23 ; τὰ πάντα, 2. 1. 1 ; εὖ ποιῶν, 1. 9. 24 ; ἐκ τῆς νικώσης (γνώμης), in accordance with the opinion that prevailed, 5. 9. 18, 10. 12.

Νίκη, ης, ἡ, victory, 3. 1. 23, &c.

Νικόμαχος, ου, ὁ (νίκη, μάχη), Nicomachus, a Thessalian, 4. 6. 20.

Νιψαῖοι, ων, οἱ, the Nipsæi, a people in Thrace.

Νοέω, ήσω, &c. (νόος), to perceive, observe, 3. 4. 44, &c.

Νόθος, η, ον, illegitimate, bastard, 2. 4. 25.

Νομή, ῆς, ἡ (νέμω), pasture, herd, 5. 3. 9, 3. 5. 2.

Νομίζω, ίσω, Att. ιῶ, νενόμικα, νενόμισμαι (νόμος), to think, consider, ἰχθῦς θεούς, 1. 4. 9, 2. 5. 39; with inf. 3. 1. 3, 1. 5. 9, 2. 5. 13, 7. 3. 8, 1. 5. 16, 1. 3. 6, 5. 9. 20; ἱκανὸς εἶναι, 2. 6. 17; acc. and inf. 1. 5. 16, 2. 5. 6, 3. 2. 29, 7. 7. 46; ὅτι—τοῦτον στασιάζειν, 5. 9. 29, where ὅτι is pleonastic; part. ἀποκτείνων, 6. 4. 24 ; τὰ νομιζόμενα, the usual pay, two Cyzicenes for the captains, four for the generals, 7. 3. 10.

Νόμιμος, η, ον (νόμος), customary, usual, 4. 6. 15.

Νόμος, ου, ὁ (νέμω), *custom*, 7. 3. 22 ; ἐστι τάσσεσθαι, 1. 2. 15 ; Θρακίῳ νόμῳ, *according to the Thracian custom*, 7. 2. 38; νόμῳ τινί, *to a kind of tune*, 5. 4. 17.

Νόος, ου, ὁ, contr. νοῦς, νοῦ, νῷ, or νοῖ or νόῳ, *mind*, *thought*, ἐν νῷ ἔχειν, 3. 3. 2.

Νοσέω, ήσω, &c. (νόσος), *to be sick*, *ill*, *in a bad state*, 7. 2. 32.

Νόσος, ου, ἡ, *sickness*, 5. 3. 3.

Νότος, ου, ὁ, *the south wind*, Lat. *notus*, 5. 7. 7.

Νουμηνία, ας, ἡ, contr. for νεο-μηνία (νέος, μήν), *the new moon*, *the first of the month*, 5. 6. 23, 31.

Νυκτερεύω, εύσω (νύξ), *to pass the night*, *bivouac*, 4. 4. 11, 6. 2. 27.

Νυκτοφύλαξ, ακος, ὁ, ἡ (νύξ, φύλαξ), *keeping watch by night*; Lat. *excubitor*, 7. 2. 18, 3. 34.

Νύκτωρ (νύξ), adv. *by night*= νυκτός, 3. 4. 35, 4. 6. 12, 7. 3. 37.

Νῦν, adv. *now*, Lat. *nunc*, but νύν, Lat. *ergo*; *now*, *then*, ὁ νῦν χρόνος, *the present time*, 6. 4. 13; τὸ νῦν εἶναι, *for the present*, 3. 2. 37, 7. 7. 46, 49 ; νῦν δή, *even now*, 7. 6. 37; καὶ νῦν, 2. 3. 26, 3. 1. 38; νῦν δέ, 6. 4. 31, *but now*; νῦν δὲ δή, *but even now*, 7. 1. 28, 6. 31.

Νύν, *now*, *ergo*, 7. 2. 26.

Νυνί, strengthened form of νῦν, *even now*, *at this moment*, 7. 3. 3.

Νύξ, νυκτός, ἡ, *night*, ἐγένετο, 4. 6. 22; προβαίνει, 3. 1. 13 ; νυκτός, *by night*=νύκτωρ, 3. 4. 34, 35, 7. 3. 37, &c.; τῆς νυκτός, refers to a particular

night, 4. 2. 14, 4. 4. 8, 15, 6. 1. 6, &c.; ταύτης τῆς νυκτός, 3. 3. 20; καὶ ἡμέρας καὶ νυκτός, 2. 6. 7 ; εἴτε νυκτός εἴτε ἡμέρας, 3. 1. 40; τὴν νύκτα φυλάττειν, *through the night*, 4. 2. 1, 5. 8. 24; ἡμέραν καὶ νύκτα, 5. 9. 14; καὶ νύκτα καὶ ἡμέραν, 7. 6. 9; διὰ νυκτός, 4. 6. 22; περὶ μέσας νύκτας, 7. 8. 12.

Νῶτον, ου, τό, *the back*, 5. 4. 32.

Ξ

Ξανθικλῆς, έους, ὁ (ξανθός, *golden*, κλέος, *glory*), *Xanthicles*, an Achæan, 5. 8. 1.

Ξενία, ας, ἡ (ξένος), *hospitality*, *friendly relations*, 6. 4. 35, 5. 9. 3.

Ξενίας, ου, ὁ (ξένος), *Xenias*, from Parrhasia in Arcadia, 1. 3. 7.

Ξενίζω, ίσω (ξένος), *to entertain*, 5. 5. 25.

Ξενικός, ή, όν, and ός, όν (ξένος), *of or belonging to a stranger*, *mercenary*=μισθοφόροι, 1. 2. 1, 2. 5. 22.

Ξένιος, α, ον (ξένος), *hospitable*; Ζεὺς Ξένιος, *Jupiter*, *the god of hospitality*, 3. 2. 4; ξένια, *friendly gifts*, *presents*, 4. 8. 24, 5. 5. 2; διδόναι, 5. 5. 14; πέμπειν, 5. 9. 15 ; δέχεσθαι, 5. 5. 3; ξενίοις δέχεσθαι, *to receive with presents*, 5. 5. 24 ; ἐπὶ ξένια καλεῖν, *to invite to dinner*, *to partake of hospitality*, 7. 6. 3.

Ξένος, ου, ὁ (ἱξ), *a guest-friend*, τινός, 2. 1. 5, &c.; τινὶ εἶναι, 1. 1. 10 ; γίγνεσθαι, 7. 1. 8 ; *mercenary soldier*, 1. 1. 10, 3. 18, 2. 6. 28.

Ξενόω——'Ο   93

Ξενόω, ώσω (ξένος), to entertain, 7. 8. 6, 8.

Ξενοφῶν, ῶντος, ὁ (ξένος), Xenophon, an Athenian, 3. 1. 5. &c.

Ξέρξης, ου, ὁ (Pers. khshayarsha, venerable king, Rawl.), Xerxes, the son of Darius Hystaspis and Atossa, king of Persia, succeeded his father, 486 B.C., died 465, was succeeded by Artaxerxes Longimanus, 1. 2. 9, 3. 2. 13.

Ξεστός, ή, όν (ξέω), polished, 3. 4. 10.

Ξηραίνω, ανῶ, ἐξήρασμαι and ἐξήραμμαι (ξηρός), to dry, 2. 3. 15.

Ξίφος, εος, τό (ξέω), a sword; Lat. ensis, straight (the crooked is μάχαιρα), from one to two and a half feet long, kept in a sheath (κολεός) and hung by a belt (τελαμών), 2. 2. 9, &c.

Ξόανον, ου, το (ξέω), an image carved of wood, 5. 3. 12.

Ξυήλη, ης, ἡ (ξύω = ξέω), a sickle-shaped dagger, 4. 7. 16, 8. 25.

Ξυλίζομαι, ίσομαι (ξύλον), to gather wood, 2. 4. 11.

Ξύλινος, η, ον (ξύλον), made of wood, wooden, 5. 2. 25.

Ξύλον, ου, τό (ξύω), wood, 4. 5. 5, &c.

O

'Ο, ἡ, τό, def. art. the, ὁ μέν—ὁ δέ, the one—the other, some—others, 1. 10. 4, 5. 4. 12; τὰ μέν—τὰ δέ, sometimes, at one time—sometimes, at another time, 4. 1. 14, 5. 6. 24; τὰ μὲν ἔπαθεν, he suffered some hurts, 1. 9. 6; with gen. οἱ

ἐκείνου, his friends, his soldiers, 1. 2. 15, 1. 5. 11; τὰ Κύρου, the affairs of Cyrus, 1. 3. 9; τὰ ἐκείνων, their property, 5. 1. 9, 6. 2. 11; τὰ τῶν στρατιωτῶν, the circumstances of our soldiers, 3. 1. 20; with adj. ὁ τοιοῦτος, 3. 1. 13; τὸ πλεῖον, 7. 6. 16; οἱ σύμπαντες, 1. 2. 9: with numerals to specify round numbers, ἀμφὶ τὰ εἴκοσι, 1. 7. 19; with part. τῶν ἐθελόντων, 1. 9. 15; τοὺς ἐλάσσοντας, 7. 7. 55, &c.; with inf. διὰ τὸ διεσπάρθαι, 2. 4. 3, 2. 6. 8; with adv. οἱ ἔνδον, 2. 5. 32; οἱ οἴκοι, 1. 2. 1, 7. 4; οἱ τότε, the men of that time, 2. 5. 11; ἢ τὸ πρόσθεν, than before of time, 1. 10. 11; τὰ οἴκοι, the advantages at home, 1. 7. 4; with prep. and case, οἱ σὺν αὐτοῖς, 3. 2. 11; τὸ κατ' αὐτούς, the part opposed to them, 1. 8. 21; τὸ ἀμφ' αὐτόν, sc. στράτευμα, 4. 1. 6; τὰ ὑπὲρ τοῦ λόφου, 1. 10. 14, what was going on beyond the hill; τὰ περὶ Προξένου, the fate of, 2. 5. 37; τὰ παρὰ βασιλέως, the messages from the king, 2. 3. 4; τὰ παρὰ σοῦ, the money due by you, 7. 7. 31; τὸ πρὸς ἑσπέραν, towards the west, 6. 2. 4; τὰ πρὸς τὸν πόλεμον, the matters connected with the war, 4. 3. 10; τὴν πρὸς τοὺς ἐναντίους, sc. ὁδόν, 6. 3. 10; τὰ πρὸς σέ, as regards your own interest, 7. 7. 30; in apposition, ὁ Ζεὺς ὁ σωτήρ, 3. 2. 9; ἡ πόλις οἱ Ταρσοί, 1. 2. 26; χεὶρ ἡ δεξιά, 1. 10. 1; it marks the subject, πολλοὶ ἦσαν οἱ τετρωμένοι, 3. 4. 30, 4. 8. 20, 5. 2. 1, 6.

4; it stands for the poss. pron. Κῦρος ἀναβὰς ἐπὶ τὸν ἵππον τὰ παλτὰ εἰς τὰς χεῖρας ἔλαβε, *his horse, his darts, his hands*, 1. 8. 3; the art. is not used with the king of the Persians, except 2. 4. 4: in 2. 5. 38, ὁ βασιλεύς, is *our king*; πολλοί, *many*; οἱ πολλοί, *the majority, the mob*; ὀλίγοι, *few*; οἱ ὀλίγοι, *the nobles*: ἄλλοι, *others*: οἱ ἄλλοι, *the rest*; πᾶν, *everything*; τὸ πᾶν, *the universe*; αὐτός, *himself, ipse*; ὁ αὐτός, *the same, idem*; it is used as a distributive, 1.3.21, τοῦ μηνὸς τῷ στρατιώτῃ, *each month to each soldier*, Lat. *singulis mensibus, singulis militibus*; the position of the art. when attributive is before the adj. as ἡ φιλία χώρα or ἡ χώρα ἡ φιλία, or even χώρα ἡ φιλία, *the friendly country*; the adj. as a predicate has no art. as, φιλία ἡ χώρα, or ἡ χώρα φιλία, *the country is friendly*; διὰ φιλίας τῆς χώρας, *through the country that is friendly*, 1. 3. 14; διὰ τῆς φιλίας χώρας, *through the friendly country*, as compared with other countries; διὰ φιλίας τῆς χώρας, *through the country now friendly*, as compared with itself at other times.— *Buttm.*

Ὀβελίσκος, ου ὁ (dim. from ὀβελός, *a spit*), *a spear*, 7. 8. 14.

Ὀβολός, οῦ, ὁ (ὀβελός), *an obol*, symbol Ο, a copper coin = eight χαλκοῖ, or a little more than three half-pence, 1. 5. 6.

Ὀγδοήκοντα, indecl. num. *eighty*, 4. 8. 15.

Ὄγδοος, η, ον (ὀκτώ), *eighth*, 4. 6. 1.

Ὅδε, ἥδε τόδε, *this*, referring frequently to what is coming, while οὗτος refers to what goes before, 2. 1. 20; it never stands between the art. and the noun, ὅδε ὁ ἀνήρ, or ὁ ἀνὴρ ὅδε, 2. 3. 19; τάδε, *so and so*, 2. 1. 17; in 7. 3. 47, supply to τάδε ἐστὶ or γίγνεται, *the very things* (*are happening*).

Ὁδεύω (ὁδός), *to go, travel*, 7. 8. 8.

Ὁδοιπορέω (ὁδός, πόρος), *to walk, go*, 5. 1. 14.

Ὁδοποιέω, ήσω (ὁδός, ποιέω), *to make a road*, ὁδόν, 4. 8. 8, 5. 1. 13; τινι, 3. 2. 24.

Ὁδός, οῦ, ἡ, *a way, road*, 1. 2. 13, 6. 2. 9, &c.; στενή, 3. 4. 19, &c.; ἀτριβής, 7. 3. 42; εὔπορος, 5. 1. 13; ὀρθή, 6. 4. 38; *journey*, δώδεκα ἡμερῶν, 7. 3. 16, 2. 2. 12, *march*, 1. 4. 11, 3. 4. 24; πᾶσαν τὴν ὁδόν, 1. 5. 9, often understood, εὐοδωτάτη, 4. 2. 9; ταχίστη, 4. 3. 24; μακροτάτη, 7. 8. 20; λοιπή, 3. 4. 46; τὴν πρός, 6. 3. 10; ἡ ἐπὶ Βαβυλῶνα, ἡ πρὸς ἕω φέρει, 3. 5. 15.

Ὀδρύσης, ου, ὁ, *an Odrysian*, οἱ Ὀδρύσαι, the Odrysæ were a people in Thrace, 7. 2.32, 5. 1.

Ὀδυσσεύς, έως, ὁ,* *Ulysses*, a famous Greek hero, king of Ithaca, 5. 1. 2.

Ὅθεν, adv. *whence*, 1. 2. 8, 2. 1. 3, 4. 7. 20, 2. 3. 14, with persons, *from whom*, 2. 5. 26.

---

* ὠδύσσομαι. Lat. odi, *child of hate*, Hom. Od. 19, 407; or Ὀλυσσεύς, Ὀλισσεύς, ἀλύγχ, *the little one, the dwarf*.

Ὅθενπερ, adv. strengthened form of ὅθεν, 2. 1. 3.

Οἷ, adv. whither, 1. 6. 10, al. οἷς.

Οἴκαδε (οἶκος), adv. to home, homewards, 7. 7. 57.

Οἰκεῖος, α, ον and ος, ον (οἶκος), of or belonging to a house, domestic, πρὸς τοὺς οἰκείους, to our families, 3. 2. 26, 39; τις τῶν οἰκείων, one of the household, 3. 3. 4; οἰκειότατος Ἀριαίῳ, very intimate with, 2. 6, 28.

Οἰκείως, adv. in a friendly way, 7. 5. 16.

Οἰκέτης, ου, ὁ (οἶκος), a domestic servant, 4. 5. 35, 6. 1; slave, 2. 3. 15.

Οἰκέω, ήσω, ᾤκηκα, ᾤκημαι, to inhabit, live, 1. 1. 9, 2. 3. 18; παρὰ θάλατταν, 5. 1. 13, ἐπί, 1. 4. 6, πρό, 5. 4. 15, ἐν, 4. 8. 22, &c., πόλις οἰκουμένη, a well-inhabited city, 1. 2. 6. &c.

Οἴκημα, ατος, τό (οἰκέω), a dwelling, 7. 4. 15.

Οἴκησις, εως, ἡ (οἰκέω), the act of dwelling, a dwelling, 7. 2. 38.

Οἰκία, ας, ἡ (οἶκος), a house, 4. 2. 22.

Οἰκίζω, οἰκιῶ, ᾤκισμαι (οἶκος), to found, settle, πόλιν, 5. 6. 17, 6. 2. 14; Pass. 5. 3. 7, 6. 4. 3.

Οἰκοδομέω, ήσω ᾠκοδόμηκα, ᾠκοδόμημαι (οἶκος, δέμω), to build a house, 5. 4. 26, to build, τεῖχος, 2. 4. 12, 3. 4. 7.

Οἴκοθεν (οἶκος), adv. from home, 4. 8. 25.

Οἴκοι, adv. (οἶκοι, pl. of οἶκος), at home, 7. 8. 4, 1. 1. 10; οἱ οἴκοι, the people at home, 1. 2. 1, 7. 4; τὰ οἴκοι, vitæ conditio in patria, 1. 7. 4.

Οἰκονόμος, ου, ὁ (οἶκος, νέμω), a manager of a household, a manager, 1. 9. 19, hence economy, economist, &c.

Οἶκος, ου, ὁ, a house, home, Lat. vicus, 2. 4. 8.

Οἰκτείρω, οἰκτερῶ, 1 aor. ᾤκτειρα (οἶκτος), to pity, 1. 4. 7, 3. 1. 19.

Οἶνος, ου, ὁ, wine, Lat. vinum, 1. 2. 13, ἡδύς, 1. 9. 25, παλαιὸς εὐώδης, 4. 4. 9; φοινίκων, palm-wine, 2. 3. 14; κρίθινος, beer or whisky, 4. 5. 26.

Οἰνοχόος, ου, ὁ (οἶνος, χέω), a cup-bearer, 4. 4. 21, 7. 3. 24.

Οἴομαι, οἰήσομαι, 1 aor. ᾠήθην, inf. οἰηθῆναι, impf. ᾠόμην and ᾤμην, and so in pres. οἶμαι, to think, 1. 9. 22, 3. 1. 35; βέλτιστον εἶναι, 5. 1. 8; ἡμᾶς τοιαῦτα παθεῖν, 3. 2. 3; οὐκ ἂν ἱκανὸς εἶναι, 1. 3. 6, 2. 1. 12, 3. 1. 17, &c.

Οἷος, οἴα, οἶον (ὅς, ἥ, ὅ), what sort of, such as, Lat. qualis. correl. τοιοῦτος, Lat. talis. ἄνπερ οἵαν ἐδύναντο ταρέσχον, 4. 8. 8, 5. 8. 3, 3. 1. 15, 7. 4. 1, 1. 7. 4; οἶον, such as, 4. 1. 14, 7. 3. 32; ὥρα οἵα ἄρδειν, the proper season for watering, 2. 3. 13; οἷός τέ εἰμι, I am able, οἷόν τέ ἐστι, it is possible, οὐχ οἷον, &c., it is impossible, 1. 3. 17, 3. 3. 9, &c.; without ἐστι, 2. 2. 3, 3. 3. 15, 7. 7. 51; ὡς οἷόν τε μάλιστα πεφυλαγμένως, 2. 4. 24.

Οἷόσπερ, οἵαπερ, οἷόνπερ, strengthened form of οἷος, 4. 4. 16, 5. 4. 13; οἷόσπερ = τοιαύτη πρὸς οἷόσπερ, 1. 3. 18, οἷόσπερ, ας, 1. 8. 18.

Ὄις, οἴος, ἡ, also οἷς, pl. ὄιες, or οἷς, 4. 5. 25, 5. 3. 11, 10. 3.

'Οϊστός, οῦ, ὁ (φέρω, οἴσω), also οἰστός, an arrow, 2. 1. 6.

Οἰταῖος, α, ον, Œtœan, near Œta, a mountain in Thessaly, 7071 feet, 4. 6. 20.

Οἴχομαι, οἰχήσομαι, οἴχωκα and ᾤχωκα, οἴχηκα and ᾤχηκα, οἴχημαι and ᾤχημαι, to be gone, as perf. 1. 4. 8; εἰς τὸ πρόσθεν, 1. 10. 5; ἄλλην ὁδόν, 3. 5. 1; ᾤχετο πλέων, he sailed away, 2. 6. 3, ἀπιών, 3. 3. 5, φερόμενοι, 4. 7. 14.

Οἰωνός, οῦ, ὁ (οἶος, alone), a solitary bird, bird of prey, hence an omen, τοῦ Διός, sent by Jupiter, 3. 2. 9, 5. 9. 23, 6. 3. 21.

'Οκέλλω (=κέλλω, Lat. cello), to run ashore, 7. 5. 12.

'Οκλάζω, ἄσω (κλάω), to bend the knee, to sink on bended knee, in dancing, 5. 9. 10.

'Οκνέω, ήσω (ὄκνος), to shrink from, with inf., 1. 3. 17; to be afraid, μή with conj. 2. 3. 9, with opt. 6. 4. 5.

'Οκνηρῶς (ὄκνος), with reluctance, 7. 1. 7.

Ὄκνος, ου, ὁ, reluctance, unwillingness, 4. 4. 11.

'Οκτακισχίλιοι, αι, α, eight thousand, 5. 3. 3.

'Οκτακόσιοι, αι, α, eight hundred, 1. 2. 9.

'Οκτώ, eight, 1. 2. 6.

'Οκτωκαίδεκα, eighteen, 3. 4. 5.

Ολεθρος, ου ὁ (ὄλλυμι), ruin, destruction, 1. 2. 26.

'Ολίγος, η, ον, few, small, little, 1. 5. 12, 5. 5. 1; κατ' ὀλίγους, in small parties, 7. 6. 29; ὀλίγον ποιεῖσθαι, to hold of small account, 6. 4. 11; ὀλίγας (πληγὰς) παίειν, to strike (too) few blows, 5. 8. 12;

small, χωρίον, 3. 3. 9; little, χρόνος, 3. 4. 46; ὀλίγον ὕστερον, 7. 2. 20; Comp. μείων, Superl. ὀλίγιστος.

'Ολισθάνω, or αίνω, ὀλισθήσω, ὠλίσθηκα, 2 aor. ὤλισθον (ὄλισθος, λεῖος), to slip, 3. 5. 11.

'Ολισθηρός, ά, όν (ὀλισθάνω), slippery, 4. 3. 6.

'Ολκάς, άδος, ἡ (ἕλκω), a ship of burden, merchantman, 1. 4. 6, Eng. hulk.

'Ολοίτροχος, ὁ, ἡ, and ὀλοίτροχυς (ὀλοός, τρέχω, destructive rollers, or ὅλος, τρέχω, quite round), a round stone, sc. λίθος, 4. 2. 3.

'Ολοκαυτέω (ὅλος, καίω), to bring a burnt offering, 7. 8. 4.

Ὅλος, η, ον, whole, ὅλη ἡ νύξ, 4. 2. 4; ἡ ἡμέρα ὅλη, 3. 3. 11.

'Ολυμπία, ας, ἡ, Olympia, a town in Elis, where the Olympic games were celebrated, 5. 3. 7.

'Ολύνθιος, α, ον, Olynthian, or a native of Olynthus, a town on the isthmus of Pallene, 1. 2. 6.

'Ομαλής, ής, ές (ὁμός), level, even, 4. 6. 12.

'Ομαλός, ή, όν (ὁμός), even, level, smooth, 4. 2. 16; adv. ὁμαλῶς, in an even line, =ἐν ἴσῳ, 1. 8. 14.

Ὅμηρος, ου, ὁ (ὁμός, ἄρω), a hostage, τοῦ ἐκπέμπειν, for the sending, 3. 2. 24, 7. 4. 12.

'Ομιλέω, ήσω (ὅμιλος, ὁμός, ἴλη), associate with, τινί, 3. 2. 25.

'Ομίχλη, ης, ἡ (ὀμίχω), a mist, fog, 4. 2. 7.

Ὄμμα, ατος, τό (ὄπτω), the eye, 7. 7. 46.

'Όμνυμι and ὀμνύω, ὀμοῦμαι, ὀμώμοκα, ὀμώμομαι and ὀμώμοσμαι, to swear, θεούς, by the *gods*, 5. 9. 31; with inf., μὴ προδώσειν, 2. 2. 8; ἡμῖν νομιεῖν, 2. 5. 39; ἢ μὴν πορεύεσθαι, 2. 3. 27, 6. 4. 17.

Ὅμοιος, α, ον, or ος, ον (ὁμός), *like*, πυρεία ὁμοία φυγῇ, 4. 1. 17; ὅμοια ἅπερ ἄν, *just as they would have done*, 5. 4. 34; ὅμοιοι ἦσαν θαυμάζειν, *they seemed to wonder*, 3. 5. 13; ἐν τῷ ὁμοίῳ, *on a level*, 4. 6. 18; οἱ ὅμοιοι, *of the same rank, the peers*, citizens who had equal right to hold state offices, 4. 6. 14; ὁμοίως, adv. *in like manner*, 7. 6. 10; ὥσπερ, 6. 3. 31, *just as if*; πάντες ὁ. *all alike*, 1. 3. 12.

Ὁμολογέω, ήσω, &c. (ὁμός, λέγω), *to confess*, 6. 4. 17; τι, 1. 6. 7; ἄδικος γεγενῆσθαι, 1. 6. 8, 5. 8. 3; *to acknowledge*, 5. 9. 27, 28; *to agree*, 7. 4. 13, 22; *confess*, pass., 1. 9. 1, 14, 20, 6. 1. 9. ὁμολογουμένως ἐκ πάντων, *by the acknowledgment of all*, 2. 6. 1.

Ὁμομήτριος, α, ον (ὁμός, μήτηρ), *of the same mother*, 3. 1. 17.

Ὁμοπάτριος, α, ον (ὁμός, πατήρ), *of the same father*, 3. 1. 17.

Ὁμόσε (ὁμός), adv. *to the same place* = *cominus, to come to close quarters, engage in close combat, hand to hand*, ἰέναι, 6. 3. 23; θεῖν, 3. 4. 4; χωρεῖν, 5. 4. 26.

Ὁμοτράπεζος, ος, ον (ὁμός, τράπεζα), *a companion at table*, 1. 8. 25.

Ὁμοῦ (ὁμός), adv. *together*, 1. 10. 8; εἶναι, 5. 6. 32, 7. 1. 28; ἀλλήλοις, 4. 6. 24; γίγνεσθαι, 4. 2. 22, 5. 4. 25, 4. 5. 29, 5. 2. 14, 3. 9.

Ὀμφαλός, οῦ, ὁ, *the navel*, Lat. umbilicus, 4. 5. 2.

Ὅμως (ὁμός), adv. *yet, nevertheless*, 2. 2. 17, 4. 23, 1. 8. 23, 3. 1. 10, 2. 16; after καίπερ, 5. 5. 17; ὅμως δέ, *but yet*, 4. 4. 21, 5. 6. 6, 7. 23.

Ὄναρ, τό, only in nom. and acc., ὄνειρος, ου, ὁ, is used in the sing., and ὀνείρατα in the pl., *a dream*; ὄναρ, 3. 1. 12; ὀνείρατα, 4. 3. 13; ὄναρ εἶδεν, *had a dream*, 4. 3. 8.

Ὀνίνημι, ὀνήσω, 1 aor. act. ὤνησα; pass. ὠνήθην, *to benefit*, τὸ στράτευμα, 3. 1. 38, 5. 9. 32, 7. 1. 21; τινά τι, 5. 6. 20; ὀνηθῆναί τι, 5. 5. 2.

Ὄνομα, ατος, τό (γιγνώσκω), *a name*, 4. 7. 21, 1. 5. 4, 2. 4. 13; ὀνόματι, *by name*, 1. 4. 11, or acc. 2. 4. 28, 1. 4. 4, 5. 10; τοὔνομα, 5. 2. 29; *a name=fame*, 5. 6. 17; κτᾶσθαι, 2. 6. 17; 5. 9. 20, 7. 3. 19.

Ὀνομάζω, άσω, ὠνόμακα, ὠνόμασμαι (ὄνομα), *to name* or *call*.

Ὀνομαστί, adv. (ὄνομα), *by name*, 6. 3. 24.

Ὄνος, ου, ὁ and ἡ, *an ass, a wild ass*, ὄνος ἄγριος, 1. 5. 2; ὄνος ἀλέτης, *a mill-stone*, 1. 5. 5.

Ὄξος, εος τό (ὀξύς), *vinegar, an acid drink*, 2. 3. 14.

Ὀξύς, εῖα, ύ, *sharp, sour*, 5. 4. 29.

Ὅπη, adv. *where*, 4. 2. 12, 24, 6. 2. 3, &c.; *in what way, as*, 2. 1. 19, 4. 5. 1, 5. 9. 21.

Ὁπηνίκα, adv. *when*, 3. 5. 18.

Ὄπισθεν (as ὄπις from ἕπομαι), *behind*, opp. πρόσθεν, 5. 4. 12;

ἔπεσθαι, 4. 7. 22, 5. 6. 9;
ποιεῖσθαι, 1. 10. 9; ὅ. τῶν
ὑποζυγίων, 4. 2. 9, 1. 7. 9;
ἐκ τοῦ ὅ., 4. 1. 6; εἰς τοὔπισθεν, 3. 3. 10; τὰ ὅ., the rear,
3. 4. 40; οἱ ὅ., those in the
rear, 4. 2. 25, 3. 7.

'Οπισθοφυλακέω, ήσω (ὄπισθεν,
φυλάσσω), to guard the rear,
2. 3. 10, 3. 2. 36, 4. 1. 15,
4. 5. 7, &c.

'Οπισθοφυλακία, ας, ἡ (ὄπισθεν,
φύλαξ), the command of the
rear-guard, 4. 6. 19.

'Οπισθοφύλαξ, ακος, ὁ, one of the
rear-guard; οἱ ὁ., the rear-
guard, 3. 3. 7, 4. 1. 17, &c.;
ὁπλῖται, 4. 1. 6; εὐζωνότατοι,
4. 3. 20; λοχαγοί, 4. 7. 8.

'Οπίσω, adv. (as ὄπις from
ἕπομαι), back, behind his back,
5. 9. 8.

'Οπλίζω, ίσω, &c. (ὅπλον), to
arm, ὡπλισμένος, 1. 8. 6, 2.
6. 25.

"Οπλισις, εως, ἡ (ὅπλον), warlike equipment, 2. 5. 17.

'Οπλιτεύω, εύσω, to serve as a
hoplite or heavy-armed soldier,
5. 8. 5.

'Οπλίτης, ου, ὁ (ὅπλον), a
hoplite or heavy-armed soldier, having a helmet, κράνος;
a cuirass, θώραξ; greaves,
κνημῖδες; a shield, ἀσπίς; a
curved sword, μάχαιρα; and
a spear, δόρυ, 1. 1. 2, &c.

'Οπλιτικός, ή, όν (ὅπλον), of or
belonging to the hoplites, τὸ
ὁπλιτικόν=οἱ ὁπλῖται, 7. 6.
26, 4. 8. 18, &c.

'Οπλομαχία, ας, ἡ (ὅπλον, μάχομαι), the fighting of the
hoplites, military tactics, 2.
1. 7.

"Οπλον, ου, τό, pl., ὅπλα, arms,
7. 3. 40; λαμβάνειν, 1. 2. 2,
3. 7; ἔχειν, 1. 10. 3, 5. 7. 9;
ἐν τοῖς ὅπλοις εἶναι, to be
under arms, 3. 2. 28; κατα-
τίθεσθαι, 5. 2. 15, to put
aside; τίθεσθαι (1) to halt
under arms, 1. 5. 14, 10. 16,
4. 2. 16, &c.; (2) to station
themselves, arrange themselves,
1. 6. 4, 5. 2. 19, 2. 2. 21;
(3) to lay up their arms, 1. 5.
17; ἔκειντο τὰ ὅπλα, 4. 2. 20,
=ὁπλῖται, so 2. 2. 4, 3. 2.
36; πρὸ τῶν ὅπλων, in front
of the arms, the arms were
piled in one place in the
camp, 2. 4. 15, 3. 1. 33, 5.
7. 21.

'Οπόθεν, adv. (πόθεν), whence,
5. 7. 6; οὐκ εἶχον ὁπόθεν
λαμβάνοιεν, they had no place
from whence to take, 3. 5. 3,
so 2. 4. 5, 5. 10. 4; ὁπόθεν
οἴχοιτο, wherever he was gone,
3. 1. 32; to a place where, 5.
2. 2.

"Οποι (ποῖ), adv. whither, where,
1. 9. 13, 3. 5. 13, 17; ὅποι
δύεται, where it sets, 5. 7. 6;
ὅποι ἂν ἐλθόντες ἀγορὰν μὴ
ἔχωμεν, wherever we go and
have no market, 5. 5. 16;
οὐχ ἕξουσιν ὅποι φύγωσιν,
they will have no place to
flee to, 2. 4. 20, 5. 1. 8, 7.
7. 5.

'Οποῖος, α, ον (ποῖος), what sort
=Lat. qualis, 3. 1. 13; ταῦτα
ὁ., those things which, 5. 6.
28, 5. 2. 3, 6. 1. 2; ἄλλα
ὁποῖα ἂν δύνωνται κράτιστα,
and such other things as they
can with the greatest effect, 7.
7. 15; ἡγεῖται τοῦ στρατεύματος ὁποῖον ἂν ἀεὶ πρὸς τὴν
χώραν συμφέρῃ, that part of

the army leads that is always
suited to the country, 7. 3.
37; whatever, 2. 2. 2.

Ὁπόσος, η, ον (πόσος), how
great=Lat. quantus, ὁπόσοι,
how many, however many, 1.
1. 6; as many as, 5. 6. 28;
ὁπόσον ἐβούλετο, as much as
he pleased, 4. 3. 8; like rel.
who, which, whoever, whatever,
4. 1. 12, 5. 2. 16, 1. 10. 3;
with opt. 1. 2. 1, 7. 2. 33;
with opt. and ἄν, 3. 2. 12;
with ἄν and conj. 3. 2. 21, 7.
2. 36, 3. 10; ὁπόσον—το-
σοῦτον, however far—so far,
3. 3. 10, with opt., so 5. 1. 16,
ὁπόσα, whatever.

Ὁπόταν (ὁπότε, ἄν), whenever,
with conj. after a pres. 2. 3.
27, after a fut. 5. 7. 8, 6. 3.
15, 7. 3. 36; after a historical
tense, 5. 2. 12, 7. 1. 12.

Ὁπότε (ποτε), when, whenever,
with ind. 1. 6. 7, 2. 1. 1, 4.
7. 16; with opt. 3. 2. 36, 4.
6. 20, 7. 3. 18, 7. 17, 1. 5. 7,
1. 9. 25, 2. 6. 27, &c.

Ὁπότερος, α, ον (πότερος), which
of two, Lat. uter, 3. 4. 42, 7.
7. 18; with ἄν and conj. 3.
1. 21.

Ὅπου (ποῦ), adv. where, where-
ever, with ind. 1. 5. 9, 3. 1.
3, 7. 2. 18, &c.; with ἄν and
conj. 1. 3. 6, 2. 3. 26, 3. 2. 9;
with opt. 1. 9. 15, 27, 3. 1.
32, 4. 5. 30.

Ὀπτάω, ήσω, &c., to roast, bake
of bread, 5. 4. 29.

Ὀπτός, ή, όν, shortened for ὀπ-
τητός, from ὀπτάω, roasted,
baked of bread, burnt of bricks,
2. 4. 12.

Ὅπως (πῶς), how, with ind. of
aor. 1. 6. 11; fut. 1. 1. 4, 4.

6. 7, 8. 9; with ἄν and opt. 3.
1. 7, 2. 5. 7, 4. 3. 14, 5. 7. 7,
&c.; that, see that, with ind.
fut.1.7.3, 3.1.16, 14, 4.6.10,
3. 1. 18, 7. 3. 34; with conj.
after a pres. 3. 2. 3, 4. 6. 15,
5. 1. 12; with aor. conj. 1.
3. 14, 5. 6. 21; after a past,
1. 6. 6, 2. 5. 28, 7. 4. 2;
with opt. after a pres. hist.
4. 6. 1, 7. 19; after an im-
perf. 2. 6. 21, 4. 2. 2, 7. 2.
12; after an aor. 1. 4. 5, 2.
1. 9, 4. 1. 22, 7. 6. 36.

Ὁράω, ὄψομαι, ἑώρακα, ἑώραμαι
and ὦμμαι, 2 p. ὄπωπα, 2 aor.
εἶδον, conj. ἴδω, fut. pass.
ὁραθήσομαι and ὀφθήσομαι,
impf. ἑώρων, to see, 4. 1. 20,
1. 8. 26, &c.; ὁρᾷ τὸν Κῦρον
ἃ ἐποίει, he sees what Cyrus
was doing, 4. 7. 11; τοὺς
ἀνθρώπους ὡς εἶχον, 6. 2. 23;
πάντα ὄντα, 5. 5. 24; ἀσφαλὲς
ὄν, 7. 2. 15, 5. 8. 15; ὅτι, 5.
9. 27; τοὺς πολεμίους ὅτι, 3.
2. 29; τοὺς στρατηγοὺς οἷα,
3. 2. 8; pass. 2. 3. 3, 4. 3. 5,
6. 13.

Ὀργή, ῆς, ἡ (ὀρέγω), rage, anger,
1. 5. 8, 2. 6. 9.

Ὀργίζομαι, ίσομαι or ιοῦμαι,
ὤργισμαι, Act. to exasperate;
Mid. to be enraged, 1. 2. 26,
5. 9. 30; τινί, 1. 5. 11.

Ὀργυιά, ᾶς, ἡ (ὀρέγω), the length
of the outstretched arms across
the body, a fathom, six feet,
1. 7. 14, 4. 5. 4, 7. 1. 30.

Ὀρέγω, ὀρέξω, ὤρεγμαι and
ὀρώρεγμαι, to stretch out, hand,
7. 3. 29.

Ὀρεινός, ή, όν (ὄρος), mountain-
ous, hilly; ὀρεινοὶ Θρᾷκες,
the hill Thracians, 7. 4. 11,
5. 2. 2.

Ὄρθιος, α, ον and ος, ον (ὀρθός), straight up, steep, μαστός, 4. 2. 14; ὁδός, 1. 2. 21, 4. 1. 20; ὄρθιον ἱέναι, to march up-hill, 4. 6. 12; τὸ ὄ. the decli-vity, the slope, 4. 2. 3, 8. 28; ὄρθιοι λόχοι, Liv. recti or-dines, battalions in column (φάλαγξ, in line); ὁ. τοὺς λό-χους ποιεῖσθαι, to throw the battalions into column, 4. 2. 11, 8. 10; ἄγειν, to bring up in column, 4. 3. 17, i.e. with more men in depth than in front.

Ὀρθός, ή, όν, straight, ὁδός, 6. 4. 38; ἵσταται, 4. 8. 20; τιάρα, upright, 2. 5. 23 ; Lat. rectus.

Ὄρθρος, ου, ὁ (ὄρνυμι, to raise), the dawn, 2. 2. 21, 4. 3. 8.

Ὀρθῶς, adv. from ὀρθός, rightly, κρίνειν, 1. 9. 30; λέγειν, 7. 3. 39, 2. 5. 6 ; ἔχειν, it was right, 3. 2. 7.

Ὁρίζω, ίσω, ὥρικα, ὥρισμαι (ὅρος), to bound, 4. 3. 1, 8. 1, 2 ; to define, 7. 7. 36 ; ὁρί-ζεσθαι ·στήλας, to set up pillars for boundaries, 7. 5. 13.

Ὅριον, ου, τό, a boundary, fron-tier, 4. 8. 8, 5. 4. 2, 10. 19.

Ὅρκος, ου, ὁ (ἕρκος, a barrier, εἴργω, to restrain), an oath, 2. 5. 3 ; θεῶν, 2. 5. 7, 3. 1. 22, 2. 10, Lat. Orcus.

Ὁρμάω, ήσω, ὥρμηκα, ὥρμημαι (ὁρμή, ὄρνυμι, to raise), to in-cite, urge, rush; Mid. to set out, ἐκ χώρας, 3. 4. 33 ; εἰς τὸ διώ-κειν, 1. 8. 25; ἐπ' αὐτούς, 4. 3. 31 ; κατ' αὐτούς, 5. 7. 25 ; ἁμιλλᾶσθαι, 3. 4. 4 (ὁδόν, to start on the way, 3. 1. 8), ἐξ Ἐφέσου, 5. 9. 23, &c.

Ὁρμέω, ήσω, &c. (ὅρμος, εἴρω,

to fasten), to lie at anchor (ὁρμίζω, to bring to anchor), 1. 4. 3, 6.

Ὁρμή, ῆς, ἡ (ὄρνυμι, to raise), movement, 3. 1. 10 ; ἐν ὁρμῇ, on the start, 2. 1. 3 ; μιᾷ ὁρμῇ, with one impulse, 3. 2. 9.

Ὁρμίζω, ίσω, ὥρμικα, ὥρμισμαι (ὅρμος), to bring to anchor, moor, 3. 5. 10 ; Mid. to come to, lie at anchor, 5. 9. 15, 10. 1, 2.

Ὄρνεον, ου, τό (ὄρνις), a bird, 5. 9. 23.

Ὀρνίθειος, α, ον or ος, ον, fowl's κρέα, flesh, 4. 5. 31, from

Ὄρνις, ῖθος, ἡ and ὁ (ὄρνυμι), a fowl, 4. 5. 25.

Ὀρόντας, ου, ὁ, Orontas, the son-in-law of Artaxerxes, satrap of Armenia. His wife's name was Rhodogune (Ῥοδογούνη), 2. 4. 8, 3. 4. 13.

Ὀρόντης, ου, ὁ, Orontes, a Per-sian put to death by Cyrus, 1. 6. 1, &c.

Ὄρος, εος, τό (ὄρνυμι), a moun-tain, 4. 7. 21; ὅρος, a boun-dary ; ὀρός or ὀρρός, whey.

Ὄροφος, ου, ὁ (ἐρέφω), thatch, 7. 4. 16.

Ὀρύττω or ὕσσω, ὕξω, ὀρώρυχα, ὀρώρυγμαι, vb. ὀρυκτός, 1. 7. 14; to dig, 5. 8. 9, 1. 5. 5.

Ὀρφανός, ή, όν (ὀρφός, Lat. orbus), an orphan, 7. 2. 32.

Ὀρχέομαι, ήσομαι, to dance (Act. to make dance), 5. 4. 34, 9. 5, 11, 12.

Ὄρχησις, εως, ἡ (ὀρχέω), a dance, 5. 9. 8.

Ὀρχηστρίς, ίδος, ἡ (ὀρχέω), a female dancer, 5. 9. 12.

Ὀρχομένιος, α, ον, Orchomenian, from

Ὀρχομενός, οῦ, ὁ, Orchomenus, a

town in Arcadia, NW. from Mantinea, 2. 5. 37.

Ὅς, ἥ, ὅ, rel. pron., *who, which*, 1. 5. 13, 7. 13, 2. 5. 27; ἐφ' ἅ, for ταῦτα ἐφ' ἅ, 1. 2. 2; so ἐφ' οὕς, 5. 1. 8; περὶ ὧν, 7. 6. 15; often the rel. precedes the demonstr., ὃ εἶπεν ἐψεύσθη τοῦτο, 1. 8. 11, 2. 6. 26, 1. 9. 29, 2. 5. 27, 6. 2. 9, 2. 3. 1; sometimes includes demonstr. and anteced. within itself, οὓς ἄνδρας for τοὺς ἄνδρας οὕς, 3. 2. 20, 5. 7. 33; ὃ δὲ λέγεις, *quod dicis, as to what you say*, 5. 5. 20; so ἃ διεπράττοντο, 3. 5. 5; Attic attraction, when the rel. is in the case of the antecedent, ἄξιοι τῆς ἐλευθερίας ἧς, 1. 7. 3, 1. 1. 8, 3. 2. 21; ταῖς ἑταίραις αἷς ἦγον, 5. 4. 33, 1. 3. 16; τῷ ἀνδρὶ ᾧ, 1. 3. 15, 2. 5. 14; ἡμέρᾳ ἕκτῃ ἀφ' ἧς for ἀπὸ ταύτης ᾗ, 5. 10. 12; ἧς κατεστρέφετο χώρας, for τῆς χώρας ἥν, 1. 9. 14; ἡμιόλιον οὗ for τούτου ὅ, 1. 3. 21, 5. 7. 13, 4. 7. 16, 1. 3. 4, 7. 7. 8, 4. 5. 17, 1. 9. 25, 28; sometimes the anteced. is attracted to the case of the rel. ἀνεῖλε θεοῖς οἷς, for θεοὺς οἷς, 3. 1. 6, 1. 4. 15; with ind. in oblique narrative, 1. 9. 28, 3. 1. 6, 5. 2. 17; impf. 2. 1. 2, 7. 3. 7; fut. 2. 1. 17, 4. 7. 20; with conj. 1. 7. 7, and ἄν, 1. 3. 15; with opt. 1. 3. 17, &c. ἐν ᾧ (χρόνῳ), *during which time*, 1. 2. 20; καὶ ὅς, *and he*; ἀφ' οὗ, *since*, 3. 2. 14; ἐξ οὗ, *in consequence of which*, 6. 4. 11; μέχρις οὗ, *unto where*, 1. 7. 6, 5. 4. 16; δι' ὅ, *on which account, wherefore*, 1. 2. 21.

Ὅσιος, α, ον, *pious*, 2. 6. 25, 5. 8. 26.

Ὅσος, η, ον, Lat. *quantus, how great*, 3. 1. 19; pl. *how many*, 2. 5. 10; *as*, after τοσοῦτος, τοσοῦτοι ὅσους, *so many as*, 2. 1. 16, 4. 26, 3. 1. 36; ταῦτα ὅσα, 3. 1. 7, 5. 1. 5; πᾶν ὅσον, 7. 6. 36; πάντα ὅσα, 4. 4. 9, 7. 1. 2; λαβόντες ὅσοι ἦσαν βόες, 7. 8. 16; with ind. 5. 3. 12, 5. 14; in oblique narrative, 4. 2. 17; with opt. iterative, 1. 9. 23; in oblique narr. 1. 5. 9, 2. 6. 25; with ἄν and conj. 5. 1. 12, 6. 1. 14, 7. 3. 20; *as far as*, 3. 3. 15, 7. 3. 9; ὅσον οὐ, *all but*, 7. 2. 5; ἐφ' ὅσον, *as wide as*, 6. 1. 19; ὅσῳ—τοσούτῳ, *the more—the more*, with comparatives, Lat. *quanto—tanto*, 7. 3. 20.

Ὁσοσπερ, ηπερ, ονπερ, *as many as*, 6. 3. 28, 4. 3. 2, 7. 4. 19; πάντες ὅσοιπερ, 1. 7. 9; ὅσῳπερ χαλεπώτερον, *how much more difficult*, 7. 7. 28.

Ὅσπερ, ἥπερ, ὅπερ, *who, which indeed*, 2. 6. 29, 3. 2. 10; ὅπερ, *what*, 1. 4. 5, 3. 2. 29; ἅπερ, 5. 4. 34, 4. 20, 8. 15.

Ὄσπριον, ου, τό, *pulse*, 4. 4. 9, 5. 26, 6. 2. 6, 4. 1.

Ὅστις, ἥτις, ὅ, τι, *who, which*, in indirect questions, with ind. 5. 7. 23, 2. 1. 2, 1. 6. 9, 2. 1. 17, 2. 4. 7, 7. 3. 29, 1. 8. 21, &c.; with conj. 1. 7. 7; opt. 3. 1. 40, 2. 3. 23, 5. 7. 6; τις ἔσται ὅστις with ind. 2. 1. 11, 4. 1. 26; *whoever*, 3. 1. 26, 2. 9, 39; a sing. after a pl. τὰ ἐπιτήδεια ὅτῳ, 4. 1. 9, 3. 3. 1, 6. 3. 7; ὅστις— πάντας, 1. 1. 5, 2. 5. 32;

ἐξ ὅτου, since, 7. 8. 4; ὅτου is for οὗτινος, and ὅτῳ for ᾧτινι, ὅτου δή, some one or other, 4. 7. 25, 5. 2. 24; μηδ' ὁντιναοῦν μισθὸν προσαιτήσας, without even asking any additional pay whatever, 7.6.27.

'Οσφραίνομαι, ὀσφρήσομαι, 1 aor. pass. ὠσφράνθην, to perceive by the smell, to smell, 5. 8. 3.

"Οταν, when, whenever, with conj. 5. 5. 20, 7. 12, 8. 20, 7.7. 47, 6. 4. 26, &c.

"Οτε, when, with ind. 1. 2. 9, 3. 4. 8, 5. 3. 6, &c.; opt. 2. 6. 12, 4. 1. 16.

"Οτι, I. that, with ind. even in oblique nar. 7. 2. 19, 2. 4. 21, &c., and also opt. 2. 2. 15, 5. 9. 16; ἔλεγον ὅτι εἴη, 3. 5. 15, 1. 10, 1. 3. 7; ὅτι in direct nar. answers to our inverted commas, and is not translated,1.6.7,8; pleonastic in some edd., with inf.5.9. 29; with ὡς, 6.2.18. II. because, 2. 6. 28, 29, 4. 8. 6; with ind. even in oblique nar. 1. 2. 21, 2. 3. 19. III. quam, with superl. ὅτι πλεῖστοι, as many as possible, 3. 1. 45, 1. 1. 6, 3. 4. 5, &c.

Οὐ, before a vowel οὐκ, before an aspirate οὐχ, when emphatic οὔ, 1. 6. 7; not, no, 2. 6. 5, &c.; οὐκ ἔφη=negavit, 1. 3. 1, 2. 5. 12; οὐ μὴ γένηται, will not prove, 5. 10. 4, 7. 3. 26, in interrog. sentences= nonne, 3. 1. 29, 7. 6. 24.

Οὗ, adv., where, 3. 4. 32, 4. 7. 27; προϊόντες οὗ, advancing to the place where, 2. 1. 6.

Οὗ, Dat. οἷ, Acc. ἕ, Pers. Pron. sui, sibi, se, himself, him, 1. 1. 8, 2. 8; σφεῖς, 5. 7. 18, 7. 5.

9; σφῶν, 4. 3. 28, 5. 6. 3; σφᾶς, 5. 7. 25, 7. 2. 16; σφίσι, 6. 4. 5.

Οὐδαμῇ, adv., nowhere, 5. 5. 3, 7. 3. 12.

Οὐδαμόθεν, adv., from nowhere, 2. 4. 23, 4. 5. 30.

Οὐδαμοῦ, adv., nowhere, 6. 1.16, 2. 2. 18, &c.

Οὐδέ, adv., and not, nor, 1. 2. 25, 1. 4. 8, 4. 7. 11; οὔτε— οὔτε—οὐδέ, neither—nor—nor yet, 1. 6. 11; οὐδὲ εἷς, not one even, 3. 1. 2, 31, 6. 1. 16.

Οὐδείς, εμία, έν, no one, none, 1. 9. 3; οὐδεὶς οὐδέν, 3. 1. 16, 1. 8. 20; οὐδέν, in no way, not at all, 7. 1. 25; so οὐδέν τι, 7. 3. 35.

Οὐδέποτε, adv., never, 2. 6. 13.

Οὐδέπω, adv., not yet, 7. 3. 24.

Οὐκέτι, adv., no longer, 1. 8. 17, 2. 6. 3; οὐκέτι μή, 2. 2. 12.

Οὔκουν, not therefore, surely not; οὐκοῦν, therefore, then, 1. 6. 7, 3. 2. 19, 6. 3. 21, 3. 5. 6, 2. 5. 24.

Οὖν, therefore, 1.4.14, 4.5.15; after γάρ, 3. 2. 30, 32, 5. 1. 4, 2. 6. 11; μὲν οὖν, 1. 7. 17, 3. 1. 19; δ' οὖν, 1. 2. 12; καὶ γάρ οὖν, wherefore, 1. 9. 8, 12, 17, 2. 6. 13.

Οὗπερ, where indeed, 4. 8. 26.

Οὔποτε, never, 2. 5. 7, 3. 1. 3, 1. 3. 5.

Οὔπω, not yet, 3. 2. 14, 1. 5. 12, &c.

Οὐρά, ᾶς, ἡ, the tail, the rear of of an army, 3. 4. 38, 42, 6. 3. 5.

Οὐραγός, οῦ, ὁ (οὐρά, ἡγέομαι), the leader of the rear-guard, 4. 3. 26, 29.

Οὐρανός, οῦ, ὁ (ὄρνυμι, to raise), heaven, 4. 2. 2.

Οὖς, ὠτός, τό, *the ear*, 7. 4. 3.

Οὔτε—οὔτε, *neither—nor*, 1. 3. 6; οὔτε—οὔτε μήν, *nor—nor indeed*, 7. 6. 22; οὔτε—τέ, *neque—et, and not—and*, 2. 5. 4, 4. 3. 6, 5. 28; οὔτε—δέ, 5. 9. 26, 6. 1. 16.

Οὔτι, *not at all, by no means*, 7. 6. 11, al. οὔτοι.

Οὖτος, αὕτη, τοῦτο, dem. pron., *this*, does not stand between the art. and noun ; οὖτος ὁ ἀνήρ, or ὁ ἀνὴρ οὖτος, 7. 5. 3 ; it is sometimes assimilated with the pred. ταύτην τὴν γνώμην ἔχω, *this is the opinion I entertain*, 2. 2. 12, 4. 8. 4, 7. 5, 3. 5. 9 ; ταῦτα φλυαρίας εἶναι, 1. 3. 18; ταῦτα, *these words*, 1. 7. 6, &c.;. τὸ κατὰ τοῦτον εἶναι, *as far as this man is concerned*, 1. 6. 9 ; τούτων τοιούτων ὄντων, *such being the case*, 2. 5. 12 ; ταῦτα, *for this reason* (διά), 4. 1. 21; καὶ οὖτος, 2. 5. 20, &c.; καὶ ταῦτα, *and that too*, 1. 4. 12, 2. 4. 15, &c.

Οὑτοσί, αὑτηί, τουτί, *this here*, Lat. *hicce*, 1. 6. 6, 7. 2. 24, 6. 12.

Οὕτω, *before a vowel* οὕτως, *so*; ὡς, *as*—οὕτως, *so*, 1. 2. 15 ; οὕτω πολλοί, 4. 8. 21, 6. 1. 12.

Οὐχί, *a strong form of* οὐ, 7. 7. 47.

Ὀφείλω, ήσω, ὠφείληκα (2 aor. ὤφελον, *O that*, Lat. *utinam*, 2. 1. 4), *to owe*, 1. 2. 11, 7. 7. 34.

Ὄφελος, τό, *only used in nom. and acc., benefit, use*, 1. 3. 11, 2. 6. 9.

Ὀφθαλμός, οῦ, ὁ (ὄπτομαι), *the eye*, 4. 5. 13.

Ὀφλισκάνω, ὀφλήσω, ὤφληκα, ὤφλημαι, *to owe, incur, be guilty*, 5. 8. 1; 2 aor. ὤφλον.

Ὀφρύνιον, ου, τό, *Ophrynium*, a town in the Troad, 7. 8. 5.

Ὀχετός, οῦ, ὁ (ὄχος, ὀχέω, ἔχω), *a canal, channel*, 2. 4. 13.

Ὀχέω, ήσω (ὄχος, ἔχω, Lat. *veho*), *to carry* ; Mid. *to ride*, 3. 4. 47.

Ὄχημα, ατος, τό (ὀχέω), *a vehicle, support*, 3. 2. 19.

Ὄχθη, ης, ἡ (ὄγμος, *a furrow*, ἄγω), *the bank* of a river, 4. 3. 3, 5, 17, 23.

Ὄχλος, ου, ὁ (Æol. ὄλχος, with dig. Lat. *vulgus*, Eng. *folk*), *people*; ὁ πολὺς ὄχλος, *the numerous multitude*, 3. 2. 36, 2. 5. 9; *trouble*, 3. 2. 27.

Ὀχυρός, ά, όν (ἔχω), *strong*, 1. 2. 24 ; *strongly-defended*, 1. 2. 22 ; ὀχυρά, *strong places*, 4. 7. 17.

Ὀψέ, adv., *late* (contr. fr. ὄπισθε, ὄπις), 4. 5. 5, 3. 4. 36, 2. 2. 16; adj. ὄψιος, α, ον (ὀψία, sc. ὥρα), *evening*, 6. 3. 31.; Comp. ὀψιαίτερος, Sup. ὀψιαίτατος.

Ὀψίζω, ίσω (ὀψέ), *to go or come, late*, 4. 5. 5.

Ὄψις, εως, ἡ (ὄπτομαι), *appearance*, 2. 3. 15 ; *sight, spectacle*, 5. 9. 9.

Π.

Παγκράτιον, ου, τό (πᾶς, κράτος), *the pancratium*, a contest in wrestling and boxing, 4. 8. 27.

Παγχάλεπος, ος, ον (πᾶς, χαλεπός), *very difficult, hard*, 5. 2. 20 ; adv. 7. 5. 16.

Πάθημα, ατος, τό (πάσχω), *suffering*, 7. 6. 30.

Πάθος, εος, τό (πάσχω), *suffering* ; τὸ αὐτοῦ πάθος, *of what he had endured*, 1. 5. 14 ; ὅ, τι τὸ πάθος εἴη, *what was the matter*, 4. 5. 7.

Παιανίζω, ίσω (παιάν, ᾶνος, ὁ), *to chant the pæan, sing a song of triumph*, 3. 2. 9; *on the making of a truce*, 5. 9. 5, 11 ; *before beginning battle*, 1. 8. 17, 10. 10, 4. 3. 19, 29, 31, 8. 16, 5. 2. 14, &c.

Παιδεία, ας, ἡ (παιδεύω), *education, training*, 4. 6. 15.

Παιδεραστής, οῦ, ὁ (παῖς, ἐράω), *a lover of boys*, 7. 4. 7.

Παιδεύω, εύσω, πεπαίδευκα, πεπαίδευμαι (παῖς), *to instruct*, 1. 9. 3.

Παιδικά, ῶν, τά (παῖς), *a darling, a favourite*, 2. 6. 6, 28, 5. 8. 4; Lat. *deliciæ*.

Παιδίον, ου, τό (παῖς), *a child*, 4. 7. 13.

Παιδίσκη, ης, ἡ (παῖς), *a young girl, maiden*, 4. 3. 11.

Παῖς, παιδός, ὁ and ἡ (παίω?), *a boy or girl, son*, 1. 1. 1, 7. 9; pl. *children*, 1. 9. 2, 4. 8. 27; ἐκ παίδων, *from childhood*, 4. 6. 14.

Παίω, παίσω (πέπαικα, πέπαισμαι), better πέπληχα, πέπληγμαι, from πλήσσω, *to strike*, 3. 1. 29; ὀλίγας (πληγάς), *too few blows*, 5. 8. 12; 6. 4. 27; πύξ, 5. 8. 16; βακτηρίᾳ, 2. 3. 11, 4. 6. 2; μαχαίρᾳ, 5. 9. 5, 1. 10. 7; λόγχῃ, 5. 8. 16, 3. 2. 19, 1. 8. 26, &c.

Παιωνίζω=παιανίζω.

Πάλαι, adv., *long*, 4. 8. 14, 4. 5. 5 ; καὶ πάλαι, *even long ago*, 7. 6. 9.

Παλαιός, ά, όν (πάλαι), *old*, 4. 5. 35; τὸ παλαιόν, *formerly, in old times*, 3. 4. 7. Comp. παλαίτερος, Sup. παλαίτατος.

Παλαίω, αίσω, πεπάλαικα, πεπάλαισμαι, *to wrestle*, 4. 8. 26.

Πάλη, ης, ἡ (πάλλω), *wrestling*, 4. 8. 27.

Πάλιν, adv., *back*; ἄγειν, 4. 8. 28; ἔρχεσθαι, 3. 1. 7 ; ἥκειν, 4. 3. 12, 6. 2. 8, &c.; *again*, 1. 10. 6, 3. 1. 29, &c.

Παλλακίς, ίδος, ἡ = πάλλαξ, *a concubine*, 1. 10. 2.

Παλτόν, οῦ, τό (πάλλω), *a spear, javelin*, each Persian horseman carried two, 1. 5. 15, 8. 3, 27 ; ὡς ἐξάπηχυ (9 ft.), 5. 4. 12, 25.

Παμπληθής, ής, ές (πᾶς, πλῆθος), *very numerous*, 3. 2. 11.

Πάμπολυς, πόλλη, πυλυ (πᾶς, πολύς), *very many*, 2. 4. 26, 3. 4. 13, 7. 7. 35 ; pl. 4. 1. 8, 6. 26 ; ἐπὶ πάμπολυ τῆς θαλάσσης, *far out into the sea*, 7. 5. 12.

Παμπόνηρος, ες, ον (πᾶς, πονηρός), *thoroughly bad*, 6. 4. 25.

Πανουργία, ας, ἡ (πᾶς, ἔργον), *knavery, villany*, 7. 5. 11.

Πανοῦργος, ον, ὁ (πᾶς, ἔργον), *a villain*, 2. 5. 39, 6. 26.

Παντάπασι(ν), (πᾶς), adv., *wholly, entirely*, 3. 4. 26, 4. 2. 3, 4. 5. 3, 5. 2. 20 ; with neg. *not at all*, 3. 1. 31, 38, 2. 5. 18.

Πανταχῇ (πᾶς) adv., *everywhere*, 2. 5. 7, al. πανταχῆ.

Πανταχοῦ (πᾶς), adv., *everywhere*, 2. 6. 7.

Παντελῶς (παντελής, πᾶς, τέλος), *completely*, 7. 4. 1.

Πάντῃ (πᾶς), adv., *everywhere*, 2. 5. 7 ; *on all sides*, 1. 2. 22, 2. 3. 3, al. παντῆ.

Παντοδαπός, ή, όν (πᾶς), *of all sorts*, 1. 2. 22, 4. 4. 9, 6. 2. 5.

Πάντοθεν (πᾶς), *from, on all sides*, 3. 1. 12.

Παντοῖος, α, ον (πᾶς), *of all sorts*, 1. 5. 2.

Πάντοσε (πᾶς), *in all directions*, 7. 2. 23.

Πάντως (πᾶς), *wholly, altogether*, 7. 7. 43.

Πάνυ (πᾶς), *very* ; ὀλίγοι, 5. 6. 7 ; *very well*, 5. 9. 31 ; οὐ πάνυ πρός, *not very near*, 1. 8. 14 ; οὐ πάνυ τι, *not at all*, 5. 9. 26 ; πάνυ μὲν οὖν, *quite so*, 7. 6. 4.

Πάομαι (ᾰ), πάσομαι, πέπᾱμαι, *to acquire*, 1. 9. 19, 3. 3. 18, 7. 6. 9 [πάομαι (ᾰ), πάσομαι, πέπασμαι, *to taste*].

Παρά, a prep. gov. Gen., Dat., Acc. ; with Gen. *from beside*, Dat. *close beside*, Acc. *to beside*. GEN.: *by*, after a Pass. vb., 1. 9. 1 ; *from*, 3. 4. 8, 5. 6. 18 ; παρὰ βασιλέως, 1. 1. 5, 2. 4. 24 ; παρ' ὑμῶν, 5. 5. 19, 7. 3. 7 ; τὰ παρὰ βασιλέως, *the messages from the king*, 2. 3. 4. DAT.: *close beside*, 1. 3. 7 ; οἱ παρ' αὐτῷ βάρβαροι, *the barbarians with him*, 1. 1. 5 ; παρ' ἀνδρὶ ἐκδεδομένη, *given in marriage to a man*, 4. 1. 24 ; τὰ παρ' ἐμοί, *my affairs*, 1. 7. 4. ACC.: *to*, πορεύεσθαι, &c., 1. 3. 7, 1. 2. 12 ; *along*, τὰς τάξεις, 3. 1. 32 ; *beside, near*, παρὰ τὴν ὁδόν, 1. 2. 13, 1. 8. 5 ; παρὰ πότον, *with wine*, 2. 3. 15 ; *contrary to*, τὰς σπονδάς, 1. 9. 8, 5. 8. 17 ; παρ' ὀλίγον, *of little importance*, 6. 4. 11.

Παραβαίνω, βήσομαι, &c., *to break*, 4. 1. 1.

Παραβοηθέω, ήσω, &c., *to come to help*, 4. 7. 24.

Παραγγέλλω, ελῶ, &c., *to tell, give orders*, 1. 8. 3, 15, 22 ; *summon*, εἰς τὰ ὅπλα, 1. 5. 13 ; *to give out*, τὸ σύνθημα, 1. 8. 16. With Inf., 1. 8, 3, 3. 4. 14, 4. 3. 17 ; with Dat., and Acc. and Inf., 1. 2. 1, 4. 3. 26, 29, 5. 2. 12 ; κατὰ τὰ παρηγγελμένα, *according to instructions*, 2. 2. 8.

Παράγγελσις, εως, ἡ, *the word of command*, 4. 1. 5.

Παραγίγνομαι, γενήσομαι, &c., *to be with* ; τινι, 5. 6. 8, 7. 2. 34 ; *to come*, εἰς Σάρδεις, 1. 2. 3 ; *to be present*, ἐν τῇ μάχῃ, 1. 7. 12.

Παράγω, άξω, &c., *to lead along, bring along*, 7. 2. 8, 6. 3 ; εἰς τὰ πλάγια, *in an oblique direction*, 3. 4. 14.

Παραγωγή, ῆς, ἡ, *conveyance*, 5. 1. 16.

Παράδεισος, ου, ὁ, *a park*, 1. 2. 7, 9, 4. 10, 2. 4. 14 ; hence, *paradise*.

Παραδίδωμι, δώσω, &c., *to hand over, give up* ; ἡγεμόνα τινί, 4. 2. 1, 6. 1, 7. 3. 40 ; χώραν, 5. 5. 10 ; ὅπλα, 2. 1. 8 ; *to give out*, τὸ σύνθημα, 7. 3. 34 ; ἢν οἱ θεοὶ παραδιδῶσι, *if the gods grant it*, 6. 4. 34.

Παραθαρρύνω, υνῶ, &c., *to encourage*, 2. 4. 1 ; τινά, 3. 1. 39.

Παραθέω, θεύσομαι, &c., *to run beyond, outrun*, 4. 7. 12.

Παραινέω, έσω, &c., *to recommend*, 5. 7. 35, 7. 3. 20 ; *address, exhort*, 1. 7. 2.

Παραιτέομαι, ήσομαι, &c., *to intercede for*, περί, 6. 4. 29.

Παρακαλέω, έσω, &c., *to send for, summon*, 3. 1. 32, 1. 6. 5 ; *to encourage, exhort*, 6. 3. 24, 3. 1. 24, 36, 44.

Παρακαταθήκη, ης, ἡ (παρά, κατά, τίθημι), *a deposit*, 5. 3. 7.

Παράκειμαι, κείσομαι, *to lie beside*, 7. 3. 22.

Παρακελεύομαι, εύσομαι,&c.,Dep. Mid. *to exhort, encourage*; ἀλλήλοις, 4. 2. 11; αἴθειν, 4. 7. 20; αὐτῷ μὴ μάχεσθαι, 1. 7. 9, 8. 11, 3. 4. 48.

Παρακέλευσις, εως, ἡ, *cheering on, encouraging*, 4. 8. 28.

Παρακολουθέω, ήσω, &c., *to follow close beside*, 3. 3. 4, 4. 4. 7.

Παραλαμβάνω, λήψομαι, &c., *to take with one*; τινά, 5. 6. 36, 7. 2. 17; *to receive*, 7. 7. 7, 47; τὰ ἐκείνου, *his command*, 6. 2. 11.

Παραλείπω, ψω, &c., *to pass over*, 6. 4. 18; *to leave behind*, 6. 1. 19.

Παραλύω, λύσω, &c., *to take off* τὰ πηδάλια, *our rudders*, 5. 1. 11.

Παραλυπέω, ήσω, &c., *to grieve along with*, οἱ π., *the troublesome, refractory*, 2. 5. 29.

Παραμείβω, ψω, *to pass by*, 1. 10. 10.

Παραμελέω, ήσω, &c., *to disregard*, 7. 8. 12; ὅρκων, 2. 5. 7.

Παραμένω, μενῶ, &c., *to remain with, continue*, 2. 6. 2.

Παραμηρίδιος, ος, ον (παρά, μηρός), *along the thighs*; τὰ π., *armour for the thighs, cuisses*, 1. 8. 6.

Παραπέμπω, πέμψω, &c., *to send along*, 4. 5. 20, 6. 1. 15.

Παραπλέω, πλεύσομαι, &c., *to sail past, along*, 5. 1. 11, 7. 15; εἰς, 5. 6. 10, 7. 2. 7.

Παραπλήσιος, ος, ον and α, ον, *like, similar*, 1. 5. 2; πρᾶξις π. οἷαπερ, *like that in which*, 1. 3. 18.

Παραρρέω, ρεύσομαι, ἐρρύηκα, *to flow past*, 5. 3. 8; *to slip off*, 4. 4. 11.

Παρασάγγης, ου, ὁ, a Persian *farsang*, a *parasang*=30 stadia, 2. 2. 6, nearly 3½ miles, or an hour's march, differing according to the difficulties of the road. One day's march (σταθμός) was on an average 5 parasangs, or about 17 miles.

Παρασκευάζω, άσω, &c., *to get ready, prepare*, 3. 1. 16, 5. 2. 13; ὡς εἰς μάχην, 1. 8. 1; ἐπὶ τοὺς πολεμίους, 3. 1. 36; θυσίαν, 4. 8. 25; τὴν ἄφοδον, 5. 2. 21; ὅπως ἀμυνούμεθα, 3. 1. 14; οἴκαδε, *to go home*, 7. 7. 57; τὴν γνώμην, *having made up our minds*, 6. 1. 17.

Παρασκευή, ῆς, ἡ (παρά, σκεῦος, εος, τὸ, a *vessel*), *preparation*, 1. 2. 4.

Παρασκηνέω, ήσω, &c., *to pitch one's tent beside or near*, τινί, 3. 1. 28.

Παράταξις, εως, ἡ (παρά, τάσσω), *arrangement*, 5. 2. 13.

Παρατάσσω, τάξω, τέτἄχα, τέτἄγμαι, *to draw up, arrange*, in order of battle, 1. 10. 10, 4. 3. 3, &c.

Παρατείνω, τενῶ, τέτἄκα, τέτᾰμαι, *to stretch out, extend*,φάλαγγα, 7. 3. 48; *to draw,make,*τάφρον, 1. 7. 15.

Παρατίθημι, θήσω, τέθεικα, τέθειμαι, *to place*; ἐπὶ τὴν τράπεζαν, 4. 5. 31; *to lay down beside one*, ὅπλα, 5. 9. 8.

Παρατρέχω, θρέξομαι or δραμοῦμαι, δεδράμηκα, δεδράμημαι, 2 aor. ἔδραμον, *to run by or past*, οἰκίαν, 7. 4. 18; *to run over*, ἡμίπλεθρον, 4. 7. 6; *run up to*, εἰς χωρίον, 4. 7. 11.

Παραχρῆμα, adv. for παρὰ τὸ χρῆμα, on the spot, straight-way, 7. 7. 24.

Παρεγγυάω, ήσω (παρά, ἐν, γυῖον, a hand), to pass from hand to hand, to order, command, ταῦτα, 7. 1. 22; εὔχεσθαι, 4. 8. 16; ἕπεσθαι, 4. 1. 17; to pass the word, στρατηγοὺς παριέναι, 6. 3. 12, 7. 3. 46.

Παρεγγυή, ῆς, ἡ, order, 6. 3. 13.

Πάρειμι, ἔσομαι (παρά, εἰμί) to be present, Lat. adesse, 1. 5. 15; εἰς τὴν ἐξέτασιν, 7. 1. 11; τινί, 1. 1. 1, 3. 1. 46, 6. 4. 20; ἀπό, 1. 10. 16; εἰς, 1. 2. 2, 7. 2. 5, 4. 6; πρός, 6. 4. 26; ἐν τῷ παρόντι, at the present time, 2. 5. 8; τὰ παρόντα (πράγματα), the present state of affairs, 1. 3. 3, 3. 1. 34, 4. 1. 26; παρόν, like ἐξόν, it being in our power, 5. 8. 3; another reading is παρόντος, being at hand.

Πάρειμι (παρά, εἶμι), to pass, 4. 5. 8, 6. 3. 12; παρὰ τὴν φάλαγγα, 6. 3. 23; 3. 2. 35, 4. 2. 19; χωρία, 5. 4. 30, 3. 4. 37; τινά, 4. 7. 12; to pass on, 3. 4. 48, 7. 3. 16.

Παρελαύνω, ελάσω or ελῶ, ελήλακα, ελήλαμαι, to march past, 1. 2. 16; ride past, 1. 8. 12, 14, 6. 1. 2. 17; ἐπὶ τοῦ ἵππου, 3. 4. 46, 3. 25; ἐφ' ἅρματος, 1. 2. 16.

Παρέρχομαι, ελεύσομαι, ελήλυθα, 2 aor. παρῆλθον, to go past, 1. 4. 4, 3. 4. 39; pass through, 1. 7. 17; to pass, 1. 7. 18; ἔξω τοῦ κέρατος, 1. 10. 6; εἴσω τοῦ τείχους, 2. 4. 12; σύνθημα παρέρχεται, passes along the line, 1. 8. 16; οἱ παρεληλυθότες πόνοι, 4. 3. 2.

Παρέχω, ἔξω or παρασχήσω, παρέσχηκα, παρέσχημαι, impf. παρεῖχον, 2 aor. παρέσχον, to furnish, supply; ἄλφιτα, 5. 3. 9; ἀγοράν, 2. 3. 26, 5. 10. 10; to render, make, τὴν χώραν φιλίαν, 2. 3. 26, 2. 5. 13, 6. 27, 7. 6. 22; to excite, φόβον, 3. 1. 18; to give up, ἑαυτὸν εἰς κρίσιν, 6. 4. 20; κρῖναι, 6. 4. 16; εὖ ποιεῖν, 2. 3. 22; Mid. to display, προθυμίαν, 7. 6. 11.

Παρθένιον, ου, τό, Parthenium, a town in Mysia, 7. 8. 15.

Παρθένιος, ου, ὁ, the Parthenius, a river in Paphlagonia, where Artemis (ἡ παρθένος) bathed, 5. 6. 9.

Παρθένος, ου, ἡ, a virgin, 3. 2. 25.

Παριανοί, ῶν, οἱ, the inhabitants of

Πάριον, ου, τό, Parium, a town in Mysia, 7. 3. 20.

Παρίημι, ήσω, &c., to yield, give way, 5. 7. 10.

Παρίστημι, παραστήσω, παρέστηκα, παρέσταμαι (παρά, ἵστημι), to place by; Intr. to stand by; pres., impf., fut., 1 aor., trans.; 2 aor., pf., plpf. intrans.; 5. 8. 10, 7. 8. 3, 5. 9. 22.

Πάροδος, ου, ἡ (παρά, ὁδός), a passage, 1. 4. 4.

Παροινέω, ήσω, &c., impf. ἐπαρῴνουν, 1 aor. ἐπαρῴνησα, double augm. (παρά, οἶνος), to act insolently under the influence of wine, 5. 8. 4.

Παροίχομαι, ήσομαι, παρῴχημαι, to be gone by, τὰ παρῳχημένα, the things that are past, the past, 2. 4. 1.

Παρρασία, ας, ἡ, Parrhasia, a town in Arcadia, on Mt. Lycæus, hence

Παρράσιος, α, ον, adj., Parrhasian, 1. 1. 2.

Παρύσατις, ιδος, ἡ, Parysatis, Persian *Pharziris*, was the dr. of Artaxerxes Longimanus, and mar. her own brother Darius Ochus. Artaxerxes Mnemon and Cyrus the Younger were her sons. She was a bold, bad woman, cruel and vindictive, 1. 1. 1, 4, 4. 9.

Πᾶς, πᾶσα, πᾶν, all, every; πᾶσα ὁδός, every way; πᾶσα ἡ ὁδός, the whole way, 2. 5. 9; πάντες οἱ στρατιῶται, 4. 3. 19, 1. 9. 3; οἱ πάντες ἄνθρωποι, 5. 6. 7, is stronger than πάντες ἄνθρωποι, 3. 1. 18; οἱ πάντες, 5. 7. 27; τὰ πάντα, completely, 2. 1. 1; also πάντα, 1. 3. 10; ἡ τοῦ παντὸς ἄρχη, the command of the whole army, 5. 10. 12, 6. 1. 1.; διὰ παντὸς πολέμου, in every kind of warfare, 3. 2. 8; πάντῃ γὰρ πάντα τοῖς θεοῖς ὕποχα καὶ πανταχῆ πάντων ἴσον οἱ θεοὶ κρατοῦσι, for in all places all things are subject to the gods, and in all directions all things the gods rule equally, 2. 5. 7.

Πασίων, ωνος, ὁ, Pasion, a Megarian, 1. 2. 3, 4. 7.

Πάσχω, πείσομαι, 2 p. πέπονθα, 2 aor. ἔπαθον, to suffer, 3. 1. 41, 4. 2; τι, 3. 1. 17, 7. 1. 28; ὅ, τι ἂν δέῃ, 1. 3. 5, 6; μηδὲν παρὰ τὰς σπονδάς, 1. 9. 8; οὐδὲν κακόν, 7. 4. 13; κακῶς, to be ill off, in an evil plight, 3. 3. 7; εὖ, to be well treated; ἀνθ᾿ ὧν εὖ ἔπαθον, for ἀντὶ τούτων ἅ, in return for the benefits I received, 1. 3. 4, 7. 7. 8; ὑφ᾿ ὧν

κακῶς ἔπασχον, by whom they were wont to be ill-treated, 5. 2. 2; ἤν τι πάθῃ, if he should meet with any misfortune, a euphemism for death, 5. 3. 6, 7. 2. 14; τί μέγα ἂν οὕτως ἔπαθον ὅτου, quid tam grave passi essent, ut, what injury could they have suffered of such magnitude as, 5. 8. 17; οἱ ταῦτα πάσχοντες, 3. 4. 20; ἀδικώτατα, 7. 1. 16; δεινά, 7. 1. 25; κακά, 2. 5. 5, 4. 3. 2; ἀγαθόν, 5. 5. 9, 7. 3. 20.

Παταγύας, or Πατηγύας, α, ὁ, Pataguas, a Persian, 1. 8. 1.

Πατάσσω, πατάξω, πεπάταγμαι, to strike, 4. 8. 25, 7. 8. 14.

Πατήρ, πατρός, ὁ, a father, 7. 6. 38.

Πάτριος, α, ον, of a father; σὺν τῷ πατρίῳ φρονήματι, with the spirit of your fathers, 3. 2. 16. Herm. says πάτρια, quæ patris sunt, of a father, Lat. patrius; πατρῷα, quæ a patre veniunt, hereditary; πατρικά, qualia patris sunt, paternal, Lat. paternus; θησαυροὶ πάτριοι, 5. 4. 27; νόμος, 7. 8. 5.

Πατρίς, ίδος, ἡ, fatherland, native country, Lat. patria, 1. 3. 6, 3. 1. 3, 4, 7. 1. 29.

Πατρῷος, α, ον and ος, ον, hereditary; οἰκία, 3. 1. 11; ἀρχή, 1. 7. 6; χώρα, 7. 3. 31, 2. 34.

Παῦλα, ης, ἡ (παύω), cessation, 5. 7. 32.

Παύω, παύσω, πέπαυκα, πέπαυμαι, to cause to cease, cause to halt; Mid. to cease, to stop, τὴν φάλαγγα, 4. 8. 10; ὑποψίας, 2. 5. 2; τινὰ ἐνοχλοῦντα, 2. 5. 13; Mid. to cease, πολέμου, 1. 6. 6; πόνων, 5. 1. 2; with part. 3. 1. 19, 5. 9. 27, 7. 6. 35.

Παφλαγονία, ας, ἡ, Paphlagonia, a district in Asia Minor ; adj. Παφλαγονικός, ἡ, όν, 5. 2. 22, 6. 6. Inh. Παφλαγών, όνος, ὁ.

Πάχος, εος, τό (παχύς), thickness, 5. 4. 13.

Παχύς, εῖα, ύ, thick, large, 4. 8. 2, 5. 4. 25.

Πέδη, ης, ἡ (πέζα), Lat. pedĭca, a chain for the feet, fetters, 4. 3. 8.

Πεδῖνός, ή, όν (πεδίον), even, level, 5. 5. 2, 7. 1. 24.

Πεδίον, ου, τό (πέδον), a plain, 1. 2. 22, 5. 1, 5. 6. 6, &c.

Πεζεύω, εύσω (πεζός), to travel on foot, or by land, 5. 5. 4.

Πεζῇ (πεζός), on foot; σπεύδειν, 3. 4. 49 ; διαβατός, 1. 4. 18 ; ἐξιόντες, 7. 1. 1 ; οὔτε π. οὔτε κατὰ θάλατταν, 5. 6. 10; πορεύεσθαι, 5. 6. 1, 6. 2. 12 ; διασωθῆναι, 5. 4. 5.

Πεζός, ή, όν (πέζα, πούς), on foot, ἡγοῦμαι, 7. 3. 45; δύναμις, infantry, 1. 3. 12.

Πειθαρχέω, ήσω, to obey one in authority, 1. 9. 17.

Πείθω, πείσω, πέπεικα, πέπεισμαι, 2 aor. ἔπιθον, 2 p. πέποιθα, I trust; to persuade, Mid. to obey; αὐτὸν πορεύεσθαι, 5. 10. 13; τὴν πόλιν ὡς ἀδικῦσι, 2. 6. 2 ; λέγων, 7. 2. 10 ; λόγοις τινά, 2. 6. 4 ; Mid. 1. 1. 3, 5. 1. 13, 1. 3. 6, 3. 2. 30 ; νόμῳ, 7. 3. 39; πειστέον, 2. 6. 8 ; to believe, πείθεται αὐτῷ μὴ εἶναι χρήματα, he believes he has no money, 7. 8. 3.

Πεινάω, ήσω, πεπείνηκα, to be hungry, contr. with η for α, 1. 9. 27.

Πεῖρα, ας, ἡ, a trial, proof, experience, 3. 2. 16, 5. 8. 15 ; ἐν πείρᾳ Κύρου, on intimate terms with Cyrus, 1. 9. 1.

Πειράω, άσω, πεπείρακα, πεπείραμαι, to try, prove; Mid. try, attempt, make trial of, 7. 2. 37, τάξεως, 3. 2. 38, 3. 5. 7 ; inf. διαβαίνειν, 4. 3. 5 ; ὅπως σωζώμεθα, 3. 2. 3, endeavour, 5. 7. 31, 7. 2. 15, 2. 5. 41, 5. 1. 8, 7. 3. 11.

Πεισίδαι=Πισίδαι.

Πειστέον, vb. fr. πείθω.

Πελάζω, άσω, to bring near, intr. approach, 4. 2. 3.

Πελληνεύς, έως, ὁ, an inhabitant of Pellene, a town in Achaia, 5. 2. 15.

Πελοπόννησος, ου, ἡ (Πέλοψ, νῆσος, the island of Pelops), the Peloponnesus, now called Morea because its shape resembles a mulberry leaf. Homer's name is Ἀπία (ἀπό, the distant land), Il. 1. 269, 3. 48, adj. Πελοποννήσιος, α, ον, 1. 4. 2.

Πελτάζω (πέλτη), to be a peltast, 5. 8. 5.

Πελταστής, οῦ, ὁ, a peltast, because armed with the πέλτη; the peltasts came between the ὁπλῖται and the ψιλοί, 1. 10. 7, 4. 3. 27, &c.; οἱ Ἕλληνες πελτασταί, 6. 3. 26.

Πελταστικός, ή, όν, of or belonging to the peltasts, τὸ π. =οἱ πελτασταί, 1. 8. 5, 7. 3. 37.

Πέλτη, ης, ἡ, a light shield, half-moon form, covered with leather, 2. 1. 6, 5. 9. 9. In 1. 10. 12 some make πέλτη a pole, a spear-shaft, but there is no need of changing the ord. meaning; the eagle was on *a shield,* and the shield was on a pole.

Πεμπταῖος, α, ον, *on the fifth* day, 6. 2. 9.

Πέμπτος, η, ον (πέντε), *fifth,* 3. 4. 23, 4. 7. 21 ; πεμπτός, vb. fr. πέμπω.

Πέμπω, πέμψω, πέπομφα, πέπεμμαι, 1 aor. pass. ἐπέμφθην, *to send,* 1. 1. 8, 2. 3. 1, 3. 1. 27 ; πρός τινα, 5. 2. 6 ; παρά τινα, 5. 9. 2 ; αὐτῷ, 1. 3. 8; εἰς αὐτούς, *into their land,* 5. 4. 2 ; τινὰ ἐρυῦντα, 2. 5. 2, 5. 2. 10, 1. 3. 14, 4. 5. 22, &c.

Πένης, ητος, ὁ (πένομαι), *a labourer, a poor man,* 7. 7. 28.

Πενία, ας, ἡ (πένομαι), *poverty,* 7. 6. 20.

Πένομαι, pr. and impf. *to be poor,* 3. 2. 26.

Πεντακόσιοι, αι, α, *five hundred,* 1. 2. 3.

Πέντε (Ϝέντε=κπέντε, *the hand*), indecl. num. *five,* 1. 2. 8.

Πεντεκαίδεκα, *fifteen,* 4. 7. 16.

Πεντήκοντα, *fifty,* 2. 2. 6.

Πεντηκοντήρ, τῆρος, ὁ, *a commander of fifty men,* 3. 4. 21.

Πεντηκόντορος, ου, ἡ, sc. ναῦς (πεντήκοντα), *a fifty-oared galley,* 5. 1. 15.

Πεντηκοστύς, ύος, ἡ, *a company of fifty men*=half a λόχος, 3. 4. 22.

Πέρ, enclit. particle, *much, very, even,* joined to εἰ, ἐάν, ὅς, ὅσος, &c.

Πέρα, adv. *longer,* 5. 9. 28 ; *beyond,* with gen. 6. 3. 7.

Περαίνω, περᾶνῶ, πεπέρασμαι (πέρα), *to finish, accomplish,* 3. 1. 47, 5. 9. 18, 3. 2. 32.

Περαιόω, ώσω (πέραν), *to convey across, carry over,* intr. *to cross,* 7. 2. 12.

Πέραν, *on the other side, across,* Lat. *trans,* εἶναι, 2. 4. 20 ; γίγνεσθαι, 6. 3. 22 ; εἰς τὴν Ἀσίαν διαβῆναι, 7. 2. 2 ; τοῦ ποταμοῦ, 1. 5. 10, 2. 4. 28, 4. 3. 3 ; τὸ πέραν τοῦ ποταμοῦ, *to the opposite bank of the river,* 3. 5. 2 ; ἐν τῷ π. *on the other side,* 4. 3. 11, 29 ; τὰ πέραν, *the affairs on the other side,* 4. 3. 24.

Περάω, περάσω, πεπέρακα (πέραν), *to go over, cross* (περάω, άσω, *to sell*); τὸ ὕδωρ, 4. 3. 21.

Πέργαμος, ου, ἡ, and ον, ου, τό, *Pergamus* or *Pergamum,* a town in Mysia, 7. 8. 8.

Πέρδιξ, ῑκος, ὁ and ἡ, *a partridge,* Lat. *perdix,* Scot. *pertrick,* 1. 5. 3.

Περί, prep. gov. Gen. Dat. and Acc. *about, round* (*all round,* ἀμφί, *on both sides*). I. With Gen. *about,* γιγνώσκειν, 2. 5. 8; λέγειν, 1. 9. 23; ἐρωτᾶν, 7. 6. 39 ; μάχεσθαι, 2. 1. 12 ; π. πολλοῦ ποιεῖσθαι, *to consider it of great importance,* 1. 9. 7, 3. 2. 4, 5. 6. 22, &c.; π. παντός, *all important,* 1. 9. 16, 2. 4. 3. II. With Dat. *close round,* χιτῶνας περὶ τοῖς στέρνοις, 7. 4. 4, 1. 5. 8. III. With Acc. *round,* π. τοὺς πόδας, 4. 5. 36 ; τὴν σκηνήν, 1. 6. 4 ; περί τι εἶναι, *to be busy about,* 3. 5. 7 ; οἱ περί τινα, *anyone's soldiers or followers,* 1. 5. 8 ; *anyone and his followers,* 2. 4. 2, 7. 4. 16, 6. 1. 25, *and sometimes the principal person alone,* so ἀμφί. Of time, *about,* π. μέσας νύκτας, 1. 7. 1, 7. 8. 12, 2. 1. 7, 6. 3. 32 ; *in regard to, with* reference to, 6. 4. 31, 3. 2. 20, 1. 6. 8.

Περιβάλλω, βαλῶ, &c. to throw round or about, 7. 4. 17 ; embrace, 4. 7. 25 ; surround, 6. 1. 3.

Περιγίγνομαι, γενήσομαι, &c. to be superior to, to excel, τῷ πολέμῳ τινός, 1. 1. 10, 2. 1. 13, 3. 2. 29; to turn out, 5. 8. 26.

Περιειλέω or περιείλω, or περιελίσσω, to wrap round, 4.5.36.

Περίειμι (περί, εἰμί), to be superior to, to excel, τινός τινι, 1. 8. 13, 1. 9. 24 ; πολύ, were much superior, 3. 4. 33.

Περίειμι (περί, εἶμι), to go round, 4. 1. 3 ; to visit, 7. 1. 33.

Περιέλκω, aor. περιείλκῦσα, to drag round, 7. 6. 10.

Περιέχω, ἕξω, &c. to surround, 1. 2. 22.

Περιΐστημι, περιστήσω, &c. to stand round, 4. 7. 2, 6. 4. 6.

Περικυκλόω, ώσω, &c. (περί, κύκλος), to encircle, 6. 1. 11.

Περιλαμβάνω, λήψομαι, &c. to embrace, 7. 4. 10.

Περιμένω, μενῶ, &c. to wait for, wait, 2. 1. 6, 3. 2, 7. 3. 41; τινά, 2. 1. 3.

Πέρινθος, ου, ἡ, Perinthus, a town on the Propontis, 2. 6. 2 ; adj. Περίνθιος, α, ον, Perinthian, 7. 2. 8.

Πέριξ, adv. round about, 2. 5. 14, 4. 4. 7 ; τῆς τύρσιος, 7. 8. 12.

Περίοδος, ου, ἡ, the circuit, circumference, 3. 4. 7, 11.

Περιοικέω, ήσω, &c. to dwell around, 5. 6. 16.

Περίοικος, ου, ὁ, dwelling round, a neighbour ; in Sparta the periœci were the free inhabi-

tants of the towns (except Sparta), a middle class between the Spartans on the one hand and the Helots on the other, 5. 1. 15.

Περιοράω, ὄψομαι, &c. 2 aor. inf. περιιδεῖν, to overlook, 7. 7. 46.

Περίπᾶτος, ου, ὁ (περί, πατέω), walking, ἔτυχον ἐν περιπάτῳ ὄντες, they happened to be walking, 2. 4. 15.

Περιπέτομαι, ἥσομαι, to fly around, 5. 9. 23.

Περιπήγνυμι, πήξω, &c. to fix round, Pass. to be frozen round, 4. 5. 14.

Περιπίπτω, πεσοῦμαι, &c. to fall upon and embrace, τινί, 1. 8. 28 ; fall upon, 7. 3. 38.

Περιπλέω, πλεύσομαι, &c. to sail round, 1. 2. 21, 7. 1. 20.

Περιποιέω, ήσω, &c. Mid. ἑαυτῷ, to get for himself, 5. 6. 17.

Περιπτύσσω, ξω, to enfold, surround, take in flank, 1. 10. 9.

Περιρρέω, ρεύσομαι, &c. to flow round, 1. 5. 4 ; to fall from around, 4. 3. 8.

Περισταυρόω, ώσω, &c. to fence about with a palisade, 7. 4. 14.

Περιστερά, ᾶς, ἡ, a dove, pigeon, 1. 4. 9.

Περιττεύω, εύσω or περισσεύω (περισσός), to outnumber, outflank, τινός, 4. 8. 11.

Περιττός or περισσός, ή, όν (περί), more than sufficient, surplus, ἔχειν, 7. 6. 31 ; τὸ π. 5. 3. 13 ; τὰ π. 3. 2. 28, 3. 1 ; οἱ π. 4. 8. 11.

Περιτυγχάνω, τεύξομαι, τετύχηκα, to fall in with, 6. 4. 7.

Περιφανῶς, adv. fr. περιφανής (περί, φαίνω), manifestly, 4. 5. 4.

Περιφέρω, οἴσω, &c. *to carry round*, 7. 3. 24.

Περίφοβος, ος, ον, *in great fear*, 3. 1. 12.

Πέρσης, ου ὁ, *a Persian*, pl. οἱ Πέρσαι, 1. 8. 1, 6, *the Persians*.

Περσίζω, ίσω, *to speak Persian*, 4. 5. 34.

Περσικός, ή, όν, adj. *Persian*, 5. 9. 10.

Περσιστί, adv. *in the Persian language*, 4. 5. 10.

Περυσινός, ή, όν (πέρυσι, adv. *last year*, πέρας), *last year's*, 5. 4. 27.

Πέταλον, ου, τό (πέταλος, *outspread*, πετάω, πετάννυμι), *a leaf*, 5. 4. 12.

Πέτομαι, πετήσομαι and πτήσομαι, 2 aor. ἐπτόμην, inf. πτέσθαι, also ἵπταμαι; 2 aor. ἐπτάμην, inf. πτάσθαι, *to fly*, 1. 5. 3.

Πέτρα, ας, ἡ, *a rock*, 4. 2. 3, 17, 4. 7. 14, 4. 2. 20.

Πετροβολία, ας, ἡ (πέτρος, βάλλω), *a stoning*, 6. 4. 15.

Πέτρος, ου, ὁ, *a rock*, 4. 7. 12, 7. 7. 54.

Πεφυλαγμένως, adv. fr. pp. of φυλάσσω, *cautiously*, 2. 4. 24.

Πῆ, adv. *how*, as an encl. part. *somehow*, πῆ μέν—πῆ δέ, *in part—in part, partly*, 3. 1. 12, 5. 9. 20.

Πηγή, ῆς, ἡ, *a fountain, source*, 1. 2. 7, 4. 10, &c.

Πήγνυμι, πήξω, πέπηχα, πέπηγμαι, *to fix, freeze*, 4. 5. 3; Pass. *be frozen*, 7. 4. 3.

Πηδάλιον, ου, τό (πηδόν, πέδον, πούς), *a rudder*, 5. 1. 11.

Πηλός, οῦ, ὁ, *clay*, 1. 5. 7.

Πῆχυς, εως, ὁ, *the forearm*, the length from the elbow to the tip of the finger, Lat. *cubitus*, *a cubit* = 1½ ft. 4. 7. 16.

Πίγρης, ητος, ὁ, *Pigres*, a Carian, 1. 2. 17, 5. 7, 8. 12.

Πιέζω, πιέσω, πεπίεσμαι, *to press* or *crush*, 3. 4. 19, 27; *oppress*, 1. 1. 10, 3. 4. 48.

Πικρός, ά, όν (πεύκη), *pointed, sharp, bitter*, 4. 4. 13.

Πίμπλημι, πλήσω, πέπληκα, πέπλησμαι, *to fill*, χόρτου, 1. 5. 10.

Πίνω, πίομαι, πέπωκα, πέπομαι, *to drink*, 5. 9. 4.

Πιπράσκω, περάσω, πέπρᾶκα, πέπρᾶμαι, *to sell*, 7. 2. 6, 8. 6, 7. 1. 36; χρημάτων, *for money*, 7. 7. 26.

Πίπτω, πεσοῦμαι, πέπτωκα, 2 aor. ἔπεσον, *to fall*, 4. 5. 7, 1. 8. 28, 9. 31, 6. 2. 9.

Πισίδης, ου, ὁ, *a Pisidian*, an inhabitant of Pisidia in Asia Minor, 1. 1. 11.

Πιστεύω, εύσω, πεπίστευκα, ευμαι (πίστις), *to trust*, τινί, 1. 3. 16, 9. 8, 5. 2. 21, 7. 2. 17; ταῖς σπονδαῖς, 3. 1. 29; μηδὲν ἂν παθεῖν, 1. 9. 8, 7. 7. 47, &c.

Πίστις, εως, ἡ, *trust, fidelity*, 1. 6. 3; πίστεως ἕνεκα, *to insure his fidelity*, 3. 3. 4; διὰ πίστεως, *through confidence in them*, 3. 2. 8; pl. *pledges*, 1. 2. 26.

Πιστός, ή, όν, *faithful, trusty, trustworthy*, 1. 4. 15; ἀνήρ, 1. 6. 3, 1. 6. 8, 7. 2. 29; τὰ πιστά, *pledges*, ἐγένετο, 2. 2. 10; λαμβάνειν, 7. 4. 22; δοῦναι, 1: 6. 7, 4. 8. 7, &c.; μὴ προδώσειν ἀλλήλους, 3. 2. 5; τὰ π. ἄπιστα ποιεῖν, 2. 4. 7.

Πιστότης, τητος, ἡ (πιστός), *faithfulness, fidelity,* 1. 8. 29.

Πίτυς, υος, ἡ, *the pine tree,* Lat. *pinus,* 4. 7. 6.

Πλάγιος, α, ον (πλᾶγος, τό, *the side,* or πλάξ), *sideways, slanting,* εἰς τὸ π., 1. 8. 10; εἰς τὰ π., *right and left,* 3. 4. 14, 6. 1. 15.

Πλαίσιον, ον, τό (πλᾶγος or πλάξ), *an oblong;* ἐν π. πλήρει ἀνθρώπων, *in solid column,* 1. 8. 9, 3. 2. 36, 7. 8. 16; ἰσόπλευρον, *a square,* 3. 4. 19, 22, 28, 43.

Πλαιάω, ήσω, πεπλάνηκα, πεπλάνημαι (πλάνη), *to cause to wander;* Mid. *to wander about,* 1. 2. 25, 5. 1. 7, 7. 7. 24.

Πλάτος, εος, τό (πλατύς), *breadth,* 5. 4. 32.

Πλάττω or πλάσσω, πλάσω, πέπλακα, πέπλασμαι, *to form, counterfeit, make up, fabricate,* ψευδῆ, 2. 6. 26.

Πλατύς, εῖα, ὑ (πλάξ), *broad,* 5. 4. 29.

Πλεθριαῖος, α, ον, *of the size of* a πλέθρον, 1. 5. 4, 7. 15, &c.

Πλέθρον, ου, τό, *a plethron=100* Greek or 101 English feet, 1. 2. 5, 3. 4. 9.

Πλεῖστος, η, ον, Superl. of πολύς.

Πλείων, ων, ον, Comp. of πολύς.

Πλέκω, ἕω, πέπλεχα, πέπλεγμαι, *to plait,* 3. 3. 18.

Πλεονεκτέω, ήσω (πλέον, ἔχειν, *to have more*), *to have or gain an advantage,* 5. 4. 15; τινός, *over one,* 5. 8. 13; τινί, *in anything,* 3. 1. 37.

Πλευρά, ᾶς, ἡ, *the side of a man,* 4. 1. 18, 7. 4; πλαισίου, 3. 2. 37, 4. 22, 28.

Πλέω, πλεύσομαι and πλευσοῦμαι, πέπλευκα, πέπλευσμαι, *to sail,* 5. 6. 12, 7. 8, 1. 10, 7. 6. 37, 1. 7. 15.

Πληγή, ῆς, ἡ (πλήττω), *a stroke, blow,* 1. 5. 11, 2. 4. 11.

Πλῆθος, εος, τό (πολύς), *a great number, multitude, mass,* τῶν ὁπλιτῶν, 5. 2. 21; δερμάτων, 4. 7. 26; *extent,* χώρας, 1. 5. 9; *length,* ὁδοῦ, 5. 5. 4; χρόνου, 7. 8. 26; πολύ, 1. 7. 4, 4. 2. 20; *the common soldiers,* 3. 1. 37; πλῆθος ὡς δισχίλιοι, *in number,* 4. 2. 2.

Πλήθω, πλήσω, πέπληθα, *to be full,* πλήθουσα ἀγορά, *full market,* the time when the market is full of people, from nine to twelve in the forenoon, 1. 8. 1, 2. 1. 7 : (1) πρωΐ, *morning ;* (2) πλήθουσα ἀγορά, *forenoon ;* (3) μεσημβρία, *midday ;* (4) δείλη πρωΐα, *afternoon;* δείλη ὀψία, *evening.*

Πλήν, adv. gov. gen. *except,* 1. 9. 9, 4. 6. 1, 5. 2. 27, 2. 4. 27, 7. 2. 29; πλήν τις ἐλέγετο, *except that,* 1. 8. 20; ὅσα ἔχομεν, 3. 2. 28, 1. 2. 1, 24.

Πλήρης, ης, ες (πλάω, πίμπλημι), *full,* ὕδατος, 2. 3. 10, 13; ἀψινθίου, 1. 5. 1; θηρίων, 1. 2. 7, 4. 9; ἀνθρώπων, 1. 8. 9; μισθοῦ, 7. 5. 5.

Πλησιάζω, άσω (πλησίος), *to draw near, approach,* 6. 3. 26; τοῖς πολεμίοις, 4. 6. 6.

Πλησίον, adv. *near,* neut. of πλησίος ; ἡ πλησίον κώμη, *the neighbouring village,* 3. 4. 9; πλησιαίτατος, *nearest,* 1. 10. 5, 7. 3. 29; with gen 5. 2. 11.

Πλήττω or πλήσσω, πλήξω, πέπληχα, πέπληγμαι, 2 p. πέπληγα, 2 aor. pass. ἐπλάγην, strike with terror, and ἐπλήγην, 5. 8. 2, 4, 12; to be wounded, 5. 9. 5.

Πλίνθινος, η, ον (πλίνθος), made of bricks, Lat. latericius, 3. 4. 11.

Πλίνθος, ου, ἡ, a brick, γηΐνη, 7. 8. 14; κεραμία, 3. 4. 7; ὀπτή, 2. 4. 12.

Πλοῖον, ου, τό (πλέω), a ship, τριήρεις, 5. 1. 4, 6. 2. 18, 4. 1; σιταγωγά, 1. 7. 15, 1. 3. 17; μακρά, 5. 1. 11; ἄγει, 5. 1. 4, 16, 6. 3. 1; κατάγειν, 5. 1. 16; συλλέγειν, 6. 4. 22.

Πλοῦς, οῦ, ὁ (πλέω), sailing, a voyage, 6. 2. 2, 5. 9. 33, pl. 5. 7. 7.

Πλούσιος, α, ον (πλοῦτος, πλέον), rich, 7. 3. 18, 7. 28.

Πλουτέω, ήσω (πλοῦτος), to be rich, 7. 7. 28, 42.

Πλουτίζω, ίσω (πλοῦτος), to make rich, enrich, 7. 6. 9.

Πνεῦμα, ατος, τό (πνέω), breath, wind, καλόν, 5. 9. 14, 10. 1.

Πνέω, πνεύσομαι and οὖμαι, πέπνευκα (πέπνευμαι and -σμαι, late, also πέπνυμαι, I am inspired), to blow, breathe, 4. 5. 3.

Πνίγω, πνίξω, πέπνιγμαι, 2 aor. ἐπνίγην, to choke, be drowned, 5. 7. 25.

Ποδαπός, ή, όν (ποῦ, ἀπό, where from), from what country? Lat. cujas? 4. 4. 17.

Ποδήρης, ης, ες (ποῦς, ἄρω), reaching to the feet, 1. 8. 9.

Ποδίζω, ίσω (ποῦς), to tie the feet, 3. 4. 35.

Πόθεν, adv. whence? 5. 4. 7, as an encl. adv. from some place or other, 6. 1. 15.

Ποθέω, ήσω, πεπόθηκα, ημαι (πόθος), to long for, wish, desire, with inf., 6. 2. 8.

Πόθος, ου, ὁ, a longing, desire, love, γονέων, 3. 1. 3.

Ποῖ, adv. whither? as an encl. somewhere, 6. 1. 10, 7. 2. 18.

Ποιέω, ήσω, πεποίηκα, ημαι, to make, do, 1. 5. 5, 4. 5. 14; δρόμον, 4. 8. 26; θυσίαν, 5. 3. 9, to sacrifice; ἀριθμόν, 1. 2. 9, to number; ἐξέτασιν, to hold a review, 1. 2. 9; ἐκκλησίαν, to hold a meeting, 1. 4. 12; κραυγήν, to raise a shout, 2. 2. 17; νίκας, to gain victories, 3. 1. 42; ἐξουσίαν, to give license, 5. 8. 22; φόβον τοῖς ἵπποις, make frightened, strike with terror, 1. 8. 18; with inf. 1. 7. 4, 2. 6. 14, 4. 1. 22, 5. 7. 27. ὥστε δόξαι, 1. 6. 6; τινί τι, 3. 2. 24, 4. 2. 23; κακῶς τινα, to treat ill, 4. 8. 6; injure, χώραν, 1. 6. 7, 2. 3. 23; εὖ, to treat well, 2. 3. 22, 7. 7. 8; εὖ τινα, 7. 8. 11; κακόν τινα, 7. 2. 33, 1. 9. 11, &c.; κακά τινα, 2. 5. 5; τοῦτον τἀναντία ποιήσετε ἢ τοὺς κύνας ποιοῦσι, you will do to this one the opposite of what they do to dogs, 5. 8. 24; ποιητέον, vb. 1. 3. 15; to put, place, 6. 3. 25, 7. 8. 16, 4. 8. 15; to consider, 2. 3. 18, 5. 9. 11, 6. 4. 11: see περί, παρά.

Ποικίλος, η, ον, variegated, tattooed, 1. 5. 8, 5. 4. 32.

Ποῖος, α, ον, of what sort, Lat. qualis, 3. 1. 14.

Πολεμέω, ήσω, &c. (πόλεμος), to make war on, τινί, 2. 6. 2, 5, 6; πρός τινα, 1. 3. 4;

ὅσα ἐπολεμήθη, *what hostilities were carried on*, 4. 1. 1.

Πολεμϊκός, η, όν (πόλεμος), *of persons, warlike*, 2. 6. 1, 5. 2. 2; πολεμικόν, *a war-cry*, 7. 3. 33; τὸ π., *the signal for battle*, 4. 3. 29; τὰ π., *warlike affairs, operations*, 3. 1. 38, 43 ; adv. κῶς, Sup. πολεμικώτατα ἔχειν, *they were very hostile*, 5. 9. 1.

Πολέμιος, α, ον and ος, or (πόλεμος), *hostile, a public enemy*; Lat. hostis (ἐχθρός=inimicus, *a private enemy*), 3. 1. 2, 2. 2. 14, 4. 3. 12, 6. 1. 22, 5. 1. 6; τινὶ γίγνεσθαι, 1. 6. 8; ἡ πολεμία (sc. γῆ, χώρα), *the enemy's country*, 3. 3. 5, 7. 6. 25, 4. 7. 20; τὰ π., *warlike affairs*, 1. 6. 1.

Πόλεμος, ου, ὁ (πέλω, *to be in motion*), *war*, 1. 9. 5, 4. 4. 1, 1. 8. 6, 5. 9; θεῶν, *against the gods*, 2. 5. 7 ; πρός, 7. 1. 27 ; ἀναιρεῖσθαι, ἐκφέρειν, ποιεῖσθαι, &c.

Πολίζω, ίσω (πόλις), *to build or found a city, colonise*, 6. 4. 4.

Πολιορκέω, ήσω, &c. (πόλις, εἴργω, ἕρκος), *to besiege, blockade*, 3. 4. 8, 4. 2. 15.

Πόλις, εως, ἡ, *a city, town*, 2. 6. 2, 5. 5. 8, 3, 6. 23, 10. 6; ἡ πόλις, *Athens*, or rather *the Acropolis*, 7. 1. 27; πόλις, *the citizens*, Lat. civitas ; ἄστυ, Lat. urbs, *the buildings*; in Athens π. *the Acropolis*; ἄστυ, *the rest of the city*.

Πόλισμα, ατος, τό (πολίζω), *a city, town*, 4. 7. 17, 6. 2. 7, 7. 8. 21.

Πολιτεύω, εύσω (πολίτης, πόλις), *to be a citizen, to live as a citizen*, 3. 2. 26.

Πολίτης, ου, ὁ (πόλις), *a citizen*, 5. 3. 9.

Πολλάκις (πολύς), adv. *often*, 5. 1. 11.

Πολλαπλάσιος, α, ον, and ος, ον (πολύς), *many times more*, 1. 7. 3, 7. 7. 25; ὑμῶν, *than you*, 3. 2. 14, 5. 5. 22, 7. 7. 27.

Πολλαχῇ (πολύς), *in many places*, 7. 3. 12, al. πολλαχῆ.

Πολλαχοῦ (πολύς), *in many situations*, 4. 1. 28.

Πολυάνθρωπος, ος, ον (πολύς, ἄνθρωπος), *full of people, populous*, 2. 4. 13.

Πολυαρχία, ας, ἡ (πολύς, ἄρχω), *the government of many*, 5. 9. 18.

Πολυκράτης, εος, ὁ (πολύς, κράτος), *Polycrates*, an Athenian, 4. 5. 24, 5. 1. 16.

Πολύνϊκος, ου, ὁ (πολύς, νίκη), *Polynicus*, a Spartan, 7. 6. 1.

Πολυπραγμονέω, ήσω (πολύς, πρᾶγμα), *to be busy, to meddle, τι, with something*, 5. 1. 15.

Πολύς, πολλή, πολύ ; Comp. πλείων, ων, ον and πλέον ; Supl. πλεῖστος, η, ον, *many, much, more, most*, ἀγαθά, 3. 1. 22, 5. 6. 4, 7. 7. 30 ; π. καὶ ἀγαθά, 4. 6. 27, 6. 2. 8, 7. 1. 33; π. τε καὶ δεινά, 5. 5. 8; φέρονται οἱ λίθοι πολλοί, for οἱ λίθοι οἳ φέρονται πολλοί εἰσιν, 4. 7. 7 ; so also τὰ ἄλλα πολλὰ διαρπάζουσιν, for τ. α. ἃ δ. πολλὰ ἦν 1. 10. 2, 4. 3. 7 ; *large*, χώρα, 5. 6. 20, 2. 4. 21; *long*, χρόνος, 1. 9. 25, 5. 2. 17 ; (ὁδός), 6. 1. 16 ; *much, far*, πολὺ πλείω, 5. 6. 5 ; μᾶλλον, 2. 3. 13 ; *with* Comp. 1. 5. 2, 16, 6. 3. 2. 15, &c.; Sup. 4. 2. 14; πολλῷ ὕστερον,

2. 5. 32, 4. 5. 36; οἱ πολλοί, *the most of them*, 2. 3. 16, 3. 1. 10, &c.; so τὸ πολύ, 1. 7. 20, 4. 6. 24; π., *a large part*, 4. 1. 11, 8. 17; *a great distance*, 1. 5. 3, 3. 3. 6; διὰ πολλά, *on many accounts*, 1. 9. 22; Comp. pl. πλείους for πλείονες, *more*, 4. 1. 11, 6. 9; τὸ πλεῖον, 7. 6. 16; φρονεῖν, 6. 1. 18; πλεῖον εἴκοσι σταδίων, 3. 2. 34, 3. 11; πλίον ἢ ἐφ᾽ ἑξήκοντα, 4. 6. 11; πλέον ἤ, 4. 2. 28, 1. 2. 11; πλεῖστος, *very many*, 1. 5. 2, 5. 2. 14; οἱ π., *the most*, 7. 4. 6. ὡς ἐδύναντο πλεῖστα, 4. 6. 1.

Πολύστρᾰτος, ου, ὁ (πολύς, στρατός), *Polystrătus*, an Athenian, 3. 3. 20.

Πολυτελής, ής, ές (πολύς, τέλος), *expensive, costly*, 1. 5. 8.

Πόμα, ατος, τὸ (πίνω), *a drink, draught*, 4. 5. 27, al. πῶμα.

Πομπή, ῆς, ἡ (πέμπω), *a procession*, 5. 5. 5.

Πονέω, ήσω, πεπόνηκα, ημαι (πόνος), *to work, labour*, 2. 6. 6; πολλά, *to go through many labours*, 7. 6. 36, 3. 31; χρήματα, *to earn money by labours*, 7. 6. 41.

Πονηρός, ά, όν (πονέω), *bad, wicked*, but πόνηρος, *unlucky, wretched*, 2. 5. 21, 5. 7. 33; ὡς π., *as a malefactor*, 2. 6. 29; τάξις, *bad*, 3. 4. 19; *useless, good for nothing*, 3.4.35; *dan-*

sea, especially the Black Sea, in full Π. Εὔξεινος, *the hospitable*, 4. 8. 22; formerly Ἄξεινος, *the inhospitable*, the Pontus Euxinus; also the district of Pontus, on the Black Sea, 5. 6. 15.

Πορεία, ας, ἡ (πόρος), *a march*, 2. 2. 10, 4. 1. 13, 4. 18, 5. 10. 4, &c.

Πορεύω, εύσω, πεπόρευκα, ευμαι (πόρος), *to cause to go, convey*; Mid. *to go, march*, 5. 3. 1; κατὰ γῆν, 5. 4. 1; ἐφ᾽ ἁμάξης, 2. 2. 14; παρὰ βασιλέως, 4. 5. 10; παρὰ βασιλέα, 1. 3. 7; ἐπὶ βασιλέα, 2. 1. 4; πορείαν, 5. 10. 4; υἱόν, 2. 2. 11, &c.

Πορθέω, ήσω, &c. (πέρθω), *to destroy*, 5. 7. 14.

Πορίζω, ίσω, πεπόρικα, πεπόρισμαι (πόρος), *to furnish, provide, supply*, ἄριστον, 2. 3. 5; πλοῖα, 5. 6. 5; τάλαντον, 3. 5. 8; θώρακας, 3. 3. 20, 2. 1. 6, 7. 6. 29.

Πόρος, ου, ὁ (πείρω), *a passage*, 4. 3. 13. 20; *means*, 2. 5, 20.

Πόρρω τινός, adv. *far from*, 1. 3. 12.

Πορφύρεος, α, ον, contr. ροῦς, ρᾶ, ροῦν, *purple*, 1. 5. 8.

Πόσος, η, ον, *how much, how great*, 7. 8. 1, 2. 4. 21; πόσον, *how far*, 7. 3. 12.

Ποταμός, οῦ, ὁ (πίνω), *a river*, 5. 4. 1, 1. 5. 10, &c.

Ποτέ *once on a time but also*

ind. 2. 2. 10, 5. 4. 2 ; with opt.
3. 1. 7 ; πότερα—ή, dir. 2. 5.
17 ; indirect with ind. 2. 1.
10, 21 ; with opt. 7. 1. 14, 6.
44.

Ποτέρως, in which way (of two),
folld. by εἰ—ή, 7. 7. 30, 33,
34.

Ποτήριον, ου, τό (πίνω), a drinking cup, 5. 9. 4.

Ποτόν, οῦ,τό (πίνω), drink, σιτίον
ή ποτόν, 1. 10. 18 :σῖτα καὶ
ποτά, 2. 3. 27, 7. 1. 33, 35,
3. 10.

Πότος, ου, ὁ (πίνω), drinking,
προὐχώρει, 7. 3. 26; παρὰ
πότον, 2. 3. 15.

Ποῦ, adv. where? πού, somewhere, 2. 4. 4, 5. 6. 17, 7. 13 ;
ἐγγύς που, 2. 2. 15 ; εἴ που,
3. 4. 23 ; ἤν που, 1. 2. 27.

Πούς, ποδός, ὁ, a foot, ἀριστερός,
4. 2. 28 ; τὰ πρὸ ποδῶν, what
lay before the feet, 4. 6. 12 ;
τραχεῖα ποσίν, 4. 6. 12 ; ἐπὶ
πόδα ἀναχωρεῖν, to retreat step
by step, slowly, 5. 2. 32.

Πρᾶγμα, ατος, τό (πράσσω), a
deed, action, thing, matter ;
Lat. res, 1. 5. 13, 15 ; pl.
affairs, state of affairs, 1. 3.
3 ; effects, plunder, 6. 1. 6 ;
ἔχειν, to have trouble, 5. 6. 5 ;
παρέχειν, to give trouble, τινί,
4. 1. 22 ; τῇ χώρᾳ, 1. 1. 11 ;
π. τι εἴη, there was something
ado, 4. 1. 17 ; οὐδέν, there
was nothing the matter, 6.
4. 8.

Πραγματεύομαι, εύσομαι, πεπραγ-
μάτευμαι (πρᾶγμα), to labour
to bring about, strive to effect,
7. 6. 35.

Πρανής, ής, ές, Att. for πρηνής
(πρό), head-foremost, with the
face downwards, Lat. pronus ;

the opp. is ὕπτιος (ὑπό), Lat.
supinus, with the face upwards,
steep, 1. 5. 8, 5. 2. 28 ; τὸ π.,
down-hill, opp. to ὄρθιος, up-
hill, 3. 4. 25 ; κατὰ τοῦ πρα-
νοῦς, down the steep, 4. 8. 28,
6. 3. 31.

Πρᾶξις, εως, ἡ (πράσσω), trans-
action, 7. 2. 30, 6. 17 ; under-
taking, 1. 3. 16, 18, 19, 2. 6. 17.

Πρᾶος, πραεῖα, πρᾶον, mild,
gentle, tame, 1. 4. 9, adv.
πράως, 1. 5. 14, better πρᾶος.

Πράττω, πράξω, πέπραχα, πέπραγμαι (2 p. πέπρᾱγα, intrans.), to do, act, Lat. ago ;
ποιέω, to make, Lat. facio, 2.
1. 1, 3. 1. 1, 5. 6. 28 ; περὶ
πλοίων, was bargaining for
ships, 7. 2. 12 ; εὖ π., to be
fortunate, fare well, 7. 6. 11,
20, so καλῶς, 3. 1. 6 ; κακῶς,
to be unfortunate, 1. 9. 10 ;
πολλὰ καὶ ἀγαθὰ π., were
making large fortunes, 6. 2. 8.

Πρέπω, ψω, to be conspicuous.
Imp. it becomes, 1. 9. 6, 3. 2.
7, 16 ; syn. προσήκει.

Πρεσβεία, ας, ἡ (πρέσβυς), em-
bassy, 7. 3. 21.

Πρεσβεύω, εύσω, &c. (πρέσβυς),
to be an ambassador, 7. 7. 6 ;
παρά τινος, 2. 1. 18 ; τινί,
7. 2. 23.

Πρέσβυς, νος or εως, ὁ, old, an
old man, only acc. and voc.,
pl. πρέσβεις, ambassadors, 3.
1. 28, 5. 5. 7, 7. 19, &c.
Comp. πρεσβύτερος, πρεσβύ-
τατος, hence, presbyter, priest.

Πρεσβύτης, ου, ὁ (πρέσβυς), an
old man, 6. 1. 10.

Πρίασθαι, only 2. aor. ἐπριάμην,
πρίωμαι, πριαίμην, to buy ;
other parts fr. ὠνέομαι, 3. 1.
20, τί τινος 1 5 6

Πρίν, *before*, with ind. after a negative, 1. 2. 26, 5. 9. 27; οὐ πρότερον πρίν, 3. 1. 16; οὐ πρόσθεν πρίν, 3. 2. 29. With ἂν and conj. 5. 7. 5, 12, 1. 1. 10; with opt. 1. 2. 2, 4. 5. 30, 7. 7. 57; with inf. after an affirmative, 1. 4. 13, 16, 10. 19, 2. 5. 2, 4. 1. 7, 5. 6. 16.

Πρό, *before*, with gen. ποδῶν, 4. 6. 12; ὀφθαλμῶν, 4. 5. 13; πύλεως, 5. 4. 15; ὑμῶν, *for your interests*, 7. 6. 27; *before in time*, τῆς μάχης, 1. 7. 13, 7. 3. 1.

Προαγορεύω, εύσω, &c., *to proclaim by herald*, 2. 2. 20.

Προάγω, άξω, &c., *to lead forward*, 6. 3. 6, 7, 11, 4. 6. 21.

Προαιρέω, ήσω, &c., 2. aor. προεῖλον, *to prefer one thing to another*, τί τινος, 6. 4. 19.

Προαισθάνομαι, αἰσθήσομαι, ἠσθήμαι, *to perceive, observe beforehand*, 1. 1. 7.

Προαναλίσκω, αλώσω, ἥλωκα, ωμαι, *to spend*, 6. 2. 8.

Προαποτρέπω, τρέψω, &c., Mid. *to turn oneself away from, leave off*, with part., 6. 3. 31.

Προβαίνω, βήσομαι, &c., *to go forward, advance*, 4. 3. 28, νύξ, 3. 1. 13.

Προβάλλω, βαλῶ, &c., *to throw forward, advance*, ἀσπίδα, ὅπλα, 1. 2. 17, 4. 2. 21, 6. 3. 16; *propose*, 5. 9. 25, 10. 6.

Πρόβατον, ου, τό (πρό, βαίνω), a *sheep*, 2. 4. 27, 6. 1. 3, 7. 6. 26, καὶ βόες, 6. 1. 22, 7. 3. 48, καὶ αἶγες, 3. 5. 9.

Προβολή, ῆς, ἡ (πρό, βάλλω), a *putting forward*, τὰ δόρατα εἰς προβολὴν καθιέναι, *to bring the* spears to the charge, couch them, 6. 3. 25.

Προβουλεύω, εύσω, &c., *to provide for a thing*, τινός, 3. 1. 37.

Πρόγονος, ου, ὁ (πρό, γίγνομαι), a *forefather, ancestor*, 3. 2. 11, 13, 7. 2. 22.

Προδίδωμι, δώσω, &c., *to give up, betray*, 1. 3. 5, 2. 2. 8, 6. 4. 17, 22, 2. 3. 22, 3. 1. 2, 14.

Προδιώκω, ώξω, *to pursue farther*, 3. 3. 10.

Προδότης, ου, ὁ (πρό, δίδωμι), a *traitor*, 2. 5. 27, 6. 4. 7.

Προδρομή, ῆς, ἡ (πρό, δραμεῖν), a *sally, sortie*, 4. 7. 10.

Προεῖδον; see προοράω.

Προειπεῖν; see προερέω.

Πρόειμι (πρό, εἶμι), *to go forward, advance*, 1. 3. 1, 4. 18.

Προελαύνω, ελάσω or ελῶ, &c., *to drive forward*, ἵππον, *to ride forward*, 1. 10. 16, 6. 1. 14, 22.

Προεργάζομαι, εργάσομαι, εἴργασμαι, *to work beforehand*, ἡ προειργασμένη δόξα, *glory won before*, 5. 9. 21.

Προερέω, ερῶ, εἴρηκα, εἴρημαι, 2 aor. προεῖπον, *to tell, intimate*, 1. 2. 17, 7. 7. 13.

Προέρχομαι, ελεύσομαι, ελήλυθα, *to go forward, advance*, 2. 3. 3; *to march*, 3. 4. 37; κατὰ τὴν ὁδόν, 4. 2. 16; τριάκοντα σταδίους, 7. 3. 7; οὐ πολύ, 3. 3. 6; εἰς, 7. 2. 1, 8. 5.

Προέχω, έξω, &c., *to excel*, ἡμᾶς, 3. 2. 19, usually τινός τινι.

Προηγέομαι, ηγήσομαι, ἥγημαι, *to lead the way*, ὁδόν, 6. 3. 10; τὰ ἴχνη προηγούμενα, *the tracks of persons gone before*, 7. 3. 42.

Προηγορέω, ήσω, &c. (πρό, ἀγορά), to speak for or in behalf of, τινός, 5. 5. 7.

Προθέω, θεύσομαι, to run forward, 5. 8. 13.

Προθυμέομαι, ήσομαι, τεθύμημαι (πρό, θυμός), to be ready, eager, 3. 4. 15, 6. 2. 22; χαρίζεσθαι, 1. 9. 24 ; διαβῆναι, 7. 2. 2 ; λαβεῖν, 4. 1. 22, 2. 4. 7, 7. 7. 47, 3. 1. 9.

Προθυμία, ας, ἡ (πρό, θυμός), readiness, eagerness, zeal, 1. 9. 18, 7. 6. 11, 7. 45.

Πρόθυμος, ος, ον (πρό, θυμός), ready, willing, eager, zealous, 1. 3. 19, 4. 15, 3. 2. 15. Adv. 5. 2. 2, 7. 7. 21, 1. 4. 9, 10. 10.

Προθύω, θύσω, &c., to sacrifice in behalf of one, τινός, 6. 2. 22.

Προΐημι, ήσω, &c., to send before, εἰ προιεῖεν αὐτῷ οἱ θεοὶ πειρᾶσθαι, if the gods should permit him to try, 7. 2. 15. Mid. to give up, 1. 9. 12, 5. 8. 14, 7. 3. 31; to abandon, 1. 9. 9. προίεσθαι εὐεργεσίαν τινί, to bestow kind offices on one, without looking for any return, 7. 7. 47.

Προΐστημι, προστήσω, &c., to set at the head of; Neut. to command, τοῦ ξενικοῦ αὐτῷ, 1. 2. 1, the mercenaries for him ; 7. 1. 30, 2. 2; to be at the head of, αὐτῶν, 5. 10. 9 ; τῆς Ἑλλάδος, 6. 4. 12.

Προκαίω, καύσω, &c., to burn before, 7. 2. 18.

Προκαλέω, έσω, &c., to call out, 7. 7. 2.

Προκαλύπτω, ύψω, &c., to cover over, ἥλιον νεφέλη, 3. 4. 8.

Προκαταθέω, θεύσομαι, to run down beforehand, 6. 1. 10.

Προκατακαίω, καύσω, &c., to burn, lay waste, all before one, 1. 6. 2.

Προκαταλαμβάνω, λήψομαι, &c., to seize beforehand, preoccupy, 1. 3. 14, 16, &c.

Πρόκειμαι, κείσομαι, to lie before, stretch forward, 6. 2. 3.

Προκινδυνεύω, εύσω, &c., to run risk beforehand, brave danger, 7. 3. 31.

Προκλῆς, έος, ὁ (πρό, κλέω), Procles, governor of Teuthrania, 2. 1. 3.

Προκρίνω, κρίνω, &c., to prefer, 5. 9. 26.

Προλέγω, λέξω, &c., to order, ἀπιέναι, 7. 7. 3.

Προμαχεών, ῶνος, ὁ (πρό, μάχομαι), a bulwark, battlement, 7. 8. 13.

Προμετωπίδιον, ου, τό (πρό, μέτωπον, the forehead), a frontlet, esp. for horses, 1. 8. 7.

Προμηρίδιον, ου, τό (πρό, μηρούς, the thigh), armour for the thighs, cuisses, supply ὅπλον, 1. 8. 6.

Προμνάομαι (πρό, μνάομαι, to woo), to sue or plead with ; τοιαῦτα προὐμνᾶτο, in such a manner did he keep suing for Seuthes, 7. 3. 18.

Προνοέω, ήσω, &c., Mid. to provide for, τινός, 7. 7. 33, 37.

Πρόνοια, ας, ἡ (πρό, νοῦς), foresight, forethought, 7. 7. 52.

Προνομή, ῆς, ἡ (πρό, νέμω), a foraging party, 5. 1. 7.

Προξενέω, ήσω, &c., to be any one's πρόξενος, to bring on one, κίνδυνον ὑμῖν, 6. 3. 14.

Πρόξενος, ου, ὁ (πρό, ξένος), a public guest, a foreign consul, but always a member of the foreign state, patron, protector, 5. 4. 2, 6. 11.

Πρόξενος, ου, ὁ, Proxenus, a

Theban, the great friend of Xenophon, 1. 1. 11, &c., 2. 6. 16.

Προοράω, ὄψομαι, &c., to see before one, 1. 8. 20, 5. 9. 8.

Προπέμπω, πέμψω, &c., to send before or forward, σκοπούς, 2. 2. 15; ἑρμηνέα, 4. 4. 5, 7. 2. 14, 19, 5. 8. 9; to accompany, 5. 9. 23.

Προπίνω, πίομαι, &c., to drink one's health, 4. 5. 32, 7. 3. 26; κέρατα οἴνου, in horns of wine, 7. 2. 23.

Προποι έω, ήσω, &c., to work for τινός, 3. 1. 37.

Πρός, a prep. towards, gov. Gen. Dat. and Acc. With Gen. by, after Pass. verbs, 1. 9. 20; so πρὸς τῆς πόλεως ὑπαιτιόν ἐστι, 3. 1. 5; π. ἡμῶν, with us, lit. from, 7. 6. 39, 2. 3. 18, 7. 6. 33; π. τοῦ Κύρου τρόπου, according to the character of Cyrus, 1. 2. 11; πρὸς τοῦ ποταμοῦ, near the river, 2. 2. 4, 4. 3. 26; ἐκφεύγει πρὸς τῶν Ἑλλήνων═πρὸς τούτους τῶν 'Ε., 1. 10. 3; πρὸς θεῶν, before the gods, 1. 6. 6, 2. 5. 20, 5. 7. 12; in swearing by, 2. 1. 17, 7. 1. 29, 6. 33. With Dat. beside, τῷ ποταμῷ, 1. 8. 4, 14, 5. 4. 25, 6. 2. 7, 7. 2. 14, 3. 21, 2. 3. 4; in addition to, π. τούτοις, 3. 2. 33, 4. 13, 7. 6. 32; but πρὸς ταῦτα, thereupon, upon this, 1. 6. 9. With Acc. towards, μεσημβρίαν, 1. 7. 6, 3. 5. 15, 5. 7. 6; ἡμέραν, 4. 5. 21; to, of place, π. τὸ στράτευμα, 3. 4. 28, 4. 2. 25, 5. 4. 5; ἐπιτήδεια, 2. 3. 9, 3. 1. 40, 4. 5. 2, 5. 10. 5; of persons, ἡμᾶς, 5. 7. 20, 3. 3. 2, 7. 3. 31; π. τινα, 5. 6. 31, 7. 6. 6, 3. 1. 34, 2. 5,

&c.; for, for the purpose of, π. τὸ ἐπιδραμεῖν, 4. 3. 31, 1. 10. 19, 2. 6. 20, 2. 5. 20; π. τὴν χώραν συμφέρει, is suitable for the ground, 7. 3. 37; to, in regard to, about, upon, 7. 1. 9, 1. 4. 9; βουλεύεσθαι, 1. 3. 19, 2. 3. 21, 5. 10. 5; διαλέγεσθαι, 2. 5. 42; στασιάζειν, 5. 9. 29; ἀκούειν, 7. 6. 23; ἀποκρίνεσθαι, 2. 5. 39, 5. 4. 8; εἰπεῖν, 1. 6. 9, 2. 1. 11, 20, 5. 5. 13; compared with, 7. 7. 41; with, φιλίαν διαπράττεσθαι πρός τινα, 7. 3. 16, 3. 5. 16, 1. 1. 10; in a hostile signification, against, ἰέναι πρὸς τοὺς πολεμίους, 2. 6. 10, 1. 1. 8, 4. 6. 25, 5. 4. 14, 1. 3. 21, 1. 4. 2, 4. 6. 11, &c.; γυμνοὶ ἐγίγνοντο πρὸς τὰ τοξεύματα, they became exposed to the arrows, 4. 3. 6; π. φιλίαν, in friendship, 1. 3. 19. Πρὸς δ' ἔτι without a case, and besides, also, 3. 2. 2.

Προσάγω, άξω, &c., to lead forward, 1. 10. 9, 4. 8. 11; πρὸς τὴν χαράδραν, 5. 2. 8, 5. 9. 14; φόβον, to bring terror before one, to utter terrible threats, 4. 1. 23.

Προσαιτέω, ήσω, &c., to ask besides, μισθόν, higher pay, 1. 3. 21; οὐδέν σε, asking nothing else of you, 7. 3. 31, 6. 27.

Προσαναλίσκω, λώσω, &c., to consume besides; χρήματα, to expend money besides, 6. 2. 8.

Προσανειπεῖν, to mention publicly in addition, 7. 1. 11.

Προσβ αίνω, βήσομαι, &c., to go to, advance, 4. 2. 28.

Προσβάλλω, βαλ ῶ, &c., to attack, 4. 6. 13; πρὸς τὸν λόφον, to

charge up the hill, 4. 2. 11,
7. 2, 5. 2. 4, 5. 2, 6. 1. 7.

Προσβατός, ή, όν (πρός, βαίνω),
accessible, 4. 8. 9.

Προσβολή, ῆς, ἡ (πρός, βάλλω),
an attack, assault, 3. 4. 2, 6.
3. 25.

Προσγίγνομαι, γενήσομαι, &c.,
to come to; πλείους προσγενέ-
σθαι, more will join them, 4. 6.
9, 7. 1. 28.

Προσδανείζομαι, ξανείσομαι, δε-
δάνειμαι, to lend in addition;
Mid. borrow besides, 7. 5. 5.

Προσδέω, impers. in act. προσδεῖ;
Mid. προσδέομαι, τινος, to be
still in need of, 3. 2. 34, 5. 6.
1, 7. 6. 27; desire, ἀρχῆς, 5.
. 9. 24.

Προσδίδωμι, δώσω, &c., to give
besides, 1. 9. 19.

Προσδοκάω, ήσω, &c., to expect,
στρατηγὸν ταῦτα πράξειν, 3. 1.
14, 5. 9. 16; πάντα, 7. 6.
11.

Πρόσειμι, to go to, come up, 1. 8.
14; αὐτῷ, 5. 9. 19; εἰς τὸ δασύ,
4. 7. 7, 7. 6. 24.

Προσελαύνω, ελάσω or ελῶ, &c.,
to drive to a place; ἵππον, to
ride up, 3. 4. 39, 4. 4. 5, 7. 3.
7, 47, 6. 1. 7; στρατόν, to
march up, arrive, 1. 5. 12, 7.
16, 3. 5. 13.

Προσέρχομαι, ελεύσομαι, ελήλυθα,
to come up or go to, 4. 8. 2, 7.
1. 33; εἰς ἐπήκοον, 4. 4. 5;
Ξενοφῶντι, 4. 3. 10, 8. 4, 3. 5.
8, 7. 3. 18, 19, 1. 3. 9.

Προσεύχομαι, εὔξομαι, εὖγμαι, to
pray to, offer up vows to, θεοῖς,
6. 1. 21.

Προσέχω, ἕξω, &c., to bring to,
τινί τι, νοῦν, to turn one's mind
to, Lat. animadverto, 1.5.9; ὡς
ἂν δύνησθε, 6.1.18; be attentive

to, τοῖς ῞Ελλησι, 2. 4.2; direct
or pay attention to, τῇ ὑδῷ, 4.
2. 2; τοῖς χρήμασι, 7. 8. 16;
ὀλίγον τινί, 7. 6. 5; μονῇ, to
think of staying, 5. 6. 22.

Προσήκω, ἥξω, to stretch, ἐπὶ τὸν
ποταμόν, 4. 3. 23; related to,
βασιλεῖ, 1. 6. 1; τούτῳ τῆς
Βοιωτίας προσήκει οὐδέν, he has
nothing to do with, 3. 1. 31;
Imp. it becomes, ἀγαθοῖς ὑμῖν
εἶναι, 3. 2. 11; ὑμᾶς ἀμείνοιας
εἶναι, 3. 2. 15, 7. 7. 18.

Πρόσθεν, adv. (1) of place, before, in front, εἰς τὸ πρόσθεν,
forwards, 1. 10. 5, 2. 1. 2, 7.
3. 41, 3. 4. 38; τῶν ὅπλων, to
the place in front of the arms,
3. 1. 33; τὰ π., the van, 3. 2.
36; ὁ π. λόγος, the previous
narrative, 3. 1. 1, 4. 1. 1;
(2) of time, before, formerly,
1. 6. 10, 7. 2. 22; π. πρίν, 1.
1. 10, 3. 2.29, Lat. priusquam;
ὁ π. χρόνος, 2. 3. 22, 5. 9. 18,
6. 4, 31; ἡ π. ἡμέρα, the previous day, 2. 3. 1, 4. 3. 7; ἡ
π. προσβολή, 3. 4. 2; οἱ π.
ἄρχοντες, 3. 2. 30, 2. 4. 5; ἡ
π. ἀρετή, 1. 4. 8, 6. 4; τὸ
π., before, 1. 10. 10, 3. 1. 23;
πρόσθεν ἤ, sooner than, 2. 1.
10.

Προσθέω, θεύσομαι, to run up to,
5. 7. 21, 6. 1. 7, 7. 1. 15, 7.
55.

Προσίημι, ήσω, &c., to let, allow,
4. 5. 5, 4. 2. 12; Mid. admit,
3. 1. 30; οὐδαμῇ προσίοιντο,
in no way permitted, 5. 5. 3.

Προσκαλέω, έσω, &c., to call to,
προσκαλῶν τοὺς φίλους, calling
to him his friends, 1. 9. 28;
call out, 7. 7. 2.

Προσκτάομαι, κτήσομαι, ἔκτημαι,
to gain besides, 5. 6. 15.

Προσκυνέω, ήσω, κεκύνηκα, 1 aor. εκύνησα or έκῦσα, *to kiss the hand to another, to do obeisance*, in the East by prostration, 1. 6. 10, 8. 21, 3. 2. 13; with the gods, *to worship*, 3. 2. 9, 13.

Προσλαμβάνω, λήψομαι, &c., *to receive in addition*, ταῦτα λαβὼν καὶ τοὺς ὁμήρους προσλαβών, 7. 7. 5; μισθόν, 7. 3. 13, 7. 6. 32, 1. 7. 3; σύμμαχον, 7. 6. 27; *to take part in*, 2. 3. 11, 12.

Προσμίγνυμι, μίξω, &c., *to mix with, approach*, τινί, 4. 2. 16.

Πρόσοδος, ου, ἡ (πρός, ὁδός), *a going to*, 5. 2. 3; *a procession*, 5. 9. 11; *income*, 7. 7. 36; *revenue*, 7. 1. 27; προσόδους ποιῶν, *improving the revenue*, 1. 9. 19.

Προσόμνυμι and -ομνύω, -ομοῦμαι, &c., *to swear in addition*, 2. 2. 8.

Προσομολογέω, ήσω, &c., *to grant, give in, surrender*, 7. 4. 24.

Προσπερονάω, ήσω, &c. (περόνη), *to fasten with a pin, skewer*, πρός τινι, 7. 3. 21.

Προσπίπτω, πεσοῦμαι, &c., *to fall upon*, τινί, 7. 1. 21.

Προσποιέω, ήσω, &c., *to add to*, τινί τι; Mid. *to pretend*, σπεύδειν, 1. 3. 14, 4. 3. 20, 6. 13; ἐπιστήμων εἶναι, 2. 1. 7.

Προσπολεμέω, ήσω, &c., *to harass in war*, τινά, 1. 6. 6.

Προστατεύω=προστατέω, 5. 6. 21.

Προστατέω, ήσω, *to stand at the head of, preside over*, ἀγῶνος, 4. 8. 25.

Προστάτης, ου ὁ (πρό, ἵστημι), *a president, leader*, 7. 7. 31.

Προστάττω, τάξω, &c., *to order, give orders to*, 1. 6. 10, 9. 18.

Προστελέω, έσω, &c., *to pay or spend besides*, 7. 6. 30.

Προστερνίδιον, ου, τό (πρό, στέρνον), *a covering for the breast of horses, breastplate*, 1. 8. 7.

Προστίθημι, θήσω, &c., *to add*; Mid. *consent to*, 1. 6. 10.

Προστρέχω, θρέξω or δραμοῦμαι, &c., *to run up to*, 7. 4. 7; τινί, 4. 2. 21, 3. 10.

Προσφέρω, οἴσω, &c., *to bring to*, 5. 2. 14; Mid. *conduct themselves*, τινί and πρός τινα, 5. 5. 19, 7. 1. 6.

Προσχωρέω, ήσω, &c., *to go to, surrender, give in*, τινί, 5. 4. 30.

Πρόσχωρος, ος, ον (πρός, χώρα), *lying near, neighbouring*, 5. 3. 9.

Πρόσω, adv. (πρό, πρός), *forward*; οὐ π., *not far off*, 2. 2. 15, 4. 5. 2, 7. 3. 17; τῶν πηγῶν, 3. 2. 22; τοῦ ποταμοῦ, 4. 3. 28, *not far from the river*; τοῦ πρόσω, gen. of portion, *any farther*, 1. 3. 1; εἰς τὸ π., *forward*, προσωτέρω, *farther*, 7. 7. 1; προσωτάτω, 6. 4. 1.

Πρόσωπον, ου, τό (πρός, ὤψ), *face, countenance*, pl. 2. 6. 18, *looks*.

Προτελέω, έσω, &c., *to pay as tribute*, 7. 7. 25.

Προτεραῖος, α, ον, a diurnal adj. ἡ προτεραία (ἡμέρα), *the day before*, 2. 1. 3, 5. 4. 23.

Πρότερος, α, ον (πρό), Supl. πρῶτος, *first* (of two), 1. 4. 12, 5. 4. 26, Lat. *prior*; προτέρα Κύρου, *before Cyrus, earlier than Cyrus*, 1. 2. 25. Adv. πρότερον, *on a former occasion*, 7. 6. 33, 4. 4. 14; almost superfluous, 1. 7. 18.

Προτιμάω, ήσω, &c., *to honour one before another*, πλέον προτιμήσεσθε, *ye shall be more highly honoured*, obs. pass. sign. 1. 4. 14, 6. 5.

Προτρέχω, θρέξω or δραμοῦμαι, &c., *to run forward*, 4. 7. 10, 1. 5. 2; τῶν ὁπλιτῶν, *before*, 5. 2. 4.

Προφαίνω, φανῶ, &c., *to. show forth*; Mid. *appear, come in sight*, 1. 8. 1.

Προφασίζομαι, ίσομαι (πρόφασις), *to set up a pretext*, 3. 1. 25.

Πρόφᾱσις, εως, ἡ (πρό, φαίνω), *a pretext*, 1. 1. 7; ποιεῖσθαι, 1. 2. 1; παρέχειν τινί, 7. 6. 22; εὑρίσκειν, 2. 3. 21.

Προφύλαξ, ακος, ὁ, *an advanced guard, outpost*, 2. 3. 2, 4. 15, 3. 2. 1, 6. 2. 26.

Προχωρέω, ήσω, &c., *to go on*, ὁ πότος, 7. 3. 26; ἔχοντι ὅ,τι προχωροίη, *having whatever might suit his convenience*, 1. 9. 13; τὰ ἱερά, *to be propitious*, 6. 2. 21.

Πρύμνα, ης, ἡ (πρυμνός, *hindmost*), *the stern, poop*, of a ship, 5. 8. 20; πρῷρα is the *prow*.

Πρωΐ (πρό), *early*, 7. 6. 6; comp. πρωϊαίτερον or πρωΐτερον, 3.4.1.

Πρῷρα, ας, ἡ (πρό), *the prow* of a ship, 5. 8. 20.

Πρῳρεύς, έως, ὁ, *the man at the prow, the look-out man*, 5. 8. 20.

Πρωτᾱγός, οῦ, ὁ (πρῶτος, ἄγω), *leading the van*, οἱ π., *the vanguard*, 2. 2. 16.

Πρωτεύω (πρῶτος), *to be first*, 2. 6. 26.

Πρῶτος, η, ον (πρό, πρότερος, πρῶτος), *first*, 2. 3. 19, 5. 1. 2, 4. 8. 18, 7. 1. 12; ὁ π. λέγων, 7. 6. 10, 6. 3. 5, 4. 8. 1; οἱ πρῶτοι, *the first, the vanguard*, 2. 2. 16, 17, 4. 2. 25,

8. 12, 7. 4. 19. Adv. πρῶτον, *first, in the first place*, 2. 3. 16, 3. 1. 15; π. μὲν—εἶτα, 1. 3. 2; πρῶτα μέν—ἔπειτα, 3. 2. 27; ἔπειτα δέ, 5. 6. 7; εἶτα δέ, 1. 2. 16; ἐπειδὴ δέ, 1. 3. 4; πρῶτον μέν—μετὰ τοῦτο, 5. 9. 5; τὸ π., 1. 10. 10; τὸ μὲν π.—ἐπειδὴ δέ, 7. 2. 18; ὡς τὸ π., 7. 8. 14, *as soon as*, Lat. *quum primum*.

Πταίω, πταίσω, ἔπταικα, ἔπταισμαι, *to stumble, strike*, 4. 2. 3.

Πτάρνῠμαι, 1 aor. act. ἔπτᾱρα, 2 aor. ἔπταρον, pass. ἐπτάρην, *to sneeze*, 3. 2. 9.

Πτέρυξ, ῠγος, ἡ (πτερόν), *a wing*, 1. 5. 3; *flaps*, 4. 7. 15.

Πυγμή, ῆς, ἡ (πύξ), *a fist, a boxing-match*, 4. 8. 27.

Πυκῐνός, ή, όν (for πυκινός, fr. πύξ), *thick, close*, σπάρτα, 4. 7. 15; δένδρα, 4. 8. 2; τύρσεις, 5. 2. 5; φάλαγξ, 2. 3. 3. Adv. πυκνά, *frequently*, 5. 9. 8.

Πύκτης, ου, ὁ (πύξ), *a boxer, pugilist*, 5. 8. 23.

Πύλη, ης, ἡ, *a gate*, 5. 2. 16, 23, 5. 20; *outlet*, 6. 3. 1; pass, 1. 4. 4. (1) Πύλαι αἱ Βαβυλώνιαι, 1. 5. 5; (2) τῆς Κιλικίας, 1. 2. 21; (3) Κιλικίας καὶ τῆς Συρίας, 1. 4. 4, also αἱ Σύριαι πύλαι, 1. 4. 5; (4) Ἀμανικαί, *the Amanian Pass*, through Mt. Amānus, near Issus.

Πυνθάνομαι, πεύσομαι, πέπυσμαι, 2 aor. ἐπυθόμην, *to ask, inquire*, ὅπως, 3. 1. 7; περί τινος, 5. 5. 25, 7. 1. 14; τινός, 6. 1. 23, 25; *to hear, learn, ascertain*, πυθομένους τὰ παρ' ἡμῖν, *having ascertained our condition*, 6. 1. 26; τινός, *from one*, 4. 6. 17; ὑμᾶς εὖ πράττειν, 7. 6. 11, 2. 1. 4, 2. 3.

Πύξ, adv. with the fists, 5. 8. 16.

Πῦρ, πυρός, τό, pl. 2. decl. fire, 2. 5. 19; προσφέρειν, 5. 2. 14; ποιεῖσθαι, 5. 2. 27; ἀνακαίειν, 3. 1. 3; καίειν, 4. 5. 5, 6; πυρὰ ἔρημα, deserted watch-fires, 7. 2. 18, 4. 4. 9, 1. 11; κατασβεννύναι, 6. 1. 25.

Πυρά, ᾶς, ἡ (πῦρ), a funeral pyre, 6. 2. 9.

Πυραμίς, ίδος, ἡ (πῦρ), a pyramid, 3. 4. 9.

Πύρᾰμος, ου, ὁ, the Pyramus, a large river in Cilicia, 1. 4. 1.

Πυργομαχέω, ήσω, &c., to storm a tower, 7. 8. 13.

Πύργος, ου, ὁ, a tower, 7. 8. 13.

Πυρέττω, έξω (πῦρ), to be in a fever, 6. 2. 11.

Πύρῐνος, η, ον (πυρός), made of wheat, wheaten, ἄρτοι, 4. 5. 31.

Πυρός, οῦ, ὁ (πῦρ), wheat, pl. 1. 2. 22, 4. 5. 5, 6. 2. 6, 4. 1.

Πυρρίας, ου, ὁ, Pyrrhias, an Arcadian, 6. 3. 11.

Πυρρίχη, ης, ἡ, a war-dance, sc. ὄρχησις, called after Pyrrichus the inventor, 5. 9. 12.

Πυρσεύω (πῦρ), to make signals, or telegraph by torches or beacon-fires, 7. 8. 15.

Πώ, yet, with negatives, οὐδείς πω, 1. 2. 26, 6. 3. 14, 7. 5. 16; οὐκ ἴσασί πω, 7. 3. 35; οὐδὲ νῦν πω, 7. 6. 35.

Πωλέω, ήσω, &c., to sell, 7. 3. 3.

Πῶλος, ου, ὁ and ἡ, a foal, 4. 5. 24, 35.

Πῶλος, ου, ὁ, Polus, a Spartan, 7. 2. 5.

Πώποτε, adv. at any time, ever, usually with neg. οὐ πώποτε, never, 1. 4. 18, 6. 11, 7. 7. 48; εἰ, 5. 4. 6.

Πῶς, how, 2. 5. 20, 5. 7. 9, 7. 6. 6; after βουλεύω, 3. 4. 40; σκοπέω, 7. 8. 16; λέγω, 3. 2. 27; πῶς μέγα ἡγοῦ, how important you considered it, 7. 7. 27.

Πώς, somehow, εἴ πως, 2. 3. 18, 5. 2, 4. 1. 8, 21; ἄλλως πως, 3. 1. 20, 26, 6. 2. 2; τεχνικῶς πως, in an artificial sort of way, 5. 9. 5; ὡδέ πως, 1. 7. 9; κατὰ μέσον πως, somewhere about the centre, 5. 10. 17; μᾶλλόν πως, somehow rather, 3. 1. 43; μεταγνόντες πως, for some reason or other, 2. 6. 3.

P.

'Ρᾴδιος, α, ον and ος, ον (ῥέω), easy, 4. 8. 13; Comp. ῥᾴων, Sup. ῥᾷστος, adv. ῥᾳδίως, 3. 5. 9.

'Ραθίνης, ου, ὁ, Rathines, a Persian, 6. 3. 7.

'Ραθυμέω, ήσω (ῥᾴδιος, θυμός), to be easy, idle, 2. 6. 6; hence

'Ραθυμία, ας, ἡ, easiness of temper, laziness, indolence, 2. 6. 5.

'Ραστώνη, ης, ἡ (ῥᾷστος, ῥᾴδιος), rest, διὰ ῥ. for the sake of resting, 5. 8. 16.

'Ρέω, ῥεύσομαι and ῥευσοῦμαι, ἐρρύηκα, 2 aor. pass. ἐρρύην, to flow, 1. 2. 7.

'Ρήτρα, ας, ἡ (ῥέω, ῥήσω, to speak), an agreement, 6. 4. 28.

'Ρῖγος, εος, τό, cold, 5. 8. 2.

'Ρίπτω and ῥιπτέω, ῥίψω, ἔρρῖφα, ἔρριμμαι, 2 aor. pass. ἐρρίφην, to throw, λίθους εἰς τὸν ποταμόν, 4. 8. 3, 3. 3. 1; to throw off, κάνδυς, 1. 5. 8; fling down, παιδία, 4. 7. 13.

Ῥίς, ῥινός, ἡ, the nose, 7. 4. 3 ; pl. the nostrils, Lat. nares.

Ῥόδιος, a, ον, Rhodian, of or belonging to Rhodes, an island on the SE. coast of Asia Minor, 3. 5. 8.

Ῥοδογούνη, ης, ἡ, Rhodogune, daughter of Artaxerxes and wife of Orontas, 2. 4. 8.

Ῥοφέω, ήσω (ῥόφος), tι. sup greedily, gulp down, 4. 5. 32.

Ῥυθμός, οῦ, ὁ (ῥέω), rhythm, time, 5. 4. 14, 9. 10, 11 ; ῥυθμούς σαλπίζειν, to play tunes, 7. 3. 32.

Ῥῦμα, ατος, τό (ῥύω), drawing, ἐκ τόξου ῥύματος, within bowshot, 3. 3. 15.

Ῥώμη, ης, ἡ (ῥώννυμι), strength, force, 3. 3. 14; also Roma, Rome.

Ῥώννυμι, ῥώσω, ἔρρωμαι, to strengthen ; τὸ ἐρρωμένον, strength of courage, 2. 6. 11.

Ῥωπάρις, α, ὁ, Rhoparas ruler of Babylon, 7. 8. 25.

Σ.

Σάγαρις, εως and ιος, ἡ, a sagaris, said to be Persian for a sword, a bill, 4. 4. 16, 5. 4. 13.

Σακίον, ου, τό, and σακκίον (σάκκος), a small bag or sack, 4. 5. 36.

Σαλμυδεσσός, οῦ, ὁ, Salmydessus, later Ἀλμυδεσσός, a town in Thrace, on the Euxine, 7. 5. 12.

Σαλπιγκτής, οῦ, ὁ (σάλπιγξ), a trumpeter, 4. 3. 29, 32, 7. 4. 19.

Σάλπιγξ, ιγγος, ἡ, a trumpet, Lat. tuba, long and straight,

usually made of metal, used in battle, 5. 2. 14, 6. 3. 27 ; σημαίνειν, τῇ σ., 4. 2. 1, 7. 4. 16 ; ὠμοβ.ίνη, 7. 3. 32.

Σαλπίζω, ἰγξω, late ίσω, to sound a trumpet, 1. 2. 17 ; σαλπιγκτής is generally understood.

Σάμιος, a, ον, Samian, of or belonging to Samos, an island in the Ægean, 1. 7. 5.

Σαμόλας, α, ὁ, Samŏlas, an Achæan, 6. 3. 11.

Σάρδεις, εων, ai, Sardis, the capital of Lydia, 1. 2. 2, 3. 1. 8.

Σάρος, ου, ὁ, the Sarus, a river in Cilicia, 1. 4. 1.

Σατραπεύω, εύσω, to be a satrap, rule as satrap, τῆς χώρας, 3. 4. 31 ; ἅπαιτα, 1. 7. 6.

Σατράπης, ου, ὁ (Sansc. kshêtra, a country, pa, to rule, Cyrop. 8. 6. 3. Malcolm translates it umbrella-carrier, Hist. I. p 271), a satrap, the governor of a province of the Persian empire, 1 1. 2, 9. 7, &c.

Σάτυρος, ου, ὁ, a Satyr, Silenus, 1. 2. 13.

Σαυτοῦ for σεαυτοῦ, of yourself, your own, εἰς τὴν σαυτοῦ (χώραν), 7. 2. 37 ; σὺ σαυτῷ, 7. 8. 3 ; σαυτόν, 7. 7. 23.

Σαφής, ής, ές, clear, manifest, 3. 1. 10.

Σαφῶς, adv. from σαφής, clearly, manifestly, 1. 4. 18, 4. 5. 8 ; without doubt, 7. 6. 43.

Σεύθης, ου, ὁ, Seuthes, a Thracian prince, 7. 1. 5, 2. 24, &c.

Σηλυβρία and Σηλυμβρία, ας, ἡ, Selymbria, a town in Thrace, 7. 2. 28.

Σημαίνω, μᾶνῶ, σεσήμαγκα, σεσήμισμαι, 1 aor. pass. ἐσημάνθην· (σῆμα), σήμα), to signify, intimate, 2. 1. 2, 7. 3. 43 ; to give

the signal, 5. 2. 12; τῇ σάλπιγγι, 3. 4. 4, 4. 2. 1, 6. 3.
25, 7. 4. 16; τῷ κέρατι, 2. 2.
4, 7. 3. 32; τὸ πολεμικόν, the
signal of attack, 4. 3. 29, 7. 2.
18; φεύγειν, 5. 2. 30, 5. 9. 24,
10.15; ὡς ἀναπαύεσθαι,2.2.4.

Σημεῖον, ου, τό (σῆμα), a sign,
signal, 5. 10. 2, 2. 5. 32; τὸ
βασίλειον σ. the royal standard, a golden eagle, 1. 10. 12.

Σησάμη, ης, ἡ, sesame, an
eastern plant, the seeds of
which are boiled and eaten
like rice, σήσαμον, ου, τό, is
the seed, 1. 2. 22, 6. 2. 6.
Hence, "Open, Sesame" of
the nursery tale.

Σησάμινος, η, ον (σησάμη), made
of sesame, χρῖσμα, 4. 4. 13.

Σιγάζω, άσω (σιγή), to bid or
force one to be silent, 5. 9. 32.

Σιγάω, ήσομαι, σεσίγηκα, σεσίγ-
ημαι, to be silent, 5. 6. 27.

Σιγή, ῆς, ἡ (σίζω), silence, adv.
σιγῇ, in silence, 1. 8. 11, 4. 2.
7; (1) σῖγα, adv. silently;
(2) σιγα, impt. of σιγάω,
hush; (3) σιγᾷ, 3 s. pres. ind.
of σιγάω, or Dor. dat. of
σιγή.

Σίγλος, ου, ὁ, sometimes σίκλος,
Heb. shekel, a Persian coin=
7½ oboli, about 11d., nearly
our shilling, but the shekel
was 3s., 1. 5. 6.

Σιδηρεία, ας, ἡ (σίδηρος), a work-
ing in iron, 5. 5. 1.

Σιδήρεος, α, ον, contr. σιδηροῦς,
α, οῦν (σίδηρος), made of iron,
5. 4. 13.

Σικυώνιος, α, ον, Sicyonian, or a
dweller in Sicyonia, a small
district between Corinth and
Achaia, 3. 4. 47.

Σιλᾱνός, οῦ, ὁ, Silanus, (1) a seer

from Ambracia in Epire, 1. 7.
18, 5. 6. 17; (2) a Macistian,
7. 4. 16.

Σίνομαι, to injure, 3. 4. 16.

Σινωπεύς, εως, ὁ, an inhabitant
of Sinope, 5. 9. 15.

Σινώπη, ης, ἡ, Sinope, a town in
Paphlagonia, on the Black
Sea, 5. 5. 7.

Σιός, Spartan for θεός, τὼ σιώ,
the Dioscūri, Castor and Pol-
lux, 6. 4. 34.

Σιταγωγός, ός, όν (σῖτος, ἄγω),
food-conveying, πλοῖα, provi-
sion ships, 1. 7. 15.

Σιτάκη, ης, ἡ, also Σιττάκη, Sit-
tace, a town in Babylonia, 2.
4. 13.

Σιτάλκας, ου, ὁ, Sitalcas, king of
the Odrysi in Thrace, 5. 9. 6.

Σιτευτός, ή, όν (σῖτος), fed up,
fatted, 5. 4. 32.

Σιτηρέσιον, ου τό (σιτηρός, σῖτος),
provisions, provision-money, 5.
10. 4.

Σιτίον, ου, τό (σῖτος), food, provisions, 1. 10. 18.

Σῖτος, ου, ὁ, pl. σῖτα, corn, 5. 4.
27, 1. 4. 19, 2. 4. 27, 3. 4.
18; bread, food, provisions,
2. 1. 6, 3. 1. 3, 5. 4. 29, &c.

Σιωπάω, ήσω, better ἥσομαι, σε-
σιώπηκα, σεσιώπημαι (σιώπη),
to be silent, pass over in silence, 1. 3. 2, 5. 8. 25.

Σκεδάννυμι, σκεδάσω, ἐσκέδασμαι
(κεάζω, κέω, to split), to scatter,
3. 5. 2.

Σκέλος, εος, τό, the leg, 4. 2. 20,
5. 8. 10.

Σκέπασμα, ατος, τό (σκεπάζω),
a tent-covering, 1. 5. 10; the
other reading is στεγάσματα.

Σκεπτέος, α, ον, from σκοπέω, 1.
3. 11, 4. 6. 10.

Σκέπτομαι; see σκοπέω. . .

Σκευάζω, ἴσω, ἐσκεύασμαι(σκεῦος), to prepare, dress out, 5. 9. 12.

Σκευή, ῆς, ἡ, equipment, dress, 4. 7. 27.

Σκεῦος, εος, τό, a vessel, pl. baggage; Lat. vasa, impedimenta, 3. 2. 28, 5. 3. 1, 8. 6; ἐσθὴς καὶ σκεύη, 7. 4. 18; λαμβάνειν, 7. 1. 7; ἀναλαμβάνειν, 6. 3. 1; καταλείπειν, 6. 2. 21.

Σκευοφορέω, ήσω (σκεῦος, φέρω), to carry baggage, 3. 2. 28, 3. 19.

Σκευοφόρος, ος, ον, carrying baggage, 3. 2. 28; τὰ σκ. (κτήνη), the beasts of burden, the baggage animals, 1. 3. 7, 10. 3, 3. 2. 36, 4. 3. 25, 7. 2. 22.

Σκηνάω, ήσω and σκηνέω, ήσω (σκηνή), &c., to live in tents, to be quartered or billeted, or encamped, 7. 4. 12, 2. 4. 14, 4. 8. 25; κακῶς, 4. 4. 14; ἐν οἰκίαις, 4. 2. 22, 5. 33, 5. 5. 20, 1. 4. 9, 5. 3. 9, 7. 3. 15.

Σκηνή, ῆς, ἡ (σκιά), a tent, 1. 2. 17, 4. 4. 21, 3. 5. 7, Eng. scene.

Σκηνόω, ώσω, &c. (σκηνή), to pitch tents, encamp, 5. 7. 31, 7. 4. 11; to be encamped, ἐν οἰκίαις, 5. 5. 11, 4. 5. 23.

Σκήνωμα, ατος, τό (σκηνή), an encampment, pl. soldiers' quarters, 2. 2. 17, 7. 4. 16.

Σκηπτός, οῦ, ὁ (σκήπτω), a thunder-bolt, 3. 1. 11.

Σκηπτοῦχος, ου, ὁ (σκῆπτρον, ἔχω), the wand-bearer, an attendant on the king, always a eunuch, 1. 6. 11, 8. 28.

Σκιλλοῦς, οῦντος, ὁ, Scillus, a town in Elis Triphylia, 5. 3. 8.

Σκίμπους, ποδος, ὁ (σκίμπτω, ποῦς), a small couch, low bed, 5. 9. 4.

Σκληρός, ά, όν (σκέλλω), dry, hard, 4. 8. 26.

Σκόλοψ, οπος, ὁ, a stake, palisade, 5. 2. 5.

Σκοπέω, σκέψομαι, ἔσκεμμαι, to keep a look-out, 5. 1. 9; τὰ ἔμπροσθεν, in front, 6. 1. 14; to observe, watch carefully, 2. 5. 4; to attend or look to, 7. 4. 8, 1. 9. 22; to look out for, 5. 7. 32; to notice, observe, consider, 3. 1. 13, 7. 3. 42, 7. 6. 33; εἰ, 7. 3. 37; πόθεν, 5. 4. 7; ὅπως, 1. 3 11; πότερον—ἤ, 3. 2. 20, 5. 2. 8, 20.

Σκοπός, οῦ, ὁ (σκέπτομαι), a spy, 2. 2. 15, 6. 1. 11.

Σκόροδον, ου, τό, contr. σκόρδον, garlic, 7. 1. 37.

Σκοταῖος, α, ον (σκότος), in the dark, 4. 1. 5, 2. 2. 17.

Σκότος, εος, τό, darkness, 2. 5. 9, 7. 4. 18; γίγνεται, 2. 2. 7, 4. 2. 4; ἐστίν, 4. 5. 17.

Σκύθης, ου, ὁ, pl. Σκύθαι, Scythians, a nation living in the north of Europe and Asia, 3. 4. 15.

Σκυθινός, οῦ, ὁ, pl. Σκυθινοί, the Scythini, a people in Asia, called Σκυθηνοί by Steph. Byz., north of the river Harpasus, 4. 7. 18.

Σκυλεύω, εύσω (σκῦλον), to strip or spoil a slain enemy, Lat. spoliare, 5. 9. 6.

Σκύταλον, ου, τό (σκῦτος, a hide, Lat. cutis), a cudgel, club, 7. 4. 15.

Σκύτινος, η, ον (σκῦτος), leathern, made of leather, 5. 4. 13.

Σμῆνος, εος, τό, a beehive, swarm of bees, 4. 8. 20.

Σμίκρης, ητος, ὁ, *Smicres*, a general from Arcadia, 6. 1. 4.

Σόλοι, ων, οἱ, *Soli*, a town in Cilicia, 1. 2. 24, hence Eng. *solecism*.

Σάς, σή, σόν, poss. adj. *thy, thine*, 7. 7. 44.

Σοῦσα, ων, τά, *Susa*, one of the capitals of Persia, the spring residence of the king, 2. 4. 25.

Σοφαίνετος, ου, ὁ (σοφός, αἰνέω), (1) *Sophænetus*, an Arcadian, 1. 2. 9; (2) a Stymphalian, 1. 1. 11, 2. 3; perhaps the same person, Stymphalus being in Arcadia.

Σοφία, ας, ἡ (σοφός), *wisdom*, 1. 2. 8.

Σοφός, ή, όν, *wise*, 1. 10. 2.

Σπανίζω, ίσω, Att. ιῶ (σπάνις), *to be in want of*, τινός, 2 2. 12, 7. 7. 42.

Σπάνιος, α, ον, *scarce*, 1. 9. 27; from

Σπάνις, εως, ἡ, *scarcity, want*, πάντων, 7. 2. 15.

Σπάρτη, ης, ἡ, *Sparta* or *Lacedæmon*, the capital of Laconia; hence

Σπαρτιάτης, ου, ὁ, *a Spartan*, 4. 8. 25, 6. 4. 30.

Σπάρτον, ου, τό (σπείρω), *a rope, cord*, σ. πυκνὰ ἐστραμμένα, *thick cords twisted*, 4. 7. 15.

Σπάω, σπάσω, ἔσπάκα, ἔσπασμαι, *to draw*, τὸ ξίφος, 1. 8. 29, 7. 4. 16.

Σπείρω, σπερῶ, ἔσπαρκα, ἔσπαρμαι, *to scatter, sow*, 5. 9. 8.

Σπένδω, σπείσω, ἔσπεικα (late), ἔσπεισμαι, *to pour out a libation*, 4. 3. 13; Mid. *make a truce, a treaty*, τῳ for τινί, *with one*, 1. 9. 7; so also πρός τινα, 3. 5. 16; ἐφ' ᾧ, *on this condition that*, 4. 4. 6.

Σπεύδω, σπεύσω, ἔσπευσμαι, *to urge on, make haste, hasten*, 2. 3. 13; ταῦτα ἐγὼ ἔσπευδον, *on this account I made haste*, for διὰ ταῦτα, 4. 1. 21, 3. 4. 49, 4. 8. 14; τὴν ὁδόν, 1. 5. 9; πορεύεσθαι, 1. 3. 14, 4. 8. 2.

Σπιθριδάτης, ου, ὁ, *Spithridates*, a Persian, 6. 3. 7.

Σπολάς, άδος, ἡ, *a leather garment, buff-jerkin*, sometimes στολάς, 3. 3. 20.

Σπονδή, ῆς, ἡ (σπένδω), *a libation*, pl. *a truce, treaty*, 5. 9. 5, 4. 3. 14, 2. 3. 24; αἰτεῖν, 3. 1. 28; ποιεῖσθαι, 2. 3. 8; παραβαίνειν, 4. 1. 1; λύειν, 2. 5. 38, 3. 2. 10; παρὰ τὰς σ. 1. 9. 8, 2. 4. 5; 2. 3. 1, 3. 1. 1, 4. 1. 1; λοιβή (λείβω), *a libation* in a religious sense, χοή (χέω), *to the dead*.

Σπουδάζω, άσω, usu. άσομαι, ἐσπούδακα, ἐσπούδασμαι (σπουδή), *to make haste, to be busy, eager, earnest*, 2. 3. 12.

Σπουδαιολογέω, ήσω (σπουδή, λέγω), *to speak seriously, engage in earnest conversation*, 1. 9. 28.

Σπουδή, ῆς, ἡ (σπεύδω), *haste*, 4. 1. 17; σπουδῇ, *in haste*, 6. 3. 14; σὺν πολλῇ, 1. 8. 4; κατὰ σπουδὴν φεύγειν, 7. 6. 28.

Στάδιον, ου, τό (ἵστημι), pl. στάδιοι and στάδια, *a stade* = 100 ὀργυιαί = 600 Grk. ft. = 606 Eng. ft, *about* ⅛th of a *mile*; *a race*, ἀγωνίζεσθαι, *to run*, 4. 8. 27.

Σταθμός, οῦ, ὁ (ἵστημι), *a station*, or *stage*, on the royal road, where the king rested when travelling; hence a day's journey, usually five parasangs,

· or 17½ miles, 1. 8. 1, 10. 1, &c.

Στασιάζω, άσω (στάσις), to rebel, revolt, τινί against one, 2. 5. 28; to excite factions, πρὸς ἄρχοντα, 5. 9. 29, 7. 1. 39, 2. 2.

Στάσις, εως, ἡ (ἵστημι), sedition, revolt, 5. 9. 29.

Σταυρός, οῦ, ὁ (στάω, ἵστημι), an upright pale or stake, a palisade, 5. 2. 21, 7. 4. 14, 17.

Σταύρωμα, ατος, τό (σταυρός), a palisade, 5. 2. 15, 19.

Στέαρ, στέατος, τό (ἵστημι), fat, tallow, 5. 4. 28.

Στέγασμα, ατος, τό (στεγάζω, στέγη), a covering, 1. 5. 10.

Στέγη, ης, ἡ, a roof, εἰς στέγας, under cover, Lat. tectum, 4. 4. 14, 5. 5. 20.

Στεγνός, ή, όν (στέγη), covered, roofed, 7. 4. 12.

Στείβω, στείψω, ἐστίβηται, to tread, παρὰ τὰς ὁδοὺς στειβομένας, along the (beaten) travelled roads, 1. 9. 13.

Στέλλω, στελῶ, ἔσταλκα, μαι, 1 aor. ἔστειλα, 2 aor. pass. ἐστάλην, to send, send for, equip, 3. 2. 7, to march, κατὰ γῆν, 5. 6. 5, 10. 13.

Στενός, ή, όν, old form στεινός, hence, comp. στεινότερος, supl. στεινότατος, narrow, χωρίον, 4. 1. 16, 2. 24, ὁδός, 3. 4. 19, 1. 4. 4, κατάβασις, 5. 2. 28; τὸ στενόν, a narrow part of the road, 4. 1. 14, 4. 4. 18, 5. 1.

Στενοχωρία, ας, ἡ (στενός, χώρα), a narrow road, 1. 5. 7.

Στέργω, στέρξω, ἔστοργα, ἔστεργμαι, to love, natural affection, as a father loves a son; ἀγαπάω is love founded on esteem (ἄγαμαι), ἐράω, sexual love, φιλέω, love in general, special-

ly of friends, 2. 6. 23. See ἀγαπάω.

Στερέω and στερίσκω, στερήσω, ἐστέρηκα, ημαι, Mid. στεροῦμαι, στερίσκομαι and στέρομαι, to deprive, τινά τινος, 2. 5. 10, ποδῶν, 1. 9. 13, 1. 4. 8, 4. 5. 28, 2. 1. 12, στέροιτο and στεροῖτο, 7. 6. 16.

Στέρνον, ου, τό, the breast, 1. 8. 26, used by Homer for the breast of males only, while στῆθος is used of both sexes.

Στερρῶς, adv. stiffly, obstinately, 3. 1. 22.

Στέφᾰνος, ου, ὁ (στέφω), a wreath, garland, crown, χιλοῦ, 4. 5. 33, χρυσοῦς, 1. 7. 7, for tombs, 6. 2. 9; hence Eng. Stephen, Stephanie. διάδημα (διὰ, δέω) is a band, diadem.

Στεφανόω, ώσω, ἐστεφάνωκα, ωμαι, to wreathe, or crown, for sacrifice, 7. 1. 40, for battle, 4. 3. 17.

Στήλη, ης, ἡ (ἵστημι), a pillar, 5. 3. 13, a boundary post, 7. 5. 13.

Στιβάς, άδος, ἡ (στείβω), a bed of straw, rushes, or leaves, 5. 9. 4, al. σκίμποσιν.

Στίβος, ου, ὁ (στείβω), a trodden way, a track, 1. 6. 1, 6. 1. 24, 7. 3. 43.

Στίζω, στίξω, ἔστιγμαι, to prick, tattoo, 5. 4. 32.

Στῖφος, εος, τό (στείβω), a body of men in close array, a close column, 1. 8. 13, 26, 6. 3. 26.

Στλεγγίς, ίδος, ἡ, a flesh scraper, used in the bath, 1. 2. 10.

Στολάς, άδος, ἡ (στέλλω), al. σπολάς, 3. 3. 20, a coat, jerkin.

Στολή, ῆς, ἡ (στέλλω), a robe, 4. 7. 13, 5. 9. 2, βαρβαρική, 4. 5. 33, Περσική, 1. 2. 27.

K

Στόλος, ου, ὁ (στέλλω), march=
πορεία, εἰς Πισίδας, ἐπὶ βασιλέα, 3. 1. 9, 10, ποιεῖσθαι,
1. 3. 16, 3. 3. 2, army, array,
1. 2. 5, πολὺν ἔχειν, 2. 2. 12,
παμπληθής, 3. 2. 11.

Στόμα, ατος, τό, mouth, opening,
to a dwelling, 4. 5. 25, of a
river, 5. 10. 1, sea, 6. 2. 1, 7.
1. 1, the front, 5. 2. 26, opp. to
οὐρά, 3. 4. 42.

Στρατεία, ας, ἡ (στρατός), an
expedition, 3. 1. 9, 5. 4. 18.

Στράτευμα, ατος, τό, an army, 1.
2. 18, &c.

Στρατεύω, εύσω, &c. (στρατός),
to march, εἰς Πισίδας, 1. 1. 11,
ἐπ' Αἴγυπτον, 2. 1. 14, 2. 3.
20, &c. Mid. to serve as soldiers,
1. 2. 3, 5. 4. 34, to make war,
ἐπὶ, on, 2. 1. 1.

Στρατηγέω, ήσω (στρατός, ἄγω),
to command, lead an army, 1.
3. 15, 2. 6. 28, 2. 13.

Στρατηγία, ας, ἡ, the office of a
general, στρατηγός, 1. 3. 15,
5. 6. 25, 7. 1. 41, generalship,
2. 2. 13.

Στρατηγιάω, desid. of στρατηγέω,
to wish to be a general, 7. 1. 33.

Στρατηγός, οῦ, ὁ (στρατός, ἄγω),
a general, 1. 1. 2. &c.

Στρατιά, ᾶς, ἡ (στρατός), an
army, 1. 2. 27, &c.

Στρατιώτης, ου, ὁ (στρατιά), a
soldier, 1. 3. 21, &c.

Στρατοκλῆς, έος, ὁ (στρατός,
κλέος), Stratocles, a Cretan, 4.
2. 28.

Στρατοπεδεύω, εύσω, &c. (στρατόπεδον), to encamp, 7. 6. 24,
4. 4. 8, &c.

Στρατόπεδον, ου, τό (στρατός,
πέδον), a camp, 1. 10. 1, &c.

Στρατός, οῦ, ὁ (στορέννυμι,
στράω, to spread), an army.

Στρεπτός, ή, όν (στρέφω), sc.
κύκλος, a chain, 1. 8. 29; περὶ
τοῖς τραχήλοις, 1. 5. 8, χρυσοῦς,
1. 2. 27.

Στρέφω, στρέψω, ἔστροφα, ἔστραμ-
μαι, 2 aor. pass. ἐστράφην, to
turn, πρός, 4. 3. 26 ; vid.
σπάρτα, 4. 7. 15.

Στρουθός, οῦ, ὁ and ἡ (στρίζω, τρύ-
ζω, στρύζω), a sparrow, but
ὁ μέγας στρ., the ostrich, also
κατάγαιοι, χερσαῖοι, birds that
do not fly off the ground, 1.
5. 2.

Στρωματόδεσμος, ου, ὁ, and ον,
ου, τό (στρῶμα, δέω), a bed-
sack, a bag for bed clothes, 5.
4. 13.

Στυγνός, ή, όν (στύξ, στυγέω, to
hate), hateful, gloomy, 2. 6. 9.

Στυμφάλιος, α, ον, Stymphalian, adj. from

Στύμφαλος, ου, ἡ, Stymphalus, a
town in Arcadia, 1. 1. 11.

Σύ, pers. pron. thou, 2. 1. 12,
17.

Συγγένεια, ας, ἡ (συγγενής),
relationship, affinity, 7. 3. 39.

Συγγενής, ής, ές (σύν, γίγνομαι),
related, οἱ σ., kinsmen, 7. 2.
31.

Συγγίγνομαι, γενήσομαι, &c., to
be with, have intercourse with,
τινί 1. 1. 9, 2. 27, 2. 5. 2, 7.
2. 19, 4. 5. 23, 2. 6. 17, 1. 2.
12, 5. 4. 33.

Συγκάθημαι, to sit together, 5. 7.
21.

Συγκαλέω, έσω, &c., to call together, 1. 4. 8, 7. 2, &c.

Συγκάμπτω, ψω, to bend together,
bend up, 5. 8. 10.

Συγκατακαίω, καύσω, to burn
down along with, τινί τι, 3. 2.
27.

Συγκατασκεδάννυμι, σκεδάσω, &c.,

Mid. *to pour over oneself at the same time,* 7. 3. 32.

Συγκαταστρέφω, στρέψω, &c., *to reduce along with, aid in reducing,* 2. 1. 14.

Συγκατεργάζομαι, άσομαι, &c., *to help in obtaining, τινί τι,* 7. 7. 25.

Σύγκειμαι, κείσομαι, *to be agreed upon, εἰς τὸ συγκείμενον, to the spot agreed on,* 6. 1. 4, *κατὰ τὰ συγκείμενα, according to the terms of the agreement,* 7. 2. 7.

Συγκλείω, κλείσω, &c., *to shut, τὰς πύλας,* 7. 1. 15.

Συγκομίζω, ίσω, &c., *to bring together,* 6. 4. 37.

Συγκύπτω, ψω, *to bend together towards each other,* 3. 4. 19, 21.

Συγχωρέω, ήσω, &c., *to yield,* 5. 2. 9.

Σύειος, α, ον (σῦς), *pig's, swine's, χρῖσμα σ., hog's lard,* 4. 4. 13.

Συέννεσις, εως and ιος, ὁ, *Syennesis,* king of Cilicia, 1. 2. 12, 21.

Σῦκον, ον, τό, *a fig,* 6. 2. 6.

Συλλαμβάνω, λήψομαι, &c., *to seize, lay hold of,* 1. 1. 3, 4. 8, 6. 4, 4. 4. 16.

Συλλέγω, λέξω, συνείλοχα, είλεγμαι, *to gather, collect together,* 5. 1. 15, φρύγανα, 4. 3. 11, χόρτον, 2. 4. 11, στράτευμα, 1. 1. 7, 9, 5. 6. 37; ἀγοράν, *to convene an assembly,* 5. 7. 3, Pass. 4. 1. 10, 11, 6. 1. 6, 4. 8. 9, 7. 4, 8.

Συλλογή, ῆς, ἡ (συλλέγω), *a gathering, σ. ποιεῖσθαι, to make a levy,* 1. 1. 6.

Σύλλογος, ον, ὁ (συλλέγω), *a gathering, assembly, meeting,* 5. 6. 22, 7. 2.

Συμβαίνω, βήσομαι, &c., *to happen, take place,* 3. 1. 13.

Συμβάλλω, βαλῶ, &c., *to throw, bring* or *heap together,* 3. 4. 31, 1. 1. 9,ξενίαν,*to contract friendly relations,* 6. 4. 35; *to agree upon,* 6. 1. 3; *to talk,* 4. 6. 14.

Συμβοάω, ήσομαι, βεβόημαι, *to cry aloud, shout to, ἀλλήλους,* 6. 1. 6.

Συμβοηθέω, ήσω, &c., *to join in giving aid,* 4. 2. 1, 7. 8. 17.

Συμβολή, ῆς, ἡ (συμβάλλω), *a meeting, encounter,* 6. 3. 32.

Συμβουλεύω, εύσω, &c., *to advise, counsel, give advice,* 5. 7. 35, 1. 8, 6. 3, 10. 14, εὖ, 5. 6. 4, 12, ἐκποδὼν ποιεῖσθαι, 1. 6. 9, μὴ παραδιδόναι, 2. 1. 18, 19, 7. 8. 4, 3. 1. 5, Mid. *to ask advice, consult,* 1. 7. 2, 2. 1. 16, αὐτῷ, 1. 1. 10.

Συμβουλή, ῆς, ἡ (σύν, βουλή), *advice,* 5. 6. 11, *there is a Greek proverb ἱερὸν ἡ συμβουλή, advice is sacred,* 5. 6. 4.

Σύμβουλος, ου, ὁ (σύν, βουλή), *a counsellor, adviser,* 1. 6. 5.

Συμμανθάνω, μαθήσομαι, &c., *to learn along with, ὁ συμμαθών, one that is accustomed to a thing,* 4. 5. 27.

Συμμαχέω, ήσω, *to be an ally, to help,* 5. 4. 30.

Συμμάχομαι, ήσομαι, &c., *to fight along with, help, τινί,* 5. 4. 10.

Συμμαχία, ας, ἡ, *alliance,* 5. 4. 3, 8; *from*

Σύμμαχος, ου, ὁ (σύν, μάχομαι), *an ally,* 7. 6. 3, 5. 4. 9, 4. 6, 7. 7. 25; σύμμαχος, ος, ον, adj. *auxiliary;* ἱππεῖς, 2. 4. 6, 7, 3. 1. 2; δύναμις, 2. 5. 11, 5. 4. 7.

Συμμετέχω, συμμεθέξω, &c. (σύν,

μετά, ἔχω), to take part in, τινός, 7. 8. 17.

Συμμίγνυμι, or νύω, μίξω, &c., to mix together, unite with, join, τινί, 2. 1. 2, 4. 2. 9, 7. 8. 24; to meet in battle, 4. 6. 24.

Συμπαρασκευάζω, άσω, &c., to get ready with, to help in providing, 5. 1. 8, 10.

Συμπαρέχω, έξω, &c. (σύν, παρά, ἔχω), to afford, ἀσφάλειαν, 7. 6. 30, φόβον τινί, to help to strike one with terror, 7. 4. 19.

Σύμπας, ασα, αν (σύν, πᾶς), all, the whole, σύμπασα ἡ ὁδός, 7. 8. 26; οἱ σ. 1. 2. 9, τὸ σ., upon the whole, 1. 5. 9.

Συμπεδάω, ήσω, to bind together, benumb, of cold, 4. 4. 11.

Συμπέμπω, πέμψω, &c., to send along with, 3. 4. 42, 6. 4. 18, τινὶ ἡγεμόνας, 5. 5. 15, τινί τινας ἐροῦντας, 5. 6. 21.

Συμπεριτυγχάνω, τεύξομαι, &c., to fall in with at the same time, τινί, 7. 8. 22.

Συμπίπτω, πεσοῦμαι, &c., to fall in, οἰκία, 5. 2. 24; fall upon, 4. 8. 11; fall off, 1. 9. 6.

Σύμπλεως, ως, ων, full, δένδρων, 1. 2. 22.

Συμπολεμέω, ήσω, &c., to make war, join in war, τινὶ πρός τινα, 1. 4. 2, τινὶ ἐπί τινα, 3. 1. 5.

Συμπορεύομαι, εύσομαι, to march or journey together, 1. 3. 5, 4. 9, 4. 1. 28.

Συμποσίαρχος, ου, ὁ (σύν, πίνω, ἄρχω), the president at a drinking party, toast-master, 5. 9. 30, like the ἀρχιτρίκλιιος of John 2. 8, ' the governor of the feast,' the arbiter bibendi of Hor., our chairman at a public dinner.

Συμπράττω, άξω, &c., to act along with, co-operate with, 7. 7. 19, ὥστε λαβεῖν, 7. 8. 23; αὐτῷ ταῦτα, 1. 1. 8; αὐτῷ ταῦτα ὧν ἐπιθυμεῖ, 5. 5. 23; σφίσι τὰς σπονδάς, to aid them in getting a truce, 7. 4. 13, περὶ τῆς διόδου, 5. 4. 9.

Συμπρέσβεις, εων, οἱ, fellow-ambassadors, 5. 5. 24.

Συμπροθυμέομαι, ήσομαι, &c., to share in the desire that, to unite zealously with, 7. 1. 5, 2. 24, μεῖναι αὐτόν, 3. 1. 9.

Συμφέρω, συνοίσω, συνενήνοχα, συνενήνεγμαι, to bring together, gather, 6. 2. 9, 3. 4. 31, 6. 3. 6; to endure with one, τινί τι, 7. 6. 20, to be useful, profitable, advantageous, 7. 3. 7; τῇ στρατιᾷ, 3. 2. 27; πρὸς τὴν χώραν συμφέρῃ, is suitable for the ground, 7. 3. 37 ; ἐπὶ τὸ βέλτιον, to contribute for the better, it would be for his advantage, 7. 8. 4. συμφέρον ἐστί, it is advantageous, ἀποδοῦναι, 7. 7. 21. τὸ ἐμὲ προκριθῆναι, 5. 9. 26.

Σύμφημι, φήσω, to agree, confess, ταῦτα, 5. 8. 8, 7. 2. 26.

Σύν, Prep. with, gov. Dat. (σῦν is acc. of σῦς, a pig), 1. 3. 5, 6, 2. 5. 9, &c., σὺν τοῖς θεοῖς, by the help of the gods, 3. 1. 23, 42, 2. 8, 11, 14 ; Τισσαφέρνης καὶ οἱ σὺν αὐτῷ, 3. 5. 3, 2. 2. 8, 4. 1, 5. 40; βασιλεὺς καὶ οἱ σὺν αὐτῷ, 1. 10. 1, 2; οἱ σὺν βασιλεῖ, 1. 10. 18, 3. 1. 19; Πέρσαι καὶ οἱ σὺν αὐτοῖς, 3. 2. 11; σὺν τῷ δικαίῳ, by just means, opp. to μετὰ ἀδικίας, with injustice, 2. 6. 18.

Συνάγω, άξω, &c., to bring together, χρήματα, 5. 10. 8, 3.

·5. 14, 4. 4. 10, 19, 1. 3. 9, 5.
· 10, 6. 2. 10, 4. 11, 29.

Συναγείρω, γερῶ, &c., to gather
· together, 1. 5. 9.

Συναδικέω, ήσω, &c., to do wrong
with one, τινί, 2. 6. 27.

Συναθροίζω, ίσω, &c., to collect
· together, 7. 2. 8, 6. 3. 30.

Συναινέω, έσω, &c., to agree with,
αὐτοῖς ταῦτα, them in this, 7.
7. 31.

Συναιρέω, ήσω, &c., to take together, ὡς συνελόντι εἰπεῖν, to
speak concisely, briefly, 3. 1.
38.

Συνακολουθέω, ήσω, &c., to follow along with, 2. 5. 30, 35,
3. 1. 4, 10, 7. 7. 11.

Συνακούω, ακούσομαι, &c., to
hear, ἀλλήλων, 5. 4. 31.

Συναλίζω, ίσω, &c., to gather
· together, 7. 3. 48.

Συναλλάττω, άξω, &c., to inter-
change, reconcile, πρός τινα,
1. 2. 1.

Συναναβαίνω, βήσομαι, &c., to
go up along with, τινί, 1. 3.
· 18, 5. 4. 16.

Συναναπράττω, άξω, &c., to help
· or join in exacting payment,
μισθὸν παρά τινος, 7. 7. 14.

Συνανίστημι, αναστήσω, &c., to
make to stand up together,
Intr. to stand up or rise together or at once, 7. 3. 35.

Συναντάω, ήσω, to fall in with,
· to meet, 1. 8. 15, τινί, 7. 2. 5.

Συνάπειμι, to go away together,
· 2. 2. 1.

Συναπολαμβάνω, λήψομαι, &c.,
to receive in common, μισθόν,
· 7. 7. 40.

Συνάπτω, άψω, &c., to join together, μάχην ἀλλήλοις, if ye
· engage in any fighting with one
another, 1. 5. 16.

Συνάρχω, άρξω, &c., to rule
jointly with, τινὶ στρατεύματος,
5. 9. 32.

Σύνδειπνος, ου, ὁ (σύν, δεῖπνον),
a companion at dinner, 2.5.27.

Συνδιαβαίνω, βήσομαι, &c., to
cross over together, 7. 1. 4.

Συνδιαπράττω, πράξω, &c., to
negotiate with one, ὑπέρ τινος,
4. 8. 24.

Συνδοκέω, δόξω, &c., to seem good,
πᾶσι, 6. 3. 9.

Σύνειμι, to be with, 2. 6. 20;
φιλικῶς τινι, to be on friendly
terms with one, 6. 4. 35.

Σύνειμι, to go together, to come
to close quarters, ὡς μαχού-
μενος, 1. 10. 10.

Συνεισέρχομαι, ελεύσομαι, &c.,
to go with one, εἰς τὸ ἔρυμα,
4. 5. 10.

Συνεισπίπτω, πεσοῦμαι, &c., to
fall along with one, εἰς τὴν
θάλατταν, 5. 7. 25 ; to rush
together, εἴσω τῶν πυλῶν, 7.
1. 18.

Συνεκβαίνω, βήσομαι, &c., to go
out together, ἐπὶ τὸ ὄρος, 4. 3.
22.

Συνεκβιβάζω, άσω, &c., to help
in bringing out, τὰς ἁμάξας ἐκ
τοῦ πηλοῦ, 1. 5. 7.

Συνεκκόπτω, κόψω, &c., to help
to cut out, or away, δένδρα, 4.
8. 8.

Συνεκπίνω, πίομαι, &c., to drink
up with one, 7. 3. 32.

Συνεκπορίζω, ίσω, &c., to help
in procuring, 5. 8. 25.

Συνεξέρχομαι, ελεύσομαι, &c., to
go out with, τινί, 7. 8. 11.

Συνεπαινέω, έσω, &c., to consent,
agree to, τι, 7. 3. 36.

Συνέπομαι, έψομαι, to follow
along with, τινί, 3. 1. 2, 5. 2.
4, 1. 3. 9, 4. 17, &c.

Συνεπεύχομαι, εὔξομαι, &c., to vow at the same time, τοῖς θεοῖς θύσειν, 3. 2. 9.

Συνεπιμελέομαι, ήσομαι, &c., to join in taking care of, to have joint charge of, τῆς στρατιᾶς, 5. 9. 22.

Συνεπισπεύδω, εύσω, &c., to join or assist in forcing onwards τὰς ἀμάξας, 1. 5. 8.

Συνεπιτρίβω, τρίψω, &c., to destroy at once or utterly, 5. 8. 20.

Συνεπόμνυμι, ομοῦμαι, &c., to swear in addition, 7. 6. 19.

Συνεργός, ός, όν (σύν, ἔργον), helping a person in a thing, - a fellow-worker, τινί τινος, 1. 9. 20.

Συνέρχομαι, ελεύσομαι, &c., to come together, meet, ἄνδρες καὶ κτήνη, 4. 7. 2, 5. 9. 30, 2. 3. 21, 2. 1. 2, 5. 3, &c.

Συνεφέπομαι, έψομαι, to follow along with, 7. 4. 6; αὐτοῖς, 4. 8. 18.

Συνέχω, έξω, &c., to keep together, στράτευμα, 7. 2. 8.

Συνήδομαι, ησθήσομαι, to rejoice with, 7. 7. 42; τινὶ ὅτι, to congratulate one that, 5. 5. 8, 7. 8. 1.

Συνθεάομαι, άσομαι, &c., to view together, τὰ ἱερά, 6. 2. 15.

Σύνθημα, ατος, τό (σύν, τίθημι), an agreement, 4. 6. 20; watch-word, παραγγέλλειν, πιραδι-δόναι, to give the word, 1. 8. 16, 7. 3. 34, 39; παρέρχεται, the word is passing round, 1. 8. 16; Lat. tessera militaris.

Συνθηράω, άσω, &c., to hunt with, 5. 3. 10.

Συνιδεῖν, see συνοράω, 1. 5. 9, to perceive plainly.

Συνίστημι, συστήσω, συνέστηκα, ἕσταμαι, to place with or set

together, introduce, recommend, τινά τινι, 3. 1. 8, 5. 9 23; Intrans. to stand together, 5. 7. 16; ἐπὶ λόφου, on a hill, 6. 3. 28; holding together, 7. 6. 26.

Σύνοδος, ου, ἡ, a coming together, assembling, 6. 2. 9; engagement, 1. 10. 7, hence synod.

Σύνοιδα, inf. συνειδέναι, to know with, to be conscious, with part. ἐψευσμένος, 1. 3. 10, 7. 6. 18.

Συνολολύζω, λύξομαι, to raise a loud cry, scream, shriek together, esp. of women, 4. 3, 19.

Συνομολογέω, ήσω, &c., to agree to, ταῦτα, 4. 2. 19, 7. 8. 3; with one, τινί, 7. 5. 10; αὐτῷ ταῦτα, with him in this, 5. 7. 15.

Συνοράω, ὄψομαι, &c., to see at the same time, see plainly, 4. 1. 11, 5. 2. 13; ἡ ἀρχὴ οὖσα, that the government was, like δῆλος, 1. 5. 9.

Συνουσία, ας, ἡ (σύνειμι), a being with, meeting, 2. 5. 6.

Συντάττω, τάξω, &c., to put together in order, draw up in battle array, 1. 2. 15, 7. 14, 8. 14, 3. 14, 10. 5, &c., 6. 1. 21.

Συντίθημι, θήσω, τέθεικα, τέθειμαι, to put, place together; Mid. to make an agreement, τινί, 1. 9. 7, 2. 5. 8; arrange, settle, τι, 4. 2. 2, 6. 21, 5. 1. 12; φυλάττειν, 4. 2. 1, 7. 1. 35.

Σύντομος, ος, ον (σύν, τέμνω), short, ὁδός, a short way, 2. 6. 22.

Συντράπεζος, ος, ον (σύν, τρά-πεζα), a companion at table, messmate, 1. 9. 31; so ὁμοτρά-πεζος.

Συντρέχω, θρέξομαι, &c., to run together, 5. 7. 4, 7. 6. 6.

Συντρίβω, τρίψω, &c., to crush completely, 4. 7. 4.

Συντυγχάνω, τεύξομαι, &c., to meet with, τινί, 1. 10. 8. .

Συνωφελέω, ήσω, &c., to join in helping, οὐδέν, contribute no advantage, 3. 2. 27.

Συρακόσιος, α, ον, sometimes Συρακούσιος, α, ον, Syracusan, of or belonging to Syracuse, Συράκουσαι, a town in Sicily, 1. 10. 14.

Συρία, ας, ἡ, Syria, a country at the eastern extremity of the Mediterranean, 1. 4. 4 ; adj. Σύριος, α, ον, Syrian, 1. 4. 5 ; Σύρος, ου, ὁ, a Syrian.

Συρρέω, ρεύσομαι, &c., to flow or flock together, 4. 2. 19, 6. 1. 6, 5. 2. 3.

Σῦς, συός, ὁ and ἡ, like ὗς, acc. σῦν (σεύω), a boar, pig, 5. 3. 10, 7. 24.

Συσκευάζω, άσω, &c. (σύν, σκεῦος), to pack up the baggage, 1. 3. 14, 2. 2. 4, 4. 5. 1 ; ἃ εἶχον, 2. 1. 2; p. p. part. συνεσκευασμένοι, 3. 5. 18, 7. 1. 11.

Σύσκηνος, ος, ον (σύν, σκηνή), dwelling in one tent, a mate, 'chum,' 5. 7. 15, 8. 5, 6. .

Συσπάω, άσω, &c., to draw, sew together, διφθέρας, 1. 5. 10.

Συσπειράω, άσω, &c., to bring into close order, 1. 8. 21.

Συσπουδάζω, άσω, &c., to make haste along with, to share in one's zeal, 2. 3. 11.

Συστρατεύομαι, εύσομαι, &c., to serve along with, to share in an expedition, 5. 10. 15, 7. 5. 9, 12; τινί, 7. 3. 14, 6. 14; σύν τινι, 5. 6. 24; ἐπὶ τὸ ὄρος, 7. 4. 20; ἐπὶ βασιλέα, 1. 4. 3.

Συστράτηγος, ου, ὁ, a fellow-general, 2. 6. 29.

Συστρατιώτης, ου, ὁ, a fellow-soldier, comrade, 1. 2. 26.

Συστρατοπεδεύομαι, εύσομαι, &c., to encamp along with, σύν τινι, 2. 4. 9.

Συστρέφω, ψω, &c., 2. aor. pass. συνεστράφην, to turn, face about, 1. 10. 6.

Συχνός, ἡ, όν (σύν, ἔχω), long, considerable, χρόνος, 1. 8. 8, 5. 8. 14; συχνοί, many, 5. 4. 16, 18, 7. 16, συχνόν, a considerable distance, 1. 8. 10.

Σφαγιάζομαι, άσομαι (σφάγιον, σφάζω), to slay a victim, sacrifice, 6. 2. 25, 4. 3. 18, 5. 4, 6. 3. 8.

Σφάγιον, ου, τό (σφάζω), a victim, καλά, 1.8.15, 4.3.19, 6.3.21.

Σφάζω, see σφάττω.

Σφαιροειδής, ής, ές (σφαῖρα, εἶδος), ball-like, 5. 4. 12, the lower end rounded of the wood itself.

Σφάλλω, σφαλῶ, ἔσφαλκα, μαι, 2 aor. pass. ἐσφάλην, to trip up, deceive; Mid. stumble, 7. 7. 42, τι, in anything.

Σφάττω, and σφάζω, σφάξω, ἔσφαγμαι, to slay, 4. 5. 16; sacrifice, 2. 2. 9, εἰς ἀσπίδα, letting the blood into a shield.

Σφενδονάω, ήσω, to sling, hurl from a sling, 3. 3. 7, 15, 17, 18, 4. 3. 30; from

Σφενδόνη, ης, ἡ, a sling, Lat. funda, Περσικαί, 3. 3. 16; ἐφέροντο, 5. 2. 14; ἐξικνοῦντο, 3. 4. 4, 4. 3. 29, ἐπιέζοντο ὑπὸ σ., 7. 8. 18.

Σφενδονήτης, ου, ὁ (σφενδόνη), a slinger, 3. 3. 6.

Σφόδρα, adv. very (σφόδρος, σπουδή, σπεύδω), 2. 3. 16, 4.

18; λευκοί, 5. 4. 32, 2. 6. 11, 13.

Σφοδρός, ά, όν, and ός, όν (σπουδή, σπεύδω), great, ἔνδεια, 1. 10. 18.

Σχεδία, ας, ἡ (σχέδιος, sudden, ἔχω), a raft, 1. 5. 10, 2. 4. 28.

Σχεδόν (ἔχω), adv. almost, nearly, τρία, 4. 7. 6, 7. 6. 1, 4. 8. 15 ; mostly, 1. 8. 25, σ. τι πᾶσα, nearly in some sort the whole, 6. 2. 20.

Σχέτλιος, α, ον (ἔχω), cruel, 7. 6. 30.

Σχῆμα, ατος, τό (ἔχω), form, 1. 10. 10.

Σχίζω, ίσω, ἔσχισμαι, to split, cleave, ξύλα, 1. 5. 12, 4. 4. 12 ; τὸ στράτευμα ἐσχίσθη, divided, 6. 1. 1; Eng. schism.

Σχολάζω, άσω (σχολή), to have leisure, 7. 3. 24, 2. 3. 2.

Σχολαῖος, α, ον (σχολή), at one's leisure, slow, πορεία, 4. 1. 13 ; σχολαίτερος, αίτατος and αἰότερος, αιάτατος, 1. 5. 9; adv. σχολαίως, 1. 5. 8.

Σχολή, ῆς, ἡ (ἔχω), leisure, time, ἥν ἰδεῖν 4. 1. 17 ; ἐστὶν εὖ ποιεῖν, 1. 6. 9, 5. 1. 9; σχολῇ, slowly, 3. 4. 27, 4. 1. 16, opp. to ταχύ ; Eng. school.

Σώζω, σώσω, σέσωκα, σέσωμαι, and σέσωσμαι, to save, preserve, 1. 10. 3, 3. 2. 10, 11, 5. 5. 8, 2. 3. 25, 3. 2. 4 ; ἀρχήν, 2. 5. 11; τὰ ἑαυτῶν, 3. 2. 39; σέσωσται, 7. 7. 56 ; Pass. 2. 1. 19, 6. 1. 5, 16, to return safely, go in safety, 3. 1. 6, 3. 4, 5. 3. 6 ; εἰς τὴν Ἑλλάδα, 6. 2. 8; ἐπὶ θάλατταν, 6. 3. 20 ; ἔνθα βουλόμεθα, 5. 6. 31 ; ὅπῃ θέλει ἕκαστος, 6. 4. 18.

Σωκράτης, εος, c. ους, ὁ (σῶς,

κράτος), (1) Socrates, the philosopher, 3. 1. 5. (2) An Achæan general, 1. 1. 11, 2. 5. 31, 6. 30.

Σῶμα, ατος, τό (σώζω), the body; 3. 2. 20; (life), 2. 1. 12, 4. 6. 10, 5. 5. 13 ; (person), 1. 9. 12, 27.

Σῶος, α, ον, contr. σῶς, σῶα, σῶν, safe, 2. 2. 21, 3. 1. 32, 5. 1. 16, 2. 32, 8. 7.

Σῶσις, εως, ὁ, and Σωσίας, ου, ὁ (σῶς), Sosias, a Syracusan, 1. 2. 9.

Σωτήρ, ῆρος, ὁ (σώζω), a saviour, Ζεύς, 3. 2. 9, 4. 8. 25.

Σωτηρία, ας, ἡ (σωτήρ), safety, 2. 1. 19, 5. 2. 24, 6. 3. 18 ; ἀσφαλής, sure, 5. 2. 20; σωτηρίας δεῖσθαι, 6. 3. 14 ; τυγχάνειν, 3. 1. 26; τὴν σ. κατεργάζεσθαι, 5. 10. 10.

Σωτηρίδας, α, ὁ (σωτήρ), Soteridas, a native of Sicyon, 3. 4. 47.

Σωτήριος, ος, ον (σωτήρ), saving, indicative of safety, 2. 6. 11 ; salutary, 3. 3. 2; τὰ σ., thank-offerings for deliverance, 3. 2. 9, 5. 1. 1.

Σωφρονέω, ήσω (σώφρων=σῶς, φρήν), to be of sound mind, to be wise, 5. 8. 24, 10. 11, 7. 3. 17, 6. 41; τὰ πρός σε, to act more prudently in what concerns you, for your interest, 7. 7. 30.

Σωφρονίζω, ίσω (σώφρων), to bring to reason, 7. 7. 24, 5. 9. 28.

Σωφροσύνη, ης, ἡ (σώφρων), moderation, self-control, 1. 9. 3.

T.

Τάλαντον, ου, τό (τλάω, Lat. tuli), a balance, a talent,

usually of silver=60 minæ,
or 243*l*. 15*s*., 1. 7. 18, 5. 6.
18, 2. 2. 20.

Ταμιεύομαι, εύσομαι (ταμίας, a steward, τέμνω), to manage, 2. 5. 18; to determine with how many we may wish to fight, or parcel out into such parts as we may wish to fight with.

Ταμώς, ώ, ὁ, Tamos, an Egyptian from Memphis, the admiral of Cyrus' fleet, 1. 2. 21, 4. 2.

Τἀναντία=τὰ ἐναντία, 5. 6. 4.

Ταξίαρχος, ου, ὁ (τάξις, ἄρχω), a taxiarch, commander of a taxis, a brigadier, 3. 1. 37.

Τάξις, εως, ἡ (τάσσω), order, battle-array, 1. 2. 18, 7. 20, 2. 3. 10; ἐν τάξει ἰέναι, 5. 1. 2, 8. 13; ἕπεσθαι, 1. 8. 19, 5. 4. 24; τὰ περὶ τὰς τάξεις, military tactics, 2. 1. 7; ἐν ταῖς τ. εἶναι, εἰς τὰς τ. θεῖν, the ranks, 2. 2. 14, 1. 8. 10, 5. 8. 13; a company, 1. 2. 16, 8. 8, 3. 4. 14 (consisting of 200 men, 6. 3. 11), 2. 3. 2, 3. 1. 32, 4. 4. 8, 7. 3. 15; applied to hoplites, 1. 5. 14, 4. 7. 2; peltasts, 4. 3. 22; cavalry, 4. 3. 17.

Τάοχοι, ων, οἱ, the Taochi, a hill tribe on the borders of Armenia, 4. 4. 18, 6. 5, 7. 1.

Ταπεινός, ή, όν (τάπης, a carpet, δάπις, δάπεδον, the ground, like humilis, fr. humus), humble, lowly, submissive, 2. 5. 13.

Ταπεινόω, ώσω (ταπεινός), to humble, 6. 1. 18.

Ταπίς, ίδος, ἡ, later form of τάπης, ητος, ὁ, a carpet. 7. 3. 18, 27, al. τάπις.

Ταράσσω, or ταράττω, άξω, τε-

τάραγμαι, to throw into disorder, 6. 3. 9, 3. 4. 19, 23, 5. 10. 9, 2. 4. 18.

Τάραχος, ου, ὁ, for ταραχή, confusion, disorder, 1. 8. 2.

Ταριχεύω, εύσω, &c. (τάρῖχος, an embalmed body, a mummy), to preserve, 5. 4. 28.

Ταρσοί, ῶν, οἱ, or Ταρσός, οῦ, ἡ (fancifully derived from ταρσός, a hoof, because the horse Pegasus lost a hoof here), Tarsus, a town in Cilicia, 1. 2. 23.

Τάσσω or τάττω, τάξω, τέτᾱχα, τέταγμαι, to arrange, 1. 2. 15; κατὰ τοὺς Ἕλληνας, opposite, 2. 3. 19; order, 2. 3. 11, 3. 1. 25, 1. 5. 7, 4. 3. 30, 2. 6. 13, 5. 5. 10, 4. 6. 22, 1. 6. 6, 5. 4. 16.

Ταῦρος, ου, ὁ, a bull, Lat. taurus, 2. 2. 9.

Ταύτῃ, in this direction, 1. 10. 6, 4. 2. 4; there, 4. 8. 12, 5. 5. 20; οἱ τ. ἵπποι, 4. 5. 36; οἱ ταύτῃ, the people there, 7. 4. 24; in this way, ὁδῷ, 2. 6. 7; εἰ δέ τι ἄλλο βέλτιον ἢ ταύτῃ, if there be any other better course than this, 3. 2. 32.

Τάφος, ου, ὁ (θάπτω), a tomb, 1. 6. 11.

Τάφρος, ου, ἡ (θάπτω), a ditch, 6. 3. 3, 5. 2. 5, 2. 3. 10, 4. 13.

Τάχα, adv. from ταχύς, quickly, 4. 4. 12, 1. 8. 8, 5. 7. 21; presently, 5. 2. 17; ταχέως, 2. 2. 12, also ταχύ under ταχύς.

Ταχύς, εῖα, ύ (θέω, to run), Comp. θάσσων, supl. τάχιστος, quick, 1. 2. 20, 1. 3. 14, 3. 3. 16, 4. 3. 24; ταχύ, adv. quickly, 2. 3. 6, &c.; βάδην ταχύ, with

a quick step, quick march, 4.
6. 25 ; ὅτι τάχιστα, as quickly
as possible, 4. 3. 29, 32, 5. 6.
18, &c.; so ὡς τάχιστα, 1. 3.
14, 3. 1. 38, 4. 6. 9, &c.; ὡς
ἐδύνατο τάχιστα, 3. 4. 48; ᾖ
ἐδύνατο τάχιστα, 1. 2. 4, 4. 5.
1, 6. 1. 21 ; ὡς τάχιστα, as
soon as, Lat. quum primum,
4. 3. 9; so ἐπεὶ τάχιστα, 6. 1.
21, 7. 2. 6, 3. 1. 9, 4. 6. 9.

Τέ, and, enclitic particle, Lat.
que, τέ—τέ, both—and, not only
—but also, 4. 5. 12 ; three
times repeated, 6. 3. 21, 7. 7.
30 ; joined to ἐάν, εἴτε, μήτε,
οὔτε, often τέ—καὶ, both—and,
not only—but also, 5. 4. 21,
5. 1, 7. 5. 6, &c.; σύ τε γὰρ
Ἕλλην εἶ καὶ ἡμεῖς, for you
are a Greek and we too (are
Greeks), 2. 1. 16, 7. 1. 21 ;
τε καί—καί, 1. 9. 7, &c.; τέ
—δέ, 7. 8. 11, &c.

Τέθριππον, ου, τό (τέσσαρες, ἵπποι), sc. ἅρμα, Lat. quadrigæ,
a four-horse chariot, 3. 2. 24.

Τείνω, τενῶ, τέτακα, τέταμαι, to
stretch, 4. 3. 21.

Τειχίζω, ίσω, &c. (τεῖχος), to
build a wall, fortify, 7. 2.
36.

Τεῖχος, εος, τό, a wall, 3. 4. 11,
5. 5. 6, &c.; εἰς τὸ τεῖχος,
within the city wall, 5. 5. 6, 7.
1. 38, 2. 13; a fortress, castle,
3. 4. 10, 7. 3. 19, 5. 8.

Τεκμαίρομαι, μαροῦμαι, 1 aor.
ἐτεκμηράμην (τέκμαρ), to infer,
4. 2. 4, τῷ ψόφῳ.

Τεκμήριον, ου τό (τέκμαρ), a sign,
proof, 3. 2. 13, 1. 9. 30.

Τέκνον, ου, τό (τίκτω), a child, 1.
4. 8.

Τελευταῖος, α, ον (τέλος), last, 4.
1. 10, 3. 24, 5. 22, 7. 3. 39.

Τελευτάω, ήσω, &c. (τέλος), to
end, βίον, to die, 1. 9. 1, 2. 1.
1, 4, 6. 2. 11 ; τελευτῶν, at
last, at length, 4. 5. 16, 6.
1. 8.

Τελευτή, ῆς, ἡ (τέλος), end, τοῦ
βίου, 1. 1. 1, 9. 30 ; without
βίου, 2. 6. 29, 3. 2. 7.

Τελέω, έσω, τετέλεκα, τετέλεσμαι
(τέλος), to end, to pay, 3. 3.
18, 7. 1. 6, 2. 27, 6. 16.

Τέλος, εος, τό, an end, τῆς
ἡμέρας, 1. 10. 18; ἐξόδου, 5.
2. 9; ἔχειν, 6. 3. 2 ; τέλος
(διὰ), at last, 1. 10. 13, 2. 3.
26, 5. 5. 3, &c.; τὰ τέλη, the
magistrates in Sparta, the
Ephors, 2. 6. 4, 7. 1. 34.

Τέμαχος, εος, τό (τέμνω), a slice,
δελφίνων, 5. 4. 28.

Τεμενίτης, ου, ὁ, an inhabitant of
Temenus, a place in Sicily,
Steph. Byz.; others make it
Τημενίτης, fr. Temenium, a
place in Argolis, Strab.; and
others Τημνίτην, fr. Temnos, a
place in Æolis, Schn. 4. 4. 15.

Τέμνω, τεμῶ, τέτμηκα, τέτμημαι,
2 aor. ἔτεμον or ἔταμον, to cut,
5. 8. 18.

Τέναγος, εος, τό (τείνω), a shoal,
a shallow, 7. 5. 12.

Τερεβίνθινος, η, ον, made from
the turpentine tree, τερέβινθος;
χρῖσμα, turpentine, 4. 4. 13.

Τεσσαράκοντα, forty, 1. 5. 13.

Τέσσαρες, ες, a (old form πέτορες
= με (for μεῖς, εἶς) + τρες,
1+3), four, 1. 2. 15.

Τέταρτος, η, ον, fourth, 3. 4. 31.

Τετρακισχίλιοι, αι, α, four thousand, 1. 1. 10.

Τετρακόσιοι αι, α, four hundred,
and sing. τετρακοσία ἀσπίς, 1.
7. 10.

Τετραμοιρία, ας, ἡ (μοῖρα), a

fourfold portion, 7. 2. 36, 6. 1.

Τετραπλοῦς, ῆ, οῦν, fourfold, 7. 6. 7.

Τευθρανία, ας, ἡ, Teuthrania, a town and district in Mysia, so called from Teuthras, an ancient king of Mysia, 2. 1. 3.

Τεῦχος, εος, το (τεύχω), a vessel, 5. 4. 28.

Τεχνάζω, ἀσω=τεχνάω (τέχνη), to practise artifice, 7. 6. 16.

Τέχνη, ης, ἡ (τίκτω, τεκεῖν), artifice, art, πάσῃ τέχνῃ καὶ μηχανῇ, by every art and contrivance, 4. 5. 16, 7. 2. 8.

Τεχνικῶς, adv. fr. τεχνικός (τέχνη), in an artificial way, 5. 9. 5.

Τέως, adv. corr. to ἕως, for a while, 4. 2. 12, 5. 4. 16, 6. 1. 5; before, ere this, up to this time, 7. 5. 13, 6. 29, 7. 55.

Τῇ μέν—τῇ δέ, here—there, 4. 8. 10; τῇδε, here, 7. 2. 13.

Τήκω, τήξω, τέτηκα intr., τέτηγμαι, to melt, make liquid, 4. 5. 15.

Τημενίτης, see Τεμενίτης.

Τήμερον=σήμερον, to-day, 1. 9. 25, 3. 1. 14, 4. 6. 8; ἡ τ. ἡμέρα, 4. 6. 9, the present day.

Τηνικαῦτα, adv. then, at that time, 4. 1. 5, 4. 2. 3.

Τήρης, ους or ου, ὁ, Teres, a king of the Odrysi in Thrace, 7. 5. 1, 2. 22.

Τηρίβαζος, ου, ὁ, Teribazus, a lieutenant-governor (ὕπαρχος) of Armenia, under Orontas the satrap, 3. 5. 17, 4. 4. 4, 17, 21, 7. 8. 25.

Τιάρα, ας, ἡ, a turban, a tiara, the Persian head-dress, worn

upright, ὀοθή, by the king, 2. 5. 23, also called κίδαρις and κίταρις and κυρβασία.

Τιαροειδής, ής, ές (τιάρα, εἶδος), shaped like a tiara, 5. 4. 13.

Τιβαρηνοί, ῶν, οἱ, the Tibareni, a people in Pontus, 5. 5. 2, 7. 8. 25.

Τίγρης, ητος, ὁ, also Τίγρις, ιδος, the Tigris, a river in Asia, 1. 7. 15, 4. 4. 3.

Τίθημι, θήσω, τέθεικα, τέθειμαι, 2 aor. ἔθην, to put, set, place, θέντας, 1. 5. 13; 7. 3. 22; ἀγῶνα, instituted a contest, 1. 2. 10. Mid. 7. 3. 23, τὰ ὅπλα τίθεσθαι, to put up their arms, κατὰ χώραν, in their accustomed place, 1. 5. 17; to ground arms, 1. 10. 16; to halt under arms, 4. 2. 16, 3. 17, 5. 2. 8, 1. 5. 14, 1. 6. 4, 6. 3. 3; εἰς τάξιν, to station themselves under arms in the order, &c., 2. 2. 21, 5. 4. 11; ἐν τάξει, 2. 2. 8, 7. 1. 22; ἀντία τὰ ὅπλα, halted under arms opposite them, 4. 3. 26.

Τιμασίων, ωνος, ὁ, Timasion, a Dardanian, 3. 1. 47, 2. 37, 5. 9. 32, 5. 6. 19, 6. 1. 14, 3. 28, 7. 3. 46, 5. 10.

Τιμάω, ήσω, τετίμηκα, ημαι (τιμή), to honour, 1. 8. 29; τὸν ἄξιον, 7. 3. 10; τοὺς ἀγαθούς, 1. 9. 14; καί με—τά τε ἄλλα ἐτίμησε καὶ ἔδωκε, both in other respects did he honour me, and in particular he gave me, 1. 3. 3, 5. 5. 14, 7. 3. 28; δώροις, 1. 9. 14, 7. 3. 19.

Τιμή, ῆς, ἡ (τίω), honour, 7. 3. 28; γίγνεται, 5. 9. 20; τιμὴν φέρειν τινί, 2. 1. 17; ἐν τιμῇ εἶναι, 2. 5. 38; price, 7. 5. 1, 8. 6.

Τιμησίθεος, ου, ὁ (τιμή, θεός), Timesitheus, 5. 4. 2, 4.

Τίμιος, α, ον (τιμή), valuable, 1. 2. 27.

Τιμωρέω, ήσω, &c. (τιμή, ἀείρω, to lift an equivalent; τιμωρός, an avenger, helper), to avenge, punish, τινά, 1. 9. 13, 2. 5. 27, 6. 29; Mid. to avenge oneself on, take vengeance on, punish, 7. 6. 7, 7. 17; τινά τινος, 7. 1. 25, 4. 23.

Τιμωρία, ας, ἡ (τιμωρός), punishment, παρ, ἐκείνου, 2. 6. 14.

Τριβαζος, see Τηρίβαζος.

Τις, τις, τι, g. τινος, &c., Indef. pron. one, a certain one, 3. 4. 23; χαλκός τις, something like brass; μελανία τις, a kind of blackness, 1. 8. 8; ἄλλην τινὰ ἀτέλειαν, some other privilege, 3. 3. 18; πρᾶγμά τι, something ado, 4. 1. 17; τοιοῦτός τις, somewhat as follows, 5. 8. 7; ποῖός τις, what sort of, 7. 6. 24; ὁποῖός τις, 2. 2. 2, 3. 1. 13, 5. 5. 15; πόσος τις, 2. 4. 21, 6. 3. 20, how large a kind of; ὀλίγοι τινές, some few, 4. 1. 10, 5. 1. 6; οἱ μέν τινες, some; οἱ δέ τινες, 2. 3. 15, 3. 3. 19, 4. 3. 33, 5. 7. 16; τὰ μέν τι, sometimes a little, 4. 1. 14; εἴ τις, some 5. 3. 3; εἴ τίς τι, if anyone, 1. 9. 18, 3. 2. 32, 4. 1. 14, 5. 7. 10; εἴ πού τι, 4. 5. 8; εἴ τί που, 6. 1. 15; τίςwith pl. following,1.4.8, 5.1, 9. 16, 5. 5. 14, &c.; τὶ connected with a pl., 5. 1. 16; εἴ τις δύναιτο, 4. 5. 17, for ἡμεῖς, 3. 4. 40, 7. 6. 25, for ὑμεῖς, 2. 3. 23, 4. 1. 25, &c., τινές, some, 3. 3. 18, 4. 6. 19, 5. 1. 8, 7. 4. 8; τί, some place, 1. 10. 16, 2. 4. 4; a part,

τῆς φάλαγγος, 1. 8, 18; διαφέρειν τι, in some respect, 3. 1. 37; οὐδέν τι, not at all, 7. 3. 35; μᾶλλόν τι, somewhat more, 4. 8. 26; ἧττόν τι, 5. 8. 11.

Τίς, τίς, τί, Interrog. who, what; εἰπὲ τίνα γνώμην ἔχεις, 2. 2. 10, 4. 8. 5, 3. 3. 18, 1. 10. 14, 2. 5. 15; ἀφήγησαι τί σοι ἀπεκρινάμην, 7. 2. 26, 7. 25, 1. 7. 8, 2. 1. 10; ἠρώτων τίνες εἶεν, 4. 5. 9, 2. 3. 4, 3. 5. 14, 4. 4. 5, 7. 4, 6, 6. 1. 23; τί, what, why, 2. 4. 3, 19, 5. 22, 3. 4. 39, 6. 1. 25; τί γάρ, 5. 7. 10, 7. 2. 28; τί οὖν, 1. 4. 14; ἐκ τίνος, wherefore, 5. 8. 4.

Τισσαφέρνης, εος contr. ους, ὁ, Tissaphernes, satrap of Ionia and Caria, 1. 1. 2, 3, &c., 2. 5. 15, 31, 3. 4. 13, 7. 6. 1, 8. 24.

Τιτρώσκω, τρώσω, τέτρωμαι, 1. aor. pass. ἐτρώθην, to wound, 1. 8. 26, 2. 2. 14, 5. 33.

Τλήμων, ων, ων, gen. ονος (τλάω), wretched, unfortunate, 3. 1. 29.

Τοί, encl. particle, strictly old dat. for τῷ, therefore, in truth, verily, assuredly, 3. 1. 18, 6. 4. 34, 5. 24, 3. 1. 37.

Τοιγαροῦν (τοί, γάρ, οὖν), wherefore, 1. 9. 9, 15, 18, 2. 6. 20·

Τοίνυν (τοί, νυν), therefore, then, 5. 1. 2, 2. 1. 22, 3. 5, 5. 41, 5. 1. 13, 6. 4. 28, 7. 7. 49; νῦν τοίνυν, 3. 1. 39, 7. 2. 29, &c.; μὲν τοίνυν, 5. 1. 2, 7. 2. 13, 3. 10, 5. 3, 10; μὴ τοίνυν μηδέ, nay then not even, 7. 6. 19.

Τοιόσδε, τοιάδε, τοιόνδε=τοῖος corr. of οἷος, of such kind, such, 5. 4. 31.

Τοιοῦτος, τοιαύτη, τοιοῦτο, stronger than τοῖος or τοιόσδε, such, πρόγονοι, 3. 2. 13; καιρός, 3. 1. 44, 5. 8. 3; γνώμη, 7. 6. 35; πράγματα, 2. 1. 16; ἀνομία, 5. 7. 33; ὡς τοιούτῳ, in that capacity, 3. 1. 30; such a one, such a man, 6. 4. 28, 7. 7. 47, 6. 4. 23, 3. 1. 30, 7. 7. 23, 5. 7. 33; τ. οὐδέν, no such thing, 2. 5. 5; τούτων τοιούτων ὄντων, such being the case, 2. 5. 12; εἰ ταῦτα τοιαῦτα ἔσται, if these things are to be so, 5. 7. 26; τοιούτων ἡμῖν εἰς φιλίαν ὑπαρχόντων, when we have such strong inducements to be friends, 2. 5. 24; ἐν τοιούτῳ τοῦ κινδύνου, in such a situation of, 1. 7. 5; ἐν τῷ τ., at such a juncture, 5. 8. 20; εἰς τὰ τ., for such services as these, 4. 1. 28.

Τοῖχος, ου, ὁ, the wall of a house, Lat. murus; τεῖχος is a city wall, Lat. mœnia, 7. 8. 14.

Τολμάω, ήσω, τετόλμηκα, μήμαι (τόλμη, τλάω), to dare, 5. 4. 34; have the heart or courage to, διδάσκειν, 3. 2. 32; σχίζειν ξύλα, 4. 4. 12, 7. 7. 46, 3. 2. 11, 16.

Τολμίδης, ου, ὁ, Tolmides, the herald, from Elis, 2. 2. 20, 3. 1. 46.

Τόξευμα, ατος, τό (τόξον), that which is shot, an arrow, 3. 4. 17, 4. 3. 6, 2. 28; ἐφέρετο, 5. 2. 14; ἐξικνεῖται, 1. 8. 19, 3. 4. 4; ἐχώρει, 4. 2. 28; τοξεύμασι κατέτρωσαν, 4. 1. 10; ἐπιέζετο ὑπὸ τ., 7. 8. 18.

Τοξεύω, εύσω, &c. (τόξον), to shoot with a bow, 3. 4. 17; τινά, 4. 2. 12, Pass., 1. 8. 20, 4. 1. 18.

Τοξική, ῆς, ἡ (τόξον), sc. τέχνη, archery, 1. 9. 5.

Τόξον, ου, τό (τυγχάνω?), 3. 4. 17, 4. 4. 16.

Τοξότης, ου, ὁ (τόξον), a bowman, 3. 3. 6, 4. 2, 5. 4. 22.

Τόπος, ου, ὁ, a place, 1. 5. 1, 4. 4. 4, &c., Eng. topics, topaz, &c.

Τοσόσδε, τοσήδε, τοσόνδε, so great, so many, 6. 3. 19.

Τοσοῦτος, αύτη, οῦτο, so great, 4. 1. 20; ποταμός, 3. 5. 7; followed by ὥστε and ὡς, τοσοῦτον ὥστε, such a distance that, 3. 4. 37, 4. 6. 13; τ. ὥστε, so much that, 1. 8. 13; τ. ὅσον, so far that, 3. 1. 45; ὅτι, 5. 8. 8; τοσούτῳ, with Comp. 1. 5. 9; so many in number, 2. 1. 16, 3. 1. 36, 7. 1. 21, 7. 25; τοσαῦτα εἶπε, 2. 1. 9; sing. thus much, 1. 3. 14.

Τότε, then, but ποτέ, now and then, 1. 1. 6, 7. 18, 1. 3. 2; κῆρυξ ἄριστος τῶν τότε, the best of the heralds of that time, 2. 2. 20; τότε δέ, 4. 1. 17, 3. 4. 21; ὅτε—καὶ τότε, 3. 2. 13; τότε δή, even then, 2. 4. 22, 4. 1. 10; ἐπεὶ—τότε, 4. 2. 4; τοτὲ μέν—τοτὲ δέ, at one time—at another, 5. 9. 9.

Τοὐλάχιστον = τὸ ἐλάχιστον, 5. 7. 8.

Τοὔμπαλιν = τὸ ἔμπαλιν, 1. 4. 15.

Τοὔπισθεν = τὸ ὄπισθεν, 3. 3. 10.

Τράγημα, ατος, τό (τρώγω, to eat), sweetmeats, 2. 3. 15, 5. 3. 9.

Τράλλεις, εων, αἱ, Tralles, a town in Lydia, 1. 4. 8.

Τρανίψαι, ων, οἱ, the Tranipsæ, 7. 2. 32, a tribe in Thrace, in some editions Θρανίψαι, probably the Νιψαῖοι of Herod., 4. 43.

Τράπεζα, ης, ἡ (τέτρα or τέσσαρες, πέζα, a foot), a table, 7. 2. 33, 3. 22, 23.

Τραπεζοῦς, οῦντος, ὁ and ἡ (τράπεζα), Trapezus, Trebisond, a town in Pontus on the Black Sea; Inh., Τραπεζούντιοι, 4. 8. 22, 23.

Τραῦμα, ατος, τό (τιτρώσκω), a wound, 4. 6. 10.

Τράχηλος, ου, ὁ (τραχύς), the neck, 1. 5. 8, 7. 4. 9.

Τραχύς, εῖα, ύ, rough, 4. 6. 12, 3. 6, 2. 6. 9.

Τρεῖς, τρεῖς, τρία, three, 6. 4. 36, 1. 5. 5.

Τρέπω, τρέψω, τέτριφα, τέτραμμαι, 1 aor. pass. ἐτρέφθην, 2 aor. ἐτράπην, to turn, 1. 8. 24, 3. 1. 41, 5. 4. 23, 3. 5. 13, 15, 7. 1. 18, 4. 8. 19, 5. 4. 24; πρός τινα, 4. 5. 30; ἐπί τινα, 5. 9. 19; ἐπὶ ῥᾳθυμίαν, 2. 6. 5; to put to the rout, 5. 4. 16, 9. 13, 6. 1. 5, 3. 26; 1 aor. ἐτρεψάμην, to turn an enemy away from oneself, put to flight, but 2 aor. ἐτραπόμην, to turn oneself away from an enemy, to flee.

Τρέφω, θρέψω, τέτροφα, τέθραμμαι, 1 aor. pass. ἐθρέφθην, 2 aor. ἐτράφην, to nourish, support, feed, 1. 1. 9, 10, 5. 1. 12, 7. 3. 13; ἐκ τῶν κωμῶν, 7. 4. 11; χιλῷ, 4. 5. 25; σίτῳ, 6. 3. 20; καρύοις, 5. 4. 32.

Τρέχω, θρέξω or δραμοῦμαι,

Τριακόντορος, ου, ἡ, sc. ναῦς (τριάκοντα), a war ship with thirty banks of oars, 5. 1. 16, 7. 2. 8.

Τριακόσιοι, αι, α, three hundred, 3. 4. 43.

Τριβή, ῆς, ἡ (τρίβω), exercise, practice, 5. 6. 15.

Τριήρης, ους, ἡ, sc. ναῦς (τρεῖς, ἄρω), a ship with three banks of oars, a trireme, 1. 4. 7, 8, 5. 1. 4, 9. 16, 10. 14, &c.

Τριηρίτης, ου, ὁ, one who goes in a trireme, a sailor or marine, 6. 4. 7.

Τρίπηχυς, υς, υ, g. εος (τρεῖς, πῆχυς), three cubits, about 4½ feet, 4. 2. 28.

Τριπλάσιος, α, ον, three times as much, 7. 4. 21.

Τρίπλεθρος, ος, ον, three plethra broad, or 300 Grk. ft., 303 Eng. ft., 5. 6. 9.

Τρίπους, ους, ουν, g. οδος (τρεῖς, πούς), having three feet, τράπεζα, 7. 3. 21; a contradictio in adjecto, so Il. 6. 93, 115; a hecatomb of 12 oxen, τοῖσι σκέλεσι ἐχειρονόμησε, he manœuvred with his legs, Her. 6. 129; dilapidated books, a green blackberry, &c. &c.

Τρίς, three times, thrice, 6. 2. 16, 19.

Τρισάσμενος, better τρὶς ἄσμενος, very glad, 3. 2. 24.

Τρισκαίδεκα, thirteen, 1. 5. 5.

Τρισμύριοι, αι, α, thirty thousand,

τρίτῳ, on the third signal, 2. 2. 4.

Τριχῆ, adv., or τριχῆ or τρίχα, in three parts or divisions, 4. 8. 15, 5. 10. 16.

Τρίχινος, η, ον (θρίξ), from or of hair, 4. 8. 3.

Τριχοίνικος, ος, ον, consisting of three chœnices=7. 3. 23.

Τρῳάς, άδος, ἡ, or Τρῳάς, the Troad, the district round Τροία in Mysia, so called from Τρώς, the king of Troy, 5. 6. 24, 7. 8. 7; Τροία, sc. γῆ, is also the Troad for Τρῳάς, 7. 8. 7.

Τρόπαιον, ου, τό (τρέπω), a trophy, 3. 2. 13; στήσασθαι, 4. 6. 27, 6. 3. 32, 7. 6. 36.

Τροπή, ῆς, ἡ (τρέπω), a rout, a defeat, 1. 8. 25, 4. 8. 21.

Τρόπος, ου, ὁ (τρέπω), (but τρυπός, a thong), manner, 2. 5. 20; τῷ αὐτῷ τρόπῳ, 4. 2. 13; οὐδενὶ τ. in no way, 3. 4. 8; τόνδε τὸν τρόπον, in this way, 1. 1. 9, 6. 1. 1; κατὰ πάντα τ., by all means, 6. 4. 30; so ἐκ παντὸς τρόπου, 3. 1. 43, 7. 4. 17; disposition, character, 7. 4. 8, 1. 2. 11, 2. 6. 8, so in pl. τρόποι, Lat. mores, 1. 9. 22.

Τροφή, ῆς, ἡ (τρέφω), nourishment, food, 1. 1. 9; ἔχειν, 7. 3. 8; λαμβάνειν, 5. 6. 32, syn. ἐπιτήδεια.

Τροχάζω, άσω (τρέχω), to run quickly, 7. 3. 46.

Τρυπάω, ήσω, &c. (τρύπη), to bore, pierce, τὰ ὦτα τετρυπημένος, 3. 1. 31.

Τρωκτός, ή, όν (τρώγω), eatable, τὰ τ., fruit for dessert, 5. 3. 12.

Τρωτός, ή, όν (τιτρώσκω), vulnerable, liable to wounds, 3. 1. 23.

Τυγχάνω, τεύξομαι, τετύχηκα, 2 aor. ἔτυχον, (1) to hit, τινός, 3. 2. 19; (2) to find, ὁποίων ἡμῶν ἔτυχον, what sort of persons they found us to be, 5. 5. 15; (3) to obtain, 3. 1. 28, 5. 9. 26; τιμῆς, 7. 1. 30. 6. 4. 16; meet, 2. 6. 29, 3. 2. 7; ταῦτά σου, this from you, 6.4.32; πάντων ἐπαίνου, praise from all, 5. 7. 33, 1. 4. 15; (4) with a Part. to happen, λέγων, 3. 2. 10, 1. 1. 2, 2. 1. 7, 2. 20, 4. 2. 8, 5. 7. 25, 9. 2, 6. 3. 22; τεταγμένος, 1. 9. 31; ἑστηκώς, 1. 5. 8; θυόμενος, 2. 1. 9, 1. 10. 3, 2. 3. 2, 5. 3. 8, 7. 1. 2; with Part. to be supplied, ὡς ἐτύγχανον ἕκαστοι ηὐλίζοντο, 2. 2. 17, 5. 4. 34; (5) τυχόν, acc. neut. of 2 aor. used absol. perhaps, 5. 9. 20, like ἐξόν δέον, &c.

Τυριαῖον, ου, τό, Tyriæum, a town in Lycaonia, 1. 2. 14.

Τυρός, οῦ, ὁ, cheese, 2. 4. 28.

Τύρσις, εως, ἡ, a tower, Lat. turris, 7. 2. 21, 8. 12, 13, 5. 2. 5, 4. 4. 2; Gen. τύρσιος, 7. 8. 12.

Τύχη, ης, ἡ (τυγχάνω), fortune, 2. 2. 13, 5. 2. 25.

Τῷ, dat. of art. ὁ, ἡ, τό, but τῷ, 2. 5. 14, Att. for τινί.

Υ

Ὑβρίζω, ίσω, ὕβρικα, ὕβρισμαι (ὕβρις), to act insolently, 5. 8. 1, 3, 22; ἀποθνήσκειν ὑβριζομένους, to die an ignominious death, 3. 1. 13, 29; δεινά τινα ὑ., 6. 2. 2, to inflict wanton injuries.

Ὕβρις, εως, ἡ (ὑπέρ), (as Lat. superbus, super, Eng. up, uppish), insolence, 3. 1. 21; οὐχ ὕβρει, not wantonly, 5. 5. 16, 8. 19; viciousness, 5. 8. 3.

Ὑβριστός, ή, όν (ὕβρις), Comp. ὑβριστότερος, τόγατος, insolent, 5. 8. 3, 22.

Ὑγιαίνω, ὑγιανῶ, 1 aor. ὑγίανα, Ion. ηνα (ὑγιής), to be in, or recover health, 4. 5. 18.

Ὑγρότης, τητος, ἡ (ὑγρός), suppleness, 5. 8. 15.

Ὑδροφορέω, ήσω (ὕδωρ, φέρω), to carry water, 4. 5. 9.

Ὑδροφόρος, ου, ὁ and ἡ (ὕδωρ, φέρω), a water-carrier, 4. 5. 10.

Ὕδωρ, ὕδατος, τό (ὕω), water, 4. 3. 21, ἡδύ, 6. 2. 4; ἐξ οὐρανοῦ, rain, 4. 2. 2.

Ὑιδοῦς, ου, ὁ (υἱός), a son's son, a grandson, 5. 6. 37.

Ὑιός, ου, ὁ (ὕω, Ϝύω=φύω, filius), a son, 4. 6. 3, 5. 8. 18.

Ὕλη, ης, ἡ, a wood, a forest (silva = ὕλϜα), 5. 2. 31 (ξύλον is cut wood), 1. 5. 1, 3. 5. 10.

Ὑμέτερος, α, ον, poss. fr. ὑμεῖς, your, yours, 5. 5. 19 = your dependants, καὶ τὰ μὲν δὴ ὑμέτερα τοιαῦτα, and such then is the state of your affairs; so τὰ ἐμά, 7. 6. 33.

Ὑπάγω, άξω, ῆχα, ῆγμαι, to lead or go slowly on, 3. 4. 48, 4. 2. 16; Mid. suggest, ταῦτα, threw out these hints, 2. 1. 18; to lead on, induce, 2. 4. 3; μένειν.

Ὑπαίθριος, ος, ον, and α, ον (ὑπό, αἰθήρ), in the open air, 5. 5. 21, 7. 6. 24.

Ὑπαίτιος, ος, ον (ὑπό, αἰτία), under accusation, guilty, μή τι πρὸς τῆς πόλεώς οἱ ὑπαίτιον εἴη, lest there should be any ground of accusation against

him on the part of his country, 3. 1. 5.

Ὑπακούω, ἀκούσομαι, &c., to listen, 7. 3. 7; hear, καλούντων, 4. 1. 9.

Ὑπαντάω, ήσω, &c., to come or go to meet, 4. 3. 34.

Ὑπαντιάζω, άσω = ὑπαντάω, 6. 3. 27.

Ὑπάρχω, άρξω, &c., to begin, εὖ ποιῶν, 2. 3. 23, 5. 5. 9; to be, 7. 1. 27, 28, 5. 1. 10, 2. 2. 11, 7. 7. 32; to be on one's side, τινί, 1. 1. 4; ἐκ τῶν ὑπαρχόντων, according to one's means, 6. 2. 9.

Ὕπαρχος, ου, ὁ (ὑπό, ἄρχω), commanding under another, a lieutenant-governor, 1. 2. 20, 8. 5, 4. 4. 4.

Ὑπασπιστής, οῦ, ὁ, a shield-bearer, 4. 2. 20.

Ὑπείκω, ξω, to yield, τινί, 7. 7. 31.

Ὕπειμι, to be under, 3. 4. 7.

Ὑπελαύνω, άσω, &c., to ride under, into, or up to, 1. 8. 15.

Ὑπέρ, prep. gov. gen. and acc. (1) With Gen. over, above, 3, 4. 29, 4. 7. 4, 5. 4. 13, &c.; (2) beyond, τοῦ ὄρους, 1. 10. 14; (3) for, in behalf of, in defence of, ὑ. τινος πονεῖν, 7. 3. 31; μάχεσθαι, 1. 8. 27, 5. 7. 10; βοηθεῖν, 3. 5. 6; τιμωρεῖσθαι, 1. 3. 4; ἀποθανεῖν, 1. 9. 31, 7. 4. 9; βουλεύεσθαι, 5. 7. 12, &c.; (4) in the name of one, 7. 7. 3, 21; (5) on account of, 1. 7. 3; about, in regard to, 5. 6. 27. 28. With Acc. over, above, ὑπὲρ τεσσαράκοντα ἔτη, 5. 3. 1; ὑπὲρ ἥμισυ, 5. 10. 10.

Ὑπεράλλομαι, to leap over, 7. 4. 17.

Ὑπερβαίνω, βήσομαι, &c., to go or cross over, ὄρη, 7. 3. 43, 8. 7; εἰς πόλιν, 7. 1. 17.

Ὑπερβάλλω, βαλῶ, &c., to go over, 4. 6. 10; ὄρος, 4. 4. 20, 6. 8; ἄκρον, 4. 5. 1; κατὰ λόφους τινάς, 6. 3. 7; πρός τινα, 7. 5. 1; τὸ ὑ. τοῦ στρατεύματος, the part of the army that gained the height, 4. 1. 7.

Ὑπερβολή, ῆς, ἡ (ὑπερβάλλω), crossing, 1. 2. 25; the pass, 4. 1. 21, 6. 6; ὄρους, 4. 4. 18, 6. 24; ὀρέων, 3. 5. 18, 4. 6. 5, 1. 2. 25; ὑπερβολαὶ τοῦ ὄρους, 4. 6. 7.

Ὑπερδέξιος, ος, ον, above on the right hand, 3. 4. 37; τὰ ὑ., the heights on the right hand, 5. 7..31.

Ὑπερέρχομαι, ελεύσομαι, &c., to go over, pass over, τὰς πηγάς, 4. 4. 3.

Ὑπερέχω, έξω, &c., to be above (τοῦ ὕδατος), 3. 5. 7; ὑπερέχουσα πέτρα, impending, 4. 7. 4.

Ὑπερθεν, adv. above, 1. 4. 4.

Ὑπερκάθημαι, to sit above, take their station above, ἡμῶν, 5. 1. 9; ἐπὶ τῶν ἄκρων, 5. 2. 1.

Ὑπερόριος, ος, ον, and α, ον (ὑπέρ, ὅρος), over the boundaries, ἡ ὑ. (χώρα), the foreign territory, opp. to ἐνδήμων, home, 7. 1. 27.

Ὑπερύψηλος, ος, ον, exceeding high, 3. 5. 7.

Ὑπέρχυμαι, ελεύσομαι, &c., to go or come under, advance slowly, 5. 2. 30.

Ὑπέχω, ὑφέξω or ὑποσχήσω, ὑπέσχηκα, ημαι, to undergo, δίκην, punishment, 5. 8. 18.

Ὑπήκοος, ος, ον (ὑπὸ, ἀκούω), giving ear, obedient, subject, 1.

6. 6, 7. 7. 29; τινός, 5. 4. 6, 5. 5. 1.

Ὑπηρετέω, ήσω, &c. (ὑπηρέτης), to serve, assist, 2. 5. 14; τινί τι, 1. 9. 18, 7. 7. 46; ὧν δέομαι, 3. 5. 8.

Ὑπηρέτης, ου, ὁ (ὑπό, ἐρέσσω, to row), an assistant, a servant, 1. 9. 27, 2. 1. 9; ἔργου, α helper in a work, 1. 9. 18, 2. 5. 14; δοῦλος is a slave, fr. δέω, to bind, Lat. servus; ἀνδράποδον is a slave taken in war (ἀνήρ, ἀποδόσθαι), Lat. mancipium; θεράπων (θέρω), one who serves from friendship, οἰκέτης, for pay (οἶκος), a domestic slave, Lat. famulus.

Ὑπισχνέομαι, ὑποσχήσομαι, ὑπέσχημαι (ὑπό, ἔχω), to promise, μισθόν, 7. 6. 5, 5. 6. 36; πολλά, 1. 7. 5, with inf. fut. 7. 2. 24, 5. 9; ἀπιέναι, 7. 7. 14; συστρατεύεσθαι, 7. 7. 31; μεμνῆσθαι, 7. 6. 38; παύσασθαι, 1. 2. 2; βουλεύσασθαι, 2. 3. 20.

Ὕπνος, ου, ὁ (ὑπό), sleep, 3. 1. 11. Lat. somnus, sopor.

Ὑπό, prep. gov. Gen. Dat. Acc., under: With Gen. μαστίγων, 3. 4. 25; ἁμάξης, 6. 2. 22, 25; after pass. vbs. by, 6. 4. 22; and neut. vbs. πάσχειν, 4. 3. 2, 5. 5. 9; ἀποθνήσκειν, 5. 1. 15, 7. 5. 13, &c.; ὑ. Ἑλλήνων εὔκλειαν ἔχων, being honoured by the Greeks, 7. 6. 33; αἰτίαν ἔχειν, 7. 6. 11, 15; ὑπὸ τῆς αἰθρίας, in the open air, 4. 4. 14; from, by reason of, τῆς αἰσχύνης, 7. 7. 11; πόνων, 5. 8. 3, 2. 15, 4. 29. With Dat. under, ὑ. τοῖς ξίφροις ἔρεπανα, 1. 8. 10; ὑ. δένδρῳ εἶναι, 4. 7. 10; ἀκροπόλει, 1. 2. 8, 3. 4.

L

24, 6. 4. 4; αὐτῇ τῇ πέτρᾳ, 6. 4. 4; ὑπό τινι γίγνεσθαι, 7. 2. 2, 7. 32. With Acc. *under*, ὑ. τὰ δένδρα ἀπῆλθον, 4. 7. 8; ὑ. τον λόφον στήσας τὸ στράτευμα, 1. 10. 14; ὑ. τὸν ὀφθαλμόν, 1. 8. 27 ; with vbs. of rest, 3. 4. 37, 7. 4. 5 ; ὑ. τὸ ὄρος, 7. 4. 11, 8. 21.

Ὑποδεής, ής, ές (ὑπό, δέομαι), *deficient* ; Comp. ὑποδεέστερος, *inferior*, 1. 9. 5.

Ὑποδείκνυμι, δείξω, &c., *to show secretly, gradually*, 5. 7. 12.

Ὑποδέχομαι, δέξομαι, δέδεγμαι, *to receive*, 6. 3. 31; *kindly, to welcome*, ὡς φίλον, 1. 6. 3.

Ὑποδέω, δήσω, &c., *to bind or tie under*, ὑποδεδεμένοι, *with their shoes on*, 4. 5. 14.

Ὑπόδημα, ατος, τό (ὑποδέω), *a sandal*, 4. 5. 14.

Ὑποζύγιον, ου, τό (ὑπό, ζεύγνυμι), *under the yoke*, prop. an adj. with κτῆμα or κτῆνος understood, *a beast of burden*, 1. 3. 1, 5. 5 ; νέμεται, 2. 2. 15 ; syn. σκευοφόρα, 3. 2. 36 ; ἀνατίθεσθαι ἐπὶ τὰ ὑ., 2. 2. 4, &c.

Ὑποκαταβαίνω, βήσομαι, &c., *to go down by stealth*, 7. 4. 11.

Ὑποκρύπτω, κρύψω, &c., *to hide under, conceal*, 1. 9. 19.

Ὑπολαμβάνω, λήψομαι, &c., *to take under one's protection*, τοὺς φεύγοντας, 1. 1. 7 ; ὑπολαβὼν εἶπεν, *interrupting him he said*, 2. 1. 15, 3. 1. 31, 6. 3. 14.

Ὑπολείπω, λείψω, &c., *to leave behind*, Mid. *to lag behind*, 1. 2. 25, 4. 5. 15, 5. 8. 16, 7. 2. 6 ; τοῦ στόματος, *the front, the van*, 5. 4. 22, 4. 3. 25.

Ὑπολόχαγος, ου, ὁ, *an under-captain, a lieutenant*, 5. 2. 13.

Ὑπολύω, λύσω, &c., *to loosen, unbind*, 4. 5. 13.

Ὑπομαλακίζομαι (ὑπό, μαλακός, *soft*), *to become a little soft; grow cowardly*, 2. 1. 14.

Ὑπομένω, μενῶ, &c., *to stay behind, halt*, 3. 4. 21, 4. 1. 16, 19, 3. 15, 5. 23 ; *to remain*, 4. 4. 21, 6. 3. 25, 29 ; *to wait for*, τινά, 4. 1. 21.

Ὑπόμνημα, ατος, τό (ὑπό, μιμνήσκω), *a remembrance, memorial*, 1. 6. 3.

Ὑποπέμπω, πέμψω, &c., *to send secretly as a spy*, 2. 4. 22 ; vb. ὑποπεμπτός, 3. 3. 4; al. ὑπόπεμπτος.

Ὑποπίνω, πίομαι, &c., *to drink slowly*, ὑποπεπωκὼς ἐτύγχανε, *he happened to be rather tipsy*, 7. 3. 29.

Ὑποπτεύω, εύσω (ὑπό, ὄψομαι, fr. ὁράω), Lat. *suspicor, to suspect*, τελευτὴν τοῦ βίου, 1. 1. 1 ; ἰέναι, 1. 3. 1 ; βασιλέα ἀφεικέναι, 2. 3. 13, 5. 28, 4. 2. 15, 7. 8. 6 ; μὴ πλήρεις εἶναι τὰς τάφρους, 2. 3. 13.

Ὑποστρατηγέω, ήσω, *to be a lieutenant-general*, τινί, *under some one*, 5. 6. 36.

Ὑποστράτηγος, ου, ὁ, *a lieutenant-general*, 3. 1. 32.

Ὑποστρέφω, στρέψω, &c., *to turn back*, τοὔμπαλιν, 6. 4. 38, 7. 4. 18; *to elude*, 2. 1. 18.

Ὑπουργός, ός, όν (ὑπό, ἔργον), *conducive*, εἶναι, *contributed*, 5. 8. 15.

Ὑποφαίνω, φανῶ, &c., *to show a little, to break*, ἡμέρα, 3. 2. 1, 4. 2. 7 ; ἕως, 4. 3. 9.

Ὑποφείδομαι, σομαι, *to spare a little*, 4. 1. 8.

Ὑποχείριος, ος, ον, *under the hand, subject*, τινί, 3. 2. 3, 7. 6. 43.

Ὕποχος, ος, ον (ὑπέχω), *under control, subject,* τινί, 2. 5. 7.

Ὑποχωρέω, ήσω, &c., *to go back,* 1. 7. 17; *make way,* 4. 5. 20; *give way to, yield,* Κύρῳ, 1. 4. 18.

Ὑποψία, ας, ἡ (ὑπό, ὄψομαι, fr. ὁράω), *suspicion, distrust,* 2. 5. 5; ἐστί τινι ὅτι, 1. 3. 21; παρέχειν, 2. 4. 10; ὑποψίαι, 2. 5. 1, 2.

Ὑρκάνιος, ου, ὁ, *a Hyrcanian.* Hyrcania lay between Media and Persia and the Caspian Sea, 7. 8. 15.

Ὕς, ὑός, ὁ and ἡ, Lat. *sus, a sow,* 5. 2. 3.

Ὑστεραῖος, α, ον (ὕστερος, ὑπό), *the day after,* ἡμέρα, 6. 2. 10; τῇ ὑστεραίᾳ without ἡμέρᾳ, 2. 2. 18, 3. 4. 37, &c.; *on the following day.*

Ὑστερέω, ήσω (ὕστερος), *to come too late for,* τῆς μάχης πέντε ἡμέρας, 1. 7. 12.

Ὑστερίζω, ίσω (ὕστερος), *to come late,* ἦττον ἂν ὑστερίζειν, *there would be less coming late, less delay,* 5. 9. 18.

Ὕστερος, α, ον (ὑπό), *later, after,* 2. 2. 17, opp. to πρῶτοι, 1. 5. 14; ὑπέμενον ὕστεροι, *stayed a little behind,* 3. 4. 21; Adv. ὕστερον, *afterwards,* χρόνῳ συχνῷ ὕστερον, 1. 8. 8; τότε μὲν——ὕστερον δέ, 1.3.2, 3.2.13.

Ὑφειμένως, adv. fr. p. p. of ὑφίημι, *slackly, quietly,* 7. 7. 16.

Ὑφηγέομαι, ήσομαι, &c., *to lead slowly,* 4. 1. 7, 6. 3. 25.

Ὑφίημι, ήσω, εἶκα, εἶμαι, *to send down, put under, concede,* 3. 5. 5; Mid. *put in one's power,* τινί, 6. 4. 31; *yield, give in,* 3. 1. 17, 2. 3, 5. 4. 26.

Ὑφίστημι, ὑποστήσω, ὑφέστηκα,

ὑφέσταμαι, *to place under, undertake,* τὴν ἀρχήν, 5. 9. 19, 31; ὑποστάς, *having engaged to go,* 4. 1. 26, 28; Intr. *stand secretly,* 4. 1. 14; *withstand,* 7. 3. 44; τινί, 3. 2. 11.

Ὑφοράω, ὑπόψυμαι, &c., *to suspect,* τινά, 2. 4. 10.

Ὑψηλός, ή, όν (ὕψος), *high,* ὄρη, 5. 6. 6; χώρα, 5. 4. 31; τὸ ὑ., *the height,* 3. 4. 25; ὑψηλὰ ἄλλεσθαι, 5. 9. 5.

Ὕψος, εος, τό (ὕψι. ὑπό), *height,* (τὸ) ὕψος, *in height,* 3. 4. 7, 9, 10, 6. 2. 3.

Φ.

Φαγεῖν, 2 aor. inf. of ἐσθίω, τι, 4. 5. 8, 2. 3. 16; τῶν κηρίων, 4. 8. 20.

Φαιδρός, ά, όν (φαίνω), *bright, beaming with animation,* 2. 6. 11.

Φαίνω, φανῶ, πέφαγκα, πέφασμαι, 1 aor. act. ἔφηνα, 2 aor. pass. ἐφάνην (φάω, *to shine*); Act. *to show,* Mid. *appear,* 4. 3. 13, 3. 2. 9; Mid. πῦρ, 7. 4. 16; καπνός, 2. 2. 15, 18; πηλός, 1. 5. 7; ἴχνη, 1. 6. 1; ἔλαφος, 5. 7. 24, &c. With Part. φαίνεται φθονῶν, 1. 9. 19, 2. 5. 38, 5. 7. 5, 10, 33, 9. 9; συμβουλεύσας φανῶ, 5. 6. 4, 4. 5. 28. With Inf. φαίνεται εἶναι, 1. 9. 15, 2. 3. 13, 5. 4. 29; φαίνεται ὤν, *he manifestly is,* but φαίνεται εἶναι, *he seems to be.*

Φάλαγξ, αγγος, ἡ, *a phalanx,* 1. 8. 17, 10. 10; πυκνή, 2. 3. 3, &c.

Φαλῖνος, ου, ὁ, *Phalinus*, a Greek from Zacynthus, 2. 1. 7, 8.

Φανερός, ά, όν (φαίνω), *manifest, visible*, ἔκβασις, 4. 2. 1; ὁδός, 4. 1. 23, 2. 6. 19; ἴχνη, 1. 7. 17; ὠτειλή, 1. 9. 6; ἐπιβουλή, 2. 5. 1. With Part. ἐπιβουλεύων ἡμῖν φανερός ἐστι, *he is manifestly plotting against us*, 3. 2. 20, 1. 9. 11, 2. 6. 23, 3. 1. 36, 2. 24, 4. 3. 24, 33, 7. 7. 24; εἰς τὸ φανερόν, *in a conspicuous position*, 7. 7. 22; ἐν τῷ φανερῷ, *openly*, 1. 3. 21; adv. φανερῶς, 1. 9. 19.

Φαρέτρα, ας, ἡ (φέρω), *a quiver*, 4. 4. 16.

Φάρμακον, ου, τό, *physic, medicine*, 6. 2. 11.

Φαρμακοποσία, ας, ἡ (φάρμακον, πίνω), *the drinking, taking of physic*, 4. 8. 21.

Φαρνάβαζος, ου, ὁ, *Pharnabazus*, satrap of Phrygia and Bithynia, 6. 4. 24, 7. 1. 2.

Φασιανός, οῦ, ὁ, *a Phasianian*. The Phasiani lived on the Phasis, in Western Armenia, 4. 6. 5.

Φᾶσις, ιδος and ιος, ὁ, (1) *the Phasis, a river in Colchis*, hence *pheasant, Phasiana avis*; (2) *the Araxes*, mistaken by the Greeks for the Phasis, 4. 6. 4, 5. 6. 36, 7. 1.

Φάσκω=φημί, *to say*, 4. 4. 21, 8. 4, 5. 8. 1.

Φαῦλος, η, ον, and ος, ον, *poor, worthless, trifling*, 6. 4. 11, 12.

Φέρω, οἴσω, ἐνήνοχα, ἐνήνεγμαι, 1 aor. act. ἤνεγκα, 2 aor. ἤνεγκον, 1 fut. pass. ἐνεχθήσομαι and οἰσθήσομαι, 1 aor. ἠνέχθην or ἠνείχθην, *to bear, bring, carry*, τοὺς τετρωμένους,

3. 4. 32; ἄλφιτα, 7. 1. 37; ἄγειν καὶ φέρειν, Lat. *ferre et agere, to plunder completely*. ἄγειν, *to lead away* live stock, φέρειν, *to carry* valuables, 5. 5. 13, 2. 6. 5; φέρειν βαρέως, *to take it ill, be annoyed*, or *vexed*, Lat. *ægre ferre*, 2. 1. 4; so χαλεπῶς, *moleste ferre*, 1. 3. 3, 5. 7. 2; *to receive*, μισθόν, 1. 3. 21, 7. 6. 7; *bring*, δῶρα, 7. 3. 31, 2. 1. 17; *pay*, δασμούς, φόρους, 5. 5. 7, 10; *produce*, ἡ γῆ κριθάς, 6. 2. 6; *lead*, of a road, 5. 2. 19, 22, 5. 2. 23; so ἄγειν. Pass. 2. 1. 6; *to rush, roll, fly*, ἅρματα, 1. 8. 20; βέλος, 3. 3. 16, 5. 2. 14; λίθοι, 4. 2. 3, 7. 6, 10, 12. Mid. ὕδωρ, 7. 4. 3; πυρούς, 6. 4. 1.

Φεύγω, φεύξομαι or φευξοῦμαι, πέφευγα, πέφυγμαι, 2 aor. act. ἔφυγον, *to flee*, 1. 10. 11, 3. 3. 9, 5. 4. 18, 7. 6. 36, &c.; *to be banished*, οἴκοθεν, 4. 8. 25; οἱ φεύγοντες, *the exiles*, 1. 1. 7, 9. 9, 1. 3. 3, 7. 1. 33.

Φημί, φήσω, *to say*, 7. 7. 9; ἔφη, 2. 3. 24, 7. 3. 9, 4. 1. 20, &c.; εἶπεν and ἔφη both occur in 2. 5. 24, 5. 9. 31, 7. 3. 24, 6. 41; also ἔλεξεν— ἔφη, 5. 1. 2, 7. 1. 13; ἀποκρίνεται—ἔφη, 4. 1. 20. With Inf., ἔφη ἐθέλειν, 4. 8. 7, 2. 2. 1, 1. 4. 14, 6. 7; and Nom. when the subj. of the Inf. is the same as the subj. of the gov. vb., ἔφη οὗτος εἶναι, 7. 2. 20, 4. 1. 24, 4. 4. 17, 5. 10. 13, &c. With Acc. and Inf., πολλοὺς ἔφη βελτίους εἶναι, 2. 2. 1, 1. 4. 12, 3. 2. 23, 1. 3. 18; οὐκ ἔφη, *he refused*, 1. 3. 7, 4. 5. 15, 1. 3. 1.

Φθάνω, φθάσω(ᾶ), or φθήσομαι, ἔφθακα, 1 aor. ἔφθασα, 2 aor. ἔφθην· (φθῶ φθαίην φθῆναι φθάς), to get before, anticipate, 4. 6. 11 ; φθάσαι πρὶν παθεῖν, 2. 5. 5, 4. 1. 4, 21 ; βουλόμενος φθάσαι πρῶτος = ὥστε εἶναι πρῶτος, 3. 4. 20 ; τι in anything, 5. 9. 18; ἔφθασα καταλαβών, I was the first to seize, anticipated them in seizing, 1. 3. 14, 5. 6. 9; φθάνουσιν ἐπὶ τῷ ἄκρῳ γενόμενοι τοὺς πολεμίους, they reach the height before the enemy, 3. 4. 49 ; φθάνει αὐτὸν πορευόμενον ἡμέρα γενομένη, daylight overtakes him on the march, 5. 7. 16.

Φθέγγομαι, φθέγξομαι, ἔφθεγμαι (ἐφθεγξαι, &c.), to utter a word, 6. 4. 28 ; to sound, κέρας, 7. 4. 19 ; σάλπιγξ, 4. 2. 7, 5. 2. 14, 6. 3. 27; to cry, of an eagle, 5. 9. 23 ; to shout, of men, 1. 8. 18.

Φθείρω, φθερῶ, ἔφθαρκα, ἔφθαρμαι, 1 aor. act. ἔφθειρα, 2 aor. pass. ἐφθάρην, to destroy, lay waste, χώραν, 4. 7. 20.

Φθονέω, φθονήσω, 1 aor. pass. ἐφθονήθην, to envy, τινί, 1. 9. 19, 5. 7. 10.

Φιάλη, ης, ἡ, a cup, hence Eng. phial, φ. ἀργυρᾶν, 4. 7. 27, 7. 3. 27.

Φιλέω, φιλήσω, πεφίληκα, πεφίλημαι (φίλος), to love, Lat. amare, 1. 9. 28.

Φιλήσιος, ου, ὁ (φιλέω), Philesius, an Achæan, 3. 1. 47, 5. 3. 1, 6. 27, 7. 1. 32.

Φιλία, ας, ἡ (φίλος), friendship, Κορύλα, friendship for Corylas, 5. 6. 11 ; φ. τῇ σῇ, for you, 7. 7. 29 ; ἡ πρόσθεν, 1.

6. 3 ; διαπράττεσθαι, 7. 3. 16; χρῆσθαι, 1. 3. 5 ; see διά, πρός.

Φιλικός, ή, όν, friendly, 4. 1. 9 ; adv. φιλικῶς, in a friendly way, 6. 4. 35.

Φίλιος, α, ον, friendly ; ἄνθρωποι, 5. 7. 12 ; στράτευμα, 6. 1. 22 ; χωρία, 5. 7. 13 ; πόλις, 5. 7. 33 ; γῆ, 5. 1. 1 ; χώρα, 2. 3. 26, 5. 4. 2, 5. 1 ; φιλίαν ὑμῖν παρέξει τὴν χώραν, 2. 3. 26; ὡς διὰ φιλίας τῆς χώρας ἀπάξει, and also διὰ τῆς χώρας ὡς διὰ φιλίας ἀπάξει, 1. 3. 14, 4. 1. 8, 5. 4. 2 ; πορεύεσθαι ὡς διὰ φιλίας, 2. 3. 27; 5. 5. 3 ; ἐν φιλίᾳ, 7. 3. 13; εἰς τὴν φ., 6. 4. 38.

Φίλιππος, ος, ον (φιλέω, ἵππος), a lover of or fond of horses, 1. 9. 5.

Φιλόθηρος, ος, ον (φίλος θήρα), fond of hunting, of the chase, 1. 9. 6.

Φιλοκερδέω, ήσω (φίλος, κέρδος), to be greedy of gain, 1. 9. 16.

Φιλοκίνδυνος, ος, ον (φίλος, κίνδυνος), fond of danger, venturesome, 2. 6. 7, 1. 9. 6.

Φιλομαθής, ής, ές (φίλος, μανθάνω), fond of learning, 1. 9. 5.

Φιλονεικία, ας, ἡ (φίλος νεῖκος), love of strife, rivalry, 4. 8. 27.

Φιλόξενος, ον, ὁ (φίλος, ξένος), Philoxenus, from Pellene in Achaia, 5. 2. 15.

Φιλοπόλεμος, ος, ον (φίλος πόλεμος), fond of war, 2. 6. 1.

Φίλος, η, ον, a friend, friendly, γίγνεσθαι, 2. 1. 14; τινί, 4. 4. 4, 7. 7. 16; εἶναί τινι, 2. 1. 20, 7. 7. 18, &c.; πόλις, 1. 4. 2 ; Κύρῳ φιλαίτερος, 1. 9. 29; φίλος is usually pass. one loved, amatus; φίλιος, act. friendly to, amans, and φιλικός, fit for friendship. .

Φιλόσοφος, ου, ὁ (φίλος, σοφία), a philosopher, 2. 1. 13.

Φιλοστρατιώτης, ου, ὁ (φίλος, στρατιώτης), a friend of the soldiers, 7. 6. 4, 39.

Φιλοτιμέομαι, ήσομαι, &c. (φίλος, τιμή), to love honour, be jealous, ὅτι, 1. 4. 7.

Φιλοφρονέομαι, ήσομαι (φίλος φρονέω, φρήν), to be kindly disposed, 2. 5. 27, 4. 5. 29; to greet, ἀλλήλους, 4. 5. 34.

Φλιάσιος, α, ον, Phliasian, from Phlius, a town between Sicyon and Argolis, 7. 8. 1.

Φλυαρέω, ήσω (φλύαρος, φλύω, to swell), to talk nonsense, 3. 1. 26, 29.

Φλυαρία, ας, ἡ (φλύω), nonsense, pl. fooleries, 1. 3. 18.

Φοβερός, ά, όν (φόβος), causing fear, dreadful, frightful, 5. 5. 17; ὄχλος, ἐρημία, 2. 5. 9; νύξ, 5. 2. 23; νάπος, 6. 3. 19; ὡς φοβερώτατον τοῖς πολεμίοις, as dreadful a thing as possible for the enemy, 3. 4. 5; φοβεροὶ ἦσαν μή, they excited fear lest, 5. 7. 2.

Φοβέω, ήσω, &c. (φόβος), to frighten, τοὺς πολεμίους, 4. 5. 17; Mid. to be afraid, fear, dread, περὶ πόλεως, 5. 5. 7; τιμωρίαν, 2. 6. 14; ὡς ἐνεέραν οὖσαν, 5. 2. 30; τὸ στράτευμα μὴ στρατεύηται, 7. 1. 2; τὸ ἀπεχθάνεσθαι, 2. 6. 19; ἔπεσθαι, 1. 3. 17.

Φόβος, ου, ὁ (φέβομαι), fear, ὁ ἐκ τῶν Ἑλλήνων εἰς τοὺς βαρβάρους φόβος, the fear which the Greeks excited among the barbarians, 1. 2. 18; φ. ἀπὸ

Λακεδαιμονίων ᾖ, if something to deter us should arise from the L., 7. 2. 37; τῶν βαρβάρων φόβος πολὺς καὶ ἄλλοις, and the rest of the barbarians were much afraid, 1. 2. 18; φόβος ἐστί τινι στρατεύειν, 2. 4. 3; φ. κενός, 2. 2. 21; ἐμπίπτει 2. 2. 19; ἐντίθεναι, 7. 4. 1; παρέχειν τινὶ τοῦ στρατεῦσαι, 3. 1. 18; ποιεῖν, 1. 8. 18; προσάγειν, 4. 1. 23.

Φοινίκεος=φοινικοῦς.

Φοινίκη, ης, ἡ, Phœnicia, a district in Syria, 7. 8. 25.

Φοινίκιος, α, ον (φοῖνιξ), red, purple, 1. 2. 16.

Φοινικιστής, οῦ, ὁ (φοῖνιξ), a wearer of purple, a nobleman of high rank. Zonaras makes it a dyer of purple, Larcher the bearer of the purple standard, 1. 2. 21.

Φοινικοῦς, ῆ, οῦν (φοῖνιξ), purple, red, 1. 2. 16.

Φοῖνιξ, ικος, ὁ, the palm-tree, date-palm, 2. 3. 10; αἱ βάλανοι τῶν φ., 2. 3. 15; οἶνος ἐκ, 1. 5. 10, 2. 3. 14; see ἐγκέφαλος; also a Phœnician, also purple.

Φολόη, ης, ἡ, Pholoë, a mountain between Arcadia and Elis, 5. 3. 10.

Φορέω, ήσω, &c. (φέρω), to carry, wear, ξύλα, 5. 2. 26; στρεπτόν, 1. 8. 29; ἀλωπεκίδας ἐπὶ ταῖς κεφαλαῖς, 7. 4. 4.

Φόρος, ου, ὁ (φέρω), tribute= δασμός, 5. 5. 7. .

Φορτίον, ου, τό (φορέω), a burden, load, 5. 2. 21, 7. 1. 37.

Φράζω, φράσω, πέφρακα, πέφρασμαι, to tell, say, 6. 4. 20; syn. εἰπεῖν, 5. 1. 8; φράζουσιν ἅ λέγει, 2. 4. 18; ὁδόν, 4. 5. 34; οἶνον ἔνθα ἦν, 4. 5. 29; ὅτι, 7. 8. 9; τινί τι, 2. 3. 3; τοῖς ἱππεῦσιν ὑποδέχεσθαι αὑτόν, 1. 6. 3.

Φρασίας, ου, ὁ (φράζω), *Phrasias*, an Athenian, 6. 3. 11.

Φρέαρ, ᾱτος, τό, *a well*, 4. 5. 25.

Φρονέω, ήσω, &c. (φρήν), *to think of*, οἷα δεῖ, 2. 2. 5; μέγα, *to be in high spirits*, 3. 1. 27; μεῖζον, *to have higher notions*, 5. 6. 8; πλέον, *to have superior wisdom*, 6. 1. 18.

Φρόνημα, ατος, τό (φρονέω), *confidence*, 3. 1. 22; πάτριον, *the spirit of our fathers*, 3. 2. 16.

Φρόνιμος, ος, ον (φρονέω), *prudent, sensible*, 1. 10. 7, 2. 6. 7, 2. 5. 16.

Φροντίζω, φροντίσω or ιῶ, πεφρόντικα, πεφρόντισμαι (φρήν), *to think, consider*, ὅπως ἕξει, 2. 6. 8; *to be anxious*, 2. 3. 25.

Φρουρά, ᾶς, ἡ (πρό, ὁράω), *a guard*, 1. 4. 15.

Φρούραρχος, ου, ὁ (φρουρά, ἄρχω), *the commander of a guard*, 1. 1. 6.

Φρουρέω, ήσω (φρουρά), *to keep watch, guard*, 1. 4. 8, 5. 5. 20.

Φρούριον, ου, τό (φρουρά), *a guard*, 1. 4. 15.

Φρουρός, οῦ, ὁ (πρό, ὁράω), *a guard*, 7. 1. 20.

Φρύγανον, ου, τό (φρύγω, *to roast*), *a dry stick, fagot*, 4. 3. 11.

Φρυγία, ας, ἡ, *Phrygia*, a district in Asia Minor, 5. 6. 24.

Φρυνίσκος, ου, ὁ, *Phryniscus*, an Achæan, 7. 2. 1, 29, 5. 10.

Φρύξ, Φρυγός, ὁ, *a Phrygian*.

Φυγάς, άδος, ὁ (φεύγω), *an exile*, 1. 1. 9, &c.

Φυγή, ῆς, ἡ (φεύγω), *flight*, 3. 2. 17, 4. 2. 12; *banishment*, 7. 7. 57.

Φυλᾰκή, ῆς, ἡ (φυλάσσω), *watch, guard, supervision*, ἐν φυλακῇ ἔχειν, 4. 5. 29, 5. 8. 1; φυλακὰς φυλάττειν, *to keep watch*, 2. 6. 10; ποιεῖν, 5. 7. 31; ποιεῖσθαι, 6. 1. 21; καθιστάναι, 4. 5. 21; *the guard*, 2. 4. 17, 23, 3. 1. 40, 4. 2. 14; *a watch of the night*—the Greeks had *three watches*, the Romans *four*, Lat. *excubiæ*, 4. 1. 5; *a being on one's guard*, πρὸς φίλους, *against friends*, 7. 6. 22; Lat. *cautio*.

Φύλαξ, ᾰκος, ὁ, *a guard*, 4. 2. 5, 6, 5. 1. 9, 16, 6. 2. 27, 4. 4. 19, 6. 3. 4; *a body-guard*, 1. 2. 12.

Φυλάσσω or φυλάττω, άξω, πεφύλαχα, πεφύλαγμαι, *to guard*; Mid. *to be on one's guard*, τινά, 4. 6. 1, 6. 1. 11; *to act as guard*, 1. 2. 22, 4. 5, 5. 4. 26; τὰς ἀκροπόλεις, 1. 2. 1, 4. 4; εἰσβολήν, 1. 2. 21, 4. 1. 20, 2. 1; στρατόπεδον, 5. 2. 1; *to watch*, 4. 6. 11; *to keep*, τοῖς θεοῖς, 5. 3. 4; Mid. 2. 5. 37, 6. 24, 4. 7. 8; ἱκανοῖς φύλαξι, 6. 2. 27, 7. 2. 21; μὴ ὑμῖν ἐπιθῶνται, 2. 4. 16, 2. 16; ὥστε μὴ ληφθῆναι, 7. 3. 35; ὡς μή, 7. 6. 22; τινά, *against one*, 1. 6. 9, 2. 4. 10, 5. 3; βέλος, 7. 3. 33; πέτρους, 7. 7. 54.

Φυσάω, ήσω, &c. (φῦσα, *a bellows*), *to blow up*, 3. 5. 9.

Φύσκος, ου, ὁ, *the Physcus*, a river in Assyria, 2. 4. 25.

Φυτεύω, εύσω, &c. (φυτόν, φύω), to plant, 5. 3. 12.

Φύω, φύσω, πέφυκα, to produce, 1. 4. 10, pres. impf. fut. and 1 aor. are trans., but perf. plp. and 2 aor. ἔφυν are intrans.

Φωκαΐς, ίδος, ἡ, a woman of Phocæa, a town in Ionia; the name of the woman in 1. 10. 2, was Milto, so called from her red cheeks (μίλτος, red earth).

Φωνή, ῆς, ἡ (φάω, root of φημί), a sound, speech, 4. 8. 4.

Φῶς, φωτός, τό (φάω, to shine), a light, 3. 1. 12, 6. 1. 2; φώς, φωτός, a man, fr. φάω, φημί, φώς, φωδός, contr. for φωῖς (φώζω), a blister, φῶς, light, contr. for φάος fr. φάω, to shine, root of φαίνω.

X.

Χαίρω, χαιρήσω, κεχάρηκα, κεχάρημαι and κέχαρμαι, 2 aor. pass. ἐχάρην, to rejoice, be glad, Imp. χαῖρε, at meeting, Hail! Luke i. 28; Lat. Ave Maria; also at parting, Farewell, good-bye; Lat. vale; τὸ μὲν διαρρίπτειν εἴα χαίρειν, he bade the throwing about good-bye, gave it up, 7. 3. 23; χαίρων, with impunity, 5. 6. 32.

Χαλδαῖοι, ων, οἱ, the Chaldeans, south of the Carduchi on the Tigris, 4. 3. 4, &c.

Χαλεπαίνω, ανῶ, 1 aor. ἐχαλέπηνα, pass. ἐχαλεπάνθην, to be offended, to be angry, 1. 5. 11, 4. 5. 16; ὅτι, 1. 5. 14; τινί, with one, 1. 4. 12, 5. 8.

20, 7. 6. 39; τῷ Ἐκατωνύμῳ τοῖς εἰρημένοις, for what had been said, 5. 5. 24; χάρις ὧν ἐμοὶ χαλεπαίνετε, for τούτων ἅ, thanks for these things on account of which you are angry with me, 7. 6. 32, 4. 6. 2.

Χαλεπός, ή, όν, difficult, πορεία, 5. 6. 10, 4. 5. 3; πρόσοδοι, 5. 2. 3; χωρίον, 4. 8. 2, 5. 1. 17, 6. 3. 18; ταῦτα χ. ποιεῖν, 3. 4. 35; ἐχθρός, bitter, 1. 3. 12; κύνες, vicious, 5. 8. 24; harsh, 2. 6. 9; τὸ χ. τοῦ πνεύματος, the severity of the wind, 4. 5. 4, 2. 6. 11; τὰ χαλεπώτατα, the greatest hardships, 3. 1. 13; χ. διαβαίνειν, 5. 6. 9; ἀποκρίνεσθαι, 7. 7. 4; μένειν, 6. 4. 13, 7. 4. 14. Adv. χαλεπῶς φέρειν, to take it ill, be vexed, Lat. moleste ferre, 3. 4. 47; ἀναχωρεῖν, with difficulty, 3. 3. 13; ἔχειν=φέρειν, 6. 2. 16, 7. 5. 16.

Χαλινόω, ώσω (χαλινός, a bridle, χαλάω, to loosen), to bridle, 3. 4. 35.

Χάλκεος, α, ον (χαλκός), made of bronze or iron, πέλται, 5. 2. 29.

Χαλκηδών, see Καλχηδών.

Χαλκός, οῦ, ὁ (χαλάω, to loosen), iron or bronze, a mixture of copper and tin; brass, a mixture of copper and zinc, was unknown to the ancients, 1. 8. 8.

Χάλκωμα, ατος, τό, a copper vessel, 4. 1. 8.

Χάλος, ου, ὁ, the Chalus, a river in Syria, 1. 4. 9.

Χάλυψ, υβος, ὁ, Χάλυβες, οἱ, the Chalybes, a people in Pontus,

5. 5. 1, 4. 4. 18, 4. 7. 15, 7. 8. 25. As a com. n. steel, Eng. chalybeate.

Χαράδρα, ας, ἡ (χαράττω, to furrow), a gully, a ravine, 3. 4. 1, 5, 4. 2. 3, 5. 2. 3, 4.

Χαράκωμα, ατος, τό (χάραξ, χαράσσω), a palisade, 5. 2. 26.

Χαρίεις, εσσα, εν (χάρις), graceful, elegant, pleasing, ἐνθύμημα, a clever contrivance, 3. 5. 12.

Χαρίζομαι, ίσομαι and ιοῦμαι, κεχάρισμαι (χάρις), to oblige, gratify, favour, τινί, 2. 3. 19, 7. 6. 2; τῷ θυμῷ, 7. 1. 25; τινί τι, 2. 1. 10, 5. 3. 6, 7. 7. 10.

Χάρις, ιτος, ἡ, thanks, τοῖς θεοῖς, sc. ἔστω, 3. 3. 14; χάριν εἰδέναι τινί, 1. 4. 15, to feel grateful to one, τινός, for anything, 7. 6. 32; so also ἔχειν τινί, 2. 5. 14, 5. 9. 26; ἀποδιδόναι, to return a favour, χάριν εἴσεται καὶ ἀποδώσει, 1. 4. 15.

Χαρμάνδη, ης, ἡ, Charmande, a large town on the Euphrates, 1. 5. 10.

Χαρμῖνος, ου, ὁ, Charminus, a Spartan, 7. 6. 1.

Χειμών, ῶνος, ὁ (χέω, to pour), winter, 7. 3. 13, 6. 9; cold, 1. 7. 6, 5. 8. 3; ἰσχυρός, 5. 8. 14; πολύς, 4. 1. 15; a storm, 5. 8. 20.

Χείρ χειρός, ἡ, dat. du. χεροῖν, pl. χερσί, a hand, 1. 8. 24; δεξιά, 1. 10. 1, 3. 1. 17, &c.; εἰς χεῖρας ἔρχεσθαι, ἰέναι, 1. 2. 26, 4. 7. 15; δέχεσθαι, 4. 3. 31.

Χειρίσυφος, ου, ὁ (χείρ, σοφός), Cheirisophus, a Spartan general, 1. 4. 3, 2. 1. 5, &c.

Χειροπληθής, ής, ές (χείρ, πίμπλημι), hand-filling, as large as can be held in the hand, λίθος, 3. 3. 17.

Χειροποίητος, ος, ον (χείρ, ποιέω), made by hand, artificial, ὁδός, 4. 3. 5.

Χειρόω, ώσω, usually χειρόομαι, χειροῦμαι, χειρώσομαι, κεχείρωμαι (χείρ), to subdue, 7. 3. 11.

Χείρων, ων, ον (χείρ), gen. χείρονος, comp. of κακός, worse, χεῖρόν ἐστιν αὐτῷ, 7. 6. 4, 39, 5. 2. 13.

Χερσόνησος, ου, ἡ, or Χερρ. (χέρσος, land, νῆσος, an island), the Chersonese, in Xen. the Thracian, ἡ Θρᾳκία or Θρᾳκινή, καταντιπέρας Ἀβύδου, 1. 1. 9, &c.

Χηλή, ῆς, ἡ (χάω, χαίνω), a hoof, the pier or breakwater, 7. 1. 17.

Χήν, χηνός, ὁ and ἡ (χαίνω), a goose, 1. 9. 26.

Χθές, an adv., yesterday, sometimes ἐχθές, 6. 2. 18.

Χίλιοι, αι, α (χέω), a thousand, 1. 2. 3, &c.

Χιλός, οῦ, ὁ (χέω), fodder, grass, ξηρός, hay, 4. 5. 33, 1. 5. 7, &c.

Χιλόω, ώσω (χιλός), to put out to pasture, 7. 2. 21.

Χίμαιρα, ας, ἡ, a she-goat, 3. 2. 12.

Χῖος, α, ον, Chian, from Chios, an island in the Ægæan Sea.

Χιτών, ῶνος, ὁ, an under garment, coat, Lat. tunica, 5. 2. 15; περὶ τοῖς μηροῖς, 7. 4. 4, 1. 5. 8.

Χιτωνίσκος, ου, ὁ, dim. of χιτών, a short tunic, 5. 4. 13.

Χιών, όνος, ἡ (χίω, χέω), snow, 4. 4. 8, &c.

Χλαμύς, ύϊος, ἡ, a cloak, 7. 4. 4.

Χοῖνιξ, ῖκος, ἡ, a chœnix=(1·92) two pints or one quart, 1. 5. 6.

Χοίρειος, α, ον (χοῖρος), swine's, κρέα, 4. 5. 31.

Χοῖρος, ου, ὁ, a swine, hog, pig, 7. 8. 5.

Χορεύω, εύσω, κεχόρευκα, ευμαι (χορός), to dance, 4. 7. 16, 5. 4. 17.

Χορός, οῦ, ὁ, a dance, a troop of dancers, 5. 4. 12.

Χόρτος, ου, ὁ, fodder, provender, grass, 1. 5. 5; κοῦφος, hay, 1. 5. 10.

Χράομαι, χρήσομαι, κέχρημαι, 1 aor. pass. ἐχρήσθην, to use, gov. dat., 1. 9. 17; χρίσματι, 4. 4. 13; τί βούλεται ἡμῖν χρῆσθαι, in what service he wishes to employ us, 1. 3. 18, 1. 9. 18, 4. 1. 22; to find, 4. 6. 3, 2. 6. 13, 4. 6. 13; αὐτῷ, to use one's services, 2. 6. 27; to treat, 5. 7. 5; σοὶ φίλῳ, as a friend, 7. 2. 25, 2. 6. 25; οὐκ οἶδα ὅ,τι ἄν τις χρήσαιτο αὐτοῖς, I do not know in what service one could employ them, 3. 1. 40, 6. 4. 20.

Χρή, χρήσει, ἔχρησε, Imp. it is necessary, it behoves, 1. 3. 11, 2. 1. 2, 16, 7. 5. 9, 6. 13; ὑμᾶς χρὴ διαβῆναι, 1. 4. 14.

Χρῄζω, χρήσω, to want, wish, ask, 3. 4. 41; with Inf. 1. 3. 20, 8. 22, 2. 5. 2, 4. 8. 5, 5. 5. 2, 7. 17.

Χρῆμα, ατος, τό (χράομαι), a thing, that which may be used or exchanged, pl. property, τὰ χ. ἐκ τῶν ἀγρῶν συνῆγον, 5. 10. 8, 2. 4. 27, 5. 2. 4, 7. 8. 11; cargoes, γαυλικῶν, 5. 8. 1; money, 1. 2. 27, 4. 12, 5.

6. 15, 6. 2. 8, 7. 1. 27; τῆς μισθοφορᾶς, 5. 6. 35.

Χρηματιστικός, ή, όν (χρῆμα), fitted for money-making, οἰωνός, an omen portending gain, 5. 9. 23.

Χρήσιμος, ος, ον and η, ον (χράομαι), useful, 1. 6. 1; τοξεύματα, 3. 4. 17; Κρῆτες, 4. 2. 28, 5. 6. 1, 2. 5. 23.

Χρῖσμα, ατος, τό (χρίω), ointment, unguent, oil, σύειον, hog's lard, 4. 4. 13, Eng. chrism.

Χρίω, χρίσω, κέχρισμαι and κέχριμαι, to anoint, 4. 4. 12; Χριστός, Christ, the anointed.

Χρόνος, ου, ὁ, time, 7. 7. 47, 5. 8. 1; πολλοῦ χρόνου, for a long time, 1. 9. 25; ἡμίσει χρόνῳ, in half the time, 1. 8. 22; χ. τινα, some time, 3. 4. 36; τὸν πάντα χρόνον, 7. 8. 19, 3. 4. 12; χρόνῳ συχνῷ, a considerable time, 1. 8. 8.

Χρύσεος, α, ον, contr. χρυσοῦς, ῆ, οῦν (χρυσός), golden, 1. 2. 27, 5. 3. 12.

Χρυσίον, ου, τό (χρυσός), gold (money), 1. 1. 9, 7. 8. 1.

Χρυσόπολις, εως ἡ, Chrysopolis (golden city), a town in Bithynia on the Bosphorus, 7. 1. 1.

Χρυσός, οῦ, ὁ (perhaps χράομαι, cf. χρήματα), gold, 3. 1. 19.

Χρυσόχαλινος, ος, ον (χρυσοῦς, χαλινός), with gold-studded bridle, 1. 2. 27.

Χώρα, ας, ἡ, a country, district, territory, land, 1. 7. 4, 5. 6. 25, 3. 2. 23, 4. 8. 22, &c.; pl. 1. 9, 14; place, position, 1. 8. 17; ἐκ τῆς χ. ὁρμᾶν, 3. 4. 33; ἐν ταῖς χώραις ἕκαστοι ἐγένοντο, 4. 8. 15; κατὰ χ. ἀπιέναι, to return

to the same order as, &c., 6.
2. 11; τίθεσθαι τὰ ὅπλα, 1. 5.
17; ἐν οὐδεμιᾷ χ. εἶναι, to
have no place, be in no esteem,
Lat. nullo loco haberi, 5. 7.
28; ἐν ἀνδραπόδων χ., to pass,
be regarded, as slaves, 5. 6.13.

Χωρέω, ήσω, κεχώρηκα (χώρα), to
go, proceed, march, 2. 4. 10,
4. 7. 11, 1. 10. 13, 5. 4. 26;
ἐπί τινα, 4. 2. 15; τὰ τοξεύματα ἐχώρει διὰ τῶν ἀσπίδων,
4. 2. 28; to contain, ἡ δὲ
καπίθη δύο χοίνικας ἐχώρει,
1. 5. 6.

Χωρίζω, ίσω, Att. ιῶ, κεχώρισμαι
(χωρίς), to separate, set apart,
with Inf. 6. 3. 11; κεχωρισ-
μένοι τῶν, differed from, 5. 4.
34.

Χωρίον, ου, τό (χώρα), a place,
4. 7. 6; στενόν, 4. 1. 16;
ὀχυρόν, 1. 2. 24; a post, fort,
ἐπιθαλάττιον, 5. 5. 23; ἐρυμ-
νόν, 5. 5. 2; ἰσχυρόν, 4. 7. 1;
τετειχισμένον, 7. 2. 36; ἐπί-
μαχον, 5. 4. 14; ἁλώσιμον, 5.
2. 3, and applied to towns, 1.
4. 6, 5. 4. 31, 16, 23, 26, 27,
30.

Χωρίς, adv. apart, τῶν ἄλλων, 1.
4. 13, 6. 4. 2, 3. 5. 17.

Χῶρος, ου, ὁ (χάω, χανδάνω), a
place, enclosure, 5. 3. 11, 13,
κατὰ τοὺς χώρους, up and
down the country, 7. 2. 3.

Ψ.

Ψέγω, ψέξω (ψέω, ψύω, to touch),
to blame, disparage, τινά, 7.
7. 43.

Ψέλιον, ου, τό (ψέω), a bracelet,
Lat. armilla, 1. 2. 27, 8. 29;
· περὶ ταῖς χερσίν, 1. 5. 8.

Ψευδενέδρα, ας, ἡ (ψευδής, ἐνέδρα), a false, sham ambus-
cade, Lat. insidiæ simulatæ,
5. 2. 28.

Ψευδής, ής, ές, false, 2. 4. 24.

Ψεύδω, ψεύσω, ἔψευσμαι, to deceive, Mid. to lie, report falsely, deceive, ἐψεύσθη τοῦτο, 1.
8. 11, 2. 2. 13, 3. 2. 31;
Mid. μηδέν, 1. 9. 7; πάντα
ἐψευσμένος αὐτόν, 1. 3. 10;
χρήματα, they played false as
to the money, 5. 6. 35; περὶ
αὐτοῦ, to speak falsely concern-
ing him, 2. 6. 28; περὶ τοῦ
μισθοῦ, 7. 6. 15; πρὸς ἐκεῖνον
ψεύσασθαι, 1. 3. 5, to prove
false to him.

Ψηφίζω, ίσω, ἐψήφισμαι (ψῆφος),
to reckon with pebbles; Mid.
to vote, resolve, determine on,
ταῦτα, 7. 6. 14, 3. 2. 33; εἴθ'
ὑμᾶς προσῆκεν ἀπιέναι, 7. 7.
18; ἔπεσθαι, 1. 4. 15, 3. 2. 31,
5. 6. 11; πλεῖν αὐτόν, 5. 1. 4,
5. 10. 12.

Ψῆφος, ου, ἡ (ψάω), a pebble for
voting, 5. 8. 21; ψ. ἐπῆκτο
αὐτῷ περὶ φυγῆς, a vote of
banishment had been passed
against him; ψ. ἐπάγειν, to
put to the vote, 7. 7. 57.

Ψιλός, ή, όν (ψίω), bare of vege-
tation, χώρα, 1. 5. 5; bare,
without a helmet on, 1. 8. 6;
lightly armed, 3. 3. 7, 5. 2.
16.

Ψιλόω, ώσω, ἐψίλωμαι (ψιλός),
to strip, clear, ἐψιλοῦτο ὁ λόφος
τῶν ἱππέων, 1. 10. 13.

Ψιττάκη, see Σιττάκη.

Ψοφέω, ήσω (ψόφος), to make
a noise, ring, clash, 4. 3.
29.

Ψόφος, ου, ὁ, noise, 4. 2. 4.

Ψυχή, ῆς, ἡ, soul, 3. 1. 23, 2.

20; ἐκ τῆς ψυχῆς φίλος, *from the heart*, 7. 7. 43.

Ψῦχος, εος contr. ους, τό, *cold*, pl. 3. 1. 23.

Ω.

'Ω, sign of the voc.

'Ωδε, adv. (ὅς, ὅδε), *thus, as follows*, 1. 5. 10, 5. 4. 12; εἶπεν ὧδε, 2. 1. 18, 5. 1. 3, 7. 2. 32; ὧδε εἶπεν, 5. 6. 3; λέγει ὧδε, 1. 5. 15, 3. 3. 1, 5. 7. 4, 3. 1. 34, 27, 2. 1. 4, 4. 6. 7, 5. 1. 2, 5, 7. 6. 10, &c; ὧδέ πως, 1. 7. 9.

'Ωιδή, ῷδή, ῆς, ἡ (ᾄδω), *a song*, ῷδὰς ᾄδειν, 4. 3. 27.

Ωδοπεποιημένος, see ὁδοποιέω, 5. 3. 1.

'Ωθέω, ἤσω or ὤσω, ἔωκα, ἔωσμαι, impf. ἐώθουν, 1 aor. ἔωσα (ὤθω), *to push, thrust*, 5. 2. 18, 3. 4. 48.

'Ωθισμός, οῦ, ὁ (ὠθέω), *a pushing, justling, struggling*, 5. 2. 17.

'Ωμηβύειος, ος, ον, or α, ον, or ὠμοβόϊνος, η ον (ὠμός, βοῦς), *of raw ox-hide*, 4. 7. 22, 26, 7. 3. 32.

'Ωμός, ή, όν, *raw*, ὠμοὺς δεῖ καταφαγεῖν, *we must eat them up raw*, borrowed fr. Il. 4. 35, ὠμὸν βεβρώθοις Πρίαμον Πριάμοιό τε παῖδας, 4. 8. 14, by Hyperbole for *to destroy utterly*; 2. 6. 12, *harsh*.

Ωμος, ον, ὁ (ὁμός, ὁμοῦ, *together*, Lat. *humerus*), *the shoulder*, 6. 3. 25.

'Ωνέομαι, ἤσομαι, ἐώνημαι, 1 aor. ἐωνησάμην (ὦνος, *a price*), *to buy*, 7. 2. 38; ὠνουμένους ζῆν, 7. 3. 13, 2. 3. 27, 5. 5. 14;

χωρίον τῇ θεῷ, 5. 3. 7 (οὐκ ἔστιν) ὅτου ὠνησόμεθα, 5. 1. 6.

"Ωνιος, α, ον (ὦνος), *to be bought, for sale*, Lat. *venalis*, τὰ ὤ., *commodities, market-wares*, 1. 2. 18.

'Ωπις, ιδος, ἡ, *Opis*, a town at the junction of the Physcus with the Tigris, 2. 4. 25.

'Ωρα, ας, ἡ, *a season*, a part of the year, 1. 4. 10, 2. 3. 13; *an hour*, a part of the day, 4. 8. 21; generally, *time*, ὤ. λέγειν (ἐστί), 1. 3. 12, 3. 2. 32, 4. 40, 4. 6. 7; ἀπιέναι, 3. 4. 34, 4. 6. 16, 1. 3. 11; ὁπηνίκα καὶ δοκοίη τῆς ὥρας, *whenever, then, it should seem to be time*, 3. 5. 18.

'Ωραῖος, α, ον (ὥρα), *in the bloom of youth*, 2. 6. 28.

"Ως (ὅς), for οὕτως, *thus*, in οὐδ' ὥς, *not even thus*, 1. 8. 21, 3. 2. 23, 6. 2. 22.

'Ως, as, Lat. *ut*, with vbs. ὡς ὁμολογεῖται, 1. 9. 1; ὡς αὐτὸς σὺ ὁμολογεῖς, 1. 6. 7, 10. 18, 4. 5, 7; τὴν κρίσιν ὡς ἐγένετο, *the trial how it was, how the trial took place, was conducted*, 1. 6. 5; ὡς ἐδυνάμην, 5. 8. 25; ὡς ἂν δυνώμεθα ἀσινέστατα, 3. 3. 3; ὡς οἵόν τε, 2. 4. 24. With subst. and adj., ὡς φίλιον, 1. 6. 3; ὡς πολεμίους, 2. 5. 3; ὡς φίλον, 1. 1. 2, 3. 3. 2; ὡς λινοῦ, 5. 4. 13; ὡς μικρός, 5. 3. 12. With Part., ὡς γιγνώσκων, 5. 6. 29, 4. 2. 5, 1. 4. 7, 1. 1. 11, 1. 2. 1, &c.; with ἄν, ὡς μένοντας ἄν, *as likely to remain*, 7. 7. 30. With Fut. *in order to*, ὡς μαχούμενοι, 7. 8. 16, 1. 10; πολεμήσων, 1. 1.

11, 3, 2. 6. 2, 4. 3. 12, &c.
With Gen. Abs. ὡς εὖ εἰπόν-
τος αὐτοῦ, since he had spoken
well, 5. 9. 30, 6. 3, 7. 1. 19;
ὡς πολέμου ὄντος, that there is
war, 2. 1. 21; ὡς ἐπιβουλεύον-
τος, as though he were plotting,
1.1.6; ὡς ἐφεψομένης δυνάμεως,
as a force was going to follow,
3. 4. 3, 1. 10. 6; ὡς ἡγεμόνος
ἐσομένου, as there was to be a
guide, 6. 2. 23. With Acc.
Abs. that, ὡς οὐδὲν δέον, 6. 2.
22; δεῆσον, 5. 2. 12, 1. 3. 15.
With Prep., ὡς εἰς μάχην, as if
for battle, 1. 8. 1; πόλεμον,
1. 9. 23; ὡς ἐπὶ τούτους, as if
against them, 1. 2. 1, 7. 1. 37;
ὡς ἐπὶ πῦρ, as if for a fire, 4.
3. 11; μείζων ἢ ὡς ἐπί, too
great to be intended for, 1. 2.
4; ὡς πρὸς τὴν ἔκβασιν, 4. 3.
21, 5. 9. 9.
I. With numbers about, Lat.
circiter, 1. 6. 1, 7. 16, 3. 3. 6,
&c.; ὡς ἐπὶ τὸ πολύ, for the
most part, in general, 3.1. 42,
4. 35.
II. With Superl. Lat. qvam,
μέγιστος, as great as possible,
2. 5. 14; ἀσφαλέστατα, 1. 3.
11, 3. 2. 27; τάχιστα, 1. 3.
14, 6. 9, 5. 1. 4; ῥᾷστα, 4.
6. 10; κράτιστα, 4. 6. 15.
With the Pos. how, ὡς ἄβατα,
4. 1. 20; ἀθύμως, 3. 1. 40.
III. Inasmuch as, since, 2.
4. 17, 5. 8. 10, 9. 30, 32.
IV. That, Lat. acc. and inf.,
λέγειν ὡς, 2. 1. 14, 4. 2.17, 6.
2. 14; ἐπεῖ, 1. 3. 5, 4. 8; with
opt. ὡς δέοι, 2. 6. 10, 5. 6. 34,
7. 7. 44, 1. 1. 3.
V. In order that, Lat. ut,
with Conj. after a Pres. 4. 6.

15, 2. 4. 4, 3. 1. 35, &c.;
ὡς μή, 2. 4.17; with ἄν, 2.
5. 16; after a historical tense,
1. 9. 27; with Opt. 1. 3. 14,
9. 21, 28, 5. 7. 18, 7. 6. 16;
ὡς μή, 6. 3. 30, &c.; with Inf.
ὡς συνελόντι εἰπεῖν, 3. 1. 38.
VI. With Inf. so as to, 1. 8.
15; ὡς μή, 1. 5. 10, 2. 3. 10,
3. 5. 7, 4. 3. 29, 6. 13, 5.
6. 12; βραχύτερα ἢ ὡς ἐξι-
κνεῖσθαι, too short to reach, 3.
3. 7.
VII. A Prep. Lat. ad, gov.
acc. with a person only, 1. 2.
4, 2. 3. 29, 6. 1.
Ὡσαύτως (ὡς, αὔτως), strengthened for ὡς, in like manner,
just so, 3. 2. 23, 4. 7. 13, 5.
6. 9.
Ὥσπερ (ὡς, περ), as if, ὀργῇ, 1.
5. 8, 2. 6. 12, 7. 3. 10; οὕτως
ὥσπερ, so as, just as, 7. 2. 27;
ὁμοίως ὥσπερ, just as if, 6. 3.
31; ὥσπερ βοῦν, just like, 4.
5. 32, 7. 3. 10, 1. 4. 12, 1. 8.
8, 10. 10; ὥσπερ ἐξόν, just
as if we were at liberty, 3. 1.
14; ὥσπερ δή, as indeed, 3. 1.
29, 7. 4. 17.
Ὥστε (ὡς, τε), so that, with Ind.
almost=wherefore, 1. 3. 10,
5. 5. 10; Fut. 5. 4. 20;
Impf. 2. 3. 25, 4. 2, 6. 12, 3.
5. 13, 4. 26, 48, &c.; Aor. 4.
5. 4, 5. 2. 15, 6. 27; with
οὐ and Pres. 1. 7. 7, 9. 28,
3. 1. 40; Impf. 2. 6. 11; Aor.
2. 2. 17, 3. 4. 37; with Opt.
and ἄν, 5. 6. 20; with Inf. 1.
4. 8, 6. 2, 7. 4. 12; with μή,
3. 3. 14, 4. 21; ἄν, 5. 9. 31;
on condition that, 5. 6. 26.
Ὠτειλή, ῆς, ἡ (οὐτάω), a wound,
1. 9. 6, a scar, Lat. cicatrix.

'Ωτίς, ίδος, ἡ (οὖς), a bustard, so
called from its long ear-
feathers, 1. 5. 2, 3.
Ὤφελεν, see ὀφείλω.
'Ωφελέω, ήσω, ηκα (ὄφελος), to
aid, benefit, τινά, 1. 1. 9, 3. 4;
τινά τι, 5. 6. 30; ὠφελοῦντες
ὠφελοῦνται, they who benefit
are benefited, 5. 1. 12.
'Ωφέλιμος, η, ον, and ος, ον (ὠφε-
λέω), useful, serviceable, profitable, 1. 6. 2, 4. 1. 23.

MONEY.

½ obol (ἡμιοβόλιον)=¾d., symbol) or ((1. 5. 6.).
1 obol (ὀβολός)=6½ far., symbol O (1. 5. 6.).
1 drachma (δραχμή) = 6 obols = 9¾d., the Roman *denarius*.
1 daric (δαρεικός)=20 Attic silver drachmæ=16s. 3d. (Hussey, 21s.).
1 mina (μνᾶ)=100 drachmæ=4l. 1s. 3d.
1 talent (τάλαντον)=60 minæ=243l. 15s.
1 cyzicene (κυζικηνός) = 28 drachmæ=1l. 2s. 9d.
1 siglus (σίγλος)=7½ obols, about a shilling (1. 5. 6).

------

6 obols=1 drachma.
100 drachmæ=1 mina.
60 minæ=1 talent.

LENGTH.

1 foot (πούς)=12·135 inches.
1 cubit (πῆχυς)=1½ ft.
1 fathom (ὀργυιά)=6 ft.
1 plethron (πλέθρον)=100 Grk. ft., or 101 Eng. ft.
1 stadium (στάδιον)=6 plethra=606 Eng. ft.
1 parasang (παρασάγγης)=30 stadia=18,180 ft., nearly 3½ miles.

------

100 feet=1 plethron.
6 plethra=1 stadium.
30 stadia=1 parasang.

DRY AND LIQUID MEASURE.

1 cyathus (κύαθος)=¹⁄₁₂ pint.
1 sextarius (ξέστης)=12 cyathi=1 pint.
1 chœnix (χοῖνιξ)=24 cyathi=2 pints.
1 capitha (καπίθη)=2 chœnices=4 pints.
1 modius (ἕκτος)=8 chœnices=2 gallons or a peck.
1 medimnus (μέδιμνος)=6 modii=12 gallons, or 1½ bushels.

------

12 cyathi=1 sextarius.
2 sextarii=1 chœnix.
2 chœnices=1 capitha.
4 capithæ=1 modius.
6 modii=1 medimnus.

KINGS OF PERSIA.

	B.C.		B.C.
Cyrus the Elder	r. 559–529	Darius Nothus	r. 424–405
Cambyses	529–522	Artaxerxes Mnemon	405–359
Darius Hystaspes	521–485	Artaxerxes Ochus	359–338
Xerxes	485–465	Darius Codomannus	336–331
ArtaxerxesLongimanus	464–425		

CONSTITUTION OF THE GREEK ARMY.

The Greek army was divided into 6 μόραι, each μόρα into 4 λόχοι, each λόχυς into 2 πεντηκοστύες, and each πεντηκοστύς into 2 ἐνωμορίαι; so that, if the πεντηκοστύς contained 50 men, as the name implies, there would be 25 men in each ἐνωμορία, 100 men in each λόχυς, 400 men in each μόρα, and 2,400 men would constitute an army. Thus:—

⎧ ἐνωμοτάρχης	ἐνωμορία					=	25 men
πεντηκοστήρ	2	πεντηκοστύς				=	50 „
Officers. ⎨ λοχᾱγύς	4	2	λόχυς			=	100 „
μορᾱγύς	16	8	4	μόρα		=	400 „
⎩ στρατηγύς	96	48	24	6	στράτευμα	=	2,400 „

The term τάξις is sometimes used by Greek writers. In Athens it signified the men of the tribe (φυλή), and as there were ten tribes there were ten τάξεις. Ordinarily, the τάξις contained 2 λόχοι, and the commander was called ταξίαρχος. The cavalry (ἱππεῖς) were arranged in troops (φυλαί, εἶλαι or ἴλαι), each containing 64 men, usually arranged 16 in front and 4 deep. The officers were 2 ἵππαρχοι and 10 φύλαρχοι. The chief weapons of the cavalry were long lances and swords. The horses had for defensive armour προμετωπίδια for the head, προστερνίδια for the breast, and παραπλευρίδια for the sides.

The marching order of the ἐνωμορία was usually 4 men in front, and 6 deep, and the officer alongside, making 25 in all. When there were more men in depth than in front, the men were said to be drawn up *in column*, ὄρθιοι λόχοι, *recti ordines*. Hence, ὀρθίους τοὺς λόχους ποιεῖσθαι, *to throw the battalions into column*; ἄγειν, *to bring them up in column*, 4. 3. 17, 4. 2. 11; ἐπὶ κέρως or κατὰ κέρας πορεύεσθαι, *to march in column*; so κατὰ κέρας ἄγειν, also ὀρθία φάλαγξ, ὀρθία ἐπαγωγή, Lat. *longum agmen.* The van was called κέρας τὸ ἡγούμενον or οἱ ἡγούμενοι ; the rear, οὐρά, and the rear-guard, ὀπισθοφύλακες. When the troops were drawn up *in line,* i.e. in battle array, they were said to be ἐπὶ φάλαγγος, when there were more men in front than in depth. This was fighting order. A hollow square was πλαίσιον; an oblong, πλίνθιον ; a circle, κύκλος (7. 8. 16).

The Ordinary Pay

of a hoplite was 4 obols, or sixpence, a day. Officers received twice as much, horsemen three times as much, and generals four times as much (7. 6. 1, 3. 10).

The Heavy-armed Soldiers

were called ὁπλῖται, from ὅπλα, *arms, armour,* because they carried heavy weapons and wore defensive armour. Their uniform was scarlet. They wore :—1. Greaves, κνημῖδες, *ocreæ,* to protect the front of the leg from the knee to the ancle. These were usually made of metal, and lined inside with leather, felt, or cloth. 2. A cuirass, θώραξ, *lorica,* to protect the breast. It was usually made of metal and richly ornamented. On the lower edge were fastened straps of leather (πτέρυγες) covered with small bits of metal, or a fringe of twisted ropes (4. 7. 15), to protect the lower part of the body. The girdle, ζωστήρ, and the belt, μίτρα, also contributed to protect this part (Hom. *Il.* 4. 132–137). 3. The long sword, ξίφος, *gladius, ensis,* or the short sword, μάχαιρα, ξυήλη. 4. The shield, ἀσπίς, *clypeus,* large and round, or θυρεός, *scutum,* oblong. 5. The helmet, κόρυς, κόρυθος (κάρα, τίθημι), or κράνος, *galea.* 6. The spear, δόρυ, ἔγχος, *hasta.* It had a shaft, usually of ash, μελία, a point, αἰχμή, of iron, or rather bronze, χαλκός, and was altogether 7 or 8 ft. long. Each soldier usually had two.

The Light-armed Soldiers

were called ψιλοί, γυμνοί, γυμνῆται, γυμνῆτες. They had no shield or breastplate, and commonly fought (1) with javelins, and were called ἀκοντισταί; or (2) with slings, and were called σφενδονῆται; or (3) with bows and arrows, and were called τοξόται.

The Peltasts,

πελτασταί, were so called from wearing the small shield, πέλτη, *pelta.* They were not so heavily armed as the hoplites, ὁπλῖται, but were better armed than the γυμνῆται. Their chief weapon was the javelin, παλτόν, about 5 ft. long. It was commonly thrown by the hand by means of a thong, or strap of leather, ἀγκύλη, *amentum*, attached to the shaft. The lance, λόγχη, *lancea*, was slender, and the dart, ἄκων, ἀκόντιον, *spiculum*, *jaculum*, resembled the lance in form, but was smaller. It was usually made of cornel wood.

The Words of Command,

παραγγέλλειν, παρεγγυᾶν, ἀπὸ παραγγέλσεως, were given sometimes by the voice, sometimes by signal, σημαίνειν, and sometimes by sound of trumpet or horn by a herald, σαλπίζειν, κηρύσσειν (2. 2. 20, 5. 2. 18, 3. 1. 46, 3. 4. 36). The following were used in drill:—ἄνω τὰ δόρατα, '*present arms*'; κάθες τὰ δόρατα, '*ground arms*,' '*stand at ease*'; ἐπὶ δόρυ κλῖνον, '*right turn*'; ἐπ' ἀσπίδα κλῖνον, '*left turn*'; ἐπὶ δόρυ ἐπίστρεφε, '*right about turn*'; ἐπ' ἀσπίδα ἐπίστρεφε, '*left about turn*'; ἐπὶ δόρυ μεταβάλλου, '*right wheel*'; ἐπ' ἀσπίδα μεταβάλλου, '*left wheel*'; πρόαγε, '*march*,' '*forwards*'; ἄγε εἰς τὰ ὅπλα, παραστῆτε παρὰ τὰ ὅπλα, '*to arms*,' '*attention*.' Immediately before a battle the password, σύνθημα, *tessera*, was given by the general, and passed along the ranks from mouth to mouth. Among the Romans a small rectangular piece of wood, with the word inscribed on it, called *tessera*, was passed from hand to hand. At the battle of Cunaxa the password was Ζεὺς σωτὴρ καὶ νίκη (1. 8. 16). At the battle in Bithynia the word was Ζεὺς σωτὴρ, Ηρακλῆς ἡγεμών (6. 3. 25). A password was used at night also in presence of the enemy (7. 3. 34).

Marching.

When the soldiers were to march in the morning, or move their camp, κινεῖν τὸ στρατόπεδον (*castra movere*), the trumpet was sounded three times, τῷ κέρατι (σαλπιγκτὴς) ἐσήμηνε. On the first signal the soldiers had to pack up their baggage, συσκευάζειν or συσκενάζεσθαι; on the second signal they had to place the baggage on the beasts of burden, ἀνατιθέναι ἐπὶ τὰ ὑποζύγια; and on the third signal they began their march, or, as Xenophon says, they followed their leader, ἕπονται τῷ ἡγουμένῳ (2. 2. 4, 3. . 18).

The first halt took place usually between 10 and 11, for luncheon, καταλῦσαι τὸ στράτευμα πρὸς ἄριστον (1. 10. 19). After resting for an hour or two, the journey was continued until dinner, usually about 5 o'clock in the afternoon, when the day's march ended, στρατοπεδευώμεθα προελθόντες ὅσον ἂν δοκῇ καιρὸς εἶναι εἰς τὸ δειπνοποιεῖσθαι (6. 1. 14). The two chief meals were thus the ἄριστον and the δεῖπνον, luncheon and dinner, or better perhaps, like labourers in our own country, dinner in the middle of the day and supper at the close. Xenophon does not mention either breakfast, ἀκράτισμα, so called because it was simply bread dipped in unmixed (ἄκρᾱτος) wine, or supper, δόρπον. The dinner usually consisted of beef, mutton, or pork, roast or boiled, bread, wheaten or barley, and vegetables and wine. The luncheon, ἄμιστον, was a much more simple meal.

A day's march was usually five parasangs, or 17½ miles, sometimes 7 or 8, i.e. 24½ or 28 miles. Each encampment or halting place was called σταθμός, a station. The pace was probably the same as our own, 30 in. slow or quick time, and 33 in. double time. In slow time 75 paces are taken in a minute; in quick time 116, and in double time 165 paces are taken in a minute, or 3 miles 520 yards, and 5 miles 275 yards, in an hour.

Fighting.

Immediately before a battle the soldiers were drawn up in line, ἐπὶ φάλαγγος, εἰς μάχην ταχθῆναι, συντάσσεσθαι, παρατάσσεσθαι, and ἀντιπαρατάσσεσθαι (1. 7. 1, 1. 2. 15, 1. 3. 14). The usual depth of the line was 8 men; sometimes, however, it was more, ἐπὶ πολλούς, sometimes less, ἐπ' ὀλίγων (4. 8. 11). The whole line was divided into the centre, τὸ μέσον, the right wing, τὸ δεξιὸν κέρας, and the left wing, τὸ εὐώνυμον. The light-armed had no fixed place. Sometimes they were in front of the hoplites, sometimes behind, sometimes on one wing, sometimes on both wings (6. 5. 25). The cavalry were usually on the flanks. When the troops were arranged, the password, σύνθημα (1. 8. 16, 6. 3. 25), was given, and often the general gave an address to his soldiers, παρακαλεῖν (4. 8. 14). Vows were offered, εὐξαντο, and a hymn was sung, παιανίσαντες (4. 8. 16). The hoplites had their spears on their right shoulders, the peltasts took hold of the strap of their javelins, the archers bent their bows, and the slingers had their wallets, διφθέραι, full of stones. On approaching the opposing line, the hoplites and peltasts struck their spears against their shields (1. 8. 18, 4. 3. 29), the trumpets sounded, σαλπίζειν (1. 2. 17), σημαίνειν τὸ πολεμικόν (4. 3. 29), σημαίνειν τῇ σάλπιγγι (6. 3. 25, 27), a cheer is raised, ἀλαλά, ἐλελεῦ (1. 8. 17), and the excited soldiers quicken their march to a run, δρόμῳ ὁρμᾶν, and rush upon the foe (4. 3. 31). The hoplites bring their spears to the charge, καθιέναι, προβάλλεσθαι τὰ ὅπλα (6. 3. 25), *infensis s. infestis hastis provolare*, and the light-armed discharge their missiles. The Persians never waited, ὑπομένειν (6. 3. 29, 4. 4. 21), to come to close quarters, εἰς χεῖρας δέχεται (4. 3. 31), with the Greeks, but always gave way, ἐκκλίνει (1. 8. 19), and fled, φεύγει (1. 8. 19). The Greeks at Cunaxa forced their way through the enemy's line (1. 8. 19), διακόπτειν (4. 8. 11, 13). If the spears were broken the hoplites drew their swords—*pugna ad gladios venit*, Liv. 2. 46.

When the enemy were defeated, ἡττηθῆναι τῇ μάχῃ, τρέπεσθαι (4. 6. 26, 5. 4. 24), the pursuit followed, διώκειν, ἕπεσθαι, ἐφέπεσθαι (1. 8. 19, 6. 3. 17, 28). When the general thought the pursuit had gone far enough, the soldiers were called back by sound of trumpet, ἀνακαλεῖσθαι τῇ σάλπιγγι, *receptui canere* (4. 4. 22), and returned to the main body, ἀποχωρεῖν, ἀποτρέχειν (5. 7. 16, 6. 3. 17, 5. 2. 6). To commemorate the victory a trophy usually was set up, τρόπαιον στησάμενοι (6. 3. 32, 4. 6. 27, 7. 6. 36). It was generally made of heaps of stones and earth. The dead were buried (6. 3. 5, 6), and a cenotaph, κενοτάφιον (6. 2. 9), was erected in honour of those whose bodies could not be found, and wreaths of flowers were placed upon it, στεφάνους ἐπέθεσαν (6. 2. 9).

The Commissariat.

Every Greek soldier was usually paid two obols a day as wages, μισθός, and two obols as provision-money, σιτηρέσιον; and hence the soldiers usually bought their own provisions. A portion of the camp was set apart as a market, ἀγορά (1. 2. 18); those who brought provisions into the market were called ἀγοραῖοι, and the retail dealers κάπηλοι. The overseers of the market, or the market superintendents, ἀγορανόμοι (5. 7. 2, 23, 29), settled all disputes, fixed the price of provisions, punished all cheating and theft, and received the market dues. The provisions, σῖτος, ἐπιτήδεια, were conveyed on waggons and beasts of burden, ὑποζύγια. The inhabitants of the districts through which the march was made usually supplied a market, ἀγορὰν παρέχειν (1. 3. 14, 5. 10), to the Greeks, but when the inhabitants refused to give supplies (5. 5. 16), or when money began to fail, the soldiers took what they could get, ἄγειν καὶ φέρειν (5. 5. 13), by plunder, καθ᾽ ἁρπαγήν; and they often went from the camp expressly to get supplies, ἐπὶ λείαν ἐξιέναι (5. 1. 17), ἰέναι or πορεύεσθαι ἐπὶ τὰ ἐπιτήδεια (5. 1. 6, 6. 2. 23), τὰ ἐπιτήδεια λαμβάνειν (5. 2. 1). All the plunder got in these expeditions was put into a common stock, τὸ κοινόν (5. 1. 12), out of which presents (4. 7. 27) and rewards (3. 3. 18) were given. The prisoners taken were sold as slaves (5. 3. 4), and the money realised was distributed among the soldiers.

LONDON: PRINTED BY
SPOTTISWOODE AND CO., NEW-STREET SQUARE
AND PARLIAMENT STREET

www.ingramcontent.com/pod-product-compliance
Lightning Source LLC
Chambersburg PA
CBHW020228030726
47497CB00009B/2997